ALONG THE EDGE OF ANNIHILATION

ALONG THE EDGE OF ANNIHILATION

The Collapse and Recovery of Life in the Holocaust Diary

DAVID PATTERSON

A Samuel & Althea Stroum Book

University of Washington Press Seattle & London

This book is published with the assistance of a grant from the Stroum Book Fund, established through the generosity of Samuel and Althea Stroum.

Printed in the United States of America
Designed by Audrey Meyer

Library of Congress Cataloging-in-Publication Data

Patterson, David
Along the edge of annihilation : the collapse and recovery of life in the Holocaust diary / David Patterson.
p. cm.
"A Samuel & Althea Stroum book."
Includes bibliographical references and index.
ISBN 0-295-97782-5 (cloth : alk. paper).—ISBN 0-295-97783-3 (paper : alk. paper)
1. Holocaust, Jewish (1939–1945)—Personal narratives—History and criticism. 2. Jews—Diaries—History and criticism. I. Title.
D804.195.P36 1999
940.53′18—dc21 98-43862
CIP

The paper used in this publication is acid-free and recycled from 10 percent postconsumer and at least 50 percent pre-consumer waste. It meets the minimum requirements of American National Standard for Information Sciences—Permanence of Paper for Printed Library Materials, ANSI A39.48-1984.

Cover illustration: page from the diary of Tobi Gerson, of Lodz Ghetto and Auschwitz

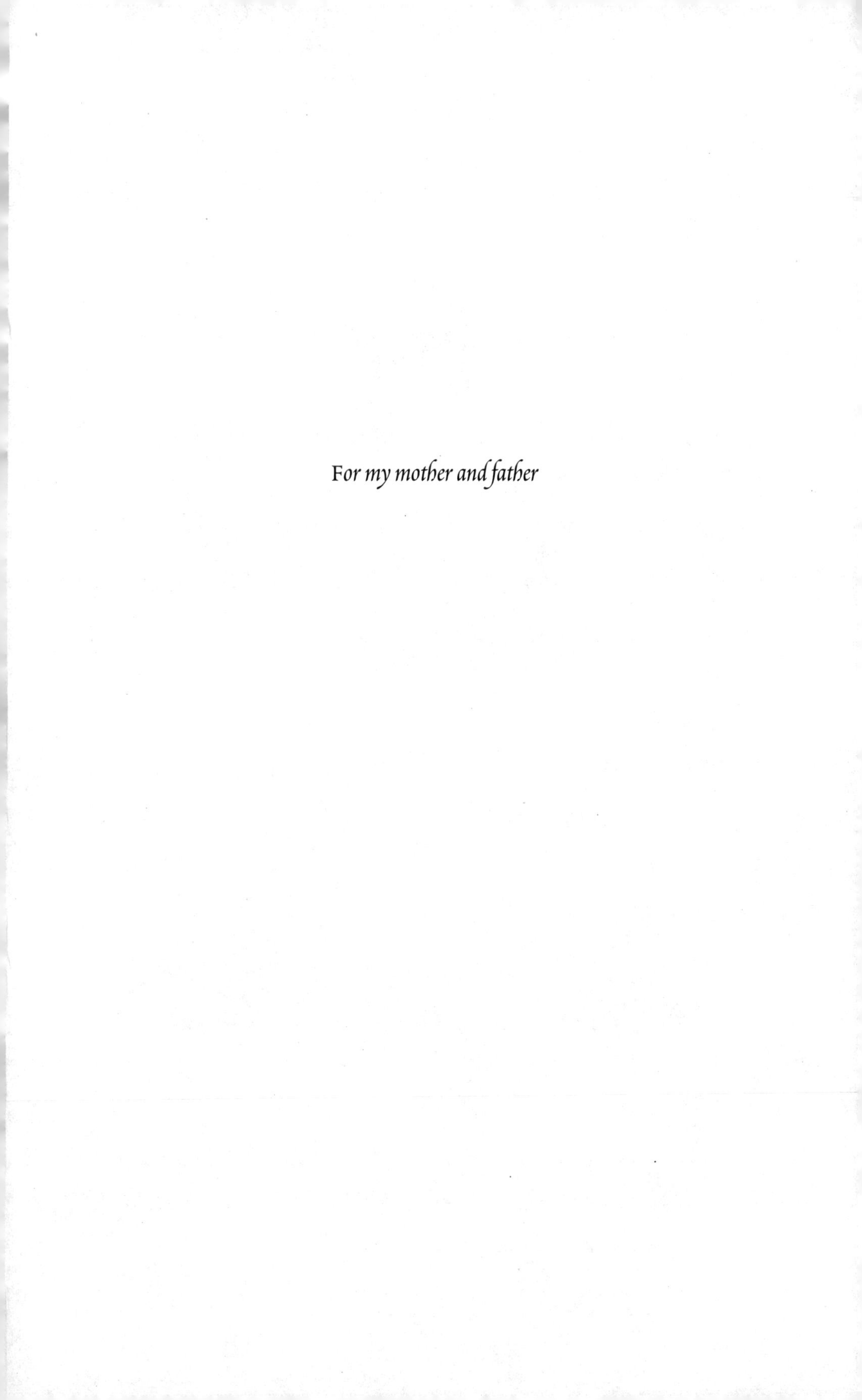

For my mother and father

CONTENTS

PREFACE

THAT ANY BOOK COULD BE WRITTEN ABOUT THE DIARIES that come to us from along the edge of *this* annihilation is something of a miracle. For the very impetus to record the truth—truth itself, truth as the good, the holy, the thing that sanctifies life—was targeted for annihilation. Indeed, most of these texts survived the annihilation by nothing short of miraculous means, just as most of their authors perished by murderous means. And yet those of us who, contrary to every rational expectation, receive these testimonies are the ones for whom the diaries are perhaps most intended. Written in secret, these diaries were not aimed at a contemporary audience. Written in silence—or in a shriek of silence—they often took on an aspect of prayer, seeking the ear of a God who seemed to have gone deaf. Written from a sense of debt and duty to the murdered, there is a sense in which the dead themselves constitute the diaries' audience—the dead and those whom they might have borne into the world.

That is why we incur a debt and a duty when we become their audience: we are the future denied the diarists, the generation whose ear the diarists so desperately sought. This desperate seeking after the ear of those who were far off characterized what hope the diarists had. In most cases they wrote without any rational hope that either they or their message would survive the slaughter that raged around them. Nevertheless they wrote, thus engaging in a profound form of spiritual resistance by refusing to allow their despair to silence them.

This spiritual dimension of the diaries is not determined by the belief system of a particular diarist. It is characterized, rather, by an embrace of the sacred, by a sense of urgency that leads one to write even at the risk of one's life, by an *ahavat Yisrael*, a love for the community of Israel. Such a concern unfolds in the testimony and commentary, both positive and negative, on the religious aspects of Jewish life, traditions, values, and texts—all of which were subject to annihilation with the annihilation of the Jewish people. The Jewish teachings and traditions that form the foundations of Jewish origins have religious significance whether the diarists believe in those teachings and traditions or not; the diarists do not have to believe in God in order for their comments to have religious implications or for their ultimate concern to be a religious concern. Inasmuch as they are interested in the sanctity of life, they have a religious interest.

Who, then, are these diarists? What became of them? And how have their diaries come to us? There is no particular profile that characterizes the authors, except that they are Jews writing about the annihilation of Jews. They come from every walk of life, every age group, every philosophical and religious outlook. Of the fifty diarists selected for this study, only a few survived, and nearly all who survived were young adults during the years of the Shoah. Among them are those who had been in hiding, such as Ruth Andreas-Friedrich, Julian Stanford, Tuvia Borzykowski, Helena Elbaum Dorembus, Michael Zylberberg, and David Kahane; those who were involved in armed resistance movements, such as Abraham Lissner and Yitzhak Zuckerman; and even those who had endured the horror of the camps, such as Renata Laqueur, Hanna Levy-Hass, and Leon Wells. In most cases those who survived managed to retrieve their own diaries or arranged for friends to preserve their testimonies for publication later. But what about those who did not survive? How did their diaries emerge from the Kingdom of Night into the light of day?

In some cases, the diaries were found in containers buried in the earth that was covered with the ashes of their authors. Resurrected from that darkness to speak to all humanity were the diaries written by members of Emmanuel Ringelblum's *Oneg Shabbat* circle, which consisted of a group of people in Warsaw who devoted themselves to the task of recording every act of horror and heroism that they witnessed. These diaries include those written by Shimon Huberband, Menahem Kon, Abraham Levin, Peretz Opoczynski, S. Sheinkinder, Hersh Wasser, and of course Ringelblum himself. Diaries similarly disinterred were written by members of the *Sonderkommando* of Auschwitz-Birkenau: Salmen Gradowski, Leib Langfus, and Salmen Lewental. In other instances the diarists anticipated their impending deaths and entrusted their words to the care of friends. Chaim Kaplan gave his diary to a friend in Warsaw, and Janusz Korczak had his delivered to Igor Newerly; Avraham Tory gave his notes from the Kovno Ghetto to a priest named Vaickus; Aryeh Klonicki-Klonymus turned his journal over to a peasant family near Pinsk; and Yitzhak Katznelson's *Vittel Diary* was given to a laundress named Marcelle Rabichon for safekeeping.

Still other diaries were simply discovered among the scattered papers and silent ruins of the lives destroyed by the Nazis. So it happened in the cases of Adam Czerniakow and Anne Frank, for example. Moshe Flinker's diary was discovered by his sisters in the basement of the building where they had lived in Brussels. Agnes Zsolt, the mother of Éva Heyman, found her daughter's diary after Éva had been sent to Auschwitz; she then placed it in the care of their cook. Sore Voloshin discovered the diary of Yitskhok Rudashevski in the ruins of the Vilna Ghetto and turned it over to Avrom Sutskever, an important poet and partisan who also preserved the writings of Vilna diarists Herman Kruk and Zelig Kalmanovitch; similarly the diaries of Sarra Gleykh and the sculptor Rivosh were delivered to authors Ilya Ehrenburg and Vasily Grossman, who included them in their edition of the Russian *Black Book*. Dawid Rubinowicz's diary remained hidden among a myriad of papers until it was discovered by Maria Jarochowska in 1959, and a certain A. Jonkman of Amsterdam kept the manuscript of the diary written by Philip Mechanicus until its publication in 1964.

Written along the edge of massive annihilation, these diaries bear witness not only to a collapse of life but to the evil of that collapse; therefore they bear witness to the good—to the holy—that came under a savage assault. Attesting to this evil, theirs is a testimony that confronts us with a recovery of the life that they desperately sought to recover, a recovery of the good and the holy that impart meaning and value to life. For what was slated for destruction then—the life of the holy and the image of humanity—is faced with destruction now. Who, then, is ultimately the audience of this outcry? All who have ears to hear—above and below.

ACKNOWLEDGMENTS

I WOULD LIKE TO EXPRESS MY THANKS TO THE NATIONAL Endowment for the Humanities, the South Central Modern Language Association, and the Oklahoma Foundation for the Humanities for their assistance in covering research costs for this book.

ALONG THE EDGE OF ANNIHILATION

OPENING REMARKS

"IF MY LIFE ENDS," READS THE LAST LINE OF CHAIM Kaplan's *Warsaw Diary*, "what will become of my diary?" (400). Kaplan's life ended in the death camp Treblinka in December 1942 or in January 1943; the exact date is uncertain. It is certain, however, that, apart from surviving the Shoah—which in itself borders on the miraculous—very little has become of his diary. Very little, in fact, has become of any of these diaries composed with courage and trepidation, in times and places where, by all that is rational, they should not have been composed at all. Yet, from little girls to old men, Jews *did* set their hands to blank pages in the midst of a world that had gone blank. Precisely when every trace of all that was meaningful and sacred in life was being erased, Jews of every ilk—but nonetheless Jews—struggled to utter a word that might transcend this erasure. Precisely when writing a diary became a crime, it became most needful for the recovery of a life that had been deemed criminal. Contrary to all that reason might have predicted, thousands of pages from these diaries have reached our hands. And, far from an egotistical concern for the fate of himself or his memory, Kaplan's question about the fate of his diary is a question concerning the fate of the truth, to which the fate of humanity is tied.

According to the Talmud, it is a religious duty to "carry out the wishes of the deceased" (*Gittin* 14b); just so, it is a religious duty to respond to Kaplan's question and to the cries of those who shared his fate. Like it or not, the voices of these victims and the truth that they sought persist. That is why this book delves into their diaries. Written from a Jewish perspective, it is a Jewish response to Jewish outcry.

Which is to say, it is a book that examines a searing question rising up from these scrolls of agony: how is the interior turmoil of the human diarist linked to the exterior annihilation of humanity? Or: what is the connection between the response to the collapse of life and the effort to regain a life? Or: what does writing the diary have to do with living a life, when both are under assault? These are a few variations on a single question. It is above all a Jewish question, which, like the Covenant entered into for the sake of "all the nations of the earth" (Genesis 18:18), is a question that concerns all humanity. "There comes a time," Elie Wiesel has written, "when one cannot be a man without assuming the Jewish condition" (*Beggar* 77), and assuming the Jewish condition has come to entail addressing the Jewish question that arises from these diaries. Kaplan himself believed that the time for this confrontation is precisely the time now upon us, in the post-Holocaust era. After the Shoah, he asserts in his entry for 10 October 1940, "either humanity would be Judaic, or it would be idolatrous-German" (130)—either *yehidutiyt* or *germaniyt-eliyliyt* in his Hebrew (201), suggesting an embrace either of the truth or of the lie, either of meaning or of the void. And Kaplan's concern for the fate of his diary is inextricably tied to this either/or.

The project here undertaken is an attempt to embrace the truth and meaning, both terrible and sublime, that Kaplan and other Jewish diarists sought to embrace. Once again, in contrast to most others who have examined these diaries, I wish to emphasize the word *Jewish* and, in that emphasis, adopt a premise set forth by Emmanuel Levinas: "*Jewish existence itself is an essential event of being; Jewish existence is a category of being*" (*Difficult* 183). How that category is distinguished will be seen in the ways in which the Holocaust diary is distinguished from other diaries; generally speaking, these distinctions are outlined in the titles of the chapters that go into this study. Seeking a link between those Jewish lives lost and our own lives, moreover, its method is phenomenological, in the sense that Levinas ascribes to phenomenology when he says, "Phenomenology is a way of becoming aware of where we are in the world, a *sich besinnen* that consists of a recovery of the origin of meaning in our life world, or *Lebenswelt*" ("Dialogue" 14–15). In the Holocaust diary, to be sure, this recovery of meaning in life is attempted in the midst of a *Todeswelt*, death world. And yet the diary lives. Hence we are faced with a phenomenological question: how do the collapse and recovery of life in the Holocaust diary implicate us in our own pursuit of life? But before we explore this huge question, we must consider other questions. Let us begin with the question concerning the critical contexts for the investigation.

THE CRITICAL CONTEXTS FOR THE INVESTIGATION

While the Shoah has invoked a great deal of research and even a great deal of genuine testimony, there has been very little embrace of the truth, very little response to the larger question before us, in the responses to these voices that arose from the very depths of the whirlwind. Renata Laqueur Weiss's doctoral dissertation on concentration camp diaries is, to my knowledge, the only book-length study of Holocaust diaries. When the diaries do come under investigation in the occasional chapter or article, their consideration is usually combined with a discussion of Holocaust memoirs, as if there were no significant generic distinctions between the two. And they are rarely approached as Jewish texts that bear implications for an understanding of Jewish life and tradition, that is, of Jewish existence as a category of being. The scholarly contexts for this investigation, then, are sparse. But the spiritual context—the context of the truth and of the soul's struggle for life—is immense, though little explored.

Before going into a critique of existing studies of the diaries, however, at least two exceptions to the claim that their truth has been ignored must be noted. While one comes soon after the Event, the is other much later, and both arise in reaction to the popular acclaim for Anne Frank's *Diary of a Young Girl.* In 1960 Bruno Bettelheim commented on the stage production of the diary by saying: "There is good reason why the enormously successful play ends with Anne stating her belief in the good in all men. . . . If all men are basically good . . . then indeed we can all go on with life as usual and forget about Auschwitz. . . . [Anne Frank's dramatized diary] found wide acclaim because . . . it denies implicitly that Auschwitz ever existed. If all men are good, there was never an Auschwitz" (46). And if there was never an Auschwitz, there was never an Anne Frank, never the hiding or the capture, the despair or the death—in a word, never a diary.

More thoroughly developing Bettelheim's position, Alvin Rosenfeld published a study of Anne Frank and her diary in 1991, where he argues: "In order to give the book this emphasis—one that urged readers to cherish its youthful author rather than to mourn her—one had to read the diary in such a way as to have it appear an uplifting and not a harrowing experience. The only way to do that, though, was to dehistoricize Anne Frank's story: to see it, on the one hand, as emblematic of Jewish fate during the Nazi period, to be sure, but, on the other hand, as transcending that fate" ("Popularization" 250). Therefore: "Far from being remembered as one dead child among a million or more murdered Jewish children, she was instead to be taken up and cherished as a general symbol of martyred innocence, who stood for but also transcended the lot of suffering humanity" (260). Again, to dehistoricize the diary is to eliminate it, and to make Anne Frank into a symbol is to get rid of her, as a child and as a Jew. Thus, as Bettelheim and Rosenfeld rightly suggest, we settle a burning question and silence a disturbing voice.

Dehistoricizing the diary is a means of overcoming the Event and salving our soul with the illusion that these dead Jewish children have no bearing on our humanity. To be sure, once they are stripped of their humanity and made into a symbol, our illusion goes so far as to suppose that their spirit of innocence and optimism lives on (whatever that means); hence we are redeemed. Or at least we are let off the hook of responsibility. But, as Emil Fackenheim insists, this illusion cannot bear the weight of a reality that cannot be overcome. "The edification of our soul is disrupted by the cries of the children," he maintains. "We therefore conclude: *where the Holocaust is there is no overcoming; and where there is an overcoming the Holocaust is not*. . . . So long as no way is found to confront the Holocaust and yet endure, it has the power to render questionable all overcoming everywhere" (*To Mend* 135). The responses of Bettelheim and Rosenfeld show that the effort to transcend the truth of Anne Frank has failed; which, in turn, is evidence that we have not found a way to confront the Holocaust and yet endure.

Dehistoricizing the diary and making it into a false symbol, however, is not our only means of removing it from its reality and placing it at a safe distance from ourselves. Another method of overcoming the Shoah is to bury it in history. Contrary to its elevation as a transcendent symbol, the diary is often reduced to a mere historical document or a piece of evidence. Here, lacking the courage of the diarists, we shrink from their diaries and regard them simply as eyewitness accounts and sources of information, as data, and not as the outcries of Jewish souls that might implicate us in any way. Albert Graeser, for example, omits these diaries from his study of the "literary diary" precisely because they are "documents" that arose from despair, rather than from *Kunstwille*, or the "will to art" (105). And yet to view them as art would be equally wrongheaded, since this would open the door to the false transcendence that occurred when Anne Frank's diary was made into art, that is, into drama. How, then, should these diaries be approached?

In the area of Holocaust studies, James Young is perhaps the most prominent scholar to have undertaken any detailed examination of the Holocaust diary. He too, however, fabricates a distance between ourselves and the diaries by reducing them not only to documents, evidence, and sources of information but to *problematic* documents, evidence, and sources of information. He accomplishes this task in two ways: first he raises epistemological concerns that discredit the diarist, and then he assumes a phenomenological stance that renders suspect the diary itself. And the fact that the diaries are written by Jews in the midst of the annihilation of the Jews is all but incidental to both approaches. From an epistemological standpoint, Young argues that the diarists "necessarily convert experience into an organized, often ritualized, *memory* of experience." Hence it is "difficult to distinguish between the archetypal patterns the ghetto diarist has brought to the events, those he perceived in or inferred from them, and those that exist in the narrative. As raw as they may have been at the moment, the ghetto and camp experiences were immediately refined and organized by witnesses within the terms of their *Weltanschauungen*" ("Interpreting" 414). Let us put aside for the moment our doubts as to whether Anne Frank or Dawid Rubinowicz can even have a *Weltanschauung*, at least in the same sense that Chaim Kaplan and Janusz Korczak may have one. There are more important issues to consider here. For example, if the ideological bias of the diarist stands between himself and any truth concerning the event, then it certainly stands between us and the event: once again we are safe and do not have to answer for anything, since we cannot answer for what we cannot know. How we know *that* the Event took place Young does not explain; *what* we know, he insists, is corrupted by the outlook of witnesses who transmit that knowledge.

One comparison that Young makes in order to support his contention is between Anne Frank and Moshe Flinker, two adolescents who were very different in their *Weltanschauungen*; Anne was an assimilated Jew, Young notes, for instance, whereas Moshe was a religious Jew. Further, "at the end of her diary," says Young, "Anne can declare that in spite of everything, she still believes in the goodness of humankind. In contrast, following his afternoon prayers on the last day of his diary, Moshe writes: 'The sky is covered with bloody clouds, and I am frightened when I see it. . . . They come from the seas of blood . . . brought about by the millions of Jews who have been captured.' . . . Where Anne might have seen beauty and hope in a fiery sunset, Moshe 'saw' only apocalypse. The 'vision' of the events in these diaries depended on the languages, figures, and even religious training that ultimately framed these testimonies" ("Interpreting" 415). Therefore, one is led to ask, who can know anything about the truth of what these children "saw"? Underlying this question, from Young's perspective, is not the horrendous nature of an event that thwarts the imagination and frustrates the understanding; rather, it is the tainted nature of the testimony that makes knowledge of the Event problematic, if not impossible.

Young's epistemological flight from responsibility is mirrored, moreover, by his irresponsible handling of these examples; here his own intellectual and ideological bias shows itself. Regarding the remark that he attributes to Anne Frank, it is not at the end of her diary but at the end of the contrived stage production that "Anne" asserts her belief in the goodness of humankind. Although she has her moments of optimism, what the child Anne does write near the end of her diary, on 15 July 1944, is this: "That's the difficulty in these times: ideals, dreams, and cherished hopes rise within us, only to meet the horrible truth and be shattered" (278). And is it the assimilated Anne who writes that, when gazing into the Sabbath candles, she senses "in the candle" the presence of her late grandmother, who "shelters and protects" her (177–78)? As for Moshe Flinker, it is true that his diary is full of apocalyptic foreboding and religious fervor, but he too has his moments of optimism. On 26 November 1942, for example, he writes: "It seems to me that the time has come for our redemption" (26). And later he declares: "The Lord will not be able to forsake His people. Undoubtedly He will save us" (52). Is this affirmation of faith so diametrically opposed to Anne Frank's assertion that "it is God that has made us as we are, but it will be God, too, who will raise us up again" (221)? Yes, these children come from different backgrounds and have different perspectives on the world. But far more significant to an understanding of their diaries are the things these Jewish children have in common: their struggle to respond to a world in ashes, their effort to recover some traces of life, and their questions concerning the dearness of life that implicate us all. This is precisely what Young overlooks.

Young takes up the phenomenological challenge to the validity of the diary itself in his book *Writing and Rewriting the Holocaust*. "Because the diarists wrote from within the whirlwind," he maintains, "the degree of authority in their accounts is [mistakenly] perceived by readers to be stronger than that of the texts shaped through hindsight. Operating on the same phenomenological basis as print journalism, in which the perceived temporal proximity of a text to events reinforces the sense of its facticity, diaries can be far more convincing of their factual veracity than more retrospective accounts" (25). One dubious assumption behind this statement is that a reader's primary interest in the diary lies with the facts that it conveys, and not with the questions that it may pose for the life of the soul; indeed, it is an assumption that insulates the soul from such questions and that ignores any internal aspect of the human being at work in the diary. And yet, as Wiesel has insisted, "the ultimate mystery of the Holocaust is that whatever happened took place in the soul" (*Against Silence* 1:239). If we are to find our way into these diaries, then we must find our way into our own souls. And to do this, we must begin by recognizing the difference between writing a document or a report, and keeping a diary.

Unlike Young, Alain Girard makes an important distinction between the phenomenological basis of diaries in general and print journalism: "[In the diary] internal observation plays a role analogous to the plane of individual consciousness, allowing it to escape from appearances and to communicate with itself. One could not imagine two forms of writing more opposed in their manner, their aim, and their content than the journal of journalists and the journal of diarists" (xvi–xvii). As we shall see, there are significant differences between diaries in general and the unique aspects of the Holocaust diary, but in this instance, Girard correctly notes a distinguishing feature of the diary which Young ignores: in the diary, notes Girard, "the interior landscape reflects the variations of an exterior landscape" (xvi).[1] When assessing the events reported by a journalist, we are interested in the factual nature of the report, not in the reporter's strife of the spirit. While many Holocaust diaries include accounts of what is transpiring around the diarist, none of them can be reduced to mere reports or documentation of facts, for all of them harbor an internal, human aspect that, far from isolating us from the diarist, establishes for us an essential bond with him. And the diary is a mirror held up not only to the horror but also to ourselves.

Even when it looks as though Young is about to make a distinction between the internal and the external aspects of the diary, he deftly avoids it. For example, he says: "The diarists who participated in Ringelblum's communal *Oneg Shabbat* archive were motivated to record events far different from those reported in a more personal record, like Mary Berg's diary. . . . The reasons for which the diarists wrote and the focus of their witness inescapably regulate, and at times restrict, the diarist's record. In the end, these formal and generic constraints contribute as much to the meaning and significance of these diaries as do the figures and selection of details in the diaries themselves" (*Writing* 25). There are certainly differences between Mary Berg's diary and those kept by the members of the *Oneg Shabbat* circle. But, as in his comparison of Anne Frank and Moshe Flinker, in this contrast between the *Oneg Shabbat* diarists and Mary Berg, Young oversimplifies to the point of being misleading, since there are considerable religious and ideological differences among the *Oneg Shabbat* diarists themselves.

In the study at hand we shall examine some of the diaries found in the *Oneg Shabbat* archives; among them are those written by Rabbi

Shimon Huberband, Menahem Kon, Abraham Levin, S. Sheinkinder, Hersh Wasser, and, of course, Emmanuel Ringelblum. Although they stood not in the middle of a circle but in the midst of a maelstrom, these men exemplify a talmudic tradition that goes back to Choni the Circle Drawer, who declared to the Almighty: "I swear by Thy great name that I will not move from here until Thou hast mercy upon Thy children!" (*Ta'anit* 23a). Like Choni the Circle Drawer, these diarists, and Ringelblum in particular, refused to move from where they stood; for, like Choni, they sensed a profound link between themselves as Jews and their Jewish community. To be sure, the very title of this communal group distinguishes it from other archival circles of other times: *Oneg Shabbat* means "rejoicing in the Sabbath" and implies, if not a personal stake, a deeply Jewish, human, and spiritual responsibility that far transcends any ordinary keeping of records and reporting of facts. They gave their group this Jewish name because, as Jews, they were deeply aware that the Sabbath is "*spirit in the form of time*," as Abraham Joshua Heschel states it (*Sabbath* 75), and that "what *we are* [as Jews] depends on what *the Sabbath is* to us" (*Sabbath* 89). Nor is it too much to assume that some of the members of the *Oneg Shabbat*, particularly Rabbi Huberband, were aware of the teaching in the *Zohar* that "the Community of Israel is also called 'Sabbath'" (3:198–99). The question of who we are—and of what will become of us—as a Jewish community was central to the members of the *Oneg Shabbat*; it cannot be ignored—and Young ignores it—if one is to understand what they and their diaries were about.

To be sure, the centrality of this Jewish consciousness can be seen both among the diarists of the *Oneg Shabbat* and in the texts of other diarists. "Our purpose," Abraham Levin explains the aim of the *Oneg Shabbat*, "is that our sufferings, 'the pains before the coming of the Messiah,' should be noted down for remembrance by future generations, for remembering by the whole world" (316). Mary Berg has a similar sense of purpose that goes well beyond the confines of personal interest; like the members of the *Oneg Shabbat*, she often exemplifies a sense of responsibility to others. For she is mindful of "an inner voice" that "urges" her—or rather "commands" her, which is a better translation of the Polish *nakazuje* (243)—"to write down all the terrible things" she has discovered about the Warsaw Ghetto Uprising

(227). Despite the differences between them, she and Ringelblum's diarists have this much in common: they are all conscious of a deeper responsibility to a human community which does not leave them free *not* to write. In its implications for the life of the soul, as well as for the life of humanity, this similarity surpasses the difference that Young regards as most decisive.

But even with respect to the difference that he emphasizes, there are problems with Young's division between archival information and personal anguish. On 12 July 1940, for example, Mary Berg relates that "there are now a great number of illegal schools, and they are multiplying every day," and that "two such schools were discovered by the Germans some time in June" (32). And in his archival "record" for 5 May 1942 Sheinkinder allows himself an expression of personal anguish. "Tomorrow will be the eve of *Shavuot*," he writes, noting the observance of the Revelation at Sinai. "There is no sadder hour for me than when I finish my work and make my way home, where my hungry family is waiting for me. They have prepared no dinner for me. I did not leave them anything for lunch" (260). As for Ringelblum himself, like his comrades, he seldom uses the first-person singular when making his entries, but surely he includes himself in the "we" when he writes: "Despair and a sense of hopelessness are growing. There is the universal feeling that They are trying to starve us out, and we cannot escape, save through a miracle" (157). Ringelblum's "we" extends throughout the community, to the children who attend the illegal schools and the hungry family awaiting the return of a tormented father. In these examples, then, one finds similarities that, despite all differences, lead Marie Syrkin to assert of the diaries: "The social historian trained in political thought and action [Emmanuel Ringelblum], the Orthodox Hebrew scholar [Chaim Kaplan], and the fifteen-year-old schoolgirl [Anne Frank] move from confused hopefulness to hopelessness in the same baffled progression. Though they differ in emotional intensity and intellectual resources, their basic responses are as tragically alike as the events they describe" (227). But there is an even more fundamental bond that ties Anne Frank and Mary Berg to Chaim Kaplan and Emmanuel Ringelblum, one that neither Young nor Syrkin addresses: *they are Jews* and are therefore conscious of an essential, definitive interweaving of personal and communal life. For "my soul is not by the side of my people," Martin Buber expresses this crucial point. "My people *is* my soul" (*Judaism* 20). This relation lies at the heart of the sense of responsibility to current and future generations that we find in every Holocaust diary. A Jew cannot stand alone, in isolation from other Jews, any more than a word can stand alone, in isolation from the language. (As we shall see below, this Jewish feature of the Holocaust diary proves to be one that distinguishes it from other diaries.)

Yet there are linguistic differences among the diaries, which in this study originally appear in Dutch, German, Romanian, Hungarian, Russian, Polish, Yiddish, and Hebrew. And, similar to David Roskies before him (199–212), Young makes much of these differences. "In choosing to write in Hebrew over Yiddish," he explains, for instance, "Kaplan and Kalmanovitch may not have deliberately chosen every specific allusion and figure in Hebrew over those in Ringelblum's Yiddish, but they did locate events within different linguistic realms all the same. . . . Where Hebrew tends to locate events in the sanctified linguistic sphere of Scripture, rabbinical disputation, and covenant, Yiddish (as the daily language and in many literal ways, the "*mama-loshen*," or *mother*-tongue) often brought into sharper relief the details of daily life and its hardships. Community, politics, and organization had a vocabulary in Yiddish not developed at that time in Hebrew. Conversely, questions of theodicy, covenant, scriptural antecedent, and even the interpretation of events 'as text' had a lexicon in Hebrew they did not have in Yiddish" ("Interpretation" 415). But this distinction carries weight only for those who have little knowledge of Hebrew and Yiddish. Although different languages certainly harbor different ways of organizing and conceptualizing the world, the mutual exclusion that Young ascribes to these particular languages is simply false. Bernard Martin, for example, points out that, through the work of Eliezer ben Yehudah (1858–1922) and Achad Ha-Am (1856–1927), Hebrew had become the vernacular of the Jewish community in Palestine by the early 1920s (344). It was the language of instruction and administration for the Technion, founded in Haifa in 1924, and for the Hebrew University of Jerusalem, founded in 1925. When the Jewish Agency was established in 1929 to deal "with the practical task of financing and administering the settlement of

Jews" in Palestine, Hebrew was the language in which it conducted its communal, political, and organizational business (Martin 346). And that business extended to Jewish organizations throughout the Diaspora, such as the *Hitachadut* (United Zionist Labor Party), which "championed the revival of Hebrew" as part of its political activity (Heller 267).

With regard to Yiddish and its shortcomings when it comes to interpreting events "as text," Young appears to overlook the massive Yiddish literature that eloquently explores all aspects, including the deeply religious and spiritual aspects, of East European Jewish life. As for the inappropriateness of Yiddish for delving into "theodicy" and rabbinical disputation, is it possible that Young is unaware of the fact that in Eastern Europe Yiddish was—and in some places remains—the language used for discussing and debating Torah and Talmud in the *yeshivot*? Reinforcing this point that undermines Young's characterization of Yiddish, André Neher makes a telling observation on Franz Rosenzweig and the significance of Yiddish for Jewish religious thought: "Throughout his life of Jewish studies, over and above the anxiety which assailed him sometimes when faced with the slowness of his progress in mastering the Talmud and the vastness of the intellectual realm which he still had to unravel, Rosenzweig was haunted with another worry, which gradually began to appear like an unquestionable certitude: He lacked the linguistic instrument—the truly Jewish language [of Yiddish], which the Warsaw schoolboy imbibed with the air of the ghetto—which would allow him an intuitive penetration of Talmudic knowledge" (*They* 143). In the matter of linguistic difference, then, Young ignores essential aspects of Hebrew and Yiddish that render his distinctions invalid.

The more pressing issue, however, is not Young's false generalizations concerning these differences among the diaries, but rather his ultimate aim in making these generalizations. Returning to our initial concern with his approach—namely, the reduction of the diaries to problematic evidence and dubious historical documents that pose no particular threat to spiritual life—we come to Young's own statement of a serious consequence of his approach. "The words in a translated and reproduced Holocaust diary," he argues, "are no longer traces of the crime, as they were for the writer who inscribed them; what was evidence for the writer at the moment he wrote is now, after it leaves his hand, only a detached and free-floating sign, at the mercy of all who would read and misread it. Evidence of the witness's experiences seems to have been supplanted—not delivered—by his text" (24). That there are problems with translations we readily admit; hence in this study we shall make use of the original texts for most of these diaries. But the soul and the humanity couched in the diary, the collapse and the recovery of a life reflected in it, can penetrate even the veils of a translation—if we do not decide beforehand that the diaries are "free-floating signs" or mere bodies of evidence and the diarists nothing more than reporters. Made into mere reports, the dairies are reduced to the status of "being there"; understood as human voices, they take on a capacity for calling forth, for calling *me* forth and announcing my responsibility. This is why Wiesel warns us: "Consideration for others must precede scholarship. Abstract erudition may turn into a futile game of the intellect. Words are links not only between words but also between human beings. The emphasis on the *other* is paramount in Judaism: *Achrayut*, responsibility, contains the word *Akher (Acher)*, the Other. We are responsible for the other" (*Sages* 184). Thus the response to the diary—the *Jewish* response—must be one that endeavors to establish a link with the diarist.

Remember Mikhail Bakhtin's insight: "The text as such never appears as a dead thing; beginning with any text—and sometimes passing through a lengthy series of mediating links—we always arrive, in the final analysis, at the human voice, which is to say we come up against the human being" (*Dialogic* 252–53). But coming up against *these* human beings, against these Jews, who collide with the extremity of the collapse of life and wrestle to recover it, is not just a difficult task—it is a terrifying task. For in the encounter with the human being, we encounter ourselves and there confront the questions of what we live and die for, of what we hold dear and what we fear. It is understandable, but not excusable, that Young would avoid the fearsome task of encountering the human being in the diary by getting rid of him. We can see why he invokes the free-floating sign in an eclipse of the human face: it is to flee, either knowingly or unknowingly, from a terrible responsibility. "Face and discourse are tied," Levinas points out. "The face speaks. It speaks, it is in this that it renders possible and begins all discourse. I have just refused the notion of vision to describe the authentic relationship with the Other; it is discourse and, more exactly, response or responsibility which is this authentic relationship" (*Ethics* 87–88). When the diaries are reduced to documents or signs, we do not respond to them; we examine, explain, and explicate them, but we do not respond to them. But then we betray the face that speaks from within and from beyond them. Chaim Kaplan's question once again comes to mind: "What will become of my diary?" In Young's approach to the diary we see what must *not* become of it.

But there are two other matters that must be considered before we launch our own attempt to respond to these diaries. First, in the existing approaches to the Holocaust diaries there is very little consideration of the generic features of the *diary* as such; as already indicated, when diaries get discussed or listed in bibliographies, they are often grouped together with memoirs and autobiographies. We shall proceed, then, to a brief discussion of the diary as a literary form. It will turn out, however, that, while it has some things in common with other diaries, the Holocaust diary is in a category by itself and cannot be neatly filed into the general genre of the diary. The matter of what distinguishes the Holocaust diary as *Holocaust* diary, then, is a second point that scholars thus far have not addressed and that must be addressed in these introductory remarks.

GENERIC FEATURES OF THE DIARY

According to P. A. Spalding, one distinguishing feature of the diary is that it arises from a "spontaneous impulse to record experience as such and preserve it" (12). A key term in this statement is the word *experience*. The video camera in the convenience store may record everything that transpires in the store throughout the day, but it experiences nothing. Experience belongs to the consciousness of a living soul; it arises in the encounter between world and mind. The diary, then, is not just the record of events; it is the record of a consciousness, of a sentient interaction with events. If the aim of this interaction recorded in the diary is the preservation of experience, then one might question Spalding's claim that it arises from a spontaneous impulse, as if it were void of any thought or calculation; indeed, the desire for preservation would seem to preclude spontaneity. We can come to Spalding's assistance, perhaps, by noting that, if the diary does arise from such an impulse, it is not because it is pointless or a reflexive stream of consciousness, but rather because it is not intended for a reader other than the diarist. And yet the diarist's reading of the diary is couched in the very process of writing it: the writing is itself a reading of the experience, and the diarist's pen becomes an organ of insight. Thus Yitzhak Katznelson, for example, can say, "This pen of mine, wherewith I have written most of these notes, has become a living part of me" (187)—*byichad im libiy biy, im nishmatiy biy*, reads his Hebrew text, "one with my heart, one with my soul" (87): it is an *essential* part of me. For Katznelson, the pen that produced the diary was his soul's link to whatever life he could retrieve from the ruins of the day.

Although most diarists do not see the day pass in destruction, they do see the day pass. The diarist's "impulse" to preserve his experience, then, is an attempt to lay his hands—or his pen—on a moment and a life that may otherwise slip through his fingers. This he does by inscribing a word upon a page, as though the inscription were a net that could snare the experience, or a sieve through which he might filter some significance attached to the experience. Thus the word becomes a repository of time and experience; thus the word takes on meaning, even if the experience is negative, since to deem an experience as negative is to ascribe to it a value and therefore a meaning. As the moment fills the word to overflowing, the word overflows with the gravity of the moment. Hence the soul of the diarist takes on substance in a life that is otherwise emptiness, and his time—that is to say, his *life*-time—is regained. This is what it means for Katznelson to say that his pen is one with his soul: his soul draws its breath as his pen inscribes the word, even if that breath tastes of ashes. Keeping the diary, the diarist keeps a hold on his sense of being: the daily record is a means of seizing the day. The diary may in some sense arise from a "spontaneous impulse," but the diarist's stake in the diary can be very high indeed. The diary becomes a portal through which the diarist inserts himself into a life that is otherwise closed off to him by the horizon of time. It is a means of capturing a trace of presence by seeking a trace of significance in the midst of a time that is draining into the void. It is a means of returning the sand to the empty hourglass. Or better: it is a means of filling the emptied glass with substance. How? Through the return of meaning to the words consigned to the pages of the diary. For where meaning is torn from words, a void appears, one that swallows up meaning. In order to fetch meaning from the void, the diarist returns meaning to words.

The diary's attempted recovery of time and meaning is a primary point of interest for Karl J. Weintraub in his study of autobiographical literature. "The diurnal entries of the diarist," he argues, "are governed by the very fact that a day has its end. Even if in the maturing diarist a sense of selection begins to be guided by the growing awareness of what this person values and does not value, the journal entry is the completed precipitate of each day. It has its very value in being the reflection of but a brief moment; it attributes prime significance to the segments of life" (827). In contrast to other literary genres, the significance of what the diarist records is definitively linked to the time when she records it: the entries in a diary are *dated*. If the diarist might emerge as a kind of protagonist, the antagonist is time itself; if the diarist does no more than establish a narrative point of view, time itself is narrated. And, whether we speak of protagonist and antagonist or of subject and object, the two confront each other not just in the word but in the written *record*. In contrast to other literary forms, the diarist does not simply write—she *records*; novels and poems, on the other hand, are not recorded—they are written. As "the completed precipitate of each day," the diary is written, in a sense, by the day itself, even as the day derives its significance from the writing of the diary. Unlike the daily recording of, say, the high and low temperatures or levels of rainfall, the diary is an interweaving of the time, word, and meaning that constitute a life. Which is to say: the day takes on meaning because it is the day of a life, a day lived in the *commentary upon* life, where commentary is to be understood not as explication but as interrogation. And if the diary may be viewed as a commentary on the day, then the day may be viewed as a kind of text. From a Jewish standpoint, the day is a text of the creation that comes from the hand—or the mouth—of God.[2] Unable to bear the silence of the day, the diarist inserts her voice into it so that she may hear it speak. The diary is a responding that is at once a hearing. The diarist does not first hear and then comment; rather, her hearing transpires in the midst of her commentary.

To the extent that it is lived in commentary, the day assumes significance, not because it has been brought to a halt but because it has been made part of a process of becoming through the process of interrogation.[3] If the "completed precipitate" of this day assumes significance, then it is oriented toward the next day; if the ordeal of the diarist has meaning, then it has direction, which implies a future where the diarist and the diary have yet to arrive. In the words of Adin Steinsaltz, "The never-ending conflict between the existent and not-yet-existent is at the root of man's whole inner struggle" (*Strife* 6). As the expression of an inner struggle, the diary is the diarist's response to the silence that frames the future. Recall once more Kaplan's question: "What will become of my diary?" Thus the diarist participates in a universal, or at least a communal, questioning; he may write in solitude, but he does not write in isolation. It is through this relation to a community of others that the diary establishes a relation to the future; Kaplan raises the question concerning his diary in the light of a fate that awaits not just himself but his community as well. Time, then, as Levinas has said, "is the very relationship of the subject with the other" (*Time* 39). Why? Because, he explains, "the other is the future. The very relationship with the other is the relationship with the future. It seems to me impossible to speak of time in a subject alone, or to speak of a purely personal duration" (*Time* 77). Time is contained in the word addressed to the other, inasmuch as the word seeks a hearing that is yet to happen, and the word is part of a public domain that implies the presence of another. Comprised of the word, the diary is an address to another, even if the other is the diarist herself. Hence many diaries are written in the form of letters, as in the case of Anne Frank's "Dear Kitty" or Éva Heyman's "Dear Diary."

If the word, however, implies the presence of another—either actual or potential—to whom it is addressed, in the diary it may also imply an essential division within the diarist, a condition in which the diarist is "other" to himself. In his massive study of the diary, Girard makes this point by saying, "If the individual interrogates himself with such avidity, it is because his situation has been called into question, and he must recover the basis of a new equilibrium" (xi). The peace that characterizes the soul's equilibrium arises only where meaning imparts wholeness to life, and that wholeness is the wholeness of presence. And yet the very writing that seeks to recover the basis of a new equilibrium undermines it, so that, contrary to what is possible for other literary genres, the diary has no closure other than death. Though it may escape him, the diarist seeks meaning in the word not just because meaning is absent from life, but also because he is himself absent, living "only in the event's reverberation," as Edmond Jabès phrases it (*Desert* 41).[4] The diarist may cast the net of the diary over the day, but he cannot live in that net, for the words that comprise the net increase what it would capture. And yet he cannot live otherwise.

This tension between the weight of the necessary and the longing for the needful comes out in one of the last entries in Emil Dorian's diary; it is dated 1 September 1944. There he writes: "I really have no idea why I go on jotting down things as I used to in the days of silent waiting when these trite pages were my consolation. I no longer have time now for personal thoughts, for sitting and contemplating people and events. Carried along on the impetuous wave of changes toward the labor awaiting me, I ought to give up these flimsy notes once and for all. Nevertheless, I was drawn again to the typewriter: a breathing space, a need to look around me" (347). Here we see that the diary is not merely the record of experience but is an encounter between the soul and itself as the one who, in the light of an essential absence of meaning, both experiences and seeks significance in experience—not only in experience as such but in *my* experience. "Each person has a curriculum vitae that belongs only to himself," says Girard. "In the same way, any action or work derives its meaning only to the extent that it is not anonymous but is signed" (xiii–xiv). In the diary, the man does not first inscribe his deeds and then sign his name; rather, signing his name, he inscribes the deeds and from that inscription derives his substance.[5] Whereas novels, for instance, are novels *by* someone, diaries are diaries *of* someone, where *of* is followed both by a *genetivus objectivus* and by a *genetivus subjectivus*; it is both an object created by a living subject and a window looking into the soul of the subject. If the diary is generally self-centered, moreover, it is because the soul has lost its center. The diary, therefore, becomes a means of regaining a center, and this can often take the diarist outside himself.

In the Holocaust diary it always takes the diarist outside himself. Let us consider, then, those aspects of the Holocaust diary which place it in a category of its own.

THE DISTINGUISHING FEATURES OF THE HOLOCAUST DIARY

In citing the Holocaust diaries to make a point about the generic distinctions of the diary, we have already implied that the Holocaust diary has certain things in common with the generically defined diary. And so it does. But, as we shall now demonstrate, the Holocaust diary bears certain characteristics that place it in a category of its own; to be sure, each of the chapters in this book deals with an aspect of the Holocaust diary that is peculiar to it. Still, some general remarks on the distinctive characteristics of the Holocaust diary should be made by way of introduction.

One of these distinctive features is the consciousness of a community of others to whom the diarist not only belongs but is *accountable*—a point touched upon earlier, in the discussion of the critical contexts for this project. In contrast to the generic aspects of other diaries, the Holocaust diary harbors a consciousness of accountability that is explicit and pronounced, not merely implied, and that situates the diarist before his or her community; this consciousness, indeed, is what imparts to the Holocaust diary a spirit of testimony. The Holocaust diary, then, contains a movement through the word and toward another who is other than oneself; generally speaking, such a movement is not a distinguishing feature of other diaries. Again, this movement toward another is a distinctively Jewish feature of the diary, and the Holocaust diary is above all a Jewish diary: this is the key to the diarist's accountability to and for a community, past, present, and future. To be sure, the time measured by the Holocaust diary's daily entry is made of this responsibility. For a Jew who stands alone, cut off from his fathers, neighbors, and children, is not a Jew. "Whoever sees himself as a severed branch becomes *other*," writes Elie Wiesel. "Isolate yourself within time, and time itself becomes abstraction, and so do you. Time is a link, your 'I' a sum total. Your name has been borne by others before you. Your fate is not yours alone" (*One* 217). Your fate is not yours alone because, from a Jewish standpoint, your blood is not yours alone.

Indeed, if the Holocaust diary is a record of the day's "completed precipitate," that precipitate consists of Jewish blood; in the Holocaust diary, time is made of blood, and this feature of the diary is also an important part of its Jewish aspect. That is why Avraham Tory, for example, writes on 6 April 1943, "Blood trickles into the huge cup of Jewish suffering" (280), and on 13 January 1943 Yitskhok Rudashevski laments, "The entire White Russian earth is soaked with Jewish blood" (122). Passages like these are reminders of the link between blood and time in the Jewish tradition, one that goes back at least to Abraham ibn Ezra's twelfth-century commentary on the Book of Isaiah. Writing on the verse that reads, "Their blood shall be sprinkled upon my garments" (Isaiah 63:3), he explains, "The blood is called *netsach*, literally 'time,' because through the blood man lives his time" (287). And because man lives his time through the blood, his time is inextricably tied to communal time: Jewish blood is an essential element of Jewish community. The Holocaust diary, then, characteristically includes not only the consciousness of personal experience but the consciousness of communal ordeal. "The people of Israel are compared to a lamb," we read in the *Mekilta* of Rabbi Ishmael. "What is the nature of the lamb? If it is hurt in one limb, all its limbs feel the pain" (2:205–6). As we shall see in the chapters that follow, the Holocaust diary, as a Jewish diary, is the chronicle both of a soul that has lost its equilibrium and of a community under assault, whether the diarist is Anne Frank or Emmanuel Ringelblum. For the internal condition of the Jewish soul—indeed, of the human soul, according to the testimony of the diaries—is tied to the fate of the other human being. Fathers such as Aryeh Klonicki-Klonymus are obsessed with the fate of their sons; daughters such as Sarra Gleykh are preoccupied with the fate of their parents; and men such as Adam Czerniakow, Chaim Kaplan, and Janusz Korczak dwell on the fate of the children.

If, as Barbara Foley maintains, the Holocaust diary "yields a surprisingly compelling depiction of character in the process of metamorphosis" (342), it is because the communal tradition that imparts life to that character faces an imposed "metamorphosis" that ends in annihilation. Unlike Young, Foley is aware of this definitive connection between the Jewish diarist and the Jewish community, both of whom struggle to recover a collapsed connection with life. Distinguished from other diaries, "the extremity of experience recorded in the Holocaust diary," she notes, "entails a profound readjustment of accustomed patterns of literary communication. Ordinarily serving to mediate between two aspects of the self—the one that performs, the other that records the performance in peace at the end of the day—the diary projects a self whose principal performance is the act of testimony and whose sense of identity hinges upon the recoverability of the text" (337). The act of testimony is an act of responsibility that situates the diarist and the diary within a relation to the community and its ebbing way of life—its tradition, its covenant, and its mission. God, for example, invariably finds His way into the Holocaust diary in its concern for prayer, holy days, and the sanctification of life; like the Jew himself, this Jewish diary cannot do without the relation to the God of Abraham, whether it manifests itself in Anne Frank's observance of the Sabbath or in Moshe Flinker's vision of a messianic age. What Foley sees as the effort to recover a text, moreover, is an effort to situate the Jewish text of the diary within the contexts that form the foundations of Jewish life. These contexts include a concern not only for the Holy One but for the human image, for the family, and for the tradition that, more than merely an accumulation of customs, is a history of the sacred. "Sacred history," according to Heschel, "may be described as an attempt to overcome the dividing line of past and present, as an attempt *to see the past in the present tense*" (*God* 211–12). Only when the past may be seen in such terms—may be seen as tradition—can we generate any basis for a future.

For the Holocaust diarist, however, both the past as tradition and the future it makes possible are *elsewhere*. In her study of concentration camp diaries Renata Laqueur Weiss makes a similar observation, which, with an added word of explanation, may apply to Holocaust diaries in general. The diarists of the concentration camp, says this woman who was herself a concentration camp diarist, wanted "to escape the present and hold on to an ideal or a concept in order to survive" (8). Later she explains that these diarists tried not only to bear witness but "to write themselves out of the concentration camp world"

(22); Nathan Cohen, it is worth noting, offers a similar commentary on the diaries of the *Sonderkommandos*. "All [these] authors," he says, "resort to writing as one of the means of preserving their sanity" (287). Far from being a flight from the world or from life, however, the "escape" of these diarists is a flight *to* the world from the antiworld, a flight *to* life from the kingdom of death. Their clinging to "an ideal or a concept" is not a clinging to some fantasy but to the reality of home and family, for instance, in the face of a radical unreality. This point is illustrated perfectly in Laqueur's own Bergen-Belsen diary, where she writes: "Father, Mother, I implore you, think of me for a few intense seconds. I shall do the same of you, and our thoughts will meet and merge" (45). And, commenting on two parents in a sealed train, the *Sonderkommando* diarist Salmen Gradowski writes: "Not so long ago they had given to the world a child and thus have joined the circle of eternity, have become partners in the progress and construction of the world. Just when their first steps had led them on in the world they were told to go away, to leave the place where they had started building their nest. They are not thinking of themselves now. Only one thought predominates—what will happen to their tiny, dear beloved child" (79). While there are obvious and significant differences between the conditions endured in the ghettos and in the camps, this struggle to recover a trace of the sacred in life—as it once was or as it is now threatened—is a distinctive feature of the Holocaust diary.

Thus, while other diaries seek to record and preserve the experience of the world, the Holocaust diaries seeks to recover the world itself. While other diaries offer an account of life in the "completed precipitate of each day," the Holocaust diary struggles to recover a life despite the day's destruction. While other diaries are projected toward a future that is yet to be realized, Holocaust diaries are written in the shadow of a doom that is certain to come—indeed, that is already at hand. While other diaries contain the individual's interrogation of himself in the pursuit of meaning, the Holocaust diary includes an interrogation of God and humanity after the loss of meaning. While other diaries are written for the diarist, the Holocaust diary is written for others, living, dead, and yet to be born. How can the dead be included in an audience? Through the diarist's conscientious engagement in a testimony for the sake of a future.

Such are the distinctions that go into the *why* that distinguishes the Holocaust diary. Says Syrkin: "The diaries begin with 'why' and end with 'why' though the object of the query keeps changing. At the outset the writer tries to find rational explanations for the Nazi program which in the beginning is viewed not as a new mode, *sui generis*, but as an atavistic throwback to the familiar persecutions of the past. An ancient, much-enduring people can find comfort in historic parallels. . . . The first stage in the education of the diarists . . . is the recognition of the existence of motiveless evil. . . . They are reduced to the simplest formulation: he murders because he is a murderer" (234–35). Here too, in the initial search for explanations in precedents, the diarist's ties to the community are revealed. But the seemingly motiveless evil of the Holocaust could not be accommodated by any established categories: it was, in fact, *sui generis*. And so is the Holocaust diary.

In order to acquire a better sense of these distinguishing features of the Holocaust diary, it may be helpful to consider a diary that is usually regarded as a Holocaust diary but which, in truth, is not. It is *An Interrupted Life* by Etty Hillesum. The point of this brief examination of Hillesum's diary is not to discredit it or to make light of the author's genuine suffering; rather, it is to show that not all diaries written by people who suffered during those years can be regarded as Holocaust diaries, as we have described them.

First of all, no *why* pervades Hillesum's diary. The undoing of the human image, the eclipse of God, the obliteration of mother and father, of family and home, of children—none of this poses any particular difficulty for her. At times, just when it looks as though there may be a *why* that would link Hillesum to her community, this vision is immediately undermined. The entry dated 29 June 1942 is a good example: "The English radio has reported that 700,000 Jews perished last year alone, in Germany and the occupied territories. And even if we stay alive we shall carry the wounds with us throughout our lives. And yet I don't think life is meaningless. And God is not accountable for the senseless harm we cause one another. We are accountable only to Him! I have already died a thousand deaths in a thousand concentration camps. I know about everything and am no longer appalled by the latest reports. In one way or another I know it all. And yet I find life beautiful" (127). Invoking the "we" who do senseless harm to one another, she seems to include both Germans and Jews in this one category; she does not make the distinction between "we," the Jews who are murdered, and "they," the murderers who murder because they are murderers. Although the Holocaust diarists have a sense of an essential bond between themselves and their fellow Jews who have been sent to the camps, none of them presumes to *know* everything about the camps or the suffering of the Jews in the camps, and all of them are appalled by the reports. Underlying the *why* in the Holocaust diary, moreover, is a fundamental refusal to accept the unreality of the Nazis' antiworld as real, that is, as viable or meaningful—a fact of life, yes, but not part of life's meaning. And certainly none of these diarists can regard as beautiful a life that runs red with so much blood.

Hillesum, by contrast, writes: "They are out to destroy us completely, we must accept that and go on from there. . . . Even if we are consigned to hell, let us go there as gracefully as we can" (130). And three months later, on 10 October 1942, she repeats: "Of course, it is our complete destruction they want! But let us bear it with grace" (190). What can this "with grace" mean? Is she suggesting that the mothers of the Warsaw Ghetto should send their children to the flames of Treblinka *with grace*? Does she suppose that the women of Auschwitz who bore children only to have them drowned so that they themselves might stay alive for another day could act *with grace*? And how does the *Muselmann*—that living image of death created by the Nazis, who proves, in the words of Fackenheim, that "the divine image in man *can* be destroyed" (*Jewish Return* 246)—go to the gas chamber *with grace*? If this is her advice to these victims, it is because Hillesum operates as a severed branch: she does not understand herself to be standing in a relation of responsibility and testimony to a community or a tradition. Like many diarists, but unlike any Holocaust diarist, she is far too focused on herself alone to sense any accountability or care for another. For example, on 25 April 1942 she boasts: "I make my own rules and do as I like. In all this chaos and misery I follow my own rhythm. . . . God save me from one thing: don't let me be sent to a camp with the people with whom I work every day" (162). And three days later she writes: "Ever-present in me is an almost demonic urge to watch everything that happens. A wish to see and to hear and to be present, to worm out all of life's secrets, to observe with *detachment* what people look like in their last convulsions" (166, italics added). While the Holocaust diarist responds to a horror in order to recover some shred of life, Hillesum voyeuristically and vicariously experiences this or that as part of a strictly internal structure of her self. Therefore, as long as she merely looks on from the safe distance of self-centeredness, she has no sense of a life of humanity torn to shreds.

Hence the *other* who is of primary significance for the Holocaust diarist—as parent or child, friend or sibling, God or community—is of very little significance to Hillesum. Although it is written by a Jew, hers is not a Jewish diary, since for the Jew, as Leo Baeck states it, " 'fellow man' is inseparable from 'man' " (190). When we find her asserting, "I so love being with people," we might think that this assessment of Hillesum is too harsh. But look at her next sentence: "It is as if my own intensity draws what is best and deepest right out of them" (191)—as if they owed the emergence of their best and their deepest to *me*. Only a radical blindness to the other and an extreme preoccupation with the self, could lead Hillesum to comment on her work at a community center by saying: "Whenever yet another poor woman broke down at one of our registration tables, or a hungry child started crying, I would go over to them and stand beside them protectively, arms folded across my chest, force a smile for those huddled shattered scraps of humanity and tell myself, 'Things aren't all that bad, they really aren't all that bad' " (192). If she stands there protectively, it is herself that she is protecting: her arms are folded across her own chest, not extended in an embrace of these others. And how bad do things have to become before they *are* all that bad? After all, "knowing everything," Hillesum must know that these mothers and children are undergoing registration for one thing: to be murdered. Even her confinement in Westerbork fails to draw Hillesum out of the confines of her self and into some relation of concern for others, for on 2 October 1942 she writes: "I prayed, 'Let me be the thinking heart of these barracks.' And that is what I want to be again. The thinking heart of a whole concentration camp. . . . Happen what may, it is bound to be for the good" (191). Such a sentiment is utterly alien to all other Holocaust diarists; indeed, it is not the sentiment of a Holocaust diarist but of a diarist who is so focused on herself as the center of all that she would make herself into the center of a concentration camp! As for the statement that whatever happens is for the good, it is precisely because, in the ghetto and in the camp, nothing happens for the good—because the good has been annihilated—that the Holocaust diarist takes up the diary.

If whatever happened was for the best, if things were not all that bad, and if Jews slated for murder were to go to theirs deaths with grace, then there is indeed no being appalled at the reports of those days of destruction. And if we need not be appalled, then Bettelheim's complaint about the stage production of Anne Frank's diary applies even more so to Hillesum's diary: we can forget about Auschwitz. It never happened. We are safe. These diaries can be ignored. But these are the lies that ooze from Hillesum's diary, and, in that sense at least, her diary is inauthentic. Hers, therefore, is not a Holocaust diary. For Hillesum has no notion of anything that might be called a Holocaust: things are not all that bad, she says, it is all for the good. The Holocaust diary, on the other hand, is defined by its pervasive awareness of Holocaust—Holocaust of children, mothers, fathers, home, God, community, meaning, sanctity, humanity. In the Holocaust diary things are not that bad—they are infinitely worse. In the Holocaust diary things are for the good—of the Nazis, at the utter expense of the Jews. The absolute enigma confronting the Holocaust diarist is how to respond to this annihilation, how to recover a human life from a realm that absolutely negates humanity. Yet, in a place void of humanity, to paraphrase Rabbi Hillel's remark in the Talmud, one must be a human being (*Avot* 2:6). But how?

Let us now set out on the long road ahead to explore this *how* that issues from the diarists' *why*.

THE WRITER AND THE WRITING

IN HIS BOOK ON THE HASIDIM, MILTON ARON RELATES A story about Levi Yitzhak of Berditchev and what transpired upon his return home after studying with Rabbi Dov Ber, the renowned Maggid of Mezeritch. On the day of his homecoming he was seated at the table for the evening meal, when his father-in-law said to him, "So tell me: did you learn anything special from the Great Maggid?"

"I have learned," replied the young Levi Yitzhak, "that God is in the world."

"But everyone knows that," retorted his father-in-law, who then called over their maid and asked her whether God is in the world.

"Yes," she answered without hesitation.

"You see," the father-in-law said triumphantly.

"She says," the inspired Levi Yitzhak shot back, "but I know" (168).

This Hasidic anecdote is more closely connected with the Holocaust diary than it may seem at first glance. From a Jewish standpoint, to know that God is in the world is to know that we must engage in a constant examination of our soul in a *cheshbon hanefesh*. Thus, in a similar way, many people say that an unexamined life is not worth living, but, on a level unattained by many, the diarist knows. Indeed, if he knows nothing else, the diarist knows that, unless he engages in some kind of self-examination, not only is his life without meaning—it is impossible to live in search of any meaning. For the diarist, then, writing becomes as essential to living as is eating or breathing. Girard makes this point by saying: "A tangible sign of internal observation and resulting from the attention focused on the self, the journal expresses for the subject an imperative necessity to write. The human being who observes himself, who reflects on himself, and who recalls his near or distant past, instead of giving himself over to the ordinary activities of life in a spirit of total independence, is not free to do it or not to do it. He is constituted in such a way that self-observation is for him a genuine need. The failure to satisfy this need would compromise all possible equilibrium. Even if he should incur grave dangers in meeting this need, it would be even more dangerous to refuse the summons" (526). When we consider writing and the writer in connection with the Holocaust diary, however, Girard's insight is not altogether applicable. It is true that in the Holocaust diary the writer senses a necessity to write and that he writes even at the risk of incurring grave dangers. It is also true that the writer of the Holocaust diary senses something of great import at stake in his response to a summons. But the summons does not arise from the self alone, and the task of the diarist is to engage in something more than self-observation. Here the writer's stake in his writing goes beyond a concern for inner equilibrium to include a communal salvation—or, failing that, a testimony to and for the sake of the life of a human community. The summons to which he responds arises from the truth, the tradition, and the meaning that constitute both himself and his community.

To be sure, the very language used by the diarist in writing his diary harbors a summons to respond not only to himself but to a humanity that is beyond himself. The Holocaust diary is an address that attests to being addressed. The words we speak were spoken by others before us, and by others they are bequeathed to us. Because language is a public domain—because the word lives within and imparts meaning to a community—the diarist who pursues the word does so in a response to a community, either implicitly or explicitly. And if the diarist is a Jew writing as a Jew, he responds to Creation itself. For a people who understands the world to be sustained by the word of God, the diary has the potential for becoming a part of that sustaining utterance. "Man is the language of God," said Menachem-Mendl of Vitebsk (Wiesel, *Souls* 86); therefore human beings must be as careful with their language as they are with their lives. As they speak, so is the Holy One either muted or made heard, and human life is either wounded or made whole. According to the Jewish tradition, to which these diaries belong, words decide not only truth but life and death. "For everything is in the word," Elie Wiesel expresses this idea. "It is enough to arrange certain syllables, to form certain sentences, speak certain words according to a defined rhythm, to be able to lay claim to celestial powers and master them" (*Golem* 44). Equally important to the diarist, we may add, is the process of laying claim to human life and meaning which transpires in the writing of the diary. Laying claim to life and meaning is precisely what it means to sustain the Creation. For the People of the Book this process has traditionally unfolded through the writing of the book. Indeed, the ancient mystical text known as the *Sefer Yetzirah*, or *The Book of Creation*, declares, "He made His universe with three books (*Sepharim*): with text (*Sepher*), with number (*Sephar*), and with communication (*Sippur*)" (5). Communicating with a community is communing with the word; it is the Jewish diarist's means of participating in the creation and in the recovery of life.

Given this Jewish teaching and tradition, we may perceive a more profound sense in which these words from the Book of Esther might be read: "To the Jews according to their writing, according to their language" (8:9). For the authors of the Holocaust diary, this does not mean that if they wrote well they would fare well; most of them, in fact, perished in the camps. But it does mean that by thus engaging the word they may engage the life of the soul which was threatened at every turn. It means that they may bear a witness that transforms us into witnesses who must affirm the life they would recover, and not who despair of the death that consumed them. The very fact that these writers and their writing are before us is a testament to the holy. Like the workers who occasionally descended into the Holy of Holies in *tevot*, or boxes, to make repairs, these authors also descend in *tevot*, which also means "words," not just into death but into the holy, where they struggle to retrieve the traces of life. This "diary-writing," says Renata Laqueur Weiss, who was among these diarists, "springs from the instinct to save life" (54)—not merely to despair of death. "Man's days in this world have a permanence," the Chofetz Chaim reminds us of a Jewish mystical teaching. "From each day a spiritual creation comes into existence" (*Ahavath* 126). And, day by day, the writing of these writers goes into the spiritual creation of spiritual life. Among these Jewish diarists, writing the diary is much more than a matter of the internal observation focused on the self. Springing from the instinct to save life, writing the diary is a matter of remembrance focused on the other. "In deciding to write this diary," Aryeh Klonicki-Klonymus explains, "I was motivated by the desire to leave some remembrance at least to those of my brothers fortunate enough to be living in lands untouched by the hand of Hitler" (21). Thus, if the summons to write comes from within, its voice is heard from beyond. Let us begin, then, by considering that summons more closely.

THE SUMMONS OF THE WORD

In an entry dated 28 February 1941, Emmanuel Ringelblum notes, "The drive to write down one's memoirs is powerful: Even young people in labor camps do it" (133). That the writing of the diary issues from a *drive* to write may suggest that the impetus to write arises from some innate aspect of human nature. Having noted this internal aspect of diary writing, however, we must not psychologize the phenomenon of writing and jump to the conclusion that it is reducible to a natural drive to meet a natural need. For upon further examination of the diarist's assessment of what drives him, we find that the drive to write is rooted more in moral obligation than in natural need. This is what makes the writing of the diary a response to the summons of the *word*: unlike the satisfaction of a personal need, meeting a moral obligation lies in a certain relation to others, and the medium of that relation is the word. The Westerbork inmate Philip Mechanicus, for example, realizes that he must "record the daily happenings for those who in time to come will want to get an idea of what went on here. So I have a duty to go on with my writing" (181–82). Notice here that the utterance of the word is the performance of a duty. The Dutch word rendered as "duty" in this passage is *plicht* (191), which, indeed, means "duty" or "obligation" in a *moral sense*; we are reminded of this important point when we recall that it is a root for the word *plichtenleer*, meaning "deontology," which is the study of ethics and moral obligation. In the writing of the Holocaust diary, the one summoned by the word is summoned not as a historian or a journalist or even as a victim, but as a human being who stands in a moral relation to other human beings. "Testimony," the Talmud teaches us, "is committed to men of care" (*Pesachim* 12b); whatever else this writing might be, it is above all testimony, and as men of care, these writers are men who care about others. If, as Girard states above, the diarist is not free to refrain from writing, this is not due to some inner psychological necessity but to a moral imperative that the writer encounters both outside himself and within himself, despite himself. "All my inwardness," in the words of Levinas, "is invested in the form of a despite-me, for-another" (*Otherwise* 11), and this inwardness is the soul, which is "the other in me" (*Otherwise* 191). The summons of the word that is both within and beyond is the summons of the soul. Far from being the manifestation of a natural drive, a psychological need, or a cultural phenomenon, this writing is the manifestation of a soul that seeks its life through a response to another soul, in the light of a higher responsibility for what there is to hold dear.

"Remember the yoke of responsibility that rests upon you," said Rabbi Kalonymus Kalman Shapira, the Rebbe of the Warsaw Ghetto. "All the worlds, even the fate of God's holiness in this world, depend on you" (121). The summons of the word—the summons *to* the word—is the summons of the Good that has laid claim to the writer as a human being whose humanity lies in being for the other, in answering to the other, both as person and as the One who is the Good. If the writer of the Holocaust diary has no choice in his writing, it is because the Good, in the words of Levinas, "is not the object of a choice, for it has taken possession of the subject before the subject had the time—that is, the distance—necessary for choice. There is indeed no subjection more complete than this possession by the Good, this election" (*Collected* 134–35). Hence, answering the summons of the word, the Jewish writer of this Jewish text discovers what it means to be among the Chosen. This possession by the imperative or the "thou shalt" of the Good may manifest itself in the work of any writer. But it is especially pronounced in the writer of the Holocaust diary, since he engages in his writing at the risk not only of his own life but of the lives of those around him. Thus Julian Stanford, who with his wife Elizabeth was hidden by a Dutch family, records Elizabeth's warnings concerning the dangers of writing: "We would be lost if ever there should be a house search and the Germans were to find these notes" (119). And yet without his writing of the diary Stanford's soul would be lost, for without this answering to the summons of the word he would lose the Good that is essential to the life of the soul. Diary writers such as Emil Dorian (126) and Yitzhak Katznelson (187) were careful to point out that the Nazis had made the writing of diaries and other Jewish texts illegal. And now we see why: the Nazis sought to destroy not only the body of Israel but the soul of the Jew. In order to destroy the soul, they had to destroy the Good; and in order to destroy the Good, they had to destroy the response to the summons of the word. For it is precisely in the midst of this response that the voice of the Good is heard. "The glory of the Infinite," as Levinas has said, "reveals itself through what it is capable of doing in the witness" (*Ethics* 109). And this is just what the Nazis did not want revealed.

The assault on the diary, then, is part of a metaphysical assault on the Good, on the Holy, and on the Truth; in a word, it is part of the assault on God. In the words of Emil Fackenheim, the Nazi, like Amalek of old, "singles out Israel for attack *because* Israel is singled out by God for a covenant, his aim being to destroy the covenant as he destroys Israel" (*Judaism* 178). Therefore, in the case of the *Jewish* writer of the *Holocaust* diary, the sense of ethical obligation has a metaphysical aspect; written in an ethical response to others, it harbors a metaphysical response to God, an implicit affirmation of the covenant with the divine through the response to the human. Indeed, from a Jewish standpoint, the path to the divine always leads through the human. What this means for the Jewish writer and his writing, Levinas makes clear when he explains that the other human being "is situated in a dimension of height, in the ideal, the Divine, and through my relation to the Other, I am in touch with God. The moral relation therefore reunites both self-consciousness and consciousness of God. Ethics is not the corollary of the vision of God, it is that very vision. Ethics is an optic, such that everything I know of God and everything I can hear of His word and reasonably say to Him must find an ethical expression. In the Holy Ark from which the voice of God is heard by Moses, there are only the tablets of the Law. . . . The attributes of God are given not in the indicative, but in the imperative. The knowledge of God comes to us like a commandment, like a *Mitzvah*. To know God is to know what must be done" (*Difficult* 17). This aspect of the moral obligation underlying the Jewish diarist's sense of duty takes us beyond what we may have thought we understood in Ringelblum's mention of the drive to write or Mechanicus's invocation of the duty to write. More than a matter of feeling a need or even sensing a duty, the writing of the diary arises from a condition of being commanded to write. If Zelig Kalmanovitch, a diarist of the Vilna Ghetto, declares, "Verily, each day should be recorded" (50), it is because the day itself is constituted by the commandment. Divided into days, the diary is itself an utterance of day unto day. God enters the day through the commandment, and through the day He enters into history. Thus the obligation to answer the commandment by answering others situates the diarist in a position of answerability to history.

"It is difficult to hold a pen," says Chaim Kaplan, "to concentrate one's thoughts. But a strange idea has stuck in my head since the war broke out—that it is a duty I must perform" (144). In war, we are forced to determine why we live, why we die, and why we kill; in war we are forced to attest to what transcends life and therefore to what makes life meaningful. War not only makes history—it unmakes it, and so it constitutes a breach or a fracture in the fabric of Being. But, as Levinas argues, the human being is also a "fracture in Being which produces the act of giving with hands which are full, in place of fighting and pillaging. This is where the idea of being chosen comes from" ("Revelation" 302). In Kaplan's case, a hand has taken hold of him, and so his hand takes hold of a pen; he has been given a task, and so he engages in an act of giving, which is an act of writing, that opposes the outbreak of war. Indeed, his writing is the only thing he has left to give. And if he has a sense of anything, he has a sense of being chosen. Chosen for what? For a response to this rupture in history before the God of history. Hence on 16 January 1940 he writes: "Anyone who keeps such a record [as this] endangers his life, but this does not frighten me. I sense within me the magnitude of this hour, and my responsibility toward it, and I have an inner awareness that I am fulfilling a national obligation, a historic obligation that I am not free to relinquish" (104). And this responsibility rules the writer and his writing to the very end. "Some of my friends and acquaintances," he notes on

26 July 1942, just a week before his final entry, "who know the secret of my diary urge me, in their despair, to stop writing. 'Why? For what purpose? Will you live to see it published? Will these words of yours reach the ears of future generations? How?' . . . And yet in spite of it all I refuse to listen to them. I feel that continuing this diary to the very end of my physical and spiritual strength is a historical mission which must not be abandoned. My mind is still clear, my need to record unstilled, though it is now five days since any real food has passed my lips. Therefore I will not silence my diary!" (383–84). This is not merely a case of stubbornness on the part of Kaplan. To silence the diary would be to succumb to the silence that, in the words of André Neher, becomes "a spokesman for the invincible Nothingness" (*Exile* 63). The diarist, on the other hand, becomes the spokesman for the being that opposes nothingness. Though it is written in silence, the diary is opposed to silence, opposed to the indifference that underlies death in war and despair in the human being. Notice that the issue of whether it will see the light of day or will reach an ear is irrelevant to the writing of the diary. Why? Because this writing is summoned not by the prospects for publication or readership but by the word itself, by the word that comes to the diarist from on high, in the mode of commandment.

Since this mission must not be abandoned, and since it is the word that summons this writing, many diarists speak if only to note that the word eludes them or that they cannot speak. On 22 September 1942, for example, Kalmanovitch writes: "A peculiar thing: all my thoughts have vanished. I forgot what I wanted to record" (28). The Hebrew phrase translated as "all my thoughts have vanished" is *ne'lamu kol hara'onot* (80), which may be rendered as "all the ideas" or "all the concepts are hidden." If writing entails the recovery of life, it entails the recovery of the concepts, which, as the Hebrew implies, have not exactly vanished but are hidden, as though there were light hidden in the darkness or divine sparks in the *kelipot* (shells), as the Jewish mystics might express it. In those days of destruction, as Wiesel has remarked, "there was a confusion, a total confusion of concepts and virtues" (Patterson 21), especially a confusion surrounding the categories of life and death. To release the light is to overcome not only the hiddenness but the confusion of concepts—that is the task of the diarist. The summons of the word, then, is a summons to return the word to its meaning, so that the concepts of life and death may be restored. This notion, of course, has serious ramifications for how we are to understand a statement made in Menahem Kon's diary, which was recovered from the *Oneg Shabbat* archives of the Warsaw Ghetto Underground: "No pen can write down what the eye saw, no phantasy can picture it. Still in a nightmare, we find it very hard to write at all. . . . But I shall try" (84). The difficulty in recording what was seen lies not just in the horror of the event or in the limits of the imagination but in the divorce between word and meaning. More than merely a process of describing or imagining, in the Holocaust diary writing is a process of rejoining and reconstituting, a process of recovery. This is what makes it a response not only to suffering but to the word that seeks a return to meaning in the return of meaning to life. "I've no heart for writing," says Kalmanovitch's comrade Hersh Wasser (212), because meaning has been drained from his heart and with it the life engendered by meaning.

It becomes all too clear that this draining of meaning from the heart is a draining of life from life when we read in Katznelson's diary: "Yesterday, I could not hold up my pen to continue writing about the annihilation of our people. It was a year to the day since they took away my Chanah and my sons Ben Zion, fourteen years of age, and Binyamin, eleven years of age" (128). Katznelson made this entry in his diary on 15 August 1943, during his confinement in the camp at Vittel; his wife and two sons were taken from the Warsaw Ghetto to the death camp Treblinka in August 1942. Taking hold of his pen to note that he could not hold his pen, he takes hold of a memory that comprises his only hold on life, his only connection to life. And in the diary that connection is constituted by the word. What for Katznelson creates a bond with the past establishes for Moshe Flinker a link to the future; in the process of writing the diary, the *was* of the one and the *not yet* of the other meet on the page before each of them. "For the past few weeks," writes young Moshe from his home in Brussels, "I have not written in my diary. The main reason for this is difficult to explain, but here it is: all this time I have been waiting for something" (96). In the Hebrew text of his diary we see that he is waiting *l'eyzeh davar* (88), or "for some word": the summons he would answer comes from the depths of a word not yet uttered, from the horizon of the future, where the word awaits its joining with meaning.[1] And yet the future does not reveal itself as meaning-governed until we generate meaning as we approach that future; similarly, the summons of the word does not come to the diarist until he responds to it. The writing of the diarist, then, is a means of listening, and his notation of the day is a turning from the previous day toward the next day. Thus "I have not written" can mean "I am waiting." Waiting for what? For the summons of the word. The writing of "I have not written" is a listening for what has yet to come.

This writing to record not having written is a recurring motif in the Romanian diary of Emil Dorian. On 20 December 1940, for example, he writes: "For weeks I haven't touched this notebook, despite the intimacy between us that had become habit. A psychological paralysis when faced with events; fear of misinterpretation, or at least of misconstruction of my notes; the feeling that any kind of writing is useless; the moral and intellectual hibernation into which I have sunk—all this kept me from these pages" (129). On 15 October 1941: "Again I stopped writing, unable to touch this notebook" (168–69). And on 31 March 1944: "Again, after several weeks' pause, I am returning to these pages, with some feeling of weariness and uselessness" (304). By now we realize that the issue here lies not in the question of why he stopped but in the question of why he returns. In the face of such paralysis, weariness, and uselessness, the answer can only be that writing the diary is the key to sustaining a life that would otherwise succumb to such emptiness. Even if it appears to be useless, writing is the only thing that can overcome the writer's sense of uselessness, because it is the one thing that enables him to hear the summons to write.[2] Paralysis sets in where the word leaves off. Only the summons of the word can penetrate the *rigor mortis* of paralysis, and, as we have seen, only the process of writing can make heard the summons of the word. For the summons of the word is the summons of life that arises in opposition to death, a point that becomes graphically clear when we read the entry dated 21 July 1942 in the Warsaw Ghetto diary of Janusz Korczak: "Ten o'clock. Shots: two, several, two, one, several. Perhaps it is my own badly blacked-out window. But I do not stop writing. On the contrary: it sharpens (a single shot) the thought"

(175). The shot that takes a life fuels the writing that would recover a life. As the rifle fires its bullets, the pen inscribes its words; the one metes out death, while the other seeks out life. Even when he has nothing to say, for the diarist the word is a refuge.

THE REFUGE OF THE WORD

To say that for the Holocaust diarist the word is a refuge is not to say that it is merely a realm into which he flees from death and despair; rather, as we have suggested, it is a realm in which he seeks a life. Unlike the novelist, poet, or dramatist, the diarist makes an *entry* and thereby *enters into* a place and a process of recovering life. With regard to diaries in general, Girard notes that the diary "represents an authentic measure taken, and it is the beginning of a rectification. It is the very instrument of salvation, a means for the self to conquer itself, always compromised and always begun again" (527). While in the Holocaust diary the act of writing may mark the beginning of a rectification and provide a path to salvation, it is not simply a means for the self to conquer itself. Much more than that, it is a means for the self to offer itself to another; in the offering that characterizes the relation of being for the other, as person or God, the soul seeks its salvation. And when the writing of the diarist revolves around such a relation, the writer is borne aloft by his writing.

This focus on relation rather than on the self is, to be sure, in keeping with the Jewish outlook that rules this Jewish writing and these Jewish writers. Elie Wiesel voices this outlook in his novel *Twilight*, where his character Abraham says: "Please try to understand: the Word is everything. Through the Word we elevate ourselves or debase ourselves. It is refuge for the man in exile, and exile for the righteous. How would we pray without it? How would we live without it?" (98). Wiesel's question concerning prayer indicates that our elevation through the word is an elevation determined by a relation to another, to the Holy One, from whom we derive the life and the meaning of all other relations. The Hasidic master Rabbi Nachman of Breslov (1772–1810) explains the Jewish understanding of the refuge provided by the word by saying: "However low you fall, you still have the faculty of speech. You should use it! Speak words of truth: words of Torah, words of prayer and the fear of Heaven. You should speak to God. Speak also to your friend, and especially to your teacher. The power of speech is such that at all times it enables you to remind yourself of the closeness to God, and so to bring strength to yourself, even in the places which seem furthest from holiness" (*Restore* 24). For the People of the Book, the medium is indeed the message: writing their book, they seek the life summoned through the Book. It may be the case that, unlike the writers of the Holocaust diaries, Rabbi Nachman did not realize how far a place can be from the place of holiness. But he did articulate what sort of refuge the word may have provided for these writers.

In the Holocaust diary the word offers a refuge for the diarist because there it becomes not only the means of address but also a presence to be addressed in the midst of what Alvin Rosenfeld calls "the emptiness and silence of an imposed Absence" (*Double* 15). Here we see a deeper sense in which the process of writing is also a hearing: the diary itself listens to the diarist, lending an ear in a world grown deaf. Mikhail Bakhtin maintains that "two voices is the minimum for life, the minimum for existence" (*Problems* 252), and the diary creates this minimum required for the recovery of life by positing an attentive presence opposite the voice of the diarist. Suddenly, as the diarist puts her hand to the page, the indifferent silence of the blank piece of paper becomes the responsive silence of a listener: it becomes a *you*. "How I need you, my dear diary," writes the Romanian teenager Mirjam Korber. "But it is so hard to release the words, not only orally, but also when forcing the hand to write" (109). In the foregoing section we found that, in the aspect of summons, the word in the diary poses a responsibility or a need to be met; here, in the aspect of refuge, we find that the diary meets a need. And both aspects can be found in a given diarist, whether the writer is a teenage girl or a mature man. Chaim Kaplan, for instance, declares, "Were it not for my pen, my delight, I would be lost" (233). Why? Because, as he puts it, "this journal is my life, my friend and ally. I would be lost without it. I pour my innermost thoughts and feelings into it, and this brings relief" (278). In Kaplan's entries we see quite clearly that the process of writing the diary is an integral part of the process of recovering a life when that life is threatened at every turn. The writer's outpouring of his innermost thoughts in this instance is much more than a matter of relieving stress or getting something off his chest. Beyond all that, it entails a process of entering into a relation that may sustain a presence in a world dominated by absence. The diary is not just an outlet—it is his life; the diary is not just a document—it is his friend.

If the diary is written, moreover, in order to meet a responsibility to the human community, the diarist incurs a responsibility to the diary itself. Once she views the diary as a friend, the diarist incurs a debt to her friend. Consider, for example, the entry made on 14 February 1944 by the thirteen-year-old Hungarian, Éva Heyman: "Dear diary, I promised to write Marta's story down in you, because you're my best friend and I mustn't keep any secret from you" (31). Éva's friend Marta Muenzer had been deported a couple of months prior to this date and was murdered near Kamenetz-Podolsk. Here the absence of the friend is taken over by the presence of the diary when the promise is made to the diary to inscribe the tale of the absent friend. Through the writing of this tale in the diary, the diary becomes a "friend," so that Éva can say to the diary: "Don't worry, you won't be alone; you're my best friend" (69). Similarly, in the case of Anne Frank, the diary not only assumes a presence that the friend cannot provide, but it also assumes a name. "Paper is patient," she writes, "and as I don't intend to show this cardboard-covered notebook, bearing the proud name of 'diary,' to anyone, unless I find a real friend, boy or girl, probably nobody cares. And now I come to the root of the matter, the reason for my starting a diary: it is that I have no such real friend. . . . I want this diary to be my friend, and I shall call my friend Kitty" (12–13). And: "In the end I always come back to my diary. That is where I start and finish, because Kitty is always patient. I'll promise her that I shall persevere" (57). Presenting itself as an interlocutor, the diary represents a center, a place from which to start and finish, and that center is made of the word. The word can constitute such a center for two reasons: first, it implies the presence of another to whom it is addressed; second, it is the site where meaning becomes an issue. In the Holocaust diary, the refuge of the word is the refuge of meaning created in a world where meaning is undergoing a constant collapse. In these examples from Éva Heyman and Anne Frank, meaning comes to bear in the promise. Why? Because the promise opens up the horizon of a future and defines a direction from which meaning may itself be defined. It is a going forth, as the Latin root of the English word *promittere* suggests. In the Holocaust diary, the refuge provided by the word is a refuge not in which the diarist hides, but from which the diarist goes forth.

This prospect of going forth is essential to the freedom and therefore to the life of these diarists, since, in one way or another, all of them are imprisoned. As Wiesel's character Paltiel Kossover declares from his prison cell: "I can write as much as I like, and whenever I like. And what I like. I'm a free man" (*Testament* 19). It is in this spirit that the Romanian author Emil Dorian not only writes in his diary but in his diary writes about writing. There the word offers refuge not only as a responsive presence but as a subject to be addressed and pursued. "All is not lost," he asserts, "while the hope of writing a poem is still alive" (33). This entry was made on 12 July 1938; by 15 September 1942, as one would expect, Dorian's pursuit of poetry becomes more problematic: "When you hear around you in what absurd and arbitrary ways an existence still full of inner life is destroyed in a few minutes, fear and rage overwhelm you and undermine the layer of resigned calm, plunging you into helpless despair. No doubt now is the moment when I ought to turn to poetry for its nourishing strength, its support which brings forgetfulness, direction, serenity. But today poetry comes very hard to me, although many times in the past it helped me in low moods and depression" (229). In his concern with the word, the diarist here opposes the meaningful to the absurd and the ordered to the arbitrary in an act of testimony. As when Bezalel fashioned the Ark of Testimony in the wilderness (Exodus 37:1), so Dorian and other diarists introduce the word to their wilderness. And why was Bezalel chosen for this task? Because, as the thirteenth-century thinker Nachmanides explains it in his *Commentary on the Torah*, "Bezalel knew how to combine the letters with which heaven and earth were created" (2:543). In keeping with a tradition that goes back to Bezalel, Dorian is an imitator of the Creator: like the Creator, he combines the letters and invokes a word that may introduce some order to a world returned to the *tohu v'bohu* of chaos and darkness, even if he goes no further than to declare that the word comes hard. As hard as it may come, it comes nevertheless.

For Dorian, as for many other diarists, this *nevertheless* constitutes the refuge of the word. It makes of the word, from which the diary is made, the subject matter of the diary itself. And that is how the word becomes a means of resisting death and affirming life, a means that opens up when all such means have been eliminated. Thus, like the bullet that sharpened Korczak's thought, the oppression of Jewish life sharpens Dorian's resolve to preserve that life through the preservation of the Jewish word. This effort also becomes part of his diary, as we see when on 20 October 1941 he writes: "In the last two months I managed to do something I would not have thought possible: I worked on, and almost completed, the anthology of Yiddish poets. . . . The harder the blows rained on Jews, the more passionately I plunged into work reaffirming the permanence of Jewish contributions to art" (170). The diary creates a refuge for the Holocaust diarist, inasmuch as it creates a place where he may affirm the importance of this reaffirmation of Jewish life and of this responsibility to Jewish life. As a refuge, then, the word that comprises the diary includes a commentary not only on death and destruction but on the means of resisting death and destruction and affirming life. Here we realize that the *you* addressed in the diary is not a "projection of the psyche" or some other psychological phenomenon—it is life itself. And, if we recall an observation made by Buber, we may see that through the diary's address to the *you*, the spirit speaks. "Spirit in its human manifestation is man's response to his You," says Buber. Spirit is word. . . . Spirit is not in the I but between I and You. It is not like the blood that circulates in you but like the air in which you breathe. Man lives in the spirit when he is able to respond to his You" (*I and Thou* 89). Such is the breathing space offered in the refuge of the word. "The spirit must be kept alive if you are to write, and you must write if the spirit is to stay alive," says Dorian (203). And in this saying, we hear within his voice the voice of the spirit.

THE VOICE OF THE SPIRIT

Near the end of his diary, on 3 September 1943, Moshe Flinker writes, "My diary has become a reflection of my spiritual life" (109). As strong as this statement may seem, it is even stronger in young Moshe's

Hebrew text, where we find that "reflection of my spiritual life" is a translation of *b'ikar shel chayey ruchiy* (101); using the word *b'ikar*, Moshe suggests that the process of writing his diary forms not just a "reflection" but the root, essence, and foundation of his spiritual life. Why? Because through this writing the spirit of a people finds its voice, and the soul of the individual voices its outcry. Earlier in this chapter we saw that the Nazis' assault on the diary was part of a general assault on the soul; here we may add that the assault on the soul entails the silencing of the soul. As the voice of the spirit, then, the diary is a manifestation of the soul's refusal to be silenced. "Your daily revolt treads mud," says Dorian, "cries out to a steadily leaden sky, and still you don't speak out. Most people, everywhere, are silent" (196). And yet, like the record of the lapse in writing, this remark on the failure to speak out is a speaking out, just as Dorian's comment on the paralysis that threatens him constitutes a movement forward. "Not out of this metal-gray day," he writes, "nor out of thoughts, nor books, but out of the depth of my being arises this refusal to go on, to pick up everyday living with its hollow sound. A sudden drop into deadly weariness, a total paralysis" (44). And: "Suddenly, thought is completely paralyzed, and in that moment revolt hurts like a burning wound" (197). Like the wind, which is also a meaning of *ruach*, the spirit is what it is in its movement; and its movement is the movement of the word. If there is an inner depth from which a refusal to go on arises, there is a deeper depth, one that comes not just from within but from beyond, that impels the writer to write. The depth that extends beyond, like the language in which I speak, is called spirit. To be sure, the talmudic sage Rabbi Yochanan once said, "Every single word that went forth from the Omnipresent was split up into seventy languages" (*Shabbat* 88b), which are the languages of humanity: the spirit that moved over the face of the deep moves through language itself. And the darkness that is the deep itself? According to the *Midrash Tanchuma*, it is "the Angel of Death, who darkened the face of Creation" (1:150). Death is the enemy of the word that goes into the Holocaust diary.

The limits of the word on my tongue extend beyond the limits of my soul into the near-limitless realm of language. The relation of the word that is mine to the word that is language parallels the relation between the soul and the spirit. Bakhtin explains this distinction by ing: "The soul is an image of the totality of everything that has been actually experienced—of everything that is present-on-hand in the soul in the dimension of time; the spirit is the totality of everything that has the validity of meaning—a totality of all the forms of my life's directedness from within itself" (*Art* 10). The spirit finds its voice in the utterance of the soul; when this utterance fails, so does the sense of reality of self and world, as we see when Dorian writes: "Days of an eerie sensation, like floating above the ground. My whole life, it seems, belongs to someone else. I write as if in a dream. I am not absent from reality, but remote, and this tints all levels of existence with a strange hue of unreality" (91). This disconnectedness from the ground, this distance from the real, is the result of a breach between soul and spirit which distinguishes the endeavor to return meaning to the word and the man to the world. Indeed, the diary exists precisely because this breach exists. "I can not feel my body," says the sculptor Rivosh, a resident of the ghetto established in Riga. "I can not feel my soul—it is as if I were made of wood" (343). If he is to find a way to return himself to the completeness of body and soul, then he must find a way to articulate the breach. And the diary provides that means; it constitutes a center around which all dwelling revolves in a time characterized by the collapse of life's center and by the impossibility of dwelling. For the writer of the Holocaust diary, then, the process of writing the diary is a process of returning to a life in which the soul is felt and the spirit is voiced. "The soul," says Rabbi Abraham Isaac Kook, "is full of letters that abound with the light of life, intellect and will, a spirit of vision, and complete existence" (93). Complete existence is realized only through dwelling, and these letters flow from the soul when that existence is threatened. Far more than a commentary on the day or a record of events, the diarist's process of writing is a re-membering of the elements of life that make not just living but dwelling possible.

Thus Hanna Levy-Hass notes in her Bergen-Belsen diary that composing the texts of songs brings her closer to the memory of home, closer to the dwelling place that opposes Bergen-Belsen (39). Here one will note the link between text and home, or the appearance of a text that may for a time replace the home. And the Holocaust diary is just such a text, for it is a text that reconnects life with life, spirit with soul. "Is it possible to consecrate God's name in a manner divorced from life itself?" asks Hannah Senesh during her time away from her Hungarian home. "Is there anything more holy than life itself?" (103). Her question is, of course, rhetorical. And it is altogether Jewish. "The way to God leads through your fellow man," says Wiesel in this connection. "Fervor? Yes—later. Study? Yes—later. Ecstasy? Yes—later. Not on a hungry stomach. Not with a sick child at home" (*Somewhere* 151). The difficulty confronting the Holocaust diarist, however, is more severe. There is the sick child, but there is no home. There is the sick soul, but no tie to the spirit that nurtures it. Hence, if the diary is the form of resistance to death that we have claimed it to be, it is much like the resistance that Fackenheim describes when he notes: "German resistance, such as it was, had to discover a true self to be respected. The Jewish resistance had to *recreate* Jewish selfhood and self-respect. . . . Once again the categories 'willpower' and 'internal desire' seem inadequate. Once again we have touched an Ultimate" (*To Mend* 222). Willpower and internal desire are adequate to human endeavor only when the human being has a dwelling place within which and from which he may proceed, and the German resistors had such a place: they were not removed from their homes, where mothers, fathers, and children were still mothers, fathers, and children. Despite their removal from a place in the world, on the other hand, the Jews found ways to recreate a place and with it a relation to the Place, or the *Makom*, that is spirit. And a primary means of creating such a place lay in the creation of a text. Thus, commenting on the Yiddish writers of the Warsaw Ghetto, Hillel Seidman writes: "Their faith has been so strong! And their longing to live so powerful!" (149). How is that longing made real in the midst of the unreal? Through the process of writing.

In this diarist who writes about the writers—this diarist whose writing responds to writing—we encounter the writing of a life that is both beyond him and within him. In a word, we encounter *ruach*. "The dimension of *ruach*," André Neher elaborates on this notion, "goes beyond that of physical bodies, so that it does not seize them in their localization or individualization but in their communication. In possessing the *ruach*, man has not acquired *one* life, but life itself. The *ruach* is the very spirit of life. As soon as that spirit encounters another life, it communicates with it" (*Prophetic* 94–95). The diarist's communication with life is a manifestation of his encounter with spirit, where spirit may be understood to be "the exteriority of the Infinite," as Levinas refers to it. "The exteriority of the Infinite becomes somehow an inwardness in the sincerity of a witness borne," he explains. "Inwardness is not a secret place somewhere in me; it is that reverting in which the eminently exterior, precisely in virtue of this eminent exteriority, this impossibility of being contained and consequently entering into a theme, forms, as infinity, an exception to essence, concerns me and circumscribes me and orders me by my own voice. The command is stated by the mouth of him it commands. The infinitely exterior becomes an 'inward' voice, but a voice bearing witness to the fission of the inward secrecy that makes signs to another, signs of this very giving of signs" (*Otherwise* 147). The inwardness of the diarist engaged with his diary is not his alone, since it is an inwardness that is for another. The diary that becomes a "sign of the giving of signs" to another becomes a sign of the very life that it seeks in the midst of death. The possibility of its becoming such a sign lies in its capacity to become a vehicle for the voice of that "infinitely exterior" presence that we call spirit.

It is not just Seidman, then, who cries out in the diary but the very presence of the spirit that cuts through the diary, its very writing process; it is *ruach* that cries: "Jews! Don't allow yourselves to be broken and scattered! Don't succumb to the darkness of despair! Drink deeply to life. To life! Jews, to life!" (77). We can see, moreover, how deep runs the identity of the writer with his writing when we recall Seidman's comment on the suicide of Adam Czerniakow, the head of the Warsaw Ghetto Jewish Council: "He left behind no last will or testament. No farewell letter. Only his notebook lying open on his writing table" (45). What many have regarded as an objective chronicle of ghetto life and the affairs of the Council here presents itself as the image of a man's soul offered to the remnants of the Jewish spirit. In his introduction to the English edition of Czerniakow's diary, Israel Gutman notes, "It has been reported that after Czerniakow made the last entry in his diary on July 23, 1942, he left a note to the effect that the SS wanted him to kill the children with his own hands" (70). And, according to Josef Kermisz's account in that same volume, Czerniakow had these words for his wife before taking cyanide on that date: "I am powerless, my heart trembles in sorrow and compassion. I can no longer bear all this. My act will show everyone the right thing to do" (70). How is Czerniakow's suicide related to Seidman's summons for Jews to live? In this way: both are grounded in the affirmation of life that constitutes the substance of their diaries. Seidman's diary calls upon Jews not only to survive the death and destruction around them but to embrace the dearness of life *despite* that death and in a refusal to participate in that destruction. Similarly, Czerniakow's suicide is not a rejection of life; it is a refusal to take part in the extermination of life. Where is the voice of the spirit in this? It lies in Czerniakow's joining his life and his soul to the lives of the children, and thereby to the Jewish future—or to the obliteration of it—along the horizon of which the Jewish spirit unfolds. The last act of his life, then, makes his life into a commentary on his diary, not the other way around. And so his diary becomes not merely a private record of an individual's soul but a part of life's spirit. It lies *open* on his desk—open to the people who constituted Israel.

"The people," Buber has pointed out, "is not a sum of individuals addressed by God; it is something beyond that, something essential and irreplaceable, meant by God as such, claimed by Him as such, and answerable to Him as such" (*Judaism* 216). Beyond the sum of individuals, the People of God, as such, embody the spirit of God; the *Zohar*, in fact, refers to the Community of Israel as the *Shekhinah*, or the Indwelling Presence of the Holy One (see 3:313). Among the diarists in whom this consciousness of the people as spirit is most pronounced is Yitzhak Katznelson. In his entry for 14 September 1943, for example, he writes: "The blood of the seven million cries out from within me. Where are they? The cry of the whole of my murdered people cries out into the void of this empty, wicked world" (220). In Katznelson's Hebrew text it is not just the blood that cries out but the *voice* of the blood, the *kol damiy* (99), which is the voice of the life and therefore of the spirit of this people. For the life is in the blood. And the blood is in this voice that speaks through this diary that we call the Holocaust diary. In a slightly different manner the spirit speaks through the Jewish blood that calls out from the earth and pours into the pages of Avraham Tory's diary from the Kovno Ghetto.

Commenting on a list of the victims of an *Aktion*, he writes: "From each line, and from each name, blood trickles into the huge cup of Jewish suffering. That cup filled up long ago; the blood spilling from it has turned into rivers and lakes. The spilled Jewish blood cries for revenge; the memory of Amalek shall be blotted out from under God's sky. The people of Israel shall live forever, until the end of all generations" (280). Tory's mention of Amalek is a paraphrase of Exodus 17:14, and in this allusion to Israel's biblical past he makes a point about Israel's future. And both are gathered into the diary entry for the day of 6 April 1943. This gathering of the time and the eternity of a people into the writing of the diary is what distinguishes this writing as the voice of the spirit. In the case of Chaim Kaplan, this voice manifests itself through the incorporation of other Jewish voices and Jewish texts into his own text. He closes his entry of 4 January 1942, for example, with the words "O earth, cover not thou my blood!" (280), which are taken from Job 16:18. Taking the words of Job into his own mouth, he voices the spirit of a people for whom the tale of Job is most significant; in these few words he voices all that Job's tale conveys. If spirit is word, as Buber says, it is because it manifests itself not only between an I and a Thou but across generations and throughout a tradition. In its temporal manifestation, spirit is tradition; and in Kaplan, the tradition speaks.

"They did not even have a cemetery," Wiesel laments. "We are their cemeteries" (*Against Silence* 1:168). But within us reside not only those who died but also those who *lived*. Inasmuch as the writer of the diary is aware of a link between his voice and the voices of others, he is aware of a relation to his people as the People of the Book. "Write, write, children," a family in the Vilna Ghetto tells Yitskhok Rudashevski and his friends. "It is good this way" (102). And so Rudashevski writes his diary with an eye toward a tradition and a future that are joined together in this writing and are signified by the book. "The ghetto folklore," he says, "which is amazingly cultivated in blood and which is scattered over the little streets, must be collected and cherished as a treasure for the future" (80–81). Thus, with these last few examples of the voice of the spirit at work in these writers and their writing, we come to another definitive aspect of the Holocaust diary: the consciousness of the book.

THE CONSCIOUSNESS OF THE BOOK

"FOR THE JEW," SUSAN HANDELMAN POINTS OUT, "GOD'S presence is inscribed or traced within a text" (88–89). In the Kingdom of Night, where both the Jew and the text bearing a trace of God are under attack, that text frequently manifests itself through the Holocaust diary. In the previous chapter we saw that, for the People of the Book, writing a book is a means of attending to the life and the meaning that issue from the Book. In the biblical passages appearing in the diaries of Avraham Tory (280) and Chaim Kaplan (280) we also found that the Book itself works its way into their books. Writing a book, therefore, is a means of sustaining a relation to the Book and to the One from whom the Book issues; it is a means of affirming the truth that the People of the Book are the Children of the Covenant. "From the Covenant of the flesh," says the thirteenth-century mystic Joseph Gikatilla, "man enters the covenant of language which is the reading of the Torah" (80); in the Jewish tradition the reading of the Torah entails responding to the Torah, often through the writing of a book. Here it will be recalled that the Hebrew word for "circumcision," which is the sign of the Covenant, is *milah*, a term that also means "word." And the word is the medium of the Book. Just as the sign of the Covenant with God is inscribed in the flesh, so the Book offered to the People is affirmed in the inscription of a book, which in the case at hand is the Holocaust diary.

In his diary from the Lithuanian ghetto of Siauliai, Eliezer Yerushalmi suggests these interconnections. For on 22 July 1943 he follows his invocation of the God "who has chosen us from all the peoples" with the assertion that the "aim and the truth of the Covenant made by Moses is Israel itself" (253). Making this entry in his diary, Yerushalmi makes the diary into a sign of the chosenness of the Chosen and of the Covenant with the One who chooses them. The consciousness of the Book, then, is the consciousness of another consciousness. "In Torah study," Adin Steinsaltz expresses this point, "it is not only that one thinks in terms of Torah, but also that the Torah thinks within oneself. It is an object that becomes a subject" (*Long* 28). When the Torah finds its way into the diary, the voice of the One to whom we are joined through the Covenant makes itself heard. Because the People of the Book are the Children of the Covenant, moreover, their status as the Chosen places them in the position of having to choose—between "life and death, blessing and curse," as the Torah teaches us (Exodus 30:19). This interweaving of ties between the People and the Book, the Book and the Covenant, and the People and the Covenant has profound implications for an understanding of these diaries as texts that come from the hands of *Jewish* writers.

"The difference between a Jewish writer and a writer," says Elie Wiesel, "is the following: for most writers, their work is a commentary on their life; for Jewish writers it is the opposite; their lives are commentaries on their work" (*Against Silence* 2:255). As we shall see in the ensuing discussion, among the writers of the Holocaust diaries, the lives that they are able to fetch from the ashes are engendered by the diaries they write, every bit as much as their diaries are generated out of their lives. Whether they are able to live as Jews is a matter often decided by whether they are able to write as Jews, that is, whether they might create a book that may draw them into a relation with the Book and other sacred texts that define and sustain Jewish life. Because Holocaust diaries are Jewish texts by Jewish authors, they must be assessed in the context of this relation to a tradition of texts, which has its origin in biblical texts.

Here "the Bible," Herbert Schneidau states it, "plays a role which demands that we acknowledge how precarious is our grasp of any meaning in the world at all and that we force ourselves to probe the words and forms before us in a never-ending labor. Like the dynamic incompleteness of language itself, the gap or lack that gives it an endless, never-catching-up-to-itself character, the Bible sets the problem of retracing urgent but unfixable messages, located in a series of texts which come to no real end or conclusion" (255). Just so, the Holocaust diary has no real conclusion other than the death of the diarist, which, of course, cannot be part of the diary. This fact that the end of a life lies outside its personal chronicle also underscores the point that the life of the Jewish writer is a commentary on his or her text. It tells us that, as a Jewish book issuing from the People of the Book, the Holocaust diary belongs to a series of texts and a chronicle of life that are as open-ended as the diary itself. Hence, in the words of Levi Yitzhak of Berditchev, the "Book is life beyond life" (Newman 22). This aspect of the *beyond* lies not merely in the generic aspects of the diary but above all in the diary's tie to a *sacred* textual tradition. For the dimension of the sacred that distinguishes this tradition is what makes the tradition open-ended: the sacred is infinite. That is why the tradition to which the Holocaust diary belongs is more than an accumulation of customs; it is a vessel of the eternal.

Even Primo Levi, who once declared, "There is Auschwitz, and so there cannot be God" (Camon 68), describes the stories shared among the inmates of Auschwitz as "simple and incomprehensible like the stories in the Bible"; and, he adds, "are they not themselves stories of a new Bible?" (*Survival* 59). The same may be said of the tales told and the accounts recorded in the Holocaust diary. For what unfolds in these books unfolds from the consciousness of the Book and in the contexts of an ancient connection with sacred writings, a connection that signifies a covenantal relation with the Holy One Himself. Just as these diarists respond to the Nazis' assault on Jewish life, so are they concerned with the Nazis' assault on the Jewish Book; for without the Jewish Book there is no Jewish life. One way in which the Book—that is, the texts of the Bible, the Talmud, and other religious works—is preserved and protected is through the interweaving of passages from the Book into the book that the diarist is writing. To be sure, "the Bible," Abraham Joshua Heschel reminds us, "is not a book that is sealed and completed; the Bible lives, always being written, continuously proclaimed" (*Israel* 199). This view of the Bible as process is what draws the Book into the process of writing these Jewish diaries. And, just as these writers write from a sense of responsibility to God and community, they sustain their consciousness of the Book not out of self-satisfaction or literary sophistication, but with the aim of offering to an unknown reader a tradition that transcends the diary. For the Book constitutes the center of the community to which they respond. Let us consider, then, these aspects of the consciousness of the Book in the Holocaust diary.

THE ASSAULT ON THE BOOK

The very existence of the Holocaust diary attests to the importance of books in the life of a community whose center is the Book. And in many cases the diarist affirms this importance through the diary itself. "You grow sick," writes Hanna Levy-Hass, for instance, in her Bergen-Belsen diary, "when you have no books. I have the impression that my innermost being has been crushed" (13). The sickness that Levy-Hass refers to is a sickness of the soul engineered by the Nazis, and she struggles to treat this sickness that issues from the absence of books by creating her own book, that is, by writing her diary. In contrast to the strictly personal and introverted taking stock of one's soul that characterizes many diaries outside the Shoah, in the Holocaust diary we have an effort to reconstitute the soul that has been assaulted through the assault on the Book. In her memoir of the Holocaust, Livia Bitton-Jackson provides us with a deeper sense of the link between the Jewish soul and the Jewish book, as well as the significance of the Nazis' attack on both. "The Torah scrolls!" she records the memory of an incident in a Hungarian ghetto. "The fire is dancing a bizarre dance of death with one large scroll in the middle, clutching and twisting and twisting in an embrace of cruel passion. Aged folios of Jewish wisdom and faith tumble and explode into fiery particles, spluttering pellets of ash. Volumes of the Bible, leather-bound Psalms, phylacteries turn and twist and burst into myriad fragments of agony. Pictures and documents flutter as weightless speckles of ash at the perimeter of the savage torch. Our identity. Our soul" (38). The horror of this event comes home to us when we recall that, in the Jewish tradition, religious texts—that is, texts bearing the Holy Name of God—are never thrown away or destroyed; they are buried with the Jews who studied them and devoted their lives to their teachings. The destruction of these texts, then, is central to the annihilation of those who strive to live by them.

Reading these lines from Bitton-Jackson's memoir, we realize what Adam Czerniakow was trying to save when, on 19 November 1941, he relates, "Several days ago I submitted a petition to save Elektoralna Street, the Synagogue, and the Judaic Library" (300). The Judaic Library contains the teachings of the tradition that constitutes the depth and the meaning of the Jewish community. "In the library you are always silent," says Wiesel, "because you do not raise your voice in a sanctuary: with Rabbi Akiba and Rabbi Shimon ben Yohai present, with the Ari Hakadosh and Rabbi Shneur Zalmen ben Baruch of Ladi in the room, you dare not speak except in a whisper" (*Kingdom* 38). And who are these talmudic and Hasidic sages? They are the ones whose wisdom constitutes the basis of Jewish life and Jewish community. Because the Jewish soul derives its identity and its life from its relation to a community, the Nazis began their annihilation of Jewish life with a destruction of the center that lends the community its significance and its sanctity. And that meant the obliteration of the Word. Thus, wherever a text could be saved or a home allowed to keep a book, it was an occasion for rejoicing. In his Vilna Ghetto diary, for example, Herman Kruk notes with a mixture of joy and sorrow that the police gave him permission to keep a prayer book and one other volume in his home (53). What the other volume is, he does not say. In a way, it does not matter, as long as it is a Jewish book that might help to sustain a Jewish life.

Chief among Jewish books are the books of the Bible. Hence we find Moshe Flinker asserting in his diary, "One of the eternal books—perhaps the only one—that I know is the Divine Bible, particularly the Pentateuch and the Prophetic sections. I therefore intend to concentrate on reading the Bible because its importance matches and perhaps even exceeds that of these days" (39). The scope of the Bible's importance to Jewish life becomes more clear when we recall Heschel's statement that the Bible "is not a book to be read but a drama in which to participate; not a book about events but itself an event, the continuation of the event, while our being involved in it is the continuation of the response" (*God* 254). What makes the Torah and the Bible eternal is neither their antiquity nor their longevity, but their capacity to provide a basis for the enduring, responsive presence of the Jews in a world that repeatedly tries to deny them a presence. "Our Torah permeates our being," Chaim Kaplan insists, "and we cannot exchange it or replace it with another" (157). Here the diarist is writing about a reading and a study, which in the Jewish tradition are forms of prayer. And Jewish dwelling is possible only where Jewish prayers are engaged in; hence Czerniakow's concern for the synagogue on Elektoralna Street. One function of the Holocaust diary in its effort to recover life, then, is to open up a place where prayer, even in the form of reading and studying, might happen. Failing the opportunity to establish a House of Prayer as a community center, that place must be opened up in the home—or in the hideout (a point we shall address below). "The home of the Jews is a sacred text in the middle of commentaries," notes Handelman. "The book creates meaning; the meaning creates life" (81). Meaning happens through the interaction between commentaries and sacred text, and the Holocaust diary is often a commentary on that interaction—and on what threatens it. That is why Emil Dorian notes in his Romanian diary, "Today, a decision by the Ministry of Education forbids the printing of any kind of Jewish writing" (126): this is part of a larger decision to forbid any kind of Jewish being.

The assault on the Book, of course, goes beyond anything so "harmless" as a decree. In her diary Helena Dorembus, a survivor of the Warsaw Ghetto Uprising, writes: "Thin, burnt pages of sacred books veined with sacred letters, like Jewish death lists. When I pick up one of these scorched pages, it crumbles to bits. Each bit becomes the skeleton of a word" (59). The image of the skeleton suggests that a word has a life, or that its meaning is intertwined with the meaning of a life, as flesh is intertwined with bone. This interconnection comes out more powerfully in a passage from *Phoenix over the Galilee*, a novel by the Holocaust survivor who writes under the pen name of Ka-tzetnik 135633: "The paper consumed becomes ashes. But words, where do they go? This was how they had been burned at Auschwitz, those whose bodies had turned into ash, whose lives had been unlived. Where did their souls go?" (170). Perhaps these diaries give us a clue: perhaps these souls go into the spaces in the margins and between the lines of the Holocaust diary. For these texts consigned to the flames bore the traces of lives devoured by flames. And, just as the flesh and bones of those victims were made into raw material for soap and fertilizer, so were the sacred texts used to serve a world that had become an accomplice to the assault on the Book. Recall in this connection a passage from Michael Zylberberg's diary: "It was said that there were no Jews and no symbols of Jewishness in Warsaw. But for those of us who had survived, the streets of the city were filled not only with memories of the past, but with actual objects freely seen, identified and sold. There were Jewish books that had belonged to libraries and private collections. The pages were used for wrapping goods in shops, as there was a great shortage of paper. Former Jewish-occupied flats were now in the possession of Polish tenants, and their specifically Jewish contents used to light fires. Wood and coal were in short supply too, and every day my landlord brought home sacks of Jewish books which he burned in the stove. He pointed out that the Jewish religion was going up in smoke" (119). And yet some of the ashes from those books remain: they form the words on the pages of the Holocaust diary.

We begin to see what lies behind Wiesel's assertion that "fire was the dominant image of this tragedy" (*Evil* 39). And we recall with profound trepidation a passage from the fifth-century midrashic text, the *Pesikta de-Rab Kahana*: "Since the Torah is called *fiery law*, said R. Johanan, he who is about to engage in the study of Torah should consider himself as standing within fire" (457). Fire consumed the body and the Book of Israel. And yet, in the midst of this conflagration, we have the Holocaust diary. It is a book that endeavors to recover a remnant of the Book, and, like the Book, it written with fire against a background of fire (see *Midrash Tanchuma* 1:1). This point is perfectly illustrated by David Kahane in his *Lvov Ghetto Diary*, where he comments on the Nazis' gathering up of Torah scrolls to be burned by saying, "As it is written: 'The scrolls are consumed by flames and the letters fly up in the air'" (40). What Kahane introduces into his diary with this quote is a portion of the tale of the talmudic sage, Rabbi Chanina ben Tradion. As the *En Jacob* relates it, when the Romans came to take away the Rabbi for the crime of teaching Torah, they found him in the act of reading the holy scrolls. And thereupon they determined that he should be wrapped in those scrolls and burned to death.

When the soldiers seized him, his daughter began to cry. And the Rabbi asked her, "Why the tears, my child?"

She said, "I weep for the Torah that is to be burned with you."

And he replied, "The Torah is fire, and fire cannot burn fire."

The Rabbi's disciples followed him to the site of his execution. The Roman soldiers wrapped him in scrolls of the Torah, piled faggots around him, and lit the pyre. In the moment of his agony his students cried out to him, "Rabbi, what do you see?"

And he answered, "I see the parchment consumed by the fire, but the letters . . . the letters are ascending to the heavens!" (5:154. See also Talmud tractate *Avodah Zarah* 18a.)

Thus, in his allusion to this tale from the Oral Torah, Jewish diarist David Kahane retrieves a trace of what was consumed, a trace of the Book and of the life engendered by the Book. In this way the diary becomes the bearer of the Book in the midst of the assault on the Book. But this point calls for more thorough consideration.

THE DIARY AS A BEARER OF THE BOOK

In the seventh-century midrashic text known as the *Pirke de Rabbi Eliezer* it is written, "Moses took the tables (of the law), and he descended, and the tables carried their own weight and Moses with them; but when they beheld the calf and the dances, the writing flew off the tables, and they became heavy in his hands, and Moses was not able to carry himself and the tables, and he cast them down from his hand" (355–56). This passage from one of the texts of the tradition conveys the tradition's teaching that those who bear the Torah are borne by the Torah. The Holocaust diary, then, becomes a bearer of the Book so that the Book might thereby bear the diarist. For the Book is the *Ets Chaim*, the Tree of Life (see tractate *Avot* 16:7 in the Talmud), and the one who seeks to recover or sustain some trace of life in the midst of this destruction draws the Book into the book he writes.

Thus a primary feature of the Holocaust diary which distinguishes it as a text that is tied to life is its inclusion and transmission of the sacred texts of the tradition that nurtures life. In the Holocaust diary, the consciousness of the book is a consciousness of the eternal that reveals itself through the avenue of tradition and that sustains life even when all the world seems to conspire against that life. The diarist's use of the texts of the tradition entails a "reading" of them from within the contexts of the extremity out of which he writes his diary. Here too, Kahane's diary is a good example. He relates, for instance, that when he was sent to the Janowski camp he was tattooed with the number 2250, whose digits add up to nine. "Number nine possesses wondrous qualities," he explains the tradition surrounding this number. "First it is half of eighteen, or in Hebrew *hai*, meaning alive. Eighteen is 1 + 8, 9 again. Talmudic sages say that 'the stamp of the Holy One Blessed be He is *emeth* (truth).' The three Hebrew letters making up the word *emeth* (*alef, mem, tav*) are 1, 40, and 400. Their sum is 441 (1 + 40 + 400). The three digits of this number also add up to 9 (4 + 4 + 1). I clung to my number like a drowning man clutching at a straw; to me it seemed a sign from heaven" (97). In Kahane's original Hebrew text, the word he uses for "sign" is not the usual *ot* but *remez* (115), which also designates an allegorical method of biblical interpretation. While this derivation of meaning from numbers falls into the general category of gematria as a method of interpretation, Kahane, like other diarists, reads many of the situations described in his diary allegorically by connecting various events to biblical texts. When he finds Jewish women begging for work in German quarters, for example, he writes, "The words of the prophet were thus fulfilled: 'And you will sell yourselves to your enemy as servants and housemaids and they will want you not' [Deuteronomy 28:60]" (31). Once again the diarist draws on the Book to draw the eternal into the temporal. Thus, making the day described in the diary into a day in the life of the eternal, the diarist fetches a remnant of life from the rubble.

The passage that Kahane cites is from the litany of curses known as the *Tokhehah*; it appears in Leviticus 26:14–40 and Deuteronomy 28:15–68. These are the passages that Chaim Kaplan refers to when he writes, "Sometimes you suspect the Nazis of reading the *Tokhehah* and using it as a guide" (197). This suspicion has a history that goes back to the days of Jeremiah and the Babylonian Exile, and Kaplan is aware of this history. On 14 September 1939, just two weeks into the war, he makes an entry in his diary that is a play on the opening line of Jeremiah's Book of Lamentations: "How has Warsaw, the royal, beautiful, and beloved city become desolate!" (31). Attaching this significance to Warsaw, with its comparison to Jerusalem, is yet another means of eternalizing the temporal and thereby drawing the catastrophe at hand into the current of sacred history. Similarly, Yitzhak Katznelson compares Lublin to Pumpeditha and Nehardea (100), centers of talmudic learning which date back to the Babylonian Exile and which were later replaced by the learning centers of Spain and Poland. And once a site is established as a center of sacred learning, it is tied to sacred history, as these diarists are well aware.

Indeed, Jews had viewed certain cities of Poland, as well as the land of Poland, from the standpoint of such a history since the Middle Ages, as Heschel explains: "The name of Poland was allegedly derived from the two Hebrew words *po-lin*, 'here abide,' which were inscribed on a note descended from heaven and found by the refugees from Germany on their eastward journey at the time of the Black Death and the attendant massacre of Jews" (*Earth* 57). But the Jews continued eastward, into Lithuania and Russia, and, in his Kovno Ghetto diary, Tory, like Kaplan, invokes the time of the Babylonian Exile as a point of comparison for the annihilation taking place all around him. Alluding to the lamentation heard in Ramah in Jeremiah 31:15, he writes: "The best Lithuanian Jews are no longer with us. They were erased without a trace. . . . The handful of remaining Jews are overcome with grief and sorrow. Like Rachel grieving over her sons, they grieve over their martyred brethren" (224). From such allusions, however, we must not conclude that these diarists equated Hitler's project of extermination with Nebuchadnezzar's conquest of the Kingdom of Yehudah. Katznelson, for example, states that "our exile in Babylon would now seem . . . a Garden of Eden and the dirge of Lamentations, a Festival song" (102). The point of these invocations of the Exile is not to imply an equation but to preserve a tradition; what is critical for the diarist is not only to relate an account of catastrophe but also to sustain a link with life. And for the Jew, that means connecting his text with the text that sanctifies life and thereby becomes a bearer of life, as it is written in the *Midrash Tanchuma*: "He who brings forth words of Torah brings forth life" (2:864–65).

In the Jewish tradition, the sanctity of life engendered by the Book is opposed to idolatry, and idolatry, as Maimonides defines it in the *Mishneh Torah*, is the worship of "any thing created" (1:67a). With regard to the Shoah, Emil Fackenheim argues in *To Mend the World* that "once idolatry is mentioned, there appears the spectre of Auschwitz, and with it the end of the age-old Christian claim that idolatry is vanquished" (71). Elsewhere, in a variation on Maimonides, Fackenheim defines idolatry as "the *literal* identification of finiteness and infinitude" (*Encounters* 189), and he adds: "Before Nazism happened we thought it could not happen. Now that it has happened, we resort to explanations that explain it away. We take it, in the style of Enlightenment liberalism, as a mere lapse into atavistic prejudice, superstition, or neurosis, ills that should not happen in this day and age and for which—soon if not now—there will be a cure. Or we take it, in neo-Lutheran style, as a mere case of national pride, lust for power, or xenophobia, sins will always happen because we are all sinners. Possibly we take it as a mixture of the two. In any case we resist confronting it as a modern idolatry—one might say, as *the* modern idolatry because, being unsurpassable, it reveals all that idolatry can be in the modern world" (*Encounters* 192–93). Long before psychologists, historians, and other social scientists were inventing their explanations, the diarists of the Holocaust made the comparison that Fackenheim suggests. Kaplan, for example, invokes ancient idolaters when he writes, "Midian and Moab have joined forces in order to oppress Israel" (45), and when he refers to the fear "in general of Esau and Amalek. In the light of all this our lives are no life at all" (54). So does Willy Cohn when he asserts, "'And think on what Amalek has done, and forget it not' [see Deuteronomy 25:17]—a saying that has endured throughout Jewish history" (16). Adding the biblical word to his own word and thus making his diary into a bearer of the Book, Cohn adds to the Jewish testimony against idolatry for the sake of life, even along the edge of the annihilation of that life. As Katznelson deems Germany the "Samael of the nations" (96) and the SS the "sons of Belial" (97), so Cohn and Kaplan read in the Kingdom of Night the signs of a darkness that has threatened the Light unto the Nations from the time of the Covenant. The question that haunts the diarist who would be the bearer of the Book, however, is: Has the Covenant—if one may speak thus—been abrogated?

And so in his diary recovered from Emmanuel Ringelblum's *Oneg Shabbat* archives, Abraham Levin writes: "Rejected lamb of Israel! Who will give us another Ezekiel to sing us words of comfort and show us another resurrection of the dry bones?" (318). And yet, even though the Covenant borne by the Book that bears the Jew is all but eclipsed—"We have all become orphans," Kaplan cries out (55)—the diarist nonetheless draws the book into his outcry: "Out of the depths I called to thee," writes Kaplan, invoking the opening line from the 130th Psalm (55). This "Song of Ascent," however, ends with the assertion that "He will redeem Israel." The diarist who would bear the Book and thus be borne by it turns to the Book for redemption, and not to the armies of a world that has long fed on Jewish blood. "We should not look to Russia, England, or America," says Moshe Flinker, "because salvation will come from a completely different source" (55). Young Moshe provides us with an intimation of that source when he closes his entry for 8 December 1942 by quoting Nehemiah 1:9, declaring, "Though your dispersed were in the uttermost part of heaven, yet will I gather them from thence" (37). From a Jewish standpoint, of course, the salvation promised by the Book comes from the hands of the human being; when men do nothing, the Jewish saying goes, God folds His arms. During the Shoah, one instance of doing something was the Warsaw Ghetto Uprising. But here too the diarist who was witness to the event draws the Book into his commentary on the event, which in turn is a commentary on the Book. When he hears of the Uprising, Vilna Ghetto diarist Zelig Kalmanovitch, for example, enters into his diary on 9 July 1943 a play on Psalms 37:12–15: "The wicked have drawn the sword to slay the poor and needy, to slay those whose path is upright. Their sword shall enter into their own heart, and all their bones shall be broken. The hour has come. The waters are come even unto the soul!" (58). Helena Dorembus comments on the Uprising by saying, "This almost seems like a repetition of Maccabean times, an echo of long-forgotten heroism" (59). And Michael Zylberberg writes: "I felt that from their blood a new life, full of hope, would spring—like a phoenix from the ashes. As the prophet Ezekiel had said, '*Bedamaich Chaii*'—'By your blood, you shall live' [Ezekiel 16:6]" (96). Thus the life of the remnant derives its significance not just from the witness borne by the example of those who perished but by linking that historical testimony to an eternal testament.

The eternity of the Book lies in its capacity to forever renew the lives of those who bear it, a point that Willy Cohn makes in his diary in the entry dated 18 October 1941. "Today is *Shabbat Bereshit*," he notes the renewal of the annual cycle of Torah study. "The new year of the reading of the Torah begins again. Our people will yet follow this cycle of reading, even though so much has been destroyed!" (67). And these diarists continue to incorporate this reading of the Torah into their writing. For the Torah is received inasmuch as it is conveyed to another. And these diarists bear the Book through their diaries inasmuch as they make that offering by attesting to the infinite value of the offering itself.

OFFERING UP THE TEXTS OF THE TRADITION

In his eighteenth-century Torah anthology known as the *MeAm Lo'ez*, Rabbi Yaakov Culi reminds us that the commandment to "be careful to seek new insights in the Torah" is "included in the commandment, 'be fruitful and multiply'" (129). The consciousness of the Book that impels these diarists to comment on the Book signifies a commitment to multiply the depth and the scope of Jewish life precisely at a time when that life is under its most radical assault, indeed, when the Book itself is under a radical assault. For a Jew, to be a bearer of human life is to be a bearer of Torah; and to be a bearer of Torah is to offer up the Torah to our fellow human beings. Many diarists, therefore, not only offer up the texts of the sacred tradition by weaving them into their own texts, but they also bear witness to the offering itself. Warsaw diarist Peretz Opoczynski, for example, notes that "in keeping with age-old traditions, Jews protect Torah Scrolls with devotion, saving and hiding them" (109). These scrolls are hidden, not so that they may never see the light of day, but so that the Light of the Holy One might be offered to humanity on another day. The consciousness of the Book, then, is the consciousness that Emmanuel Levinas describes as "the urgency of a destination leading to the other person and not an eternal return to the self" (*Nine* 48). And to have such a destination, where the other awaits our word, is to have a future. The preservation of the Torah is a preservation of the future; the consciousness of the Book is a consciousness of the future. The time of these diaries, then, is not confined to the dates of their entries. It includes a time yet to unfold, which is to say, it includes an aspect of the eternal.

Prominent among these diarists' entries, moreover, is the testimony not only to the hiding away and preservation of the Book but also to the opening up of the Book in places where the Nazis attempted to close it. Ringelblum, for example, points out: "There are illegal traveling libraries that circulate from house to house. There is a Talmud Torah attended by 700 students; rabbis are the teachers" (132)—a fact indicating that the consciousness of the Book found in these Jewish diaries is a reflection of a larger consciousness characterizing the Jewish community and its relation to the One from whom the Book derives. For the Talmud teaches us that "if two are sitting and studying the Torah together, the Divine Presence is with them" (*Berakhot* 6a).[1] Another member of the *Oneg Shabbat*, Rabbi Shimon Huberband, sought to draw the *Shekhinah* into the midst of the community when he, too, organized a Torah study group in the midst of a world that would eclipse every vision of heaven. In a reference to *Shavuot* 5700 (13 June 1940), which commemorates the giving of the Torah at Sinai, he writes: "I proposed that we establish a society for the study of Mishna called 'Ohel Leya,' in memory of my tragically killed wife, Rivke Leya. The assembled people enthusiastically accepted my proposal and immediately began to collect volumes of the Mishna" (65). The study of the Mishnah, or the Oral Torah, is especially appropriate to this time, since the Mishnah was committed to writing under the direction of Rabbi Yehudah Ha-Nasi in the second century of the common era, at a time when Rabbi Yehudah feared that the relative peace enjoyed by the Jews could not last and that the foundations of Judaism were therefore threatened. "Because of his apprehension," Steinsaltz explains, "he decided to violate the accepted prohibition against recording oral law and to compose a work comprising its main points. In fact, he succeeded in bringing this idea to fruition, creating a work second in importance and sanctity only to the Torah—the

Mishnah" (*Essential* 32). It happened again that when the foundations of Judaism and Jewish life—the indwelling presence of the Holy One Himself—were threatened, Rabbi Huberband turned to the Oral Torah that had sustained Jewish life for nearly two thousand years.

Other diarists record the study of other texts from the Jewish tradition, both ancient and modern. Herman Kruk, for instance, reports that people in the Vilna Ghetto had organized a group to study the writing of the twelfth-century Jewish thinker Rabbi Judah Halevi (44). The Vilna Ghetto, in fact, was unusual in this respect, that there the Jews were allowed to have a library. And they used it. Both Kruk (46) and Kalmanovitch (41) note with excitement the ghetto's celebration of the 100,000th book to be circulated through the ghetto library on 13 December 1942. In his *Diary of the Vilna Ghetto*, Yitskhok Rudashevski notes on that date the significance of this event for himself and for his people: "Today the ghetto celebrated the circulation of the 100,000th book in the ghetto library. . . . Hundreds of people read in the ghetto. The reading of books in the ghetto is the greatest pleasure for me. The book unites us with the future, the book unites us with the world" (106). Once again we discover that the study of the Torah, the Mishnah, the *Kuzari* of Judah Halevi, and other texts that are the basis of the tradition creates a link not only with the past but also with the future. Tradition is about the future, because tradition is about meaning, and the future is the site where meaning unfolds. To have meaning in life is to have direction in life, and to have direction in life is to have a place where we have *yet* to arrive. The world as such rises up where the present sets out in pursuit of a future, and in the Shoah the site of that encounter is the Holocaust diary. For it is the book that attests to the consciousness of the Book and therefore to the link with generations past and future. It *is* the link that unites the past with the future, and this makes it a ground for the present, for life, and for the affirmation of all that fosters life. What constitutes the diary as such a link? It is the diary's offering up the Book of the tradition.

For these reasons the consciousness of the Book in the Holocaust diary includes a consciousness of the school and of the children who attend the school. To be sure, a school in Hebrew is a *beit sefer*, a "house of the book," and central to a Jewish education is a study of the

Book. "If a man sends his children to schools where there is no reverence for the Torah and its laws," says the Chofetz Chaim, "it is as though he has sent them, God forbid, to a school for idolatry" (*Light* 76). The very existence of the *beit sefer* implies that the lives of the young are worth the devotion of our own lives; that there is something very sacred yet very fragile in life that must be carefully nurtured, or it will die; and that, in the midst of the present there abides a future in which our most sublime aspirations, our most moving inspirations, and our most urgent questions might be decided. Hence the Hebrew word for "education," *chinukh*, also means "consecration"; as Rabbi Kalonymus Kalman Shapira, the Rebbe of the Warsaw Ghetto, points out, this word refers "to the education of a child, the consecration of the altar in the holy temple, and the dedication of a house" (4). Therefore the house of the book is the place that makes it possible to dwell in the home, as this dwelling is made possible by a relation to the sacred that is symbolized by the altar, the place where the Book is kept. Thus with the overturning of the school, the world is itself overturned, as the Hungarian teenager Éva Heyman suggests in her entry for 9 April 1944. After taking a lunch to her father, who was locked up in a school transformed into a prison, she relates: "When I left him, it occurred to me that when I was going to elementary school, we children always used to be inside the gate and the parents would wait outside the fence to take us home after school. Now only adults, even old people, are inside the school fence, and we children are outside. There is no getting away from it: the world is topsy-turvy" (75). Realizing how deeply the status of the house of the book is interwoven with the status of the world, we realize that the consciousness of the Book in the Holocaust diary extends well beyond biblical quotes and comments on study groups. It is at the root of the Jewish consciousness of life and the diary's effort to recover the meaning that makes life possible.

Thus the diarists make note not only of schools and study groups but also of the closing and desecration of schools; closing those doors is part of closing the door on Jewish life. "The conqueror is condemning us to ignorance," writes Chaim Kaplan, for instance. "Jewish education of all kinds has ended in Poland" (82). The Hebrew word that Kaplan uses for "education" in this case is not *chinukh* but *ulpanot*

(103), which means "training," "schools," or "instruction." Its root is *alef-lamed-pey*, the letters that spell the first letter of the Hebrew alphabet, *alef*, which is the beginning of all the letters and of all the words made from the letters. The "ultimate secret of the letter *alef*," as Rabbi Yitzchak Ginsburgh explains it, is "the union of 'higher reality,' the upper *yud*, with the 'lower reality,' the lower *yud*, by means of the connecting *vav* of Torah" (25). That is what the Nazis attempt to erase: all union between what is above and what is below, the Hebrew word itself, which constitutes the Hebrew Book that consecrates Hebrew life. And that is what the diarists attempt to retrieve through their testimony to the offering up of the texts of the tradition. "There are now a great number of illegal schools," Mary Berg carefully points out, "and they are multiplying every day. . . . Two such schools were discovered by the Germans some time in June; later we heard that the teachers were shot on the spot, and that the pupils had been sent to a concentration camp near Lublin. . . . The illegal character of the teaching, the danger that threatens us every minute, fills us all with a strange earnestness. The old distance between teachers and pupils has vanished, we feel like comrades-in-arms responsible to each other" (32–33). This responsibility for one another manifests itself in the offering up of the Book and therefore of a life to one another, even if—or especially if—the one who makes the offering knows that he will not live to see it received. Such was the case for Salmen Lewental, one of the diarists of the *Sonderkommando* in Auschwitz. Near the end of his diary retrieved from the ashes he writes: "We shall continue our work, we shall try to preserve all this for the world. We shall simply hide it in the soil" (176). And so the diarist commends to the scorched earth his testimony to the Eternal which might make it possible for others to dwell upon the earth in another time.

In *The Jewish Bible after the Holocaust*, Fackenheim points out: "Once Moses offered his life in behalf of the life of the children and succeeded. Adam Czerniakow did not merely offer but gave his life for the children. However, unlike Moses he failed. The enemy was more sleepless and slumberless than the God of Israel" (47). The consciousness of the Book in the Holocaust diary does not equate the events of the Book with the events of the Holocaust. These diarists know better than anyone else that the events of the Holocaust cannot be equated with anything else. But for many of these diarists, sustaining that consciousness is an essential part of sustaining a remnant of Jewish life. On 29 November 1941 Czerniakow notes that he received "two valuable books (one of them a Bible)" for his birthday (302–3). He makes note of receiving the Bible not because it mirrors the depths of the terrible events transpiring all around him but because it is opposed to those events; he makes mention of the Book within his own book because it makes his own book not only a protest against death but an affirmation of life.

Similarly, in his diary Aryeh Klonicki-Klonymus records that he gave his newborn the most ancient of biblical names, explaining: "My son's name is Adam. I chose it for its symbolic significance. I wanted to emphasize by this that the Germans, worse than all beasts of prey, yet who call themselves supermen and deny us the right to exist—will finally be conquered by human beings. Therefore I called him Adam (human being)" (21). In the original Hebrew text of this diary Klonicki-Klonymus uses the alien word *Übermenschen* for "supermen" (17), to which he opposes the Hebrew word of his diary, the word from which the Book and his son's name are made. This is the word and the being, the meaning and the good, that, in its consciousness of the Book, the Holocaust diary opposes to the reign of evil. And in this opposition, which is an affirmation, Katznelson declares: "The Bible of Israel and its moral laws are at the root of all that is good in the nations. And the presence of a live people of Israel amongst the nations enriches them even more than the Bible of Israel. Living Jews are more vital than the Bible. Without the people of Israel, the Bible is void of content and has no meaning" (81). Heschel explains: "For God to be present there must be witnesses. Without the people Israel, the Bible is mere literature. Through Israel, the Bible is a voice, a power and a challenge" (*Israel* 45). The consciousness of the Book is not a worship of the Book. It is a worship of life. The time measured in the consciousness of the Book, therefore, is not the time of antiquity but the time of tradition, which is the life time, or the lived time, that makes possible the present time of the diary. This brings us to the next point in our investigation of the collapse and recovery of life in the Holocaust diary.

THE MEASURE OF TIME

COMMENTING ON THE TALE OF THE CREATION, ANDRÉ Neher explains that the "Hebrew word which introduces the account, *bereshit*, shows that what mattered to the narrator was not what was in the beginning but rather that there was a beginning. For that word does not mean 'in the beginning' but 'as a beginning.' The creative act occupies time. God starts creating, and He distributes creation over seven days. *Time* itself is of the uppermost importance" (*Prophetic* 131). Similarly, when the Creator repented of having created, He erased the measure of time, as Rashi suggests in his remarks on Genesis 8:22. "Day and night ceased," says the great eleventh-century commentator, "during the period of the Flood, for the planetary system did not function, so that there was no distinction between day and night" (1:36). As time was of the uppermost importance in the creation and destruction of old, so it remains for the Jewish people, in its significance as the history of a sacred tradition, as a present and a presence overflowing with life, and as a future that holds the messianic promise. In the Jewish diary known as the Holocaust diary, therefore, the measure of time is the measure of the sanctity, the truth, and the meaning of life. And yet the diary appears precisely because all of these are under assault; it appears when the measure of time is itself under assault. "At Auschwitz," Elie Wiesel points out, "not only man died, but the idea of man" (*Legends* 230). And with the destruction of the idea of man comes the destruction of the measure of time.

"Of all written texts," says Alain Girard in his study of the diary as a genre, "none informs the image of the self better than those written in the first person. The intimate journals, which appear at a precise moment in time and spread according to a history that is peculiar to them, attest to this most directly and least conventionally. These texts provide the opportunity to know, in a pure state, the representation of the self that human beings are able to create in their inner depths, of their inquietude, their interrogation, and of their response to the problems of their age. The intimate journals are marvelous documents for following the history of the notion of person" (xix–xx). There is, however, an important detail that distinguishes the diaries of the Holocaust from those examined by Girard: the diaries of the Holocaust originate from a realm of darkness in which the very notion of person is under assault. Yes, the authors of these diaries respond to the problems of their age, but chief among those problems is the annihilation of the divine image and with it the inner depths that lie at the core of *person*. Recall Emil Fackenheim's insistence on this point: "Not until this century was a world created in which the divine image was systematically destroyed. In manufacturing *Muselmaenner*—walking corpses—the Auschwitz criminals destroyed the divine image in their victims" (*Judaism* 180). And the manufacture of this creature extended beyond the confines of the concentration camp. With this destruction of the measure of the eternal within the human—with this history—comes the undoing of the measure of time we call history, both on personal and on societal levels.

Thus the writers of the Holocaust diaries who chronicle this assault on the human image also record the day-to-day destruction of days that went into the annihilation of the age. Even prior to the full-scale launching of the assault, on 11 February 1938, Romanian author Emil Dorian wrote in his diary, "One could feel every human being shiver at the intimate contact with the essence of historical events" (21). Why the shiver? Because the notion of person was already collapsing under the weight of the event in history that was an undermining of history. Nothing drives this point home more clearly than an image from an entry in Emmanuel Ringelblum's Warsaw Ghetto diary: "To a Jew who had lost his armband, a German police chief cried: '*Sie, Jude, Sie haben das zwanzigste Jahrhundert verloren!* [You, Jew, you have lost the twentieth century!]'" (129). The armband that labels the Jew as a Jew marks him precisely as one who is lost, without time or place; for the Jew, to bear the sign of the twentieth century is to be locked into a history that removes him from history. Time and history are torn asunder, so that the Jew is rendered absent not only from this century but from all of history, all of time. For the Jew, this is the century that erases the centuries. Remember Amon Goeth's remark in Steven Spielberg's film *Schindler's List*: commenting on a day that was a "great historical occasion," he declared that by the end of the afternoon the six hundred years of Jewish presence in Cracow would be nothing more than a rumor.

Girard maintains that, "affected by complex historical influences, diary writing has been in principle precisely a means invented at a particular moment in time by people of a certain character to express themselves and to arrive at what they might be in a society where they have experienced a great evil" (526). Like the diaries Girard describes, the Holocaust diary arises in an attempt to retrieve a remnant of good from a great evil. Rabbi Nachman of Breslov, in fact, associates doing good with time itself. "You must know," he once said, "that time does not exist of itself, and that days are made only of good deeds. It is through men who perform good deeds that days are born, and so time is born" (Levin 344). Unlike the diaries that concern Girard, however, the Holocaust diary responds to a great evil experienced by a people who have been removed from society and therefore from the time of society. These lines from the diary of Mirjam Korber, a Romanian teenager, are a good example: "How was it at home? I can no longer, I mustn't any longer, think about this 'at home.' We have no 'at home.' I must imagine that we are nomads. . . . But the memories are stronger than my will . . . the unforgotten past, the sad present, the desolate future" (87). Mirjam kept her diary during her family's wanderings in the East, after they had fled from Iasi. But, as her entry suggests, this flight to the East takes them out of the realm of time and into a realm of wandering. It is a realm without place or time, where one day is indistinguishable from the next, and each day consists of a struggle between a weakening resolve and an insistent memory, between false hope and terrifying certainty. Although the past is unforgotten, the desolation of the future divorces the past from any contact with the present, so that Mirjam is herself robbed of all presence, except the presence she strives to generate through her diary. Girard notes that the diary "is inscribed into time, for the page that remains blank will be filled tomorrow; it obligates the subject to advance and to position himself before himself" (537). But the Holocaust diarist does not advance; she merely wanders and waits and wanders. Already knee-deep in the rubble of any hope for tomorrow, she does not inscribe her diary in time; rather, she takes up an effort each day to inscribe time into her diary. What the diary contains, then, is not just a reflection of what the diarist endures; it is a refusal of what she endures and of what will not go away. In that refusal, time slows to a halt.

Thus on 15 October 1941 Dorian declares, "In this short time, it seems to me, I have lived twenty years" (168–69); and on New Year's Eve he looks back on 1941, saying, "I feel as if I have lived through ten years" (185). This halt of time is not due merely to hardship; it arises from the erasure of the Jews from history, from their communities, their homes, and themselves. One therefore understands why Philip Mechanicus writes from Westerbork, "Space and time have ceased to exist—man lives against a background of nothingness" (70). Indeed, in the Dutch text of Mechanicus's diary the phrase translated as "have ceased to exist" is much stronger; it is *zijn opgeheven* (64), which may be rendered "have been abolished" or "have been annulled," suggesting that some outside agent—the antiworld of the Nazis—has acted on time itself. In his introduction to the Warsaw Ghetto diary of Janusz Korczak, Igor Newerly further explains this breakdown of time, saying: "Time—in the sense of a normal perspective of days and months—did not exist. There was an ephemeral present instant—and eternity. Lying down to sleep, nobody was sure that he would not be wakened by the sound of a prison van—or shot dead in bed. Going out, nobody knew whether he would return or be rounded up in the street and find himself in a cattle truck" (68). With this erasure of the *what next*, the *is* and the *was* are obliterated. The abolition of time into nonexistence places the Holocaust diary and its measure of time into a singular category. In the Holocaust diary the measure of time is not a tracking of the days of a life; rather, it arises in a struggle to retrieve time, and with it the traces of a life. Briefly stated, the measure of time in the Holocaust diary entails the recovery of a past reconnected to a present made meaningful by a future. And yet, as we shall see, this recovery and reconnection often manifest themselves in the diary as the measure of a time lost, where the date of an entry indicates not a day lived but a day of living death and dying time, of time slaughtered in the erasure of life's horizons.

THE ERASURE OF THE PAST

The erasure of the past revealed in the Holocaust diaries entails far more than a lament over the fact that things are not as they used to be; beyond that, this erasure manifests itself in a fundamental disorientation resulting from the loss of history's reference points that might make the present intelligible and the future viable. "In all life and especially in times of crisis," Lucy Dawidowicz points out, "the patterns of the past reemerge in a person's confrontation with the present and the future. . . . [So] the Jews once again ritually dredged up the nineteenth-century arguments, hoping these would serve also in the twentieth century" (175).[1] In these remarks Dawidowicz refers to the Jews of Germany and their reactions to the Nazis between 1933 and 1938. The nineteenth-century arguments held that days of persecution had come and gone in the past; life might be difficult for a time, but attitudes change; this storm, too, could be weathered. As it was then, so it shall be. Indeed, things are bound to be better; after all, this is the twentieth century.

It would soon become clear, however, that the Jews of Germany and the rest of Europe had no past time to which they could turn in order to make sense of the time—or the antitime—of the antiworld that was upon them. From an apartment in Brussels, where he and his family were hiding from November 1942 to April 1944, for example, Moshe Flinker wondered "whether our distress is part of the anguish which has afflicted the Jewish people since the exile, or whether this is different from all that has occurred in the past." He adds, "I incline to the second answer" (26). And among the fragments of the Warsaw diary kept by Menahem Kon in 1942, uttered without a trace of Moshe Flinker's doubt, are the words "history does not know anything like this" (83)—which is a way of saying, "We cannot know this." When the past is placed under erasure, the measure of time in the Holocaust diary becomes an epistemological issue: neither the past nor the present can be known, for the categories and concepts that would connect the two and thereby make each knowable in terms of the other have broken down. Jews did not have to move to new homes—they were rendered homeless; they were not forced to hide their families—they were made into ghetto policemen who turned their families over for deportation and death; they did not have to bury their dead—they were made to dig them up from massive, unmarked graves. What are the precedents that would make such a world intelligible? The epistemological issue, moreover, pertains not only to a knowledge of the world but also to a knowledge of one's people and, therefore, of oneself. Yitzhak Katznelson makes just this observation when he says: "Those of today have no use for the people of yesterday. In alienating ourselves from our brethren we are alien to our own selves" (77). We bear the names of mothers and fathers who lived before us, but when the past is erased, so are those names, theirs and ours. Hence the erasure of the past is an erasure of the self or soul of the human being.

In the Holocaust diary, then, the life sought in the recovery of time is the life of the world and of the soul; it is the life of the soul that unfolds in the world in time. An example of the erasure of this unfolding is found in the diary of Adam Czerniakow, where he writes: "Once, long ago, I made a theoretical plan to divide my life into three parts: I. study and play; II. accomplishments; III. reconciled with God and at peace with myself. Fate would have it otherwise" (89–90). While he may have studied and played a bit in his youth, the accomplishments of his maturity were nullified, and the only peace he might have known came with his suicide. It is significant to note that in Czerniakow's Polish text the sentence "Fate would have it otherwise" is written with a German phrase added to his native tongue: *Los zrobil Strich über die Rechnung* (61), that is, fate drew "a line through the plan." The line drawn through the plan is a line drawn through time. Inasmuch as language is a vessel of time, Czerniakow's use of the Nazis' language indicates the Nazis' imposition of their time on his own. It is an antitime that erases all beginnings, all plans, and that has no place for the Jewish time and the Jewish season, for any of the seasons, or the *mo'adiym*, created on the third day of Creation (see Genesis 1:14). The Nazis, then, would obliterate not only this time but all Jewish time that comes *before*, all the way back to the beginning.

The obliteration of the beginning is what the diarist observes when he observes the anniversary of a beginning. "Have been exactly one year away from home today," wrote Mechanicus, for instance, on 27 September 1943. "The time has gone past like a film—a horrible but enthralling film. That is what it is like now that it is all behind me. I did not see the film as a member of the audience from a comfortable seat, but as an actor who had to clench his teeth as he played his part. . . . In my mind none of the events appears in perspective any more; they all stand side by side in a row, outside space and time—all the events of my life, including those before September 27th 1942" (165–66). The Talmud tells us that "remember and observe" were words that God uttered in a single word (*Rosh Hashanah* 27a). The diarist may observe the *what* of the anniversary, but he cannot remember the *when* because he cannot order the events from the time before. The dating of the diary's entry, therefore, is not so much a saying of "Here I am in time" as an asking of "Can I be here, outside of time?" And so he takes up his pen to generate a word that might restore a trace of memory.

"For a Jew," says Elie Wiesel, "nothing is more important than memory. He is bound to his origins by memory. It is memory that connects him to Abraham, Moses, and Rabbi Akiba" (*Forgotten* 71). Just so, both Wiesel (*Evil* 155) and Primo Levi (*Drowned* 31) have noted that the Shoah was a war against memory. As such it is characterized by an effort to erase time, both past and present, since the memory of the past imparts meaning to the present. Very much aware of this condition, Dorian declares that "the greatest danger" confronting the community is "the short memory of the Jews"; and he adds, "Some Jewish-Romanian writers are in almost physical pain when they hear Yiddish. Strange, how they appreciate almost any language, be it Kirghiz or Ukrainian, and find justification for the existence of any culture—but when it comes to Yiddish, they cringe in disgust" (24). One immediately notices Dorian's association of memory with language; if, as suggested above, language is the vessel of time, it is the bearer of memory and the measure of time. Which time? The time of a people and of a person, the time of a life. Thus "to be attentive to language," as Edmond Jabès has said, "is to be attentive to oneself" (*Desert* 91), for to be attentive to oneself is to attend to the measure of time that goes into the memory of a life. This attentiveness is just what

Hanna Levy-Hass endeavors to sustain when, in her Bergen-Belsen diary, she writes: "The spiritual damage runs so deep that your whole being dies away. You have the impression of meeting with a thick, massive wall that cuts you off from the normal world of before. It is as though all capacity for perception has been blunted or has disappeared. No longer do you remember yourself or your own past" (37). The dying away of memory is a dying away of being, so that the aim of writing the diary is not only to record events but, in an act of utterance, to retrieve a memory—and with it a life—even if it is no more than the utterance of memory's loss. To be sure, Rabbi Yitzchak Ginsburgh reminds us that "the word 'memory' (*zikaron*) itself, in Hebrew, means 'a source of speech'" (4); as a source of speech, it is the source of the diary. If memory cannot retrieve the past, then the diary will be the spoken sign, if not of memory's being, then of its having been. The endeavor of the Holocaust diarist is not an exercise for achieving psychological insight; it is a matter of sustaining existence itself through its sustaining utterance.

While Levy-Hass is aware of a connection between the destruction of the individual and the erasure of the past, the Nazis implemented other means of this erasure as well. Avraham Tory makes this clear in his Kovno Ghetto diary, where he writes: "Dozens of Jewish settlements, firmly rooted on Lithuanian soil for hundreds of years, have already been obliterated from the face of the earth as if they had never existed. They were replaced by mounds of poisonous earth covering large pits—fresh mass graves, without tombstones, without inscriptions or any identifying marks" (23). And so the individual's diary becomes an identifying mark for whole communities where there remains no identifying mark; it becomes a measure of time where time has been erased, both for the individual and for a people. The dates that mark an entry, the coordinates that mark a time, mark the effort to reintroduce the inscription of a life to the palimpsest of history. In his personal diary from the Vilna Ghetto, on 10 November 1942, Yitskhok Rudashevski notes such an effort undertaken on a communal scale, saying: "Today the meeting for the establishment of the Jewish history circle took place. We resolved to learn, to study Jewish history, and to deal with the problems in Jewish history that interest us and can have current application, especially most recent Jewish history" (91). As significant as his recording of what these Jews pursued in their studies of Jewish history is Rudashevski's personal notation *that* they studied. If this study of history is a means of maintaining memory and recovering the past on a communal level, the diarist's notation that it takes place is a means of recovering the time that is threatened with erasure on an personal level. "Where experience prevails in a strict sense," Walter Benjamin points out, "certain contents of the individual's past meet in memory with the contents of a collective past" ("Baudelaire," 611). During the Shoah the place where the individual and the collective met was very often the Holocaust diary.

A similar illustration of Benjamin's observation on the link between communal and personal memory appears in Willy Cohn's diary from Breslau, where, on 8 November 1941, he wrote: "Today is the eve of the notorious 9th of November! Three years ago the synagogues burned! And yet the Jewish people will outlive this time!" (73). The burning of the synagogues on *Kristallnacht* was a burning not only of places of prayer but of shrines of memory and symbols of the past, for every synagogue houses its memorials. Every synagogue *is* a memorial. Insisting that the Jews will outlive that terrible time, Cohn insists that the measure of time will survive its shrines and its symbols, that the community will outlive the individual. As just such a measure of time, his diary is itself a symbol of this survival, for himself and his community. And yet the weight of this measure, like the weight of the community, is often more than the diarist can bear, so that at times she finds herself longing now for the loss of memory, now for the return of care. "If only we could completely lose our memory," Mirjam Korber laments. "It is so hard to recall the old times, when it was warm in our home and no one was hungry" (69). But soon even the suffering of the former time becomes an object of longing. "Past cares," writes Mirjam, "where are you? I long for you, and I long for all the past" (78). What we have in these lines from Mirjam's diary is an indication not only of the erasure of a past but also of the collapse of a present. For in this longing for even the cares of the past, the diarist is removed from the present. Let us consider, then, the nature of this time in the present which is a time of longing for a time of suffering in the past.

THE COLLAPSE OF THE PRESENT

"Time there, on planet Auschwitz," writes Ka-tzetnik, "was not like time here. Each moment there revolved around the cogwheels of a different time-sphere. Hell-years lasted longer than light-years" (*Shivitti* xi). The light of the light-year could not penetrate the darkness of the hell-year. Cogs driven by blood turned wheels that belonged to no heavenly vault, and Auschwitz turned on an axis that belonged to no planet. It was its own planet, and its gravitational field extended over the face of the earth and into the other camps, into the ghettos; there the cogwheels of the different time-sphere moved by fits and starts, collapsing the present into something that was not time. "The day is endless," writes Renata Laqueur in her Bergen-Belsen diary, "the evening much too short, the night without dreams, and suddenly it is half-past four" (40). There is, of course, no clock to announce the time, no chime to ring in the hour; time here is marked by the barking of the Kapo who announces the onslaught of another day with no end other than an evening awash in blood. Time bleeds to death. Therefore *Oneg Shabbat* member Abraham Levin makes a special entry in his diary: "A night that passes without blood being shed in the ghetto is so unusual that it must be noted. We have become so accustomed to unremitting terror that if there is an hour of pause it seems to us that we are mistaken" (326). The present collapses when the hour is measured not by the passing of minutes but by the spilling of blood; if life is in the blood, as the Torah teaches us (Genesis 9:4), so is time. And when an hour of time unmarked by blood appears in the midst of this antitime, it is unrecognizable: we must be mistaken. The measure of time in the Holocaust diary is a measure of this time collapsed into blood, into a river of death rather than a river of life. Hence "some evenings seem like assassins," says Dorian (302), and he asks: "What does it matter that I jot down dates? Is there any difference between sorrow that bears a date and that lost in the void of time?" (295). The void of time in this case is the voiding of time and the time of the void, the time of tension without a tense. Although Dorian wonders whether it matters that he records the dates, he nonetheless records them. Why? Because it is his only means of fetching a shred of time and of life from those days with evenings like assassins. It is his only means of rummaging through the ruins of time collapsed.

With the present collapsed into death, the presence of the diarist collapses into a death that is an absence made into a presence. "Death is hard," says Chaim Kaplan. "Harder still are the moments before death; and even hardest of all is being condemned to a death which is inevitable, but whose time has not been set" (371). Or rather, it is a death whose time has been unset, removed from the time of nature's course and shoved into the diarist's face. This time-not-set situates the diarist's time in a non-time, in a present that is not a living but a dying, a dying for which there is no getting it over with. In the world of the human being, death may be understood as the horizon of time; but in the antiworld, that horizon collapses. Once again we see that the Holocaust diary is the chronicle not of a life but of a living death that is outside of time and without a date, a point that adds depth to Dorian's question concerning the point of jotting down dates. "The worm of extinction gnaws at the heart," Vilna Ghetto diarist Zelig Kalmanovitch expresses it, and from the heart of the diarist the worm gnaws its way into the diary. In Kalmanovitch's original Hebrew text, the word for "extinction," *avadon* (124), also means "hell" or "abyss," calling to mind Katzetnik's hell-years. The collapse of the present is signaled by the emergence of more than extinction; it unfolds in the appearance of an abyss beyond the measure of time. Nevertheless, in spite of the abyss, the diarist puts his pen to the page to chip away at the hell that eats away at him. He writes in order to avoid for a moment the death that consumes him a day at a time, even if it is to count himself among the dead. Josef Katz, for example, was sent out one day to bury his dead uncle during his stay in the camp at Jungfernhof. "Leo and I walk in front," he writes, "and two from the burial *Kommando* in back. I have a strange feeling. It is as if the dead were carrying the dead" (48). Similarly, Yitzhak Katznelson declares, "I feel I have joined those already on the road and those that have gone" (48), and Leon Wells asserts with certainty, "Today is the day I die" (149).

And yet the diarist lives to make another entry; his gnawed heart continues to beat when it should have come to a stop. The day recorded, therefore, is a day that should not be there, a day that, indeed, is not there. Where the day might have been, there is only the *avadon* into which the present has collapsed.

One can understand why, in another diary retrieved from Ringelblum's *Oneg Shabbat* archives, Hersh Wasser writes: "Nobody really has the courage to die, but the general opinion is that the dead have already passed through their vale of tears. Their ears will no longer hear the harrowing reports of German brutality. The living envy the dead" (271). Where the living embrace life, a portion of time lies in the news of the day that posits a direction for life to follow; there is a link between knowing the news and knowing the path. But when the news signals the breakdown of knowing, it signals the loss of the path, and therefore the collapse of the present.[2] Time characterized by envy of the dead (and thus, by being *for* death) is precisely antitime, a time without a present and therefore without a past or future. Why? Because what the harrowing reports make known cannot be assimilated by the categories of knowledge, since what those reports declare is not that mothers, fathers, and children have been slaughtered, but that the very notions of mother, father, and child have been undone. Whereas the measure of time is normally a measure of the "not yet," in the Holocaust diary it is the measure of the "already over" before it is over. The yet-to-be that constitutes the time of the present is made not only unknown but unknowable. The day dated by the diarist is a day without a next day, a date without a calendar; it is a day that is not a day, and a date that measures nothing but the battle with nothingness.

Unlike the diaries that appear in the world, those that emerge from the antiworld are records not of increasing insight but of increasing blindness; they are accounts not of an expanding consciousness but of a growing dread. Once more we return to the epistemological issue discussed earlier, and we realize more clearly that knowledge and time are intertwined: to know is to know what to expect. He who does not know is removed from the coordinates of time, so that the measure of time in the Holocaust diary is a measure of the annihilation of knowledge. Kon confirms this. "None of us," reads his entry of 12 September 1942, "is capable of describing everything in detail. Each of the survivors lives in mortal fear, nobody knows what the next hour may bring" (84). What we find in Kon's journal from the Warsaw Ghetto, we find also in Tory's record of the Kovno Ghetto: "There is a somber mood in the Ghetto. No one knows the reason for this, but everyone senses that living conditions have deteriorated. No one knows what tomorrow will bring" (202). And, as Wasser receives the harrowing reports that lead him to envy the dead, so Tory receives the news of the day that undermines the day: "The news about the extermination of 5,000 Jews at Ponar has been received in the Ghetto with fear and anguish. No words can express the feelings of each one of us. Suddenly we see ourselves teetering on the brink of an abyss" (282). The brink of the abyss, of the *avadon*, is the brink of the present collapsed into dread, where the dread is a dread of a nothingness that is not a mere nothing; it is instead a "something" with which the diarist is in constant communication. "Everything," writes Herman Kruk in his diary from the Vilna Ghetto, "is now focused on one thing—the dread of the following day" (56). A present that is part of time is a present that passes; a present that is made of dread is one that will not go away. The measure of time recorded in the Holocaust diary, then, is the measure not of days gone by but of the piling of day upon day; it is a weighing of the increasing weight of time—or of an antitime—collapsing on the human being whose wait is without resolution. Soon dread turns into a hunger of the soul added to the hunger of the body, a hunger for the end, regardless of what it may be.

"I hope something will happen soon now," we read in the diary of Anne Frank, for instance, "shooting if need be—nothing can crush us *more* than this restlessness. Let the end come, even if it is hard" (256). To the reader who is aware of what crushed this child, the irony of her statement is devastating. But what is at issue is not the irony that overwhelms the reader but the overturning of time that undoes young Anne, leading her to long for an end to a present that will not end and which offers no egress. The hiding place is a prison of time made into antitime, more confining than the attic space and yet without measure. It is the prison without walls that Dorian describes when he says: "All Jews endlessly chew over the one preoccupation: leaving Romania. But this is merely an obsession, a neurotic symptom of powerlessness and despair. For in actuality, nobody moves—since there is nowhere to go, there is no salvation in sight. . . . There is no way out. We scream, we groan, blood mixes with earth, we die, and a whole generation is destroyed. Then there is silence" (31). The silence that comes in this wake of vain longing is the silence of a future that will not come. Doom overtakes every inkling of destiny, so that the erasure of the past and the collapse of the present lead to a divorce from the future.

THE DIVORCE FROM THE FUTURE

"In Judaism," Franz Rosenzweig explains in *The Star of Redemption*, "man is always somehow a remnant. He is always somehow a survivor, an inner something, whose exterior was seized by the current of the world and carried off while he himself, what is left of him, remains standing on the shore. Something within him is waiting. And he has something within himself. What he is waiting for and what he has he may call by different names; often enough he may barely be able to name it. But he has a feeling that both the waiting and the having are most intimately connected with each other. And this is just that feeling of the 'remnant' which has the revelation and awaits the salvation" (405). As a form of awaiting, the feeling of the remnant is the feeling of the future; it is the sensing of the *Shekhinah*, who "is always in the west," as it is written in the *Pirke de Rabbi Eliezer* (39). This feeling of the remnant, however, is just what the Holocaust diarist has lost. What is seized by the current of the world—or rather, by the onslaught of the antiworld—is not just his exterior form but also his inner something, that place where the *Shema* stirs before it comes to the lips. What he awaits, therefore, is not the salvation of a remnant, but a doom without remnant. Thus divorced from the remnant, he is divorced from the future.

Among the first entries in Dorian's diary, one dated 30 December 1937, for example, a question harbors a foreboding that would become a dominant theme of the Holocaust diary: "What will happen now to all of us Jews? Will the collapse be total?" (4). But a question about *total* collapse is a question about something for which there is no precedent, and therefore something for which there is no measure.

Later, on 22 October 1940, when Dorian writes, "I am no longer interested in the future, I am too weary" (127), it is because he is weary of this question that no future can resolve, of this question that is tied to no quest. It is because he is divorced from the future. Just over two years later, over a thousand miles away, Moshe Flinker would respond in a similar vein to a remark made by his teacher in Brussels. "Any boy or girl who can flee to safety," his teacher told him, "represents a hope for the future"; such, indeed, is the hope of the remnant. In his diary, however, Moshe responds to this statement by saying: "I thought that here was the answer to the question I had often asked myself: 'How can I flee from my people while they are in such terrible trouble?' . . . Now I feel that I have not been saved for the future" (65). To be sure, in this same spirit—in this same darkening of the spirit—Willy Cohn writes, "The future lies dark over the earth" (27), and Renata Laqueur declares, "We do not know whether we have any future at all" (22). Here we see how the *not knowing* that signals an absence from the present is tied to a darkening of the future. In the world, salvation is the salvation of a remnant for the unfolding of a future; in the anti-world, void of any remnant, the future is nothing more than a void.

In diary after diary, regardless of the biography or the background of the diarist, we encounter this divorce from the *not yet* that gives meaning and measure to the *now*. Just a month before his death in Auschwitz, for example, the twenty-year-old German Jew Guenther Marcuse wrote from the labor camp at Gross-Breesen: "For us, the prospects of a prolonged stay are diminishing. Filled with apprehension, we await coming events" (181). Here, of course, staying in the labor camp means more than staying in one place; it means staying in one piece, staying alive, and sustaining a present. The dreaded coming event, moreover, is not another event in a series of events, not an event in time, but the event that means the end of life and therefore of time. "I simply can't imagine," says Anne Frank, "that the world will ever be normal for us again. I do talk about 'after the war,' but then it is only a castle in the air" (127–28). Earlier we spoke of Anne's imprisonment in time; here we see the lock that seals her in her cell: it is the absence of an *after*. That is why she longs for the coming event, whatever it might be: once it comes, she supposes, it will return her to an *after* (and yet it turns out to be an *after* with no afterward). Similarly, but more explicitly than in the diaries of Marcuse and Frank, in Czerniakow's diary we see a recurring dread of the coming event that divorces the human being and his community from any future. "I cannot shake the fearful suspicion," he notes on 19 January 1942, "that the Jews of Warsaw may be threatened by mass resettlement" (317); four months later, on 15 May, he writes, "The city is full of rumors about deportations" (354); and on 18 July, just five days before his last entry, he laments, "Panic in the Quarter; some speak of deportations, others of a pogrom" (382). The interplay between Czerniakow's suspicion and the Jews' panic brings to mind Benjamin's point about the connection between the individual's past and a collective past, but with a difference: here the link is between the individual's dread and a collective dread of the future. Once again, it must be remembered that in this case resettlement and deportation signify not an elsewhere but a nowhere. And to be faced with this pending nowhere is to be divorced from the future, locked into a nowhere that is not elsewhere but here.

In a world where time holds out hope for relief from hardship—that is, in a world where time is time—the future presents itself as an exit from the present; "the page that remains blank," we recall Girard's words, "will be filled tomorrow" (537). In the world where the human being retains a remnant of his image, even the blank page of a diary harbors the potential for further measuring the time of a life. But in the antiworld, antitime is measured precisely according to the absence of this potential; each date that would be a measure of time is the last date of the last entry. And so in Aryeh Klonicki-Klonymus's *Diary of Adam's Father* we read: "I do not know whether it will be possible for me to continue writing this diary. For all I know these may well be my last lines" (71). When the diarist is thus divorced from the future, the future no longer offers any escape from the erasure of the past or from the collapse of the present; indeed, as we have seen, the collapse of the latter is inextricably tied to the erasure of the former, and both result in the divorce from the future. This divorce, moreover, underscores the division within the soul that is known as despair. "Despair and hopelessness are growing," writes Ringelblum. "There is the universal feeling that They are trying to starve us out, and we cannot escape" (157); there is no *oys-veg*, to use the Yiddish word for "escape" that we find in Ringelblum's original text (118), no way, no path, out. And the absence of a path is the absence of a future, for to have a path is to have a time and a place that we have *yet* to attain. All of life turns on this *yet*; when it is absent, so is life absent. That is why Katznelson cries out, "There is not a single Jew here who believes that he will be allowed to remain alive" (47). Each day, again, is the end that does not end, so that the time measured in the Holocaust diary is the last time, the time of the last, without a remnant to follow.

A good example of the Holocaust diary's recurring measure of time as the time of the end can be found in the diary of Éva Heyman, the Hungarian child born on 13 February 1931 in Nagyvarad and murdered in Auschwitz on 17 October 1944. There, on 25 March 1944, this young teenager writes, "Agi [Éva's mother] says that this is the end of everything; we won't see the end of the war. But I want to, and I want to hide away" (62). Almost a month later, on 20 April, she notes: "Papa isn't even glad that he has been released. He said that in his opinion, this isn't the end of it, but only the beginning. What else can happen that can be worse than what has happened already? I know; it can only be Poland" (81). And in her entry for 29 May, a day before her last entry, we read, "And so, dear diary, now the end of everything has really come" (103). Before her end, this child confronts the declaration of the end from her mother and the announcement of the beginning of the end from her father. The very ones who, in the world of humanity, would hold out the promise of the next day for their child are forced into the revocation of that promise. Thus, like the erasure of the past, the divorce from the future goes into the obliteration of the mother, the father, and the child as categories of human being. If the child's diary can have a purpose under such conditions, it is to retain a hold on what is not there; or rather, it is to generate what might be there, the record of a day that leads to another day. But there is no escape from the day, and so there is no tomorrow that is other than today. Why? Because tomorrow means being caught—that is the meaning of being trapped in a day with no exit.

Thus, when her relatives are caught, another teenager, Elisabeth Block of Rosenheim, cries out: "You can imagine the fear we have for our relatives who were seized, as well as for ourselves. How easily we could meet with the same fate, now that we have nothing for the winter in this desolate land, with its near-impossible living conditions! This uncertainty, this fear for a small bit of life with no way out, is horrible" (256). Similarly, Anne Frank speaks of her fear of being caught precisely by not speaking of it, saying: "If one day we too should . . . no, I mustn't write it, but I can't put the question out of my mind today. On the contrary, all the fear I've already been through seems to face me again in all its frightfulness" (256), that is to say, in all its *verschrikking*, in all its "terror" or "horror" (201). The terror that will not allow the word to come to the lips will not allow the future to approach the present. This terror of what must not be uttered divorces this child from the future, just as it does the thirty-two-year-old Warsaw Jew, Tuvia Borzykowski, who writes, "Sooner or later we will all be caught" (123); just as it does the sixteen-year-old boy in the Lodz Ghetto, David Sierakowiak, who, before dying of starvation, says: "There is no way out. It seems that we shall be buried here" (20). These and other Holocaust diarists share in common the foreboding that they are writing from the places of their deaths; they have no future because the future is already upon them, because they are *already*, rather than *not yet*, slipping down its gullet. This imposition upon the human being of the *already* that obliterates the future is an integral part of the annihilation of the human image, a point that becomes clear when we recall a brief remark made by Sarra Gleykh in her diary, which is included in *The Black Book* compiled by Ilya Ehrenberg and Vasily Grossman. "After the Germans left," she writes, "Mama cried and said: 'They don't consider us people; we're doomed'" (72). Only people have a history; only for people is presence an issue; only people address the *not yet* that is the future. Therefore only people write diaries. And so we see why it is that, during the time of the Shoah, an essential means of measuring the time of human life and human being was the diary.

The measure of time that unfolds in the Holocaust diary is a measure of humanity. According to Jewish tradition, time also harbors a measure of divinity, as Abraham Joshua Heschel reminds us: "It is the dimension of time wherein man meets God, wherein man becomes aware that every instant is an act of creation, a Beginning, opening up new roads for ultimate realizations. Time is the presence of God in the world of space" (*Sabbath* 100). For the Jew, then, the measure of both time and humanity lies in a relation to eternity, to that "future which," Rosenzweig puts it, "without ceasing to be a future, is nonetheless present. Eternity is a Today which is, however, conscious of being more than Today" (*Star* 224). What is the Jewish portal in time, the Today conscious of being more than Today, that opens up the path to eternity? It is the Sabbath, which, Pinhas Peli reminds us, is "the meaning-giving component of human existence" (6). In the assault on time and humanity we find an assault on the eternity ushered in each Sabbath. "The Sabbath comes all over the world," says Zelig Kalmanovitch, "but not here. Here it is not admitted" (64). And yet this very entry in the diary is a means of remembering and observing the Sabbath, of creating a place where it may enter into the diarist's measure of time. Writing the diary is therefore a means of measuring and sanctifying time in the midst of the slaughter of the time of the Jews. It is a means of maintaining a hold on the holy and thus on life when both are under assault. In sum, it is the chronicle of the holy.

THE CHRONICLE OF THE HOLY

IN HIS ESSAY ON ROSH HASHANAH, THE THIRTEENTH-century sage Nachmanides maintains that "the days [of the week] and the months [of the year] are counted with reference to [the observance of] the commandments" (*Writings* 1:243). According to this teaching from Jewish tradition, the observance of the *mitzvot* (commandments or good deeds) is the measure of time; time is understood in terms of a *doing* that is expressive of a relation to the holy and to the Holy One. As Emmanuel Levinas expresses it, "time is the most profound relationship that man can have with God, precisely as a going towards God," and, he adds, "'going towards God' is meaningless unless seen in terms of my primary going towards the other person" ("Dialogue" 23). While this going towards God through the movement towards the other can transpire at any time, it is especially remembered through the observance of the *mitzvot* in the time of the holy seasons. What is a *mitzvah*? In the words of Abraham Joshua Heschel, it is "a prayer in the form of a deed" (*Quest* 69), so that the prayer is not in time, but time is in the prayer. Viewed as a prayer, the *mitzvah* situates the measure of time in a dimension of height; it ascends toward the light of heaven to create an opening through which the eternal may enter into time from on high. To be sure, the Torah tells us that the festivals or holy days are determined by the luminaries of the heavens (see Genesis 1:14); determined by the heavens, they are designated by the prayers and *mitzvot* peculiar to them. What sanctifies the days as holy is the descent of the Creator into His creation and the ascent of humanity toward the Holy One through the portals of prayers and *mitzvot*.

The Nazis cannot mount their ascent as the master race without usurping the place of the Holy One seated on high in their suppression of the human being. Their assault on time, then, includes an assault on the prayers and *mitzvot*, as well as on the human beings who observe them; it is an assailing of the eternal in an attempt to effect an absolute closure of the portals through which the holy might make an appearance in the midst of the mundane. The Nazis, certainly, were as much aware of these connections as their Jewish victims were. Mary Berg, for example, notes that "the Nazis strictly follow the Jewish calendar" (103), where, in her Polish text, the word translated as "follow" is *przestrzegaja* (111); it is a cognate of *przestrzeganie*, a noun that means "observance," but it can also mean "warning" or "admonition." The Nazis' adherence to the Jewish calendar, indeed, brought with it warnings and admonitions, since that observance took the form of even greater cruelties perpetrated against the Jews. "On the Day of Atonement," writes Chaim Kaplan on 23 September 1939, "the enemy displayed even greater might than usual" (36); indeed, just three days earlier he had written, "Holidays and festivals no longer exist" (35). Thus, according to Shimon Huberband, there was a running "joke" in the ghettos: "If we can endure for twenty-one days, then we'll be saved. Namely, eight days of Passover, eight days of Succos, two days of Rosh Hashanah, two days of Shavuos, and one day of Yom Kippur" (118). The scheduling of actions and selections to coincide with the remembrance and observance of holy time is a means of murdering the Holy One (an assault that we shall examine in detail in the next chapter) in the process of murdering the Jews. It is a way of annihilating the basis of truth and meaning in all of human time and all of human being.

"Time was hallowed by God," Heschel reminds us. "Space, the Tabernacle, was consecrated by Moses" (*Israel* 11). That is why the prayers said in their season, in the words of Adin Steinsaltz, include "the individual in something larger—the person becomes part of a people, not only the thousands of his countrymen who are similarly engaged at that moment or on that day all over the world, but also the millions of Jews who prayed this way throughout the generations. The place of worship embraces the whole world, past, present, and future" (*Being Free* 92). Here too the Nazis' assault on time is shown to be an assault on eternity; their annihilation of the individual is shown to be central to their annihilation of a people. And both are attacked in the assault on the holy days.

We have seen already, particularly in the first two chapters, that the internal life of the Holocaust diarist derives its substance from its tie to an external community. Just so, Rabbi Steinsaltz reminds us that "we should see the festivals as internal events in the life of the individual, which are reflections of the collective life of a nation" (*Being Free* 43). To be sure, the use of the Hebrew calendar, whose dates are measured from the time of the Creation, itself represents a link between Israel and the Creator, between time and the Eternal One: time ties us to the Covenant.[1] Responding to the onslaught aimed at the individual and the nation, therefore, the diarist who keeps a chronicle of the days of destruction also preserves a chronicle of the holy days by noting them, attesting to them, and affirming them, each in their season. In this way the diarist attempts to restore the dearness of life, if not life itself, by restoring a link to the Covenant. What the fourteenth-century sage Gersonides says of knowledge, moreover, is also true of this testimony: "The act of knowledge, the object of knowledge, and the knower are all identical" (1:180). The holy is at work in the diarist who becomes the chronicler of the holy.

As a chronicle of the holy, written precisely when the holy is under assault, the Holocaust diary, once again, belongs to a category all its own in its effort to recover life and meaning. There is no recovery of life without a preservation of what sanctifies life; there is no recovery of meaning without this testimony to the ground of meaning. In this chapter, then, we shall examine the endeavors of these diarists to sustain a remembrance and observance of the times and the seasons that make possible the truth, meaning, and sanctity of life. And we shall begin with the season that marks the beginning of the Jewish year: Rosh Hashanah, the High Holy Days, and Yom Kippur.

THE TIME OF JUDGMENT AND ATONEMENT

The biblical text read on the First of Tishrei, Rosh Hashanah, is the *Akedah*, the harrowing account of the Binding of Isaac. It is a tale about Abraham's raising a knife over his beloved child and therefore over the promise of a people given to him by God—by the very God who ordered the Patriarch to raise the knife and make his son, the vessel of the promise, into a burnt offering. Just as on that day Abraham and Isaac came before a terrible judgment, so does every Jew stand to be judged on Rosh Hashanah. Indeed, Nachmanides points out, "the constellation for [Tishrei] is the zodiacal sign of the Balance" (*Writings* 1:37). The judgment? It is whether our names are to be inscribed into or erased from the Book of Life. One can see why Elie Wiesel reminds us that "the theme and term of the *Akedah* have been used, throughout the centuries, to describe the destruction and disappearance of countless Jewish communities everywhere. Of all the biblical tales, the one about Isaac is perhaps the most timeless and most relevant to our generation. We have known Jews who, like Abraham, witnessed the death of their children; who, like Isaac, lived the *Akedah* in their flesh; and some who went mad when they saw their father disappear on the altar, with the altar, in a blazing fire whose flames reached the highest of the heavens" (*Messengers* 95). Given these associations with the story of Abraham and Isaac and the tale's connection with Rosh Hashanah, it is not surprising to find so many commentaries on this holiday in the pages of the Holocaust diary.

In the diary he kept during his ordeal in the Lodz Ghetto, for instance, Shlomo Frank notes: "To honor the Holy Day of Rosh Hashanah, the President today released an order that the penalties pronounced on all arrested this day would be reduced. Or rescinded" (177). What seemed as though it would not come from God or from the SS came for a day from President Mordecai Chaim Rumkowski, a man who, in the words of Lucy Dawidowicz, "ruled Lodz by force of personality, tenacity of purpose, organizational intelligence, and political shrewdness, even outwitting the SS in its attempt to displace him. His presence and authority were felt everywhere in the ghetto" (241). Whether Rumkowski issued this order to further his own authority or whether it was out of a genuine compassion for the Jews is beside the point; what is to be noted is that here the diarist enters in his diary the inscription of a few names, for a brief time, into the Book of Life. He chronicles not only the days of destruction but also a moment of salvation. The link between individual and community, at least for the moment, is sustained in the diarist's record of that link as the record of a *mitzvah*.

Similarly, Josef Katz notes in his diary the *mitzvah* of saying the holiday prayers, performed in the autumn of 1944 by Jews kept prisoner on a Nazi boat sailing to Danzig. "On the first deck," he writes, "a Jew is standing with a prayer shawl over his shoulders and a prayerbook in his hand. Softly he starts to pray. A few candles eerily illuminate the dark hold. The monotonous sing-song of the praying Jew resounds from the iron bulkheads, and is repeated in chorus by the other Jews. A solemn mood takes hold. Old familiar melodies are heard; we are humming along softly. Pictures from my childhood arise; for a moment my thoughts are at home. I see my mother and my sisters and brothers on Rosh Hashanah. . . . But the pitching and tossing of the boat calls me back to reality. It is Rosh Hashanah now, too, but I am not at home" (201). The Jew wrapped in the prayer shawl attempts to create a homelike place where the tie to the community can be reestablished; after all, it is as a community that Jews stand before God on Rosh Hashanah. But, for Katz, the pitching of the vessel on the face of the deep is more than the tie can bear. Removed from home and cast upon the waters, he is removed from the holy day itself. If a tenuous tie to the holy remains, it is sustained only by the diary: the words of the diary itself are joined with the prayers of the Jews.

Because the Jews stand on Rosh Hashanah *as a community*, joined in prayer with Jews throughout the world and throughout time, this holiday is a time of rejoicing, when one eats challah with honey instead of salt. As the chronicle of the Chosen, the chronicle of the Jewish community is itself the chronicle of the holy. But when the community is robbed of its rejoicing, it falls into a state of collapse; and when the community is thrown into a state of collapse, the holy itself undergoes a collapse. For the *Shekhinah*, or the Indwelling Presence of the Holy One, says the *Zohar*, resides only in "a place of joyfulness" (2:303). Therefore we realize what is missing when Yitskhok Rudashevski says of a Rosh Hashanah in the Vilna Ghetto: "A holiday spirit which is anything but cheerful is diffused over the few little ghetto streets. Something is missing" (49–50). Something, indeed, is missing: the *Shekhinah* is missing, which is to say, the community of Israel is missing, for the Jews of the ghetto who have lost their brethren have lost their link to the world. That is why Avraham Tory writes from the Kovno Ghetto: "Our very condition of life cuts us off from the New Year celebrations of the outside world. . . . Today we can only lament, and preserve our mourning in memory of the tens of thousands of our brother martyrs who died sanctifying God's name, the victims of a 'crime'—to be a Jew" (165). The tradition tells us that when a community of Jews is sent into exile, the *Shekhinah* goes into exile with them; but when whole Jewish communities are exiled to a place from which there is no return—to mass graves that heave and then grow still or to a sky transformed into a cemetery—the *Shekhinah* herself is left without a place.

The destruction of the community is not the only means that the Nazis employed for eliminating the Presence of the Holy One from the holy days. Since, above all else, it is the communal prayer that constitutes the community, the assault against the season includes an assault against the prayers of the season. For just as the *Shekhinah* is associated with the community, so is it associated with prayer. The Baal Shem Tov, founder of Hasidism, for instance, teaches that "when a man begins the Amidah and says the opening verse: 'O Lord, open Thou my lips!' the *Shekhinah* immediately enters within his voice, and speaks with his voice" (Newman 337); and the Koretzer Rebbe Phineas Shapiro, a disciple of the Baal Shem, insists, "no man can raise his voice in prayer except when the *Shekhinah* prays through it" (Newman 336). Therefore the annihilation of the Indwelling Presence required the annihilation of prayer, a point confirmed by the diarists. During the High Holy Days of Rosh Hashanah 5700 (14 September 1939), Rabbi Huberband notes: "The days of *Selichos* prayers passed without a single *minyan* meeting in the entire city [of Piotrkow]. On the eve of Rosh Hashanah (Wednesday), a notice was issued that Jews were required to keep their shops and businesses open on the Sabbath and all Jewish holidays" (40). And a year later, on the eve of Rosh Hashanah 5701, Chaim Kaplan writes, "Never before was there a government so evil that it would forbid an entire people to pray" (202). And yet this evil is perfectly consistent with the metaphysical dimensions of this project of extermination. A people cannot live a life of any value without the holy season that sanctifies all the other seasons of life; and the holy season cannot have any significance without the prayers that define it. "Hence," said the Nazis, "we forbid you to pray before we kill you." Once again we realize that, unlike the enemies of the past, the Nazis set out to destroy Jewish souls before they destroyed Jewish bodies. The assault against prayer demonstrates once more that the Holocaust was as much about ontology as it was about biology, that it involved the metaphysical as much as it involved the material.

The other side of Rosh Hashanah, the Day of Judgment, is Yom Kippur, the Day of Atonement. On this day the Jews come before God by purifying their souls with prayer and afflicting their bodies with fasting, to become as the angels, who neither eat nor drink. The diarists, however, added their entries to their prayers of entreaty and recorded the perversion of the season imposed by the enemy's own terrible affliction of the body of Israel. Rabbi Huberband, for example, describes how at 6:00 p.m., as the end of the first Yom Kippur of the Nazi occupation drew near, the Jews of Piotrkow, weakened by their fast, were forced to crawl on their bellies down the street leading to the town hall. Once they arrived there, "everyone wearing a beard had his beard ripped out. They weren't sheared off, or cut off with a knife or bayonet, they were literally ripped out. Then they selected a young man named Liposanik and appointed him 'rabbi.' They took him over to the wall, beat him, and forced him to curse the Jewish people. . . . Then they told him to say his last prayers, and he said the *Shma Yisroel*. One of them asked him what the words meant, and the Jew told him. He then ordered the Jew to curse God's name, but the Jew refused to do so" (51). Three years later, in Warsaw, we see from Peretz Opoczynski's diary that little had changed. "The SS men," he writes in his entry for Yom Kippur 1942, "have prepared a surprise for the Jews on the Day of Atonement. The shop-commissars themselves, without the participation of German soldiers, carried out a round-up in the houses attached to the shops, breaking in door-locks and taking people from the flats in which they had been hiding" (109). On that same date Emmanuel Ringelblum simply jots down, "The practice of torturing Jews in the cities on Yom Kippur" (314). And even as these men are making their entries for that holy day, the seventeen-year-old Mary Berg writes, "At first one could hear the words pronounced by the cantor, but soon everything was drowned in one lament and sobbing" (186). And at that same time, the fourteen-year-old Yitskhok Rudashevski writes: "A sad mood suffuses the ghetto. People have had such a sad High Holy Day feeling. I am as far from religion now as before the ghetto. Nevertheless, this holiday drenched in blood and sorrow, which is solemnized in the ghetto, now penetrates my heart" (56–57). Rudashevski could not escape the holy's penetration of his soul any more than he could escape the Nazis' extermination of his body. For the target of their extermination was this penetration of the soul made possible by inscribing this entry in his diary.

The drenching of the holy day in blood is a means of bleeding the day of its holiness. For the diarist who maintains a chronicle of the holy in such a time, it must be noted, the observance of the season is not a question of having faith, if having faith means accepting the doctrine; rather it is a matter of sustaining a Jewish link to Jewish life and therefore to what sanctifies all life. The entry in Rudashevski's diary cited above hints at this point. An entry from the diary that Leon Wells kept in the Janowska camp makes it clear. Describing the activities held on the eve of Yom Kippur 5704 (1943), he writes: "We began, in whispers, but also in a holy and dignified manner, to pray. As collective praying could get us into bad trouble with the Germans, the 'antireligious' group kept guard outside the tents. . . . Many of the nonreligious ones took part in the prayers, and many fasted the whole of the next day" (201). Even for those who are not religious, praying becomes a metaphysical means of resisting the metaphysical onslaught.[2] These prisoners, then, take part in the prayers for the same reason that the diarists take up their diaries: to join their words with the words of Jews everywhere, the living and the dead, as they have sought and continue to seek the ear of the Creator and Sustainer of life in the time of judgment and atonement. In the Holocaust diary the recovery of life entails the recovery of this time that imparts meaning to all time. For there is no meaning in life without a mission in life, and there is no mission without this judgment and atonement. That is why the High Holy Days begin on Rosh Hashanah with a reading of the *Akedah* and end on Yom Kippur with a reading of the Book of Jonah, the book about responsibility and mission and testimony—which is exactly what the Holocaust diary is about. If the diary holds out any prospect for any recovery of life and meaning that would liberate the diarist, then that recovery is possible only to the extent that the diary chronicles and thereby attests to the holy. Well aware of this necessity, the authors of these diaries, almost without exception, bear witness to the liberation that comes in the season of Passover and Shavuot.

THE SEASON OF LIBERATION

For some of the diarists, such as Leon Wells, the season of liberation comes in a memory, which in turn comes in a dream: "I dream about the Seder night. The whole family is sitting at the table. My mother serves the food, looks into the face of every child with a smile" (154). Such a memory of the season of liberation can itself be liberating. Indeed, the season of liberation is a season of remembrance; as "oblivion is at the root of exile," said the Baal Shem Tov, so "memory is at the root of redemption" (Wiesel, *Souls* 27). Memory of what? Memory of fathers and mothers and children gathered at the set table, at the center of the home from which life derives its sanctity and time its eternity.[3] Liberation happens where the Passover table is laid, where the family is gathered, where a mother smiles at her children. Why? Because the table in the home—where prayers are uttered, bread is broken, and the family is gathered—becomes the portal through which the Holy One enters the world and sets the human being free from the weight of a world reduced to mere matter. According to the teaching of the talmudic sages Rabbi Yochanan and Resh Lakish, "at the time when the Temple stood, the altar used to make atonement for a person; now a person's table makes atonement for him" (*Hagigah* 27a). As the focal point of atonement, the table is the reference point for the soul's liberation. It is the family's gathering about the table for the Passover Seder, therefore, that makes it possible to honor the Talmud's injunction that in every generation we regard ourselves as though we had been liberated from of Egypt (*Pesachim* 116b). For this liberation is a liberation not merely from forced labor but from the meaningless power struggle that characterizes idolatrous materialism in all its forms, perhaps even in its most extreme, Nazi form. That is why the *Midrash Tanchuma* tells us that, on the first day of Passover (15 Nisan on the Jewish calendar), "the decree with Father Abraham was enacted between the entrails," and "the angel brought the tidings concerning the birth of Isaac" (1:269). It is the covenant with divinity and a promise of humanity that draw human beings into a relation with God and that alone make liberation and affirmation possible.

Thus it becomes possible for Tory to write in his diary on the eve of Passover 5703 (1943): "We believe in the Exodus taking place for each generation. The more we are being enslaved, the greater is our faith. *Am Israel Hai* (the people of Israel live)" (302). Where the people of Israel live, God lives and life has meaning: that is the liberation. And so we may better understand an assertion made by Levinas, one that enables us to better understand what is at work in the Holocaust diary: "The excess of evil by which it is a surplus in the world is also our impossibility of accepting it. The experience of evil would then be also our waiting on the good—the love of God" (*Collected* 183). Affirming the good in its response to evil, the diary becomes a chronicle of the holy in its refusal to succumb to the profane; it becomes an expression of faith in its refusal to succumb to despair; and it becomes a summons for the recovery of life in its refusal to succumb to the silence of death. Indeed, Rabbi Huberband notes that, during the first Passover of the occupation, the Jews of Piotrkow celebrated in an exalted spirit. "Despite the ban on public prayer," he writes, "people assembled in all the courtyards in which several *minyans* were held" (59). And: "Piotrkow distinguished itself in one more area; every day there was a heated *mikveh* [ritual bath]. In Warsaw, this was punishable by death as an act of sabotage" (61). That the use of the *mikveh* was regarded as an act of sabotage is indicative of the Nazis' effort not only to establish their absolute authority but to usurp the divine authority. To determine that any authority other than God's is absolute amounts to idolatry, and once again we are reminded of the true nature of the liberation from Egypt: it is the liberation manifested through the sanctity of the family gathered about the Passover table. The assault on the family here takes the form of an assault on the laws of family purity, to which the *mikveh* is closely tied. To forbid the use of the *mikveh* is to forbid wives from joining with their husbands, and both from joining with the Creator in the process of bringing life into the world.

Forbidding the use of the *mikveh*, then, is an act of the Angel of Death. In contrast to the first Passover, the Angel of Death from whom the Jews sought deliverance during the Shoah was not the one sent from God; it was, instead, the Nazi angel of idolatry. And yet in many cases this reversal only heightened the Jew's need to reconnect himself with the community during the season of liberation, as liberation can be found only in the midst of the community. In the spring of 1943, for example, Michael Zylberberg relates that, even though he had found some safety outside the walls of the Warsaw Ghetto, "the Passover festival was drawing closer and this, also, made me want to return to the ghetto" (94). While he managed to get inside the ghetto for a few days before Passover, he was forced to observe the holy day in isolation: "I prepared to commemorate the festival in my own small way as best I could. I went out into the forest and heard the reverberations of the distant gunfire. Sleep was impossible; this was to be a night of wakefulness—a *Lail Shimurim*. I was to hold my own vigil and service, alone, living through their experience on this night of 'blood, fire and pillars of smoke.' These words, from the *Haggadah*, had acquired new meaning" (95). Here the chronicle of the holy includes the words from the holy text that consecrates the holy season.[4] In keeping with the movement of liberation, the diarist's endeavor to recover a remnant of life and meaning entails this retrieval of ancient words that take on new meaning. For searching out renewed meaning is essential to the establishment of a renewed link to the community.

It must not be forgotten, however, that the new meaning behind the sacred words frequently reveals a perversion of the sacred, which the diary makes manifest in its testimony to this perversion. Just as new meaning is forced into the words, so are new words, words out of place, forced into the season. Ringelblum provides us with an instance of the word out of season when on 17 April 1941 he writes, "A friend whom I wished a 'calm Passover' (that was last year's motto) replied: 'Rather wish me an easy fast' " (154)—a greeting normally reserved for Yom Kippur. In the Vilna Ghetto, Herman Kruk observes, the greeting was "may we live to see each other next year" (63), and Shlomo Frank relates that in the Lodz Ghetto there was no greeting of "*yom tov*," or "happy holiday," at all (74). These examples make it clear that when meaning is removed from words and words from their season, the season of liberation is twisted into a season of destruction. As if to drive this point home, Ringelblum notes, "Passover, when many provincial Jews fasted—because they had no food that was kosher for Passover—was a factor in the significant rise in mortality" (173). On this Passover, the Angel of Death does not pass over the Jews—it cuts a bloody path through their midst. Forced off the calendar and out of its season, drained of its meaning, "liberation" becomes a synonym for death among the Jews of Nazi Europe; hence the greeting: "May we live. . . ." The only remaining link between life and liberation is the diary itself, where the "may we live" is recorded. Yet the diary contains not only the record of the greeting and its context but also the *horror* of it. To emphasize this horror, which is the turning back on itself of the sacred, Shlomo Frank writes, "All of the plagues recorded in the *Haggadah* have been turned against the Jews of Lodz: impenetrable darkness, epidemics, madness, terror, hunger, and persecution" (73–74). And so the *Haggadah* becomes the tale not of Israel's Liberator but of Israel's murderer; the door held open for Elijah is now broken down by the SS. To be sure, the Jews are led out of their captivity, as Adam Czerniakow indicates in his comment on the Jews of Lublin: "Tomorrow Passover. News from Lublin. Ninety percent of the Jews are to leave Lublin within the next few days" (339). But there is a difference between the Jews leaving Egypt and those leaving Lublin: the Jews of Lublin go not to a parting of the sea but to a sea that will rush over them and swallow them up.

On each day of the seven weeks from Passover to Shavuot, Jews count the *omer* to indicate that the season of liberation is tied to the season of revelation. For Shavuot is the observance of the giving of the Torah at Sinai, and it is this event that consummates the liberation. As all of Israel was gathered at the Mount to hear the Voice of the Holy One, blessed be He, so nearly all of the Holocaust diarists raise their voices in this chronicle of the encounter with the One who now seems to turn toward them quite a different face. Even Czerniakow, known for his secularism, writes: "At 9:30 in the Synagogue on Tlomackie Street I carried the Torah twice around the synagogue. Toward the end of the service (Shavuot) a cantor had a dizzy spell (paralysis)" (245). If we look to the Polish text of the diary, we find that "service" is a rendition of the phrase *dnia swiatecznego* (188), which means "holy day": here the time of the holy receives its closure with the fainting of the one who chants the prayers that sanctify the day. Like the cantor, the diarist struggles to sanctify the season in his chronicle of the holy. Like the cantor, very often he swoons, and for the same reason: it is the gross incongruity of the imposition of the antiworld upon the world, the collapse of all distinction, of all *havdalah*, that makes it possible for the holy to manifest itself.

Examples of the swoon of the diarist can be found in the journals of *Oneg Shabbat* members Hersh Wasser and Abraham Levin. Chronicling the events of Shavuot 5702 (1942), Wasser writes: "All the Jews were driven out of Wojslowice, Sielec, Kumow, and Wolka Leszczanska, to Chelm, and on the way masses were 'rendered cold'—shot down by machine guns. The Jewish blood contribution to world slaughter surpasses understanding and measure" (275). Equally beyond understanding and measure, however, is the determined faith of Rabbi Shlomo Zelichowski of Zdunska Wola, who, according to Levin, sang praises to God as he and nine other Jews were hanged in a grisly *minyan* on that same Shavuot. "In Zdunska Wola," the diarist relates, "ten Jews were hanged on the eve of Shavuot, among them the Rabbi of the town. The Rabbi turned to the Jews and urged them to be happy at the privilege of being emissaries for all Israel in dying for the Sanctification of the Name" (317). In these incidents we find the extremes of souls rendered cold and a soul on fire, extremes that bespeak the extremity of the season, the extremity of the holy and of the assault on the holy. Both are instances of the insertion into the world of a Presence from beyond the world, and the pages of the Holocaust diary contain the trace of that Presence.

Other dates on the Jewish calendar mark observances of the appearance of the Eternal One in time, both in times of deliverance and in times of destruction. Here, too, however, the diarist's chronicle of the holy comes in a swoon at the time out of joint. For here, too, what is symbolized in its season is turned on end, so that the diarist seeks to set it right, even if this amounts to no more than offering a testimony to this terrible overturning.

DAYS OF DELIVERANCE AND DAYS OF DESTRUCTION

Among the most prolonged of the Jewish observances of times when the community was delivered from the enemy is Hanukkah, the Festival of Lights that lasts for eight days. It is a season for remembering not just the victory of the Macabbees over the Greeks who tried to hellenize the Jews in the second century B.C.E.; more important, these are the days for remembering the reentry of the Light of the Holy One into the world, when the Temple was rededicated, the menorah rekindled, and the faith restored, opening up a place for God to enter. During the Shoah, however, the Jews trapped in the Kingdom of Night witnessed the entry of the Nazis. On the first day of Hanukkah 5702 (December 1941), for example, Rabbi Huberband tells us that one Jew relates: "The entire *minyan* began to say the *Shma Yisroel.* We could hear Jews screaming the same words on the street. . . . We began to recite the prayers, when suddenly, we once again heard terrible screams and wails form the prison yard. We went over to the window and our blood froze in our veins when we saw a new group of seven Jews being led to the execution area" (166). This conjunction of prayers and screams is yet another example of the incongruity that forces time—the time of the return of God's light to the world—out of joint. And when the time is out of joint, the holy is out of place, and God recedes into the depths of a scream.[5] Adding his voice to the unholy conjunction of prayers and screams, the diarist joins prayer to outcry and outcry to prayer in an effort to retrieve some remnant of the holy; the chronicle of the holy creates a time in which the holy may show itself, even as it is under assault. Such, indeed, is the meaning of Hanukkah: light makes its appearance in a time and a place where, by all that reason would dictate, it should not be there. Therefore Kaplan is careful to observe, "Never before in Jewish Warsaw were there as many Hanukkah celebrations as in this year of the wall [1940]" (234). In the antiworld, when the Jewish prayers that are "out of place" make their appearance, the holy is in place.

Whereas in the first example prayers were contrasted with screams, here the contrast is between the liberating light of Hanukkah and the confining darkness of the wall. In each case, however, the diary's testimony to the light is a means of penetrating the wall. Like the Jews who pray despite the prohibition, the diarist writes despite the darkness and thereby transforms a small piece of the darkness into light. Thus responding to the first utterance of Creation—"Let there be light" (Genesis 1:3)—the diarist affirms, as a Jew, the meaning of all creation and of all life. The recovery of life and meaning in the Holocaust diary, then, amounts to the Jew's recovery of the purpose of his Jewishness.[6] And Hanukkah is an observance of that recovery.

Another day of deliverance, Purim, had particular meaning for the Jews of Nazi Europe. On this day Jews gather in remembrance of their delivery from the edict of extermination that Haman tried to imposed on them in the fifth century B.C.E., during the reign of the Babylonian king Ahasuerus. This tale of deliverance is told in the Book of Esther, which is read each year amidst joyous celebration on the night of 14 Adar (February-March). Here too, of course, the diarist was faced with a staggering disjuncture between the festive occasion and the days of destruction. While the disjuncture lay in the fact that in this instance, it seemed, the Jews would not be delivered from destruction, very often it was handled by suggesting a similarity between Haman and Hitler. Ringelblum, for example, tells us, "People hope for a new Purim—to celebrate the downfall of the modern Haman, Hitler—one that will be commemorated as long as the Jewish people exist" (139). In his diary Rudashevski's writes: "We were in the mood for Purim, so let it be Purim. We were the ones who set the tone. We sang songs, presented a 'Purim play.' . . . We laughed our fill and went to sleep. We are waiting for the real Purim. Next year we shall eat Hitler-tashn [a play on the word *Hamantaschen*, which is a pastry eaten at Purim]" (137). As Rudashevski was writing his entry in the Vilna Ghetto, from the Kovno Ghetto Tory affirmed: "Today is Purim. Hitler has promised that there will be no more Purim festivities for the Jews. I do not know whether his other predictions will come true, but this one is yet to be fulfilled. . . . None other than our little children, our Mosheles and Shlomeles, give the lie to Hitler's prediction by celebrating Purim with all their innocence and enthusiasm" (253); and, he adds: "We recalled the folk adage that all the holy days will disappear with the passing of time, but that Purim will remain for ever and ever, so that our enemies will not be comforted. Today the wonderful Ghetto children gave this saying another lease on life" (256). To be sure, in the

Jewish tradition the chronicle of the holy includes the chronicle of the children, and the Holocaust diary is no exception (the child, in fact, is so prominent in the Holocaust diary that chapter 11 is devoted to this precious figure targeted for murder).

The child and the holy days are connected by the fact that, through them, to borrow an insight from Leo Baeck, "the beyond enters this world while eternity descends upon the earth in order to reveal itself and become the future" (229). The child is the embodiment of the holy, inasmuch as the holy not only sanctifies a present but also opens up a future by opening up a moment when the eternal may enter into time. And that moment comes in the moment of our devotion to the child. "To be *for* a time that would be without me, *for* a time after my time," Levinas explains, "is not an ordinary thought which is extrapolating from my own duration; it is the passage to the time of the other. Should what makes such a passage possible be called *eternity*?" (*Collected* 92). When the other is the child, the answer to this question is yes. The deliverance of a people for a time beyond their time amounts to a deliverance of the children. Children figure prominently, however, not only in the remembrance of deliverance but also in the memory of destruction. In the *Midrash Rabbah*, for example, we read: "R. Judah said: Come and see how beloved are the children by the Holy One, blessed be He. The Sanhedrin were exiled but the *Shechinah* did not go into exile with them. When, however, the children were exiled, the *Shechinah* went into exile with them" (7:106). This midrash is a commentary on the Babylonian exile and the destruction of the First Temple, which, along with the destruction of the Second Temple and other disasters that have befallen the community, is commemorated on Tisha B'Av, or the Ninth of Av. It is an occasion for fasting and mourning and all-night vigils.

Not surprisingly, this date bears particular significance for the writers of the Holocaust diaries. On the eve of Tisha B'Av 1943, Tory, for instance, is careful to note, "In the evening we gathered in the Council office to recite Lamentations" (456), the biblical text traditionally read on this occasion. As though adding to the Book of Lamentations the latest list of the dead, on 12 August 1940, Czerniakow writes, "Now I must tell their families. One hundred fifty-eight persons are dead out of 260"; and he is careful to add: "Tomorrow is

Tisha B'Av" (184). And, as might be expected, this date was marked on the Nazis' calendar as a day for imposing on the Jews something to truly lament. Zylberberg, for instance, reports that in the Warsaw Ghetto during the summer of 1942, "the first deportation order was issued to us on the 9th of Av, the anniversary of the destruction of the Temple" (75). Here the Jews themselves take the place of the Temple. "With each hour," writes Elie Wiesel, "the most blessed and most stricken people of the world numbers twelve times twelve children less. And each one carries away still another fragment of the Temple in flames" (*Ani* 27). Like the Temple, they signify the presence of the Holy One, blessed be He, in the world, and among the chief ways in which that presence is signified is the chronicle of the Holy kept by these Jewish diarists. We discover once more that in their testimony on the destruction of the holy, the Holocaust diarists affirm the dearness of the holy. For they engage in this testimony not because of some social or psychological or political need, but precisely because there is a matter of ultimate concern that demands their testimony.

The eternity of the Jews, Franz Rosenzweig maintains, "gives simultaneity to all moments of our history. Turning back, recapturing what has remained behind, is here a permanent and life necessity. For we must be able to *live* in our eternity" (*Learning* 90). To be sure, there is no other life for the Jew, and the Jewish diarist seeks to recover that life through the recovery of the eternal, which enters time in the holy season. The Holocaust diary's chronicle of the holy is more than a diarist's record of events that transpired on certain days of the year: it is a witness borne by a human being who becomes the bearer of the holy.

One holy day that we have not mentioned in this chapter is the day for which "all these days were created," as Wiesel has suggested (*Dimensions* 5): the Sabbath. Explaining the significance of the Sabbath in this connection, Pinhas Peli cites the sixteenth-century Maharal of Prague, saying: "Everything in the material world has six dimensions, or directions, and can be weighed and measured. The six dimensions are the extent of the realm of matter created in six days. The Sabbath adds to the world a seventh dimension, the dimension of the Holy, which gives meaning to the other six" (11–12). Thus the Sabbath imparts presence to the time of the present, for presence is the presence of the holy, of truth and meaning. An older contemporary of the Maharal, Rabbi Meir ibn Gabbai of Turkey, says, "The relationship of the sixth day to Shabbat is as the relationship of this world to the World-to-Come" (17). Thus the Sabbath imparts a meaningful future to the time of the present, for the meaning derived from the holy opens up a path that leads us into a realm of the yet-to-be, into a realm of promise.

The Nazis were all too aware of this significance of the Sabbath and saw to its desecration in various ways. So, too, were the diarists aware of it, yet their invocation of the Sabbath nearly always includes an allusion to something or someone that is no more. Tuvia Borzykowski, for example, says that "the sight of the Sabbath candles brought back memories" (117)—memories of a time when the sacred was in place and a portal was opened for the entry of the Sabbath Bride into the world. In his diary Dawid Rubinowicz, the teenager from Krajno, Poland, associates the Sabbath with his absent father, whom the Nazis have taken away, saying: "In the evening we went to pray—after all it *is* Friday. We used to always go with Father" (72). And Hannah Senesh encounters the Sabbath as an emptiness exemplifying the emptiness of a world devoid of holiness: "Today is the Sabbath. An empty Sabbath which offers only a part of the day's significance: a day of rest, but not a holiday, not a day of festivity" (99). Just as the Sabbath signifies the dimension of the holy, so do the absence and the emptiness here surrounding it signify the erasure of the holy.

Therefore this day for which all the other days are created is ultimately the basis for the Holocaust diary's chronicle of the holy. Without the Sabbath such a chronicle would have no point. With the Sabbath it becomes a matter of absolute urgency. "Man brings God into the world," Leo Baeck expresses one of Judaism's basic teachings. "He sanctifies the world by sanctifying God in it" (187). One means of bringing about this sanctification is the remembrance and observance of the Sabbath. For on the Sabbath, the Holy One Himself rested from His work and settled into His creation. Compiling this chronicle of the holy, the diarist struggles to create a place where the Holy One might once more enter His creation. And because this chronicle is generated in the midst of the darkness produced by driving God out of the world, it attests to an assault on the Holy One Himself.

ASSAILING GOD

IN THIS CHAPTER WE SHALL EXAMINE IN DETAIL AN important implication of all that has been discussed thus far; namely, that in the Holocaust the assault on God's Chosen is quintessentially an assault on God Himself.[1] The validity of the claim that Israel's affliction is God's affliction rests not on a belief in God, but on a certain understanding and treatment of the human being as a creature who harbors a trace of something holy. As we shall see, now more clearly than ever, a singular and distinctive feature of the Holocaust is that it is characterized not only by an attack on human beings but also by an assault on everything that sanctifies humanity.

This singular feature of the Holocaust is reflected in the Holocaust diary and its chronicle of an assault on the human being that entails an assault on divine being. "Not only the body of Israel is being attacked," writes Moshe Flinker, for instance, "but also its spirit" (43), an observation echoed by Yitzhak Katznelson, who asserts, "It is against the great Beth Hamedrash, the spirit and soul of East European Jewry, that the nations have set this Horror" (202–3). The assault on the spirit of Israel manifests itself in the reduction of the body of Israel to mere matter that may be used as raw material for the manufacture of soap from Jewish fat, fertilizer from Jewish bones, and textiles from Jewish hair. It manifests itself in the calculated destruction not only of Jewish bodies but of Jewish souls and Jewish prayers, of Jewish texts and traditions, of Jewish homes and families—everything that goes into the fabric not only of the Jewish community but of any human community. "A community," says Martin Buber, "is built upon a living, reciprocal relationship, but the builder is the living, active center" (*I and Thou* 94). In the Jewish community, that living, active center is the God of Abraham, Isaac, and Jacob, and the community is established *as* a community through its covenantal relationship to this center. If the spirit of Israel is the community of Israel, it is because the community of Israel is grounded in the Covenant with the Holy One, blessed be He. In Hebrew the word for "community" is *e'dah*, which also means "testimony": the community inheres in its testimony to God, Whose presence, in turn, is revealed through that testimony. Therefore, invoking the word of God, the talmudic sage Rabbi Yannai declares, "'I the Lord am not greater than Israel, nor is Israel greater than I'" (Kahana 99). Assailing this relation to God that constitutes Israel as a community, the Nazis assail God Himself.

In the Jewish tradition the community of Israel is often identified with the *Shekhinah*, or the Indwelling Presence of God in the world. The *Zohar*, for example, teaches us that "wherever the truths of the Torah are expounded, the Holy One and the Community of Israel (the *Shekhinah*) are present" (3:297). As this passage suggests, the "knot" that ties God and Israel together is the Torah, which in turn is often identified with the Name of God, as well as with God Himself. "The Torah," says the *Zohar*, "consists wholly of the Name of the Holy One, blessed be He, and every letter of it is bound up with that Name" (5:73). And the sixteenth-century *Midrash Shemuel* teaches that the Torah "is an integral part of God and, thus, all-inclusive and infinite" (Chill 410). Similarly, the Koretzer Rebbe, a disciple of the Baal Shem Tov, once said: "God and Prayer are One. God and Torah are one. God, Israel and Torah are one" (Newman 147); and Rabbi Schneur Zalman, founder of the Lubavitch school of Hasidism, states repeatedly, "The Torah and the Holy One, blessed be He, are one and the same" (15, 233, 579). Such a view of the Torah situates it in an invisible realm that is both within and beyond the world. And it is precisely in such a realm that Katznelson situates the community of Israel: "The nation [of Israel], scattered and divided as it is, is continually likened to sheep. But it is like God, in whom we believe; whom we know to exist, but who is concealed from our sight. We cannot behold the nation, for it is like God, who lives in our midst but whom we cannot see" (182). The nation who is like God is like the Torah, to which God is compared and by which the nation is sustained.

One means employed by the Nazis for destroying the Jewish community, and with it the soul of Israel, was the destruction of Torah scrolls wherever they could find them. Rabbi Shimon Huberband points out, for instance, that whenever Jews were found with Torah scrolls, they were tortured and the scrolls were burned or desecrated (44). Why this attack on the Torah? Because the Nazis knew, on some level, what the thirteenth-century Kabbalist Abraham Abulafia teaches us: "God's intention in giving us the Torah is that we reach this purpose, that our souls be alive in His Torah" (Idel 37). Because they knew, on some level, what the twentieth-century Rabbi Adin Steinsaltz teaches: "*Kenesset Yisrael* [the Community of Israel] is not the passive bearer of a yoke of Torah and law that has been thrust upon it—it is an active component of the Torah" (*Being* 223).[2] Hence in the diary he kept at Westerbork, Philip Mechanicus affirms: "God and Israel are inseparable. Jews may perish but Israel is eternal" (94); hence Katznelson insists, "The God of Israel and the people of Israel are one" (122). This identity underlying Jewish life lies behind the care taken by Emmanuel Ringelblum, to cite another diarist, to attest to the desecration of eight hundred Torah scrolls (80) and to the murder in one city of all the rabbis, that is, of all who are the teachers of the Torah (48). It is for these reasons that Zelig Kalmanovitch writes in his diary from the Vilna Ghetto: "A war is being waged against the Jew. But this war is not merely directed against one link in the triad [of Israel, the Torah, and God] but against the entire one: against the Torah and God, against the moral law and Creator of the universe" (52). In these diaries written from the depths of the Event, therefore, we discover that the diarists were all too aware of the profound metaphysical implications that distinguish the Event as a *novum* in the history of humanity and divinity. This awareness reveals itself in direct ways, as one can see from the passages cited above. But it also reveals itself in other ways, particularly in the testimony to the destruction of holy sites and ritual objects, as well as in the argument with God that these diarists courageously pursue.

THE ONSLAUGHT AGAINST RITE AND RITUAL

In the *Midrash Rabbah* we read: "Thus God said to Israel: 'I have given you a Torah from which I cannot part, and I also cannot tell you not to take it; but this I would request: wherever you go make for Me a house wherein I may sojourn'" (3:415). Therefore a primary scene where the assailing of God transpired during the Holocaust was the very place where the rite and ritual of prayer unfolded. Indeed, one of the Hebrew words used to refer to God is *HaMakom*, which means "the Place," so that God was assailed in the place where His Name was invoked: in the synagogue. Very often this assault took the form of desecration, whereby synagogues were made into latrines, stables, or other such facilities: the place was desecrated by inserting into its midst what was out of place. In one of the first diaries to make its way out of the Warsaw Ghetto, published in 1943, Dr. Henryk Shoshkes writes, "The synagogue has been transformed into a warehouse for scrap iron" (75). And from the Varad Ghetto in Hungary, the teenager Éva Heyman notes that, after the synagogue was converted into an infirmary, the Holy Ark was "used to hold bowls, pots and bedpans" (93).

More often, however, the Nazis were not content merely to desecrate the houses of prayer. They put them to the torch, often with Jews inside the building, and thereby consigned God Himself to the flames. In her memoir of the Holocaust, Judith Dribben makes this point by recalling the utterance of a Nazi as he triumphantly gazed upon a synagogue ablaze: "The Jewish God is burnt to ashes!" (24). And so, from a hiding place in Holland, the German diarist Julian Stanford recalls that in Hamburg "all the synagogues were set on fire and demolished" (64); in his Romanian diary Emil Dorian notes, "The majestic Sephardic synagogue has been completely destroyed" (139); and, after an *Aktion* in the Vilna Ghetto, Yitskhok Rudashevski laments: "The old synagogue courtyard is pogromized. Phylacteries, religious books, rags are scattered under one's feet. Everything in the second ghetto is demolished, broken and abandoned. Everything is pervaded by the despair of those who have been wrenched away from here" (46). What has been wrenched away from this place is the Place that is God Himself, the One who constitutes a place of dwelling where the community may dwell. If His presence continues to be felt, it is felt in the form of a despair that is as omnipresent as God Himself.

One realizes why Adam Czerniakow, despite his secularism, labored to save the Great Synagogue in Warsaw. From November 1941 to March 1942 he records his fear that "the Synagogue cannot be saved" (301), his effort to "save the Synagogue, so far without success" (335), and his sorrow that "the Synagogue could not be saved" (337). Of course, what is to be saved in the attempt to save a synagogue is not just a wooden structure but a realm of sanctity and prayer, a place through which God may enter the world even as the world is being undone. "To worship," says Heschel, "is *to expand the presence of God* in the world" (*Man's Quest* 62). The assault on the synagogue, then, is not an assault on a building or on a space, but on the encounter between the human and the divine that transpires within and thereby consecrates this space; it is an assault on the capacity of this space to consecrate all other spaces in life. Why the assault on the encounter and the consecration? Because if the God who breathes life into the community and thus consecrates it is to be obliterated, then this encounter must be eliminated; if the substance and meaning of Jewish life are to be erased, then the union with God, from which that life derives its dearness, must be eradicated. And so, with the help of these diarists, we come once more to a realization only touched upon in the last chapter: in order to assail God, the Nazis launch an attack on the prayer that is itself divinity.[3] Prayer joins humanity with divinity; therefore prayer and the place of prayer must be demolished.

"Public worship was banned," David Kahane makes an entry in his Lvov Ghetto diary. "With the discovery of a *minyan* [ten men, the minimum number required to engage in the rites of prayer] . . . all the worshippers, together with owners of the apartment, would be taken to the Lecki prison. No one ever returned from there" (24). From the devout Hasid, Rabbi Huberband (179), to the worldly head of the Jewish Council, Adam Czerniakow (211), the diarists of the Warsaw Ghetto also bear witness to the Nazis' assault on Jewish prayer, as well as to the Jews' resistance of the assault. On the eve of Tisha B'Av 5700 (1940) Chaim Kaplan writes: "Public prayer in these dangerous times is a forbidden act. Anyone caught in this crime is doomed to severe punishment. If you will, it is even sabotage, and anyone engaging in sabotage is subject to execution. But this does not deter us. Jews come to pray in a group in some room facing the courtyard, with drawn blinds on the windows" (179). Just so, with blinds drawn on the windows, the Holocaust diarist engages his diary. To be sure, in *Le journal intime* Alain Girard compares the diarist engaged in his diary to a person engaged in prayer. Surrounding the diarist, he says, is "a silence pierced only by the scratching of his pen on the paper. The silence descends upon him as well" (539). But in the Holocaust diary there is a difference: what descends on him is the cry of a humanity and the silence of a God under a physical and metaphysical assault. The utterance of the Holocaust diarist is akin to prayer; through it, not only does a silence descend upon him, but, in a refusal of silence, he himself rises up to stand as a witness to the assault and to the resistance of the assault. His writing is a writing despite himself, for another—for God and the humanity created in His image—so that what is assailed might be sustained. Similarly, as the site where this prayer is uttered, the diary takes on a status akin to the status of the synagogue; the space that opens up when we open the Holocaust diary is a realm of the holy.

Assailing God, the Nazis launch their attack not only on the prayers said in a *minyan* but also on prayers that assume the form of rituals and that inhere in ritual objects. In the previous chapter we noted, for example, the Nazis' prohibition against the use of the *mikveh*. Here we find that the assault on the ritual bath, and therefore on the notion of any purity associated with holiness, goes well beyond a mere prohibition against using the bath. In an entry dated 12 May 1942 Czerniakow notes an occurrence in the ghetto that at first glance might seem relatively innocuous: "Avril [an SS sergeant] arrived with the filmmakers and announced that they would shoot a scene at the ritual baths on Dzielna Street. They need 20 Orthodox Jews with earlocks and 20 upperclass women" (352–53). But on 14 May Kaplan reveals the perverted, blasphemous intention behind Avril's demand: "Both sexes were forced by means of intimidation and whiplashes to remove their clothes and remain naked; afterward they were made to get into one bath together and were forced into lewd and obscene acts imitating the sexual behavior of animals. . . . While one Nazi cracked his whip over the heads of the captives, his partner set himself up in a corner with a camera. Henceforward all the world will know how low the Jews have fallen in their morals, that modesty between the sexes has ceased among them and that they practice sexual immorality in public" (331–32). From a Jewish standpoint, this incident far exceeds anything like forced pornography. Staging this outrage in the place of ritual purification, the Nazis assail the whole notion of purification as a means of approaching God. For the relation of Israel to God is often understood in terms of the conjugal relation that belongs to the sanctity of marriage. The *Midrash Tanchuma*, for example, tells us that the two tablets given at Sinai signify Israel as a bride come to meet her groom, the Holy One (1:411); Rashi declares that at Sinai the *Shekhinah* went "forth to meet them, as a bridegroom who goes forth to meet his bride" (2:100); and, in the words of the sixteenth-century mystic Rabbi Moshe Cordovero, "the people of Israel are the spouse of the Holy One" (12). Therefore, to wrap the *tefillin*, or phylacteries, around one's finger each weekday morning is to declare oneself "betrothed" to God. Since the sexual union of husband and wife, for which the *mikveh* prepares them, is a sacred expression of this sacred relation, the Nazis' desecration of the *mikveh*, is a violation of the marriage of Israel to God and is an assault on both.

In addition to the assault on holy places, the diarists bear witness to the assault on holy objects, on those symbols that assist in our effort to hear the voice of the One who forever speaks and to perceive the presence of the Omnipresent. Because they set out to exterminate the Presence, the Nazis set out to destroy the symbol. "A group of Jews," writes Ringelblum on 2 February 1941, "were locked up in the synagogue until they hacked the holy ark to bits. Heard this explanation: The only purpose is to see to it that no vestige of the Jewish past survives in Poland" (127). In Ringelblum's Yiddish, the word that has been translated as "vestige" is *shpuren* (95), which means "traces" or "marks": the assault is on the mark, on the sign and symbol, of God because, in the words of Karl Jaspers, "the symbol is *communication*. In the contact of the soul with Being it is the enkindling in which Being acquires communicative power" (39–40). When the soul is cut off from the symbol, it is severed from its source, and God is rendered mute. Forcing the Jews to do this work themselves, moreover, is a means of forcing them into a destruction of their own image as they destroy the sign of the One in whose image they are created. And, as we saw in chapter 3, to remove the vestige of the Jewish past is to obliterate the Jewish present and, with it, the Jewish future. "The opposite of the past," Elie Wiesel reminds us, "is not the future but the absence of future; the opposite of the future is not the past but the absence of past. The loss of one is equivalent to the sacrifice of the other" (*Kingdom* 239). When both are combined, they constitute the present, where the Voice calls us forth through the symbol set before us. And the divine holiness that shows itself through the symbol, in turn, opens up to us what is holy in the human being.

The synagogue, the ritual bath, and the holy ark are all components of the sacred center upon which the Jewish community is founded. Tied to that sacred center and sanctified by it is the primary component of the community itself: the home. Therefore, assailing God, the enemy launches an attack on the symbols that consecrate the home. One of the most significant of these symbols is the *mezuzah*, which is attached to the doorposts of the home and contains portions of the Torah. It is embossed with the letter *shin*, which stands for *Shaday* or "Almighty" and is one of the names of God. Another reading of the *shin* is offered by Rabbi Yitzchak Ginsburgh, who explains: "Often the letter *shin* appears alone on the *mezuzah* container, as short for *Sh.D.Y.* (the initial letters of the phrase *shomer daltot Yisrael*, 'the guardian of the doors of Israel')" (319). And so we realize the importance of the *mezuzah*: it is the sign of God's presence at the threshold of the home, a sign of the sanctity of home and family. The destruction of the *mezuzah*, then, signifies an attempt to destroy the name of God and with it the Guardian of Israel Himself, a point that is not lost on the Holocaust diarists. Ringelblum, for example, carefully notes, "At the beginning of the Ghetto period, *men of valor* [Nazis] tore down the *mezuzot* from the doorposts of Jewish apartments" (152), and Rabbi Huberband observes, "*Mezuzahs* were torn off doorposts and ripped apart" (35). This destruction of the *mezuzah* is an assault not only on the particular homes violated but on the very notion of home as a sanctuary for the sacred. For the home is not merely a place where people take their meals and spend their nights; it is the place of *dwelling*, where mothers and fathers and children create a realm in which the Place may dwell.

Well aware of these connections, the Nazis took their onslaught against ritual objects from synagogues and homes to the people that breathed life into them. They took Hebrew artifacts and *tefillin*, says Huberband, and "ripped them and burned them. They confiscated *talis kotons* in order that they be used by Jews to clean toilets" (44). And: "The Germans collected *taleysim*, *talis kotons*, and *kitls*. These holy garments were given to Jews to wash floors, automobiles, and windows" (35).

Taleysim, *talis kotons*, and *kitls* are prayer shawls, "little prayer shawls" usually worn under one's shirt, and white robes donned on High Holy Days and at Passover. Religious Jews are often buried in their *kitls*. When a Jew puts on these holy garments or lays *tefillin*, with the appropriate prayers on his lips, his very body is transformed into a symbol of the divine Presence in the world. Jews are taught that to wrap oneself in the prayer shawl is to wrap oneself in the Light of God. The *tsitsit* or fringes on the *taleysim* and *talis kotons* signify the 613 commandments of the Torah. Each fringe is made of eight threads and five knots, and, as Rashi explains: 613 equals the numerical value of the word for 'fringes' (600) plus five plus eight (4:76–77; see also *Midrash Tanchuma* 2:751). The destruction and desecration of such ritual objects, then, is an assault on the Torah, on Israel, and on God.

If wearing a *talis koton* can transform the Jew into a symbol, the body of the Jew—and particularly the face of the Jew—can itself become a symbol. Among Jewish men, the beard is the symbol that distinguishes the face as a face turned toward God. Thus Michael Zylberberg laments: "Saddest of all, perhaps, was the position of the Orthodox. They were ordered to shave their head and face completely, to remove every symbol of Jewishness" (21). Similarly, Rabbi Huberband notes: "If a bearded Jew was caught, his life was put in danger. They tore out his beard along with pieces of flesh, or cut it off with a knife and a bayonet" (35). Describing an *Aktion* staged in the Lvov Ghetto, Kahane writes: "First they seized old men with beards and sidelocks. Not even a work card could save a bearded Jew" (45). And Avraham Tory comments on a custom practiced in the Kovno

Ghetto, saying: "They [Germans and Lithuanians] shave off the beards of rabbis and yeshiva students; heads are bashed, arms are twisted" (9).

The Talmud declares that beard is the glory of the face (*Shabbat* 152a). If it is the *glory* of the face, then it makes the face into a sign of the Holy One, who sanctifies the life of the human being; and if the face is the sign of the Holy One, then, in the words of Emmanuel Levinas, "the face is what forbids us to kill" (*Ethics* 86). Such a prohibition is precisely what the Nazis must eliminate, if they are to get rid of God. And they do indeed eliminate it by eliminating those whose faces signify the glory of the One who, through the face, speaks the prohibition.

"Where are the yeshiva students from the bygone days," Tory asks, "the rabbis? For the most part they have been killed—like thousands of other Jews—for the sanctification of God's name. Only a handful have survived. They gather at night, after work, . . . to study the Torah and to pray. They carry on. They guard the holy fire and refuse to let it die out" (367). In these last few lines we see how great is the communicative power of the symbol, even when the symbol itself has been erased—or torn out. Cast out of their synagogues, stripped of their *taleysim*, and shorn of their beards, the Jews nonetheless continue to be a sign of the giving of signs that make life not only possible but meaningful. Here their refusal to succumb to darkness is itself the symbol that takes the place of the symbols. And the Holocaust diary is the symbol of that symbol.

The diarists' refusal to succumb to the Nazis, however, does not always take the form of a submission to God. While it is lamentably true that some Jews among the kapos and Jewish police resemble the enemy, Hillel Seidman points out that in the Warsaw Ghetto none of the religious Jews wind up among the ranks of the Jewish police force (252). And yet the piety of Jews who revere God—a piety that resisted the assault on God—very often reveals itself not through acquiescence to God but through an argument with Him. The Jews' assailing of God, however, is not on the same order as the Nazis' assault on God.[4] When the Holocaust diarist assails God, he does so with the aim not of assaulting the sacred but of insisting upon the sanctity of the human being and upon the divine basis of that sanctity. The diarist's assailing of God, therefore, is another means of opposing the Nazis' assault on God. To be sure, if the diarists should break off their argument with God, then the Nazis would have their victory. "There comes a time," Wiesel reminds us, "when only those who do believe in God will cry out to Him in wrath and anguish" (*Kingdom* 20).

THE ARGUMENT WITH GOD

The Jewish tradition of argument with God goes back to the first Jew, to Abraham himself, when he argued with God over the fate of Sodom and Gomorrah (Genesis 18:23–32). Why did God bother to consult Abraham in this matter? Because, says Wiesel, "God, knowing the fate of the Jews, wished to teach them the need of arguing, even against Himself" (*Sages* 378). Therefore, the Talmud teaches, "when the Holy One is conquered He rejoices" (*Pesachim* 119a); therefore, says the Talmud, when Rabbi Yehoshua refuses to heed the heavenly voice, Elijah can declare, "God smiled and said: 'My sons have defeated Me, my sons have defeated Me!'" (*Bava Metzia* 59b). This tradition arises in biblical times, unfolds throughout the talmudic period, and continues into Hasidic texts and teachings; there, in the name of a love for the humanity that is our only pathway to God, Rabbi Yaakov Yosef of Polonnoye, a disciple of the Baal Shem Tov, maintains: "It is against the Creator of the universe and the Lord of history that accusation must be hurled. Ultimately, the exile—in body and spirit—is His doing. Ultimately, therefore, He must take mercy" (Dresner 239).[5] What introduces depth to the prayer offered up to God is our love for our fellow humans beings, *ahavat Yisrael*. And so when our anger with God is stirred by this love, it is the anger of which the *Zohar* speaks: "There is anger which is blessed on high and below, and is called 'blessed' (*barukh*)" (2:203). Such anger instills our prayers with the intensity and the fervor, the *kavanah* and the *hitlahavut*, that may redeem God and humanity. Part of keeping the Covenant with God lies in insisting that He keep the Covenant with humanity.

In this insistence lies a key to the link between the teachings of our fathers and the outcry of our contemporaries. As André Neher states it: "Here on earth it is no longer a question of a man but of Job. Here on earth one no longer has the horizontal pattern of man hunted by man, but the vertical pattern of the Jew harassing God.

Thus the enigma of time is electrified by the eternity of a question" (*They* 49–50). Which of the biblical figures has been sculpted and placed near an entrance to the museum at Yad Vashem? It is Job, the one who questioned God and His justice and who, in his questioning, sought out God: "Oh, that I knew where I might find Him, that I might come even unto His seat! I would lay my case before Him and fill my mouth with arguments" (Job 23:3–4). Although God reproves Job, saying, "Who is this that darkens counsel by words without knowledge?" (Job 38:2), He nonetheless declares, "My servant Job has spoken rightly" (see Job 42:7). Why? If it is not because He approves of the content of Job's words, it is because He approves of the fact that Job spoke up in the face of what he understood to be an injustice.

The situation confronting the Jews of the Holocaust, however, exceeds even what Neher imagines to be the modern condition of the Jew, as a Job harassing God. Here we have a situation akin to what Emil Fackenheim describes when he points out that, while Nietzsche or Sartre may have found some exhilaration in the idea that God is dead or absent, "there is no exhilaration but only terror in a God present still—but become an enemy" (*To Mend* 250). He illustrates this point with a story, borrowed from Elie Wiesel, about "a small group of Jews who were gathered to pray in a little synagogue in Nazi-occupied Europe. As the service went on, suddenly a pious Jew who was slightly mad—for all pious Jews were by then slightly mad—burst in through the door. Silently he listened for a moment as the prayers ascended. Slowly he said: 'Shh, Jews! Do not pray so loud! God will hear you. Then He will know that there are still some Jews left alive in Europe'" (*God's Presence* 67). Perhaps the slightly mad, pious Jew would not have cautioned his fellow Jews about praying so loudly, if their prayers had taken the form of the harassment of which Neher speaks. Or perhaps, slightly mad, he had determined that the only way for a pious Jew to exhibit his piety was to refrain from all prayers and observances. After all, Leib Langfus, Salmen Lewental, and Salmen Gradowski—diary writers from the *Sonderkommando* of Auschwitz—"came from a religious background," Nathan Cohen reminds us, "and all three continued to observe, to some extent, the precepts of Judaism. However, at the time of writing their testimonies, they no longer regarded religious observance as a proof of man's spiritual qualities" (311). What proof might remain? Religious anger, the anger that is called "blessed."

If religious anger can become a form of piety, then, like piety, it must be cultivated; it is not the starting point but a next stage of what begins with a state of despair. Such a state of darkness that may find the light of God only by assailing God can be seen in the pages of Moshe Flinker's diary. On 9 September 1943, for example, he writes: "Each time I stand to say the Eighteen Benedictions I direct my whole soul to my lovely land, and I see it before my eyes; I see the coast, I see Tel Aviv, Jaffa, and Haifa. Then I see Jerusalem, with the Mount of Olives, and I see the Jordon as it flows from Lebanon to the Dead Sea. I also see the land across the Jordan—I visualize all of this when I stand to pray. And when I pray and do not see my beloved country before my eyes it is as if my prayer had been rejected and as if I had been praying to the wall" (81–82). The Nazis assail God by assailing prayer, and the prayer is the first casualty in this assault. One notices here that young Moshe's visions are not of heavenly hosts but of the Land, which is the symbol of God's presence in this world and of His Covenant with the Jewish people. "The Land of Israel is not something external," Rabbi Abraham Isaac Kook explains. "The Land of Israel is an essential unit bound by the bond-of-life to the People" (89). And: "Each individual of Israel has his nucleus in the Land of Israel, which is stored in the interior of his spirit with enormous longing and love" (140). But in the Kingdom of Night such visions of the Land are clouded by darkness and blood that spill into the soul of the Holocaust diarist and onto the pages of the Holocaust diary, until all hope is eclipsed and with it all life. "The moment I stop hoping," says Moshe, "I shall cease to exist. All I have is hope; my entire being depends on it. And at the same time I have nothing. What will these useless hopes bring me? I don't know what to do. Everything is becoming hollow. Formerly, when I took up my Bible and read it, it was as if I had returned to life, as if the Lord had taken pity on me; even in my darkest moments I found consolation in Him. Now even this is denied me" (99). It will be recalled that another meaning of the Hebrew word for "hope," *tikvah,* is "cord" or "thread": hope signifies a tie to something. When there is hope, there is connection. The Nazis, in assailing God, assail the connection to Him; severing that connection, they undermine all hope. And where hope is undermined, a *why* appears.

This *why* all but dominates many of the Holocaust diaries; it echoes throughout the questions that pervade these diaries. Nevertheless, the diarists do ask, even demand: Why? They are not silent. In Kahane's diary, for example, we read in the entry for Yom Kippur 5703: "The Jews of Lvov were animated by a different spirit on the Day of Atonement of 1942—the spirit of protest. Prayers were sounded as a reproach. Master of the world, why? For what sins? For what offenses have you singled us out from all people? Are the Ukrainians, the Poles, the Germans better than we are? Are other nations' moral standards higher than ours? This mood did not resemble anything that came down to us in all the chronicles" (76). The chronicles deal with Jewish suffering that results from Jewish transgression. But in the Shoah, as Fackenheim relentlessly points out: "Jews were murdered, not because they had disobeyed the God of history, but rather because their great-grandparents had obeyed Him. They had done so by raising Jewish children" (*God's Presence* 6). While the chronicles recount Jewish suffering, they do not contain an account of the enemy's assault on God, which is a *novum* in human history.

The chronicles abide in a relation to the One who is omnipresent, not in the despair over the One who appears to be omniabsent. Therefore this *why* that haunts the Holocaust diary is a *novum*, unlike other *whys* that human beings have raised to the heavens. It addresses the slumber of the One who does not slumber, as when Kalmanovitch cries out, "Awake, why sleepest Thou, O Lord?" (59); or as when Dorian relates the story about a "popular Jewish speaker who, talking in a synagogue about the Jewish massacres in the Ukraine, walks to the altar, angrily jerks aside the velvet curtain, throws open the doors hiding the Torah, and cries out, 'Lord are you asleep?'" (32). This question, aimed at the Torah scrolls, transforms the Torah that contains the Covenant with God into an outcry aimed at God. The Jews have not abandoned their prayers but have turned them into a question: Why?[6] God Himself is gathered into the question, for gathered into this *why* is the *ahavat Yisrael*, through which His presence is revealed to the world. Thus we see Him at work in the compassion that underlies Tory's tears and outcry: "I have seen, many times, these pictures of the wandering Jew—in books, newspapers, and pamphlets. And each time I am seized by terror. My soul weeps. Master of the World, why? Why?" (319). Even in His absence, or in the mode of absence, God perhaps abides in this question. For this is not "Why me?" but "Why my brother?"

In *A Beggar in Jerusalem* Wiesel reminds us that when God says, "I," it means "I who am with you, within you" (7). Even if we stretch the language to suggest that God might be present "in the mode of absence," there is nevertheless no one who is *with* the diarist, no one who answers—"Here I am"—to his own utterance of "Here I am." The *why*, then, is transformed into a *where*. "More than once," says Tory, for example, "Jewish history has seen justice being done. Until then we shall extend our hands toward the sky and cry for help. Oh Lord, where are you?" (285). This inversion of the first question put to the first man (Genesis 3:9) comes from a member of the Jewish Council of the Kovno Ghetto; it is echoed, more meekly and more pitiably, by a teenage girl in Hungary. "God," Éva Heyman utters her heartrending prayer, "it's true, isn't it, that it is only by accident that You weren't paying attention when they killed Marta, but now You are watching over us?!" (66). The child's double punctuation of her sentence punctuates her terror over an assertion that she can make only in the form of a question. For the divine absence "by accident" shows itself in human horrors perpetrated by design. This design does not escape the child anymore than it escapes a man such as Aryeh Klonicki-Klonymus, a native of the Galician town of Kovel. In an entry dated 5 July 1943 he writes: "They are burying children alive as well as adults who have not yet died. Is there a God in this world or is lawlessness at the very core of the universe?" (32). In Klonicki-Klonymus's original text this last statement, like Éva Heyman's sentence, is punctuated with a question mark and an exclamation mark. And 'is lawlessness at the core of the universe" is a loose translation of the Aramaic phrase *leyt diyn v'leyt dayan*, which literally means "there is [or is there] no justice and no judge" (23). Hence his question/exclamation concerns the absence not only of the Law but of the Author of the Law. If the Law that is Torah—if the God who is Torah—is somehow to be preserved and life's meaning to be recovered, then the site of that preservation and recovery is precisely the Holocaust diary—not in its assertion of "Here He is," but in its question of "Where is He?"

One diary in which this question, this lamentation, resounds with overwhelming depth is the *Warsaw Ghetto Diary* of Chaim Kaplan. From the beginning of the Nazis' assault, on the eve of Simchat Torah 5700 (5 October 1939), he asks: "Where are we to look for salvation? It seems as though even our Father in Heaven—the mainstay of our fathers—has deserted us. Are we indeed to sing with the poet [Ch. N. Bialik]: 'Heavenly spheres, beg mercy for me. Behold, the path to God no longer exists! God of Israel, where art Thou?'" (46). As Kaplan's diary progresses, the question of where God is takes on implications for how Israel might understand its relation to God's word. When God seems to be absent, His word seems to be drained of meaning: God dwells where meaning dwells in the word, and it is this dwelling that makes possible human dwelling. Here too the fear of God's absence expresses itself in the form of a question: "Will impoverished, homeless parents still find the heart to send their children to study Torah? Will the Eternal break His promise?" (61). The second sentence is a translation of a stronger statement in Kaplan's Hebrew text: *Haiym Netsach Yisrael yishakar?* or "Can it be that the Eternal One of Israel will have lied?" (70). God's presence is the presence of God's truth; God's eternity lies in the eternal presence of Israel as His Chosen. A lying God is an absent God, and the absence of God means the death of Israel. As this terror settles into Kaplan's soul, his soul is drained more and more of its life, and his questions turn into the assertions that may have been hidden within his questions all along. "It is good in our terrible troubles," reads his entry of 10 November 1940, "to believe that some mighty hand is guiding us, that our sufferings are seen and our sighs are heard. But we woke up, and our souls were empty" (223). What these souls awaken to, of course, is not life but death. On 23 July 1942, just a couple of weeks before his deportation to Treblinka, Kaplan comments on an *Aktion*, saying: "In these two days the emptiness of the ghetto has been filled with cries and wails. If they found no way to the God of Israel it is a sign that He doesn't exist" (383). A sign that He exists would not be a divine hand descending from heaven to strike the enemy but a human hand offering some help to the victims. Failing that, the only trace of anything divine at work is the movement of the hand across the pages of the diary.

As for the heavens themselves, they remain silent, as Helena Dorembus indicates in her diary from the Warsaw Ghetto. "I dreamed of an air raid over Warsaw during which the Jews in the ghetto might escape. But my prayers haven't reached God. The heavens are silent" (58). What, indeed, can stir the heavens, if not prayer, supplication, and a concern for our fellow human beings? In *A Warsaw Diary* Zylberberg describes one man who sought another way to stir the heavens in the aftermath of an *Aktion* that took place on Rosh Hashanah 5703 (1942): "The man kept raising his clinched fists to heaven and the poor woman who led him wept uncontrollably and shouted, 'My husband has gone mad.' 'Jews,' he called, 'collect large stones and throw them up to heaven! Why has God picked us for this torment? Give me stones to throw in defiance of heaven!' His wife was shocked at the blasphemy and tried to apologize for him, saying, 'He has had neither food nor water for days. He is terrified. He is not responsible for what he is saying'" (57). Here stones take the place of prayers; when piety fails, the man tries blasphemy, anything to break the silence. To be sure, the dead themselves cannot seem to arouse the heights, a point that Zylberberg makes by way of a midrashic commentary that comes in the wake of the massive deportations from the Warsaw Ghetto to Treblinka during the summer of 1942. "The synagogues and prayer houses in Warsaw," he writes, "are now empty, dark and sad. No traditional candles, no chanting, no prayers. The crowds of men, women and children are now assembled in Heaven. Among them are our two religious men, Reb Zalman and Reb Zishe. The crowds neither pray nor move—they are stunned into horrified silence. Suddenly Reb Zalman starts moving forward, pushing his way through the crowd. He is now less in awe of his old friend Reb Zishe. At the foot of the Throne his cry breaks the silence, '*Zu Torah ve'zu secharah?* We lived by the Torah; is this the reward?' The echo reverberates through the Halls of Heaven. There is no answer" (61). Of all the horrors recorded in the Holocaust diary, this is perhaps the most horrifying: that God might be deaf not only to the cry raised from below but also to the cry raised from on high.

According to Jewish tradition, the movement below stirs the movement above (see, for example, *Zohar* 4:385; Meir ibn Gabbai 26; Zalman 405). But, beyond anything that a historical document can contain, the Holocaust diary contains the terrible record of this terrible impotence to move the Most High from above or from below. "The God who hides His face," says Levinas, "is not, I believe, a theological abstraction or a poetic image. It is the moment when the just individual can find no help" (*Difficult* 143). When the just individual can find no help, the dimension of height that confers meaning on being is erased. And yet the Holocaust diarist struggles to recover that dimension by assailing the God on high in a response to the Nazis' assault from below. Like one in prayer, he struggles, heeding the outcry that comes to us from the pages of Wiesel's *Ani Maamin*:

> Pray, men.
> Pray to God,
> Against God,
> For God. (107)

And so it is *despite* his own despair and the Nazis' attempt to murder God that Moshe Flinker asserts, "Not from the English nor the Americans nor the Russians but from the Lord Himself will our redemption come" (73). It is *despite* being faced with "the horrible truth" (278) that Anne Frank declares: "Surely the time will come when we are people again, and not just Jews. Who has inflicted this upon us? Who has allowed us to suffer so terribly up till now? It is God that has made us as we are, but it will be God, too, who will raise us up again. If we bear all this suffering and if there are still Jews left, when it is over, then Jews, instead of being doomed, will be held up as an example. Who knows, it might even be our religion from which the world and all peoples learn good" (221). While these words from two very different Jewish children may not have reached the ear of God, they have reached our ears. And they tell us why the diarists assail God. They do so in a response to the Nazis' assault on God, even when God offers them no response. They do so in an effort to sustain the Creation, even when all creation is crumbling around them.

THE CRUMBLING OF CREATION

IN THE LAST CHAPTER WE SAW THAT THE NAZIS' ASSAULT on God and His Chosen often took the form of an assault on the Torah. We also found that, in its association with God and the people of Israel, the Torah assumes a metaphysical aspect; the Torah transcends both the words and the silence between the words inscribed on the scrolls that we bring forth from the ark. Indeed, the Torah exceeds creation itself; exceeding creation, it sanctifies creation. Hence one of the oldest portions of the *Midrash Rabbah*, the fifth-century *Genesis Rabbah*, includes the Torah—along with the Throne of Glory, the Patriarchs, Israel, the Temple, and the name of the Messiah—among the six things that "preceded the creation of the world" (1:6).[1] Preceding the Creation, the Torah is conceived as something akin to a ruling or organizing principle for the creation of the world. It is rather like the blueprint for creation, with this important difference: it appears not only before the world or beyond the world but in the midst of the world, imparting to creation that dimension of holiness which God declares to be "very good." It is through the Torah that the Infinite One is able to enter into His finite creation and sustain it: the blueprint is a pathway, as well as a living presence.[2]

According to this tradition, the revelation of the Torah is definitively linked to the creation of the world; creation is not creation, the world is not constituted as world, without studying and living by the Torah and its truth. Hence Rabbi Adin Steinsaltz teaches us, "In its widest sense, the study of Torah is a re-enactment of Creation, a transfer of primal force from one system to another" (*Sustaining* 117), that is, from Creator to creature, from creature to creation.[3] This "transfer of primal force" is what establishes the distinctions between darkness and light, heaven and earth, good and evil that impart structure and meaning to reality and thus create a sense of world. When those who study and live by the Torah are murdered, the very life of the Tree of Life is annihilated; the Creator is divorced from the Creation, and creation itself collapses.

Writing from the depths of a total assault on the Torah, the Holocaust diarist records his or her testimony in the midst of the destruction not only of a people but of a world and a civilization. For this destruction, this *churban*, is the destruction of the truth and the meaning that ordain a world and make civilization possible; it is the destruction not only of humanity's cultural and moral values but of the very ground for any such values. That is why Emil Dorian writes in his Romanian diary: "I cannot find a single peaceful thought, a single image to dream over in these pages where once I used to record other kinds of events than today's horrible ones. I recall beautiful books of poems bound in blue and red, the pleasure of touching them, of opening their silky pages to pore over them with friends, to discuss them for afternoons and evenings on end. But it must have happened in another existence" (16). Yes, in another existence, another world that was before this destruction of the world: the beautiful books themselves lose their contact with the world because the very world is crumbling. And the world is crumbling because the very notion of the book that the People of the Book introduce to the world is being obliterated. The "other existence" that Dorian refers to is not merely a time when things were going well; it is a time when the book was able to sustain the world. "The world exists because the book exists," argues Edmond Jabès. "This is so because in order for something to exist it has to be named" (*Desert* 84). The study of the Torah, which is the original study of the book, entails a process of naming the world, of naming what there is to hold dear and what there is to shun; in this sense, it is a participation in the Creation with the Creator who is known as the Name and whose Name is Torah. Dorian can find no meaning in the beautiful books because the One whose Name is the Book that constitutes the world is under assault; he can find no meaning in the books because the world itself has been bled of meaning. That is why creation crumbles during the Shoah.

The Talmud tells us that the rents in the clothing of one who mourns the burning of the Torah scrolls are not to be sewn up (*Mo'ed Katan* 26a); just so, one may wonder whether the rent in the fabric of civilization that occurs in the Shoah, with the burning of the Torah and the body of Israel, *can* be sewn up. If it can be mended, then that mending begins with the material of the Holocaust diary. Here, then, we shall consider the testimony borne by those witnesses who witnessed the end of civilization, who were plunged into the void, and who could find no refuge. The void, indeed, is that realm from which there is no refuge, and when civilization collapses, only the void remains. Let us examine these elements of the Holocaust diary.

WITNESSING THE END OF CIVILIZATION

In his entry dated 23 September 1939 Adam Czerniakow writes: "Mayor Starzynski named me Chairman of the Jewish Community in Warsaw. A historic role in a besieged city. I will try to live up to it" (76). At the time, of course, Czerniakow had no idea that his historic role would entail being part of an end to a certain history. Could he, indeed, have imagined that living up to this role would mean dying in it (refusing to comply with an order to deliver children for deportation to Treblinka, he committed suicide at the end of July 1942)? Where civilization endures, even in times of war, living up to a role normally entails living through it; Czerniakow, however, witnessed the breakdown of a civilization that did not endure but reverted backwards. Utterly undermining all evolutionary notions of progress, all Hegelian superstitions concerning a dialectic of mediation grounded in a rational principle, this sense of reversal appears in many of the Holocaust diaries. In the Warsaw diary of Abraham Levin, for instance, we read, "Humanity has gone backward more than 2,000 years" (329). And the Hungarian teenager Éva Heyman notes: "The Ghetto is going to be in the Jewish Quarter, where there used to be a Ghetto once. But that was a long time ago, because people know about it only from books" (83). And yet, to view this catastrophe as a reversion to the time of suffering under the Romans or to the persecutions of the Middle Ages is to situate it in a world and a time that belong to civilization. To witness the end of civilization, by contrast, is to see that such comparisons do not apply; civilization is not going backwards any more than a beam of light swallowed up by a black hole goes backwards. No, civilization here is going nowhere, slipping into a realm of nothingness that is nowhere, that is unworldly or antiworldly. As early as 20 March 1938 Dorian had the insight to ask: "If in 1933, in the heart of Europe, the Hitlerist takeover could lead to crimes and atrocities unparalleled even in the Middle Ages, with no intervention from abroad, how can any nation be expected to show courage and dignity? This is not merely a Jewish problem" (26). Dorian, of course, is quite correct. Four years before the construction of a single gas chamber, he saw that only the crumbling of civilization, and not merely its reversal, could make it possible to target a people for destruction.

Other diarists also detected early signs of this collapse. On 10 November 1938, the day after *Kristallnacht*—when 191 synagogues were destroyed, 7,500 stores were looted, and 30,000 Jews were arrested in Germany—Ruth Andreas-Friedrich wrote in her Berlin diary: "I knew this would come. The war against the Jews has begun. Last night at 2:00 a.m. With an assault on the entire people. And precisely on Schiller's birthday" (30). Why the mention of Schiller? Noted for his aesthetics, his poetry, and his history plays, Friedrich Schiller marks one of the peaks not only of German culture but of Western civilization; his essay "On the Sublime," for example, is viewed as an achievement of new heights in the human understanding of artistic beauty. But the diarist sees the depths to which humanity sinks on the anniversary of Schiller's birth. Whether Andreas-Friedrich understands this sign of civilization's undoing as a contradiction to or as an outcome of Schiller's thinking is ambiguous. For Yitzhak Katznelson, however, there is little ambiguity. In the entry to his Vittel diary dated 12 August 1943 he writes, "These are the generations of Goethe: Goethe begot that ugly reptile, utterly loathsome, foul-blooded filthy vermin—Hitler" (112). Katznelson implies that the end of civilization signaled by the Shoah began with one of its champions, the great Johann Wolfgang von Goethe. How is this possible?

A brief consideration of a few of Germany's intellectual lights might help us to see how. One can easily guess, for instance, what Katznelson might think of one of Goethe's most famous lines:

> What man reveres as God
> Is drawn from his own innermost being. (188)

This idea from Goethe's *Sprüche* borders on the apotheosis of the human being and is the opposite of the teaching perhaps most fundamental to Judaism, namely that the human being is created in the image of God, and not the other way around. Goethe's notion was soon followed, all too logically, by Ludwig Feuerbach's assertion that "God is the highest subjectivity of man abstracted from himself" (31); and it is not much of a leap from this statement to Nietzsche's infamous declaration that "God is dead" (90). One begins to suspect that Katznelson's remark is not so farfetched as it may seem.

To be sure, Emil Fackenheim shows that, for post-Hegelian and humanistic atheists such as Feuerbach and Nietzsche, "divinity vanishes in the process of internalization, to be replaced by a humanity potentially infinite in its modern 'freedom'" (*Encounters* 191), which becomes a "freedom" to do whatever we have the will to do. Rabbi Samson Raphael Hirsch, a contemporary of Feuerbach, had the wisdom to see that "once man endeavors to carry out not the will of God, but solely his own will, he no longer has an eye for the Law of the All-One Whom all creatures serve, and the world divides itself before him into as many gods as he sees forces at work. . . . Since all creatures seem to him not as servants of one great world scheme, but independent forces, seeking power and pleasure, he too ceases to look upon the pursuit of power and thrills as bestial and unworthy of man, but deems it divine and man's most worthy goal" (45). In German intellectual circles the thinking of Feuerbach and Nietzsche was to hold sway over that of Rabbi Hirsch, until the internalization of a human, self-styled divinity developed into the embodiment of the *Volk* in the *Führer*. "And the *Volk*," Fackenheim explains, "realizes its selfhood in blind obedience and total sacrifice. Because Nazism internalizes divinity, it is an idealism. Yet since it idolatrously identifies finiteness and infinitude, it is an idealism *totally without ideals*" (*Encounters* 194), and therefore totally without the good. There is no more definitive proof of the soundness of Fackenheim's position than the statement that Martin Heidegger made to the students of Freiburg University on 3 November 1933, "The *Führer* himself and he alone is German reality and its law, today and henceforth" (Fackenheim, *To Mend* 167–68). After the human appropriation of the divine, however, humanity's savior becomes an inhumanity incarnate, since no human being can presume to become as the gods without becoming inhuman. Perhaps Katznelson is not so misguided after all: perhaps it is indeed with Goethe, the pinnacle of German and Western civilization, that civilization's end begins.

The Holocaust diarists comment upon veiling of the end of civilization in the guise of progress, or at least in the façade of normalcy, in other ways. While hiding on the Aryan side of the wall after the Warsaw Ghetto Uprising, for example, Tuvia Borzykowski notes, "The streets looked normal; nothing indicated that on the other side of the wall the greatest human tragedy had taken place" (116). The horror of the tragedy that occurred with the Uprising lay not only in the massive suffering and destruction that it entailed; above all, it lay in the attempt, doomed beforehand, to return to its proper ground a world turned on end. In her memoir, ghetto fighter Zivia Lubetkin remembers that "absolute darkness reigned within the underground kingdom of the main bunker of the Jewish Fighting Organization on Mila 18. Outside a beautiful spring day must certainly have been shining brightly, but the order of life had been reversed in the bunker. Day had turned into night, and night into day" (206). Indeed, all of creation had been transformed into a bunker in which the order of life had been reversed, and, almost without exception, the diarists make note of this overturning. "Why is it necessary to ruin the world," Hannah Senesh asks, "turn it topsy-turvy, when everything could be so pleasant? Or is that impossible? Is it contrary to the nature of man?" (60). Toward the end of her diary, where she notes a reversal in the roles of the civilized and the uncivilized, Anne Frank uses the same expression: "The world has turned topsy-turvy, respectable people are being sent off to concentration camps, prisons, and lonely cells, and the dregs that remain govern young and old, rich and poor" (254).

Near the beginning of her diary, in the midst of her family's preparations to go into hiding, she also writes: "So much has happened in two days, it is just as if the whole world had turned upside down. But I am still alive, Kitty, and that is the main thing, Daddy says" (23). Thus the crumbling of creation frames the diary of Anne Frank. Neither Hannah Senesh nor Anne Frank, however, is still alive. In their brief lives we see that the end of civilization means far more than the end of pretty words and lofty sentiments from poets such as Schiller and Goethe; it means the end of young lives that are snuffed out with the extinguishing of those values that situate the world on its proper ground.

Therefore the ruins in which Yitskhok Rudashevski finds himself are not just the ruins of civilization's achievements but of human lives that had been sustained by the value placed upon human life. In an entry from his diary of the Vilna Ghetto dated 2 October 1942, he describes these ruins: "Strange feelings come over me as I look at black ruins shattered by the bloody storm that used to sweep over our ghetto. I look at the black holes, at the fragments of stoves. How much tragedy and anguish is mirrored in every shattered brick, in every dark crack, in every bit of plaster with a piece of wallpaper. . . . As I look at the ruins an uncanny feeling comes over me to see how Jews putter around there. I too crawl between the bricks, pieces of wallpaper, tiles, and it seems to me a lamentation ascends from the black crevices, from the stale holes. It seems to me that the ruins are weeping and importuning as though lives were hidden there" (63–64). Rudashevski drives home the point that civilization is not made merely of things, that the stuff of civilization is the stuff of life itself, and that it does not end without the massive shedding of blood. The civilization that cries out from the black holes of these ruins is made not of poetry and art, not of history and philosophy, but of blood. From the pages of the Holocaust diary it cries out, just as it cries out, like the *dam* or the blood of Abel, from the very earth, from the *adamah* of which *adam*, all of humanity, is made. "The entire White Russian earth," Rudashevski reports one survivor's account, "is soaked with Jewish blood, he exclaims. People in the house inquire about the town, about one or another corner of White Russia. 'They are no more,' he answers in such a sad voice. White Russian towns were cut down as though with a scythe. As quietly as a candle Jewish life flickered out its blood in them" (122–23). But remember Dorian's words: "This is not merely a Jewish problem" (26); it is not just Jewish life that flickers out. "In Israel's agony," Abraham Joshua Heschel expresses it, "all nations are involved" (*Prophets* 1:149). Rudashevski's allusion to the candle, then, reminds us of the status of the Chosen as a light not unto themselves but unto the nations. With the extinguishing of this light, civilization itself loses the light that civilizes it.

That is why, when he beholds the destruction of European Jewry, Rabbi Shimon Huberband wonders, "Lord Almighty, will such a good and beautiful world actually be destroyed?" (7). He asks the Creator this question about creation because not only is the world undergoing annihilation, but so too are the good and the beautiful themselves, those ideals without which there is no world, no creation, no civilization. The Creator pronounced His creation to be "very good," because the good sanctifies the blood that goes into the making of a world. When the earth is soaked with blood, the saying of "very good" is torn from the mouth of the Creator and bled away from His creation. And so we are reminded of Levin's plaintive cry of "Blood, blood, blood" (328). What remains after the blood has been drained, as Chaim Kaplan suggests, is the primeval chaos that preceded the utterance of the "very good." "Besieged Warsaw," he writes, "is now a world of primeval chaos. It is difficult to recognize the city. At times it seems to me that I am in an alien land, entirely unknown to me" (34). In Kaplan's Hebrew text, the words translated as "primeval chaos" are *tohu v'bohu* (29), a phrase taken from Genesis 1:2. In the Torah these words represent precisely what the Torah itself opposes; each of them designates emptiness, chaos, nothingness, confusion, and vanity—the void that is devoid of the good. The *Midrash Rabbah* tells us that the first word "refers to Adam, who was reduced to complete nothingness [on account of his sin]," and the second "refers to Cain, who desired to turn the world back to formlessness and emptiness" (1:16). Sin and murder are the opposite of creation; they constitute the supreme effort to kill the Creator in the midst of His creation.[4] Given the assault on the Holy One that characterizes Nazism, we see that sin and murder are not just among its byproducts but constitute its very essence. Where they reign, creation crumbles into a void.

PLUNGED INTO THE VOID

"*Toleh hagiyto 'al bliymah*," writes Kaplan on 19 July 1942 (540): "The ghetto is suspended over nothingness" (377), over the "abyss" or the "void," literally over a "being without anything." The *bliymah* is the absolutely elsewhere, utterly other to any place situated within creation. Therefore among the Holocaust diarists we discover a pronounced sense of having been cast into a realm that has been broken off from the world and set adrift, into a "being without anything." Yitzhak Zuckerman, a survivor of the Warsaw Ghetto Uprising, for instance, says that "crossing a street was like crossing the frontier" (65) and that "the ghetto walls split an organism of three-and-a-half million into thousands of cells, sunk into terrible destitution. The ghetto walls separated the Jews from the outside world and also from themselves" (64). Expressing a similar sense of being trapped in an elsewhere not of this world, Hersh Wasser, a member of Emmanuel Ringelblum's *Oneg Shabbat* circle of diarists and archivists, writes, "Everyone wants to be in Poland, i.e., on the other side of the ghetto" (230). And Ringelblum himself notes that the gate to the ghetto "looks like a border point between two countries" (87–88), or better: between creation and a crumbled creation, between world and antiworld. Those who cross over this border—those who are plunged from one side to the other—cross over not from one place to another but from place to nonplace. Nor is this realization confined to the sophisticated minds of these men from Warsaw. For in Éva Heyman's diary we read: "When we were still allowed to look outside, before that became punishable by death, we could see what was happening in Varad. Isn't it odd that I wrote: 'In Varad,' even though I'm also in Varad?!" (94). Éva wrote "in Varad" because she is *not* in Varad. She is not anywhere. Here we see a definitive feature of the void into which this flower of humanity is plunged: in the void, it is forbidden to look beyond the void. That is what distinguishes this "place" as a nonplace: the Jews are in no place from which they may look out. And that is what signals the human being's having been plunged into the abyss beyond the world, where the light of the world, the light created upon the first utterance of creation (Genesis 1:3), does not reach.

There is "no sky to be seen in the Ghetto," says Ringelblum (259), no *hiymel* (210), as his Yiddish text reads: no "heaven." In the beginning God created not only the earth but the heavens as well, and in the heavens He placed the luminaries that shed their light upon the world. "These heavenly bodies," says the fourteenth-century sage Gersonides, "provide for man more than anything else, such that all human actions are ordered by them" (2:183). It is their light that makes the earth a dwelling place and that constitutes the world as world. But in the time of the Shoah the heavenly bodies lost their shining, so that with the occlusion of the heavens comes the crumbling of the world. Instead of the luminaries of the heavens, the only star that illuminates the path forced upon the Jews is the yellow star, the dark star that "makes the selection process easier," as Andreas-Friedrich expresses it. "It illuminates the path into the darkness. This darkness is called 'ghetto'" (83). The darkness here is not the darkness of the night, which is part of a life in the world, but the darkness at noon in a world overturned, the darkness of the sun turned to darkness and the moon turned to blood. It is the Egyptian darkness, as the Vilna Ghetto diarist, Herman Kruk, describes it: "How can one write all this? How gather one's thoughts? In my room there is a silence as if in the presence of a dead person. In reality, there are many dead here. None of them is weeping or saying anything. Egyptian darkness prevails at midday. . . . What is one to say? Against whom complain? Horror of horrors and dread of dreads!" (16–17). What characterizes the "Egyptian darkness," or the *choshekh-mitsrayim*, to use the original term from Kruk's Yiddish text (55), is that "no man could see his brother" (Exodus 10:23); that is the horror of horrors. The vision of the world illuminated by the light of the heavens is a vision of our fellow human being. Just as the world is made of human relation, the antiworld into which creation crumbles is made of isolation. Plunged into the void, the human being is plunged into an unmitigated forlornness. Thus in the diary of Anne Frank we read: "Lately I have begun to feel deserted. I am surrounded by too great a void. I never used to feel like this" (66). The Dutch word translated as "deserted" here is *verlaten* (49), which means "forsaken"; it is used in the phrase *de wereld verlaten*, meaning "to give up the world" or "to depart from life," from every human contact that is a contact with life in the world.

The "void" that surrounds this child, then, is a *leegte*, an "emptiness" empty of human relation.

The forlornness of the void is a prevalent motif in the diary of another teenager, Moshe Flinker. "I am completely in the grip of this nothingness," he writes. "Lately I feel so lonely, so barren—a feeling I have never had before. I feel myself so far from all my brothers" (81). Here the Hebrew word rendered as "nothingness," however, is not *bliymah* but *riykot* (72), which, like Anne's *leegte*, also means "emptiness." What Anne implies, Moshe makes clear: the emptiness of the void into which he is plunged consists of a distance from humanity, from his brothers, so that once again we encounter the Egyptian darkness. And the theme continues throughout Moshe's diary. "Although I do not know from where this emptiness has come," he cries out, "I can feel it with my whole body. When I pray I feel as if I am praying to the wall and am not heard at all, and there is a voice inside of me that says: 'What are you praying for? The Lord does not hear you.' A few times already there has flashed through my mind the verse which I think I heard on *Simhat Torah*: 'And the spirit of Thy holiness do not take from him.' Yes, I think that the holy spark which I always felt within me has been taken from me, and here I am, without spirit, without thought, without anything, and all I have is my miserable body" (77). In these lines we see that the void characterized by a distance from humanity is a distance from divinity. In the crumbling of creation there is a crumbling of the relation to the Creator. In the world, the task that comprises a life is to turn matter into spirit and thereby to sanctify the body; spiritual life is an issue only for a being of flesh and blood, only for a being who eats. In the isolation of the void, however, the being is reduced to a body that eats and nothing more; the breath and spirit that the Creator breathed into him is drained into the emptiness. Indeed, the emptiness that plagues the diarist is the emptying of this breath that sustains creation; this isolation, this reduction, is the void itself. And as he is plunged into it, Moshe is consumed by it. On 19 May he writes, "My great complaint is against this terrible emptiness" (88); and on 23 July he cries out, "O Lord, please relieve the terrible emptiness from which I suffer. Give some meaning to the life of your servant. Please Lord, do!" (104). In the emptiness that removes us from our brother and isolates us from the Creator, creation crumbles into meaninglessness. And the words that go into the Holocaust diary, the words that would fetch a shred of meaning from the void, issue like blood from a gaping wound. That wound in the soul is the void.

Turning once more to the diary of Emil Dorian, we see that it is not only the souls of teenagers such as Anne Frank and Moshe Flinker which are so wounded. "Sometimes," says Dorian, "I am able to experience loneliness to its very limits—which verge upon nothingness. It is a state similar to a breakdown and can be traced through its finest shadings into the twilight of consciousness" (10–11). It is a state into which all the Jews of Europe, into which humanity itself, is plunged. And it shows itself in another feature of the void that we find in the Holocaust diary: abject fear. "The panic among the Jews," Dorian records on 15 September 1942, "is now permanent" (228). The permanent, universal nature of this panic suggests that it now belongs to the essence of this humanity, and so we see once again that the void is not only all around the soul but all through it. To be plunged into the void is to be plunged into panic, and in this condition we find another dominant feature of these diaries. "The terror that has been so great," writes Hillel Seidman from the pit of the Warsaw Ghetto, "now becomes even greater" (44). David Sierakowiak, a teenager who died of starvation in the Lodz Ghetto, asserts, "I'm worried and afraid" (19). From the Lithuanian ghetto of Siauliai, Eliezer Yerushalmi writes, "An even greater terror arises due to the dangerous condition of our confinement" (185). In the Vilna Ghetto, Rudashevski declares that life is "a life of helpless terror" (27). And in the Kovno Ghetto, Avraham Tory reports: "An atmosphere of fear and trepidation has set in here in the Ghetto. Breathing has become difficult" (189). Tory's brief remark demonstrates what transpires in all the ghettos, from Warsaw to Kovno: where creation collapses, breathing becomes difficult. Thus we come to another variation on a profound realization: the void that is made of dread, the void whose emptiness empties life of its spirit, will suck the very breath from the soul, the breath that the Creator breathes into the soul. To be sure, in the moment of creation it is the *ruach*, breath or spirit, of God that moves over the waters (Genesis 1:2). The sign of the undoing of that moment and that movement is the fear that takes away the breath, a fear not of this or of that but a fear that becomes an *essential* feature of an existential condition.

The breath that is stolen away is the medium of the word. "And it came to pass in those days," writes Elie Wiesel, "that terror denied all languages" (*Six Days* 5). Plunged into the void and robbed of her breath, the diarist is robbed of the word. Therefore she takes up the diary in an effort to breathe, in an effort to retrieve the word, if only to cry out. And yet, without the breath, even the outcry does not come. "As if in a nightmare," says Hannah Senesh, "I would like to scream, but no voice comes from my throat" (103). Because she cannot scream, she writes, seeking an exit for the scream. But where creation crumbles there is no exit.

NO EXIT

We began this chapter by noting the connection between Torah and creation. The *Midrash on Psalms* tells us that "the Torah is like gates and doors" (2:282): where the Torah abides in human life, gates and doors that lead into the world are open to the human being. But where the Torah is under assault, all doors are closed. Hence, in the diary he kept while hiding in Holland, Julian Stanford notes that, in this realm from which there is no escape, only escape has any meaning. "Everything else has now become meaningless," he declares. "One would gladly hand over all his possessions just to find a way out" (82). We recall that the confiscation of Jewish possessions—whether before, during, or after deportation to the camps—was one means that the Nazis used not only to accumulate wealth but to dispossess the Jews of their links to life. Stanford shows us that, in the crumbling of creation, this dispossession extends even into the hiding places; for when things no longer have meaning, they are no longer possessed. Here, of course, we are not speaking of a materialistic attachment to material goods. No, we are speaking of the signs of life's attachment to life and of the creature's participation in the creation. We are speaking not of mammon but of photographs and prayerbooks, of wedding rings and heirlooms, things that signify an embrace of the holy in the midst of the human. That embrace is the place where life unfolds, and certain things that we own, certain signs of who we are, connect us to that place.

It was pointed out earlier that only for a creature who eats can life take on a spiritual significance. That is why eating is a sacred act; that is why we pray when we eat. Among those possessions that constitute our most direct link to life, then, is food. But this is just what the Jews, plunged into the void and deprived of any place, do not possess. "How can an entire community feed itself," Kaplan asks, "when it has no place in life?" (131). Seeing that the Jews have been torn from the table of humanity, he realizes that they "have been eliminated from society" (168). This elimination runs far deeper than the imposition of laws prohibiting social contact, physical movement, or a participation in the professions. It runs even deeper than the decisions that mark the Jews for death. For this is an elimination from life before death, a ruin before ruin, a closing of the door before the closing of the last door. In a word, it is an elimination that has no exit.

"Outside—annihilation," Kaplan laments. "Inside—terror. Woe unto us for we are lost" (343). In Kaplan's Hebrew text we find that the words rendered as "outside—annihilation, inside—terror" are *michuts tishakel-cherev umechdariym eymah* (503); they are taken from Deuteronomy 32:25 and literally mean "outside the sword will bereave you of your children, and inside there will be terror." What is here understood to be an absolute annihilation, a condition of absolutely no exit, is not only the slaughter of oneself but of one's children. Bearing children is our primary and most profound means of participating with the Creator in His creation. Our children provide us with an "exit" into life where otherwise there is no exit; they provide us with a legacy to offer and a meaning to confer; they provide us with a future. But this is precisely what is lost when Kaplan cries out that *all* is lost. When making this entry, Kaplan perhaps had in mind not only the passage from the Book of Deuteronomy but the commentary on this passage which appears in the Talmud, where we are taught, "[Even where] the terror is 'within' the 'sword' will destroy [more] without" (*Bava Kama* 60b). Emmanuel Levinas comments on this teaching by saying: "One must withdraw into one's home. 'Go home until the storm passes.' There is no salvation except in the re-entry into oneself. One must have an interiority where one can seek refuge. . . . And even if 'at home'—in the refuge or in the interiority—there is 'terror,' it is better to have a country, a home, or an 'inwardness' with terror than to be outside" (*Nine* 190). In the crumbling of creation that characterizes the Shoah, however, the storm does not pass by the interior but passes into it. "Continuous mortal fear in the locked homes," writes Peretz Opoczynski. "That is the way of life today" (104). *This* condition, in which there is no exit, is one in which there is not only no exit outward but also no exit inward.

That is Kaplan's point, and it is a point made in various ways by other diarists. From the annex, the *achterhuis*, hidden within her house and finally invaded by the SS, Anne Frank writes: "Now we are so surrounded by danger and darkness that we lump against each other, as we search desperately for a means of escape. We all look down below, where people are fighting each other, we look above, where it is quiet and beautiful, and meanwhile we are cut off by the great dark mass which will not let us go upwards, but which stands before us as an impenetrable wall" (128). Where the movement inward is cut off, so is the movement upward, for it is the movement of the soul within that brings us into contact with the movement of the Creator above. Seeking what is above, the soul seeks the first things that are the basis of all things. Creation begins with this dimension of height: God created the heavens before He created the earth, and this is what imparts meaning to the world.[5] But, as Ringelblum noted earlier, in the Warsaw Ghetto there was no sky, no dimension of height, and a great dark mass will not allow Anne Frank the movement upward. The absence of an exit, which precludes the movement inward and outward, also blocks off the movement upward.

We see, then, what underlies a question so deceptively simple, so utterly desperate, as the one Hillel Seidman asks: "How are we to be saved?" (32). And we see that when Éva Heyman laments, "So it's true that I'll be taken to Poland" (79), it is a lament that the storm raging outside will enter the interior and sweep her into the great dark mass itself. Philip Mechanicus sees the storm sweeping over the Jews almost from the beginning of the diary he kept at Westerbork, for on 29 May 1943 he wrote: "I feel as if I'm an official reporter giving an account of a shipwreck. We are all together in a cyclone and feel the holed ship slowly sinking" (16). Where there is no exit out or in or up, the only avenue remaining is down. The crumbling of creation is a collapse into that dimension downward, which in this case is a downward without an upward. In contrast to the dimension of height that imparts meaning to existence, this sinking plunges the human being into a realm that is void of meaning, where even the struggle for existence becomes meaningless. Therefore, says Aryeh Klonicki-Klonymus, "All our efforts are in vain, I feel, and there is little sense in continuing our struggle for existence" (70). When the struggle for existence loses all sense, not only does creation lose its sense but the creature loses his status as creature, as a human being who bears the image of the Creator. To be without exit is to be without humanity. To make an exit from the antiworld would be to make a movement of return to a world made meaningful by human and divine relation, a world in which the divine still manifests itself from within and from above the human. With the erasure of within and above—with the collapse of all exits—the human being is reduced to the status of an animal who flees on all fours, face to the ground and oblivious of the sky.

That is why Borzykowski compares himself to an animal: "Staying night and day in this narrow confinement has a depressing effect. I cannot for one moment forget that I am a hunted animal. . . . I no longer remember that there are such things as sky, sun, fresh air. I look for hours on end at the wall. . . . An electric light is constantly on; I cannot tell the difference between night and day" (129). The electric light eclipses the sun, which, says the *Pirke de Rabbi Eliezer*, "has three letters of (God's) Name written upon its heart" (40). Once again, then, we see in the images of sky and sun the dimension of height and the source of the light, from which the man has been cut off; once again we see the impenetrable wall of the great dark mass, which here is exemplified precisely by the electric light that robs life of the distinctions between night and day. We are reminded of Rashi's observation that when the Creator Himself undid His creation in the time of the flood, "day and night ceased" (1:36). No longer situated in time, the man no longer has a place: even on the inside, in his hiding place, Borzykowski is hunted. Therefore he has no inside, just as Abraham Lissner, a Jewish partisan in Paris, has no inside. "A partisan," he notes in his diary, "must spend his entire day outdoors even when he has no special reason for being on the street" (288). When going outside is a means of hiding, there is no exit from danger. Hence there is no going outside. "Everyone," the teenager Dawid Rubinowicz writes in the diary he kept in Bodzentyn, "goes round frightened, wondering where he can hide and find somewhere safe. But where can one feel safe nowadays?—nowhere at all" (51). Somewhere safe, we notice in Rubinowicz's Polish text, is not just a hiding place but a *schronic* (63), a "shelter" or a "refuge," a place of protection and belonging. This word signifies the interior invoked in the passage from the Talmud cited above; it suggests a realm in which one might find an embrace, and not just an emptiness in which all are lumped against each other and hunted like animals.

Where an exit appears, there is safety and refuge, even if there is very little certainty. Where there is no exit, it is just the opposite, as Willy Cohn suggests in his diary from Breslau: "We used to have much safety and little certainty; now we have the certainty but very little safety" (38). What is the certainty that blocks off all exits? Zelig Kalmanovitch tells us in his diary from the Vilna Ghetto: "The war has affixed its mask to the catastrophe. But the catastrophe was certain even if there had been no war" (43). Kalmanovitch's insight that the war belies a much more profound event is as accurate as it is remarkable. The real catastrophe, the metaphysical catastrophe, is distinct from the physical catastrophe of war. For the real catastrophe is the crumbling of creation which begins before the war and makes such a war possible; it begins in the apotheosis of man, in the internalization of the *Volk* in the *Führer*, and it ends, with the certainty of a syllogism, in extermination of the light unto the nations.

"In the daytime," Mechanicus makes an entry in his diary, "the women bewail their sufferings, and at night the men heave the sighs they have suppressed during the day" (233)—the *verzuchtingen, die zij overdag onderdrukken*, as it is written in the Dutch text (257), the "lamentations" that they "keep down" or, literally, "press under" during the day. Here, where there is no exit, lamentation and suffering move downward, seeking the lowest level, like a sea, and they draw humanity into their depths. In this collapse of humanity, as Mechanicus states it, "the sorrow of the individual is drowned in that of the masses. It no longer contrasts with happiness and as a result makes scarcely any impact. The sorrow of all the separate individuals has united like innumerable drops to form a sea of sorrow which is too much for normal human feelings and in which you drown if you venture out upon it. It is so great and so universal that not only is it impossible to describe, but you cannot pick out the main features in it" (129). As we recall from the account in Genesis, the tale of creation is a tale about the introduction of distinctions and therefore of meaning to a realm that is empty and devoid of meaning: the distinctions between heaven and earth, between the waters above and the waters below, between the sea and the dry land, between light and darkness, between man and animals, between male and female, between the Sabbath and the six days of the week. When creation crumbles, these distinctions collapse; they collapse into a sea of suffering in which the world loses its distinction as a world. That is why Janusz Korczak says: "It's been a long time since I have blessed the world. I tried tonight. It didn't work" (185). It cannot work, because there is no world to bless. Therefore the blessing has no meaning. And when blessing has no meaning, nothing has meaning. It is in the face of this meaninglessness that the Holocaust diarist engages his diary in an effort to recover the traces of a meaningful life.

In his study of the diary as a genre, Alain Girard points out that, for those who write diaries, "the conception of the self, born of [the diarist's] experience, extends over an entire universe and is imperceptibly transformed into a conception of life, which is not a philosophy but a sense of existence" (551). Given all we have discovered in this chapter, however, we see once more that what Girard ascribes to the diary cannot be ascribed to the Holocaust diary. In this instance there is no universe over which the diarist's conception of self might extend. Witnessing the end of civilization, plunging into the void, and finding no exit, the Holocaust diarist undergoes an experience that robs him of all sense of self and therefore robs existence itself of all sense, of all meaning. To illustrate this point we need only recall an experience that Katznelson relates in his diary. Reflecting on a scene from the Warsaw Ghetto after an *Aktion* had taken place, he writes: "It is I that lie there in this deserted, ruined street. I lifted up a book, opened it, turned over some of the leaves and recalled things that I had long forgotten. There were the lines and the blank spaces . . . these blank spaces in between the lines somehow filled me with terror" (223–24). And so, having begun this chapter with the Book, we end it with the collapse of the Book into the blank spaces between the lines. Why did these spaces fill Katznelson with terror? Because between the lines, not merely in the letters of the words, is where meaning resides. The sea of suffering into which creation crumbles and is devoid of distinctions is just such a blank. This blank is the blank space that the Holocaust diarist struggles to fill each time he fills a space with words, and with spaces between the words. For this blank is the blank space left in the undoing of meaning.

MEANING UNDONE

WE RECALL FROM THE LAST CHAPTER MOSHE FLINKER'S plea to God: "Give some meaning to the life of your servant" (104). This plea lies at the heart of the Holocaust diary, for this plea arises from the very depths of the soul, from the core of the human being's ultimate need that Abraham Joshua Heschel identifies: "The ultimate human need is the need for a meaning of existence" (*Man's Quest* 144). Without meaning life is not life. Without its desperate struggle to recover a trace of meaning, the Holocaust diary is not the Holocaust diary, even if that recovery amounts to nothing more than an account of the undoing of meaning. In the Warsaw diary of Chaim Kaplan the account of this undoing begins within days of the diary's beginning, when on 7 September 1939 he writes: "Women cry and faint. Frightened Jews recite the Psalms, and heretics accept their judgment. No, this is not life. Life has gone off its straight course and becomes increasingly awry" (27). The undoing of meaning which Kaplan sees as a life gone awry does not lie in the advent of suffering; it is not suffering but *useless* suffering that here begins to drain life of its meaning, suffering without anything to suffer for, suffering that is nothing but suffering. It is simply there, and that is all. It is the suffering that Emmanuel Levinas describes when he writes, "The evil of pain, the harm itself, is the explosion and most profound articulation of absurdity" ("Useless" 157). Such is the suffering of which the human being can make no sense because it is the suffering born of the erasure of all sense from life. It has no cause, no purpose, no explanation. It cannot be situated in the world because it is the suffering that ensues upon the destruction of the world.

Hence "the one who is worldly-wise," says Warsaw Ghetto diarist Hillel Seidman, "is as naive as a child. And just as helpless" (181). Unlike the helplessness of the child, however, the helplessness of the man here lies not in the absence of power but in the absence of meaning. It is as though he suddenly finds himself in a place, or a nonplace, where he does not know the language. Indeed, Salmen Gradowski, a diarist from the *Sonderkommando* of Auschwitz, makes just such a comparison: "Man does not come here to live but to die, sooner or later. There is no room for life here. It is the residence of death. Our brain has grown dull, the thoughts are numbed, it is not possible to grasp this new language" (99). It is not only within the confines of Auschwitz but throughout the Holocaust Kingdom that there is no room for life. People sent to the ghettos come there not to live but to die, of disease and starvation, yes, but of more than that. They die of meaninglessness: there is no room for life in the Kingdom of Night because there is no room for meaning. This new language, then, is impossible to grasp not because it is a different language but because it is a nonlanguage, an antilanguage that houses an antiworld. "Here you forget what disgust is," as Philip Mechanicus puts it in his journal from Westerbork (91), because nothing in this life that is not a life bears any distinctions, any meaning, that would make disgust meaningful. And where nothing is meaningful, nothing is absurd, as Romanian diarist Emil Dorian points out: "Nothing is absurd any longer" (176). The absurd here is not the unintelligible over and against the intelligible but is instead the absence of such an opposition. The horror, then, is not that there is so much evil but that nothing is evil or good or anything else. The horror is that there is no horror. There is only the neutrality of what is. Period.

What is the situation of the Holocaust diarist in the midst of this undoing of meaning? Perhaps, at best, all he can do is attest to the undoing; and yet something is recovered in the testimony itself. Indeed, the very existence of the diary implies that there is something to lament, if not something to affirm. The fact that the Holocaust diary speaks where there should be no speech—where the language of the world has been transformed into the antilanguage of an antiworld—is an indication that meaning may not have been altogether undone, or at least that someone has not assented to its undoing. If Dorian can assert that "violence keeps pace with untruth, spiritual values beat a retreat" (292), it is because in this remarkable soul there still abides some notion of truth and spiritual values. If life were completely drained of meaning, he could not write: "Life, drained of meaning over so many years, is growing ever more senseless without intellectual pursuits. You read very little, you see very few people, and those you do meet exude an emptiness, a dryness, and a desperate stagnation of spiritual vitality which mirrors your own" (303). Thus the Holocaust diary not only records the undoing of meaning but opposes it in a time and a place where such opposition is as unintelligible as the antiworld into which these diarists are plunged. In the midst of a neutrality empty of value, a silence drained of sense, and an absence devoid of significance the Holocaust diary emerges, as it were, *ex nihilo*. If we are to reflect on the diary's response to the undoing of meaning, then, in the words of Emil Fackenheim: "our ecstatic thought must point to *their* resistance—the resistance in thought and the resistance in life—as *ontologically ultimate. Resistance in that extremity was a way of being. For our thought now, it is an ontological category*" (*To Mend* 248). Let us examine the features of this ontological category that is inserted into our thinking and our being through the very existence of the Holocaust diary.

THE NEUTRALITY OF BEING

Before turning to the diaries themselves, it will be helpful to begin this section with a consideration of what Emmanuel Levinas refers to as the "there is." The concept of the "there is" will be a key to all that we discuss in this chapter. Levinas introduces this idea in *Existence and Existents*, where he explains: "This impersonal, anonymous, yet inextinguishable 'consummation' of being, which murmurs in the depths of nothingness itself, we shall designate by the term *there is*. The *there is*, inasmuch as it resists a personal form, is 'being in general.' We have not derived this notion from exterior things or the inner world—from any 'being' whatever. For *there is* transcends inwardness as well as exteriority. . . . There is no longer *this* or *that*; there is not 'something.' But this universal absence is in its turn a presence, an absolutely unavoidable presence. It is not the dialectical counterpart of absence, and we do not grasp it through a thought. It is immediately there. There is no discourse. Nothing responds to us but this silence" (57–58).[1] What Levinas helps us to realize is this: in the crumbling of creation that was examined in the previous chapter, creation does not collapse into nothing but rather is reduced to what is merely there—neutral, impersonal, and meaningless, as if the fixtures around us turned out to be mere cardboard stage props. In the Shoah, the "there is" is embodied in the SS insignia of the death's head, the face made faceless, as the creature who wears it motions indifferently to the left and to the right. And there we have it: such neutral terms as "left" and "right" suddenly take on a life-and-death significance that immediately sinks back into neutrality.

Among the Holocaust diarists, Dorian invokes this phenomenon of impersonal being in terms that bear an uncanny resemblance to those used by Levinas. On 29 December 1941, for instance, he writes: "The room's loneliness, [as I lean] on the stove, gives me a feeling of total helplessness, as if drowning in an ocean of time. I stop working for a few moments and let myself get drunk on a kind of sadness so heady it almost feels good. Yet often I am soon seized, not only by anxiety itself, but by the memory of similar feelings of anxiety when I was a child left alone at home" (250–51). This anxiety is not so much over something that might happen as over the dread that whatever may happen is meaningless; it is an anxiety over anxiety itself, an anxiety that has no exit. That is what is meant by the "excluded middle," a term Levinas uses to describe the "there is" (*Ethics* 49): there is nothing between the man and the world around him that would enable him to make sense of it, enter into it, or even to be anxious about it, so that it might become the object of a subject's anxiety. What is excluded in the excluded middle, then, is every standard of value, that is to say, every dimension of height that would enable the human being to distinguish between good and evil, truth and lie, the real and the unreal. For the middle stems from above. Thus what is excluded, as we see in the Kovno Ghetto diary of Avraham Tory, is the sun, which radiates not only light but meaning: "The sun fills the world with warmth and brightness. It also sends its light and warmth to us in the Ghetto. This pretty picture is sharply circumscribed, however, by the barbed-wire fence surrounding us. . . . There is no joy in life here, no spring sunshine in our spirits, and no joy in sowing. The gray color of the Ghetto stops every ray of sun, every pleasant sound, every ounce of joy. And if you happen to leave the four walls of the Ghetto for the city—either to work or on an errand—the grayness of the Ghetto and all it entails keep tugging at your heart incessantly" (318). No joy in sowing: fecundity is the opposite of the "there is." Only life that begets life has meaning, for to beget life is to open up a future, and to have meaning is to be oriented toward the future. To have meaning is to have a direction, and to have a direction is to determine a place where we have yet to arrive, to plant a seed that has yet to grow.

Just as the neutral grayness of the ghetto eclipses the sun, so does the neutrality of being occlude the word, a point that Hersh Wasser makes in his diary from the Warsaw Ghetto. "Here and there," he writes on 2 December 1940, "one may hear a sympathetic word, but it is drowned out in the surroundings" (212). The word of sympathy, which is a word of human relation, is drowned out in the rumbling noise that incessantly returns after the cessation of every noise, swallowed up in the "it's all the same" that characterizes the "there is." This indifference is what marks the absence of every why or wherefore that Wasser notes when he reports that "German soldiers broke into the Lodz ghetto and murdered 1,100 innocent people without any why or wherefore" (242). It is the "for no reason" with which Dawid Rubinowicz collides when he records that the militia "met a Jew who was going out of the town, and they immediately shot him for no reason, then they drove on and shot a Jewess, again for no reason. So two victims have perished for absolutely no reason" (26). The death of the innocent is precisely death for no reason, and death for no reason arises not amid the accidents of nature but in a realm where life has no reason, or better: in a realm where life is forbidden all reason, all justification, and all legitimacy—everything that, in the Jewish tradition, is derived from the teaching and the law of the Torah, the essence of which is to be found in two words: "Choose life" (Deuteronomy 30:19). Albert Camus has said that "the absurd is sin without God" (30). In this case it is sin that persists after the assault on God and on the Torah that is identified with God; in a word, it is the sin of existing. Within the neutrality of the "there is," existence—or rather, being alive—is the sin, since to be alive in any *meaningful* sense is to be other than indifferent toward life; to be alive is to choose life, and to make a choice is to be non-indifferent. To *live* within the neutrality of the "there is," then, is to live illegally.

Thus we may reach a deeper level in our understanding of the implications of Abraham Lissner's statement that, in order to be a partisan, one must "abandon one's legal residence and begin living alone on an illegal basis" (288). Within the neutrality of being, those who are among the partisans are not just the youth who go underground and take up arms; rather, they include all who choose life in an endeavor to recover a shred of meaning from the gullet of the "there is." This snatching a shred of meaning from the maw of meaninglessness changes the living of life into a matter of stealing life, and, in the Holocaust Kingdom, stealing life is necessarily a capital crime. Hence, "in conditions as they are," writes Abraham Levin in his diary from the Warsaw Ghetto, "smuggling is an imperative of life" (327), and what is smuggled into the ghetto is life itself. But since the "there is" reigns in the ghetto, smuggling demands the death penalty. Other diarists of the Warsaw Ghetto make the same point. "The only way Jews can live these days," asserts Emmanuel Ringelblum, "is to break the law. No possibility of living within the law" (27–28). What is within the law is normally outside the sphere of the "there is." Like life itself, the law represents a breach in the neutrality of being; it is an *in*cluded middle, so that to choose life is to choose a life within the law. What characterizes the undoing of meaning in the Shoah is the reversal of this principle of law and life. And so, says Kaplan, "there isn't one who doesn't break the law, not one who doesn't deserve death under the penalty of the conqueror's decrees" (109). But it must be reiterated: within the neutrality of being, living illegally does not entail *doing* anything but lies instead in *being*; to declare illegal all the doing that is required for staying alive is to declare that being alive is itself criminal. And Kaplan is aware of this: "Whatever we do we do illegally; legally we don't even have the right to exist" (332–33), that is, "to be alive," *lechayot*, as Kaplan's Hebrew text reads (492). Here existing is criminal, because existing entails being alive, and being alive, again, entails choosing life.

A sense of this reversal of law that characterizes the Shoah can be found among other diarists. Moshe Flinker, for example, writes: "The law condemns us. Just as there is a law against stealing, so there is a law to persecute the Jews" (28). From the Vilna Ghetto Herman Kruk relates: "The Ghetto is in delirium. This is more than an 'action.' It has become a permanent 'action' under the cloak of legality" (57). And in the very pit of the crematoria at Auschwitz-Birkenau, Gradowski comments on the killing of an inmate, saying: "The executioner committed no transgression. On the contrary, he will be regarded as a good supervisor of workmen" (106). In the neutrality of being which opposes being within the law, a law arises which is opposed to the first and most fundamental of all Jewish laws pertaining to the relation between one human being and another. The new law, the antilaw that sends a people into delirium, is: Thou shalt murder. As Adin Steinsaltz has pointed out: "'Thou shalt not murder' is not a ruling set by some local chief or council to avoid vengeful blood feuds. It is the command of an Almighty God, and this is what gives it power and meaning" (*Strife* 85). If this is the command of an Almighty God, then a power that would destroy both God and the meaning engendered by His command must reverse the command. And this destruction must begin with the people chosen to receive the command. Therefore it is not just *permitted* to kill the Jew—it is *imperative*, a necessity of the "law" opposed to all law. The executioner is more than a good supervisor of the workmen he executes; he is a good administrator of the "there is." More than an "action," his is a permanent "action," to be regarded not as an event but as a condition imposed on the structure of being. It is the condition of irreality imposed upon reality, a condition of erasure calculated to erase all that is inscribed upon the Tablets of the Law.[2]

That is what terrifies Michael Zylberberg when he collides with the white that remains after the erasure of the meaning that derives only from law. Describing the Warsaw Ghetto, now razed, on 17 January 1945, he writes: "The whole area lay under thick snow. The whiteness, which should be a symbol of purity, frightened me. Under that whiteness flowed a sea of innocent Jewish blood. I wandered aimlessly over the ruins. There was no recognizable sign of what had once existed there. It was eerie and terrifying" (211). The white that veils the sea of blood represents the meaninglessness that, in the neutrality of being, shrouds the life that flows in the blood. It is the white of a blank indifference that bleaches out the blood-red cry of an urgent nonindifference. It is the silence that Zylberberg encountered when he surveyed the ruins of Warsaw for the first time in the summer of 1944. "The silence and the emptiness that enveloped those ruins," he says, "filled one with dread and awe. And [the] Jew who had lived in the ghetto till the Uprising of 1943 had known the streets and alleys filled with life and movement and, in spite of everything, hope. They were now an unimaginable wilderness" (167). The wilderness here is unimaginable because it is mute. Setting his words to the page, the Holocaust diarist does battle with that muteness, with that silence.

THE SILENCE

Commenting on two forms of silence in *A Beggar in Jerusalem*, Elie Wiesel writes: "There is the silence which preceded the creation; and the one which accompanied the revelation on Mount Sinai. The first contains chaos and solitude, the second suggests presence, fervor, plenitude" (108). But if the Shoah is comparable in its significance to the revelation at Mount Sinai, we may have to add a third form of silence: the silence of the crumbling of creation and the undoing of meaning. With this third manifestation, "silence," in the words of André Neher, "becomes the place of supreme aggression" (*Exile* 168). In our effort to understand the role of this silence in the Holocaust diary, Levinas will again prove helpful.

In *Existence and Existents*, it will be recalled, Levinas notes that in the "there is" nothing "responds to us but this silence" (58); in *Time and the Other* he explains further, saying that here "the absence of everything returns as a presence, as the place where the bottom has dropped out of everything, an atmospheric density, a plenitude of the void, or the murmur of silence" (46). The *murmur* of silence? In the matter at hand, perhaps better to say: the shriek of silence. For in the realm of the Shoah the absence of everything is the absence of anything meaningful, which is the presence of meaning undone. Indeed, whether shriek or murmur, this fading remnant of a sound itself loses its meaning; it too is engulfed in the gravitational field of silence. Similar to what we saw in the crumbling of creation, when the bottom drops out—when the grounds falls apart—the human being plummets downward into this silence that renders mute any voice from above. "Getting worse," writes Dorian in his desperation. "I'm plunged into silence and cannot stand company. I'm supposed to explain what the matter is with me, and I cannot" (167). Explanation is impossible, not because he cannot find the words, but because he himself now understands nothing; every link between word and meaning has been erased. Or rather, an "atmospheric density" has risen up to wall off word from meaning and life from life, as Kaplan suggests when he declares: "We are imprisoned within double walls: a wall of brick for our bodies, and a wall of silence for our spirits. Whatever happens or is done is cloaked in total silence" (359–60). In his Hebrew text Kaplan uses two different words for "silence": the first is *shetiykah* and the second is *demamah* (520); the first denotes a paralysis or absence of movement, while the second implies an absence of sound. Both announce the absence of any point of reference, any source of meaning for the one who is imprisoned within this silence that draws him ever downward.

The talmudic sage Rabbi Eleazar once said that "from the day on which the Temple was destroyed the gates of prayer have been closed," but "though the gates of prayer are closed, the gates of weeping are not closed" (*Berakhot* 32b). In the realm of the Holocaust diary, however, even tears become meaningless, for even tears do not rise upward but plunge downward, into silence. "Steady and continual weeping," says Kaplan, "finally leads to silence. At first there is screaming, then wailing; and at last a bottomless sigh that does not even leave an echo" (85–86). The sigh heaves without an echo because it is swallowed up in the "deadly silence" that "reigns in all these streets," as Peretz Opoczynski puts it (108). Note that the silence is not merely there as a feature of the ghetto's surroundings; it *reigns*, draining everything else that is there of all significance. And it rules not only in the Warsaw Ghetto, where Opoczynski makes this entry, but throughout the universe of the Shoah. Even in her hiding place Anne Frank writes, "It is the silence that frightens me so in the evenings and at night" (32). Rather than "frightens me so," a better translation of the Dutch phrase *zo zenuwachtig maakt* (20) might be "gets on my nerves so much." What gets on the nerves tears at the nerves, tears the human being from where she is, and tears the self from the soul. Thus she is torn from meaning: and as meaning is undone, so is the soul. Recall in this connection Wiesel's remarks in *The Testament*: "Silence acts on both the senses and the nerves; it unsettles them. It acts on the imagination and sets it on fire. It acts on the soul and fills it with night and death. The philosophers are wrong: it is not words that kill, it is silence" (209). For silence kills meaning, and when meaning is killed, the soul is drained of its life.

What Levinas calls "an atmospheric density" or "a plenitude of the void" assumes such an immense weight that Anne writes: "The atmosphere is so oppressive, and sleepy and heavy as lead. You don't hear a single bird singing outside, and a deadly close silence hangs everywhere, catching hold of me as if it will drag me down deeper into an underworld. . . . 'Go outside, laugh, and take a breath of fresh air,' a voice cries within me, but I don't even feel a response any more; I go and lie on the divan and sleep, to make the time pass more quickly, and the stillness and the terrible fear, because there is no way of killing them" (126). Again we see the gravitational pull of silence, here drawing the child into the silence of unconsciousness. In Anne's original text, the silence is not exactly "deadly" but "deathlike and stifling," *doodse en benauwende* (97); it does not threaten—it is the threat, the very fear itself that stifles the breath. Along with the image of being drawn downward, then, we find the breath snatched from the lips, and with it all meaning is snatched from life. For life's meaning is life's breath, its *ruach* or spirit.

If, in the words of Vilna Ghetto diarist Zelig Kalmanovitch, "silence means condemnation" (44), it is condemnation to this meaninglessness that oppresses Anne Frank and all the other Holocaust diarists. It is condemnation to the collapse of all sense and sensibility that Kruk refers to above as "delirium" and that Éva Heyman alludes to when she writes: "Dear Diary, I'm still too little a girl to write down what I felt while we waited to be taken to the Ghetto. . . . I knew that we were being taken to the Ghetto, but felt that if this silence would go on much longer we would all go crazy" (84). This silence invades her dreams—"In my dream I was very frightened of the silence" (96)—and it cuts through the people around her: "Nobody says a word. Dear Diary, I've never been so afraid" (83). Here we begin to see a closer connection between the crumbling of creation and meaning undone;

it lies in the silence of the people who make up a world, in the silence of a world that has succumbed to the indifference of the "there is" and has become the "there is" itself. "And the world falls silent," says yet another teen, a Romanian girl named Mirjam Korber (100). To the writers of the Holocaust diary, this is perhaps the most unnerving form of silence that they struggle to overcome. For this silence indicates that they have lost not only all meaning *in* the world but all contact *with* the world. Again, silence is not a space but a wall.

The questions that torment Ringelblum in this regard torment all of those who take up the Holocaust diary: "Does the world know about our suffering? And if it knows, why is it silent? Why is the world not stirred when tens of thousands of Jews are shot in Fonari [more commonly known as Ponary]? Why is the world silent when tens of thousands of Jews are poisoned in Chelmno? Why is the world silent when hundreds of thousands of Jews are massacred in Galicia and other newly occupied areas?" (296). This entry in Ringelblum's diary is dated 27 June 1942, when the leaders of the world, indeed, knew what was transpiring in Europe (in May 1942 the Jewish Labor Bund sent a report to London estimating that over 350,000 Jews had been slaughtered, and that the Nazis intended to exterminate all the Jews of Europe). But nearly two years earlier, on 10 October 1940, Kaplan anticipated this silence: "The naive among the Jews and Poles ask: Can the world sit silent?" (213). Between the time of Kaplan's question and Ringelblum's lament, on 5 February 1941, Dorian wrote that in the days of old "Europe still exhibited a hypocritical morality that protested against anti-Semitic persecution. But in the last few years, Jews have been expelled, tortured, massacred—while people, or rather countries, looked on with total indifference" (142). A year after Ringelblum's entry—a year after the massive deportation of the Jews of Warsaw to Treblinka—Yitzhak Katznelson continued to raise the cry on 21 July 1943: "With us they were free to do exactly as their heart (a German heart!) desired because no onlooker would open his mouth, would utter a word, or would ask—'Murderer, what is this you are doing? Why this slaughter of a whole nation?'" (50–51). And two and a half months later he repeats, "Whilst we were the victims of genocide at the hands of these brute beasts of the nether world, the nations of the world kept silent" (204). Throughout the war years, then, as much as they assailed God for His silence, the Holocaust diarists laid the charge of silence at the feet of humanity.

There is, however, an important difference between the silence of God and this silence of humanity: as it is represented in the Holocaust diary, the silence of the former belongs to the apparent absence of One Who has removed Himself or turned His face from the Jews, while the latter is a silence imposed upon the Jews, a silence chosen for God's Chosen. What decision did the Allies make at the Evian Conference on 5 July 1938 and at the Bermuda Conference on 19 April 1943? To remain silent. Thus the silence that rumbles over the Jews in the wake of meaning undone is the calculated silence of an imposed absence. On a metaphysical and ontological level, then, the Holocaust diary is much more than the record of events that are present in the life of the diarist; it is the refusal of an imposed absence. We shall now consider the characteristics of that absence, which is unlike any other the world has known.[3]

THE IMPOSED ABSENCE

Returning first to an elaboration on his notion of the "there is," we recall that Levinas characterizes the entrapment in the "there is" as a kind of insomnia. "In insomnia," he says, "one can and one cannot say that there is an 'I' which cannot manage to fall asleep. The impossibility of escaping wakefulness is something 'objective,' independent of my initiative. This impersonality absorbs my consciousness; consciousness is depersonalized. I do not stay awake: 'it' stays awake" (*Ethics* 49).[4] When the diarist cannot sleep, he writes, and in this way attempts to recover an "I" who may be said to remain awake. The writing of the Holocaust diary is the struggle of consciousness to become the consciousness of a living subject who is otherwise rendered absent by the silence that invades his soul and draws him downward, into a realm that is nowhere.

As in other instances already pointed out, Emil Dorian exemplifies what Levinas is talking about. "There is a void you cannot fill," he says, "either with memories or with reading. An absence of your self made worse by being cut off from everyone, by going over the same thoughts, when you lack information and often cannot push the cart of optimism out of the mire" (314). Is not this "going over the same thoughts," this isolation, a description of insomnia? Optimism, moreover, here entails far more than maintaining a positive outlook on life or some hope for life; beyond that, it is a capacity for establishing a presence within life. But since presence requires a relation to another, it requires meaning, because meaning, like the presence of the self, is derived from the contexts of relation. Signs, for example, take on significance only inasmuch as they point to something else; a sign that signifies only itself is meaningless. Therefore the man who is left only with himself is left without himself and without his life. When Katznelson, then, asserts, "All belief in life itself is dead in every one of us" (101), it is as much to say that he and his comrades are absent from life and that life is absent from them. This point is made more clearly and more powerfully in Katznelson's Hebrew text, where we find that not only is belief, or *emunah*, dead but also *'ikar* (51), a word omitted from the English translation. It means "essence" or "most fundamental principle": with the dying of the belief in life, what is most fundamental, most essential, to the life of the human being dies. And it is not only belief in life, but belief *b'etsem hachayyim*, belief "in the substance of life." Instead of this substance there is only absence, the imposed absence of meaning undone.

Katznelson addresses this absence in other ways, as when he describes a barracks in Vittel, which "contains everything, laws, discipline, order, everything harmonises, matches and is alike. Everything tallies. It has everything, everything, except a human being. The human element is simply not there. It is a choir, but without voices" (168–69). In the absence of the human element, this harmony and order are rendered meaningless, since the meaning of such order is derived from how it is situated within the lives of human beings. If everything tallies, it adds up to zero because the human being has been reduced to nothing. As a Nazi told one rabbi, Ringelblum reports, "You're not human, you're not animal, you're Jew" (24). The Jew here is not subhuman—he is sublife; absent from the kingdom of humanity as well as from the animal kingdom, he is rendered absent from all life, from all of the zoological order. This absence shows itself even outside the immediate conditions of starvation, torture, and murder, as we see from an entry in Zylberberg's diary. "I tried to be one of the crowd," he says of a moment spent among the Polish peasants after the Germans had burned and abandoned Warsaw. "But [I] could not forget for one second the gulf that separated me from them. There in that damp, dark room, among the drunken peasants and their wives, my imagination led me into another world. I saw all my relatives, my old friends, my teachers and colleagues, my students—people from that now vanished Jewish world" (198). Studying Zylberberg's statement more closely, we realize that the absence imposed upon the Jews becomes an absence of Jews imposed upon the world. And the absence of the Jews, of those who were chosen to bear witness to the meaning and the sanctity of life, imposes upon the world the absence of meaning. The silence of this imposed absence is the silence of those dead who were the substance of a vanished world, of an annihilated world. What is the choir without voices? It is the choir of the dead.

Peculiar to the relation of the Nazis to this choir of the dead is the fact that they were bent not only on murdering the choir of the living but this choir as well. In their assault not only on the living but on the dead—on cemeteries and on the memory of the dead—the Nazis imposed an absence not only on the Jews but on the significance of the Jews. The sum of the teaching and truth of the Jewish tradition was to be made absent. The meaning undone in the Shoah, then, was the meaning of Jewishness, as we see when in Kaplan's diary we read: "Our tragedy is the senselessness of it all. Our suffering is inflicted on us because we are Jews, while the real meaning of Jewishness has disappeared from our lives" (289). Or better: it was forcibly removed from their lives. With this removal came the disappearance not just of a culture or a way of life but of the light unto the nations that made possible any meaningful life among the nations. "Throughout the summer," wrote David Kahane in his diary from the Lvov Ghetto, "I have seen no green vegetation or the shape of a flower" (3), as though this absence of life from the face of the earth were emblematic of the absence of the Jews from the world. "Are there any Jews left in the world?" Kahane followed his observation with a question. "Do Jews still rise to say *Selikhot* somewhere?" (3). The *Selikhot* are penitential prayers recited in preparation for the High Holy Days. Penitence is intelligible only where there is value, good and evil, and therefore meaning in life.[5] Where the *Selikhot* prayers are absent, both life and meaning are absent, so that Kahane's question about the Jews and their prayers of repentance was a question about the presence of life and meaning in the world. Indeed, from the citations of the Talmud and the *Prike de Rabbi Eliezer* at the beginning of the last chapter, we recall that, like the Torah—which, says the Talmud, is the Tree of Life (*Berakhot* 32b)—repentance is among the seven things that preceded the Creation. Repentance precedes the Creation because meaning precedes the Creation. Thus we see once more that, where one crumbles, the other is undone.

Very often, when a diarist repents where meaning is undone, repentance is itself turned on end. For in the Holocaust diary repentance is frequently not for a transgression that might diminish life, but for the very rejoicing in life that Jews are commanded to summon. In the Talmud, for example, Rabbi Papa declares that there must be "no grief in the presence of the Holy One, blessed be He" (*Chagigah* 5b); Rabbi Yehuda Loeve, the Maharal of Prague, maintains, "The *Shekhinah* dwells only in an atmosphere of joy" (147); and Nachman of Breslov teaches, "The essence of everything is joy" (*Restore* 109). Yet we find Mirjam Korber, a young girl in the innocence of life, ashamed to admit that she had experienced a few minutes of joy, when she danced and for a moment forgot the plight of her people (57). In the case of Yitzhak Zuckerman, a survivor of the Warsaw Ghetto Uprising, the man feels shame over the mere fact of being alive (66), so absolute is this undoing of meaning; similarly, Janusz Korczak, the man who chose to go to his death with the children of his orphanage rather than save himself, writes: "I feel all smeared, bloodstained, stinking. And crafty, since I am alive" (149). Perhaps more than anything else, shame isolates us within the meaninglessness of ourselves and casts us into the condition of the "without-self"; shame, after all, is the first sign of the first man's transgression. And the one who is fallen is cast out, made absent from the place where he belongs. In the case of the Shoah, however, the Jews are cast out of the world into which the first human beings were cast, made absent even from the realm of exile.

All of this leaves us with the question: how is a human being to recover meaning and presence in life when both have been undone? In a word, the answer that we find in the Holocaust diary is: through sacrifice. In order to take on significance in life, a human being must become a sign of the sanctity of the life of the other human being, even to the point of offering up his life for the other.[6] Salmen Lewental, the diarist from *Sonderkommando* of Auschwitz-Birkenau, illustrates this truth in existential and experiential terms. Commenting on those who sacrificed themselves in the uprising staged at the crematoria on 7 October 1944, he writes: "They gave up everything, sacrificing their own selves. Is it not a sacrifice of their own lives laid down on the altar? Laid down in full consciousness, with complete self-denial?" (170). This laying down of one's own life is the opposite of being drawn down into meaninglessness. For, as Lewental points out, these lives are laid down upon an altar, and the altar raises up and gives meaning to what had been pulled down with the undoing of meaning. "Because this human being exists," we remember the words of Martin Buber, "meaninglessness, however hard pressed you are by it, cannot be the real truth. Because this human being exists, in the darkness the light lies hidden, in fear salvation, and in the callousness of one's fellow-men the great Love" (*Between* 98). Because the other human is there, the "there is" is not *all* there is. And so it happens that a man may lay himself down for another.

In some cases the diarists themselves engage in this laying down that is a rising up. On several occasions, from the very beginning, Adam Czerniakow, for instance, offered up himself for the sake of Jewish lives. On 8 November 1939, without pretense or concern for accolade, he says: "I pleaded to be arrested together with the Council in exchange for the 24 hostages. They promised to release them all tomorrow morning" (88). Later that same month he relates: "I was ordered to appear at the SS at 3 with six rabbis, six leading members of the community, five councilors. I proceeded at once to Baatz and the whole idea was abandoned. I informed Brandt of my willingness to offer myself as a hostage" (92–93). And on 1 December he writes, "According to information just obtained in the Community, the families of the 53 have been looking for a scapegoat. Who could serve this purpose better than I?" (95).[7] To be sure, this intercession and sacrifice has a place in the Jewish tradition that is as old as the midrash itself. In fact, there is a word for one who assume such a role; it is *shtadlon*, as Yisrael Gutman notes in his essay on Czerniakow and his diary. "Emancipation and civil equality," says Gutman, "eliminated the *shtadlon* from Jewish life, but the Nazis recreated him and made intercession the only possible form of contact between the Jews and the authorities" (466). And they made this the only possible form of contact not only through the imposition of an administrative procedure but through the undoing of meaning.

Lest we should ascribe this sacrificial will to some sociological, psychological, or behavioral quirk of Czerniakow, we would do well to recall an example of one who was altogether different from Czerniakow: the young Hannah Senesh. After leaving her native Hungary to settle in Israel, soon she could think of nothing but returning to offer some kind of relief to the suffering of her people. This return took the form of a military mission that ended in her being tortured and murdered. "I'm waiting to be called," she says on 29 May 1943. "I can't think of anything else. I don't think there is any outer, noticeable change in me. I do my daily work as usual, but sometimes feel as if I'm seeing things from a distance. I look at everything from one point of view only: is it, or is it not necessary for my mission?" (128). Back in Yugoslavia, on 2 May 1944, she wrote "Blessed Is the Match," the famous poem that eloquently and profoundly articulates the path toward the recovery of meaning in a realm where meaning has been undone:

> Blessed is the match consumed
> in kindling flame.
> Blessed is the flame that burns
> in the secret fastness of the heart.
> Blessed is the heart with strength to stop
> its beating for honour's sake.
> Blessed is the match consumed
> in kindling flame. (256)

The match that kindles this flame returns to the world the light of meaning which makes it possible to dwell in the world. It is the match that lights the hearth of a home where a people, all of humanity, are otherwise made homeless.

THE FRAGMENTATION OF HOME AND FAMILY

"WE ARE APPROACHING OUR NEW GRAVES, AS WE CALL our new home," writes the diarist from the Auschwitz *Sonderkommando*, Salmen Gradowski (99). As this brief remark suggests, the home that in the world constitutes the center of life and meaning becomes an abyss of death and absurdity in the antiworld. It will be remembered that during the Shoah every Jew—*every* Jew—in Europe was rendered homeless: every Jew was forced into a camp, into a ghetto, or into hiding. The Holocaust diary, then, is a diary about homelessness written by the homeless. As we shall see, this condition goes beyond the problem of establishing an address; like the annihilation of the people, the annihilation of the home has metaphysical and ontological implications. With these implications, this absence of a home imposed upon humanity is another unique feature of the Holocaust diary and of the Event to which it bears witness. In the world, diaries are normally written in the safety and seclusion of one's home; in the Kingdom of Night, they are written in hiding places that are the antithesis of a home, where, ever fearful, the diarist teeters on the edge of a grave that takes the place of the home. This grave is the black hole of emptiness that remains wherever the assault on God, Israel, and the Torah takes place. For the Torah, intertwined with God and Israel, begins with the letter *beit*, which is also the Hebrew word for "house" or "home"; all that is in the Torah, like all that comprises the sanctity of our lives, issues from the womb of this letter that is also a word. In the words of Martin Buber, "'Good' is the movement in the direction of home" (*Between* 78). That is why the Jew places the words of the Torah in a *mezuzah* and affixes it to the entrance of his home: so that the home may be blessed with the Good, which consists of the life and the truth of the Torah, and thus may become a place of dwelling.

"Why did the creation of the world begin with the letter *beit*," asks the *Midrash Tanchuma*, "even though *alef* is the first of all the letters? Because *alef* begins the word *arur* [cursed], while *beit* begins the word *barukh* [blessed]" (1:9). And blessing in the world begins in the home. The home is where the family makes its appearance, where we first hear our names uttered with love, and where we first come to the realization that we are a *something* and that life *means* something. It is the center and the origin of all our aspirations and all our seeking, the reference point for every direction that we pursue. "The dwelling," Emmanuel Levinas states it, "is not situated in the objective world, but the objective world is situated by my relation to my dwelling" (*Totality* 153); without the beacon that emanates from hearth and home, we venture not into a world but into a wilderness. Rabbi Yitzchak Ginsburgh places this philosophical insight within the contexts of Jewish thought by saying: "As an extended image, the house represents man's general frame of reference in his relation to the world. The word *beit*, 'house,' is derived either from the root *banah*, 'to build,' or *bo*, 'to come.' Through education and life experience, man builds his house and enters into it in order to attain a balanced and stable relationship to reality. On a deeper level all of reality is a house in relation to G–d" (44). God is "the dwelling place of the universe," we recall the teaching from the *Midrash on Psalms*. That is why He is referred to as *HaMakom*, "the Place" (2:93). And the space where the Place opens up is the space opened up by the Torah. In Jewish life, then, the Torah that is associated with God is at the center of the education and the life experience that make it possible to build a home. Once the Torah and its Covenant with Abraham, Isaac, and Jacob are lost, all of humanity is rendered homeless.

Having invoked the Patriarchs, we are reminded of a tradition, according to which Abraham is symbolized by a mountain, Isaac by a valley, and Jacob by a house (see, for example, Wiesel, *Messengers* 137). It was Jacob who wrestled the blessing and the name of Israel from the angel at Peniel, as he was returning to his homeland. It is from Jacob, therefore, that this people derives its name, engaged as they are in an eternal return homeward.[1] As the basis of all that is dear and meaningful in life, the home draws our glance upward, toward the heavens that were created before the earth and that sanctify our dwelling upon the earth. "The clouds that, like wads of cotton, are driven across the heavens," writes Renata Laqueur in her Bergen-Belsen diary, "take my thoughts more and more homeward" (17). The diarists who behold the crumbling of creation and the undoing of meaning thus turn their glance upward, clinging to the fragments that remain of the home, as though clinging to the fragments of the sky. That is why, desperate to remain even in the rubble that remains of her home, Ruth Andreas-Friedrich writes in her Berlin diary, "The stuffiest little corner of the home is better than any palace in an alien land" (123). And that is why, with the erasure of the dimension of height opened up by the home, Julian Stanford laments, "The Jews of Amsterdam no longer sleep in their dwelling places" (84). What constitutes a place as a dwelling place, of course, is not just this or that particular space but a family: mothers and fathers and children. But when the family is no longer able to sleep in its home, it is reduced to the status of a mere social unit, and parenthood is made into a matter of biological breeding. That is why the Talmud declares that a man is not a man without a home (*Yevamot* 63a): without a home a man is without a family and therefore without his fatherhood. And once he is without his fatherhood, he loses the capacity to address the Creator as "Our Father."[2]

The destruction to which the Holocaust diarists bear witness is the destruction precisely of these foundations. In this chapter we shall examine the ways in which the Holocaust diarists respond to this destruction of the dwelling place, the obliteration of the family, and the murder of parenthood. In this last category, we shall focus here on the father, with chapters 9 and 10 devoted to detailed discussions of the mother and of the child.

THE DESTRUCTION OF THE DWELLING PLACE

As a dwelling place, the home is not just a place where we spend our time away from work, not just a place where we eat and sleep. People can have a place to eat and sleep, a place to stay—a hotel room or a dormitory, for instance—and still be without a place to dwell. What constitutes the dwelling place as a home is the center of life and meaning that it introduces into the world. It therefore has a significance similar to the significance of the Temple, and in this we have another connection with Jacob, the one who symbolizes a home. For when he set out from his homeland, Jacob had a dream in which he saw angels ascending and descending a ladder to heaven. Awaking from his dream, he realized that "this is none other than the house of God, and this is the gate of heaven" (Genesis 28:17). Rabbi Yaakov ben Z'ev Kranz, the eighteenth-century Maggid of Dubno, points out that "the place where Jacob found himself in his dream was the very site at which, hundreds of years later, the Holy Temple was erected" (20); hence its designation as the house of God. Like the home that is a dwelling place, the house of God is a center from which is derived the truth and the holiness of life; there is no home without this house, so that the destruction of the synagogues discussed in chapter 5 has direct connection to the destruction of the dwelling place that now concerns us.[3] Thus the notion of dwelling, in Jewish thought, is laden with metaphysical significance. When God tells Isaac, for instance, to "dwell [*shekhon*] in the land" (Genesis 26:2), the *Midrash Rabbah* interprets this to mean: "cause the *Shekhinah*"—the Indwelling Presence of God—"to dwell in the land" (2:574). And the *Shekhinah* dwells in the land wherever a home that sanctifies the Name of the Holy One, blessed be He, is to be found.

But in the time of the Churban (the Destruction)—when God, Torah, and Israel were under assault—this dwelling place was targeted for destruction. Just as the Nazis' protocol for the occupation of a town included the burning or desecration of the synagogue, so did it include the ransacking of Jewish homes. In the diary of Sarra Gleykh, for example, we read: "Everything in the house was scattered and broken. We decided not to clean up the mess. If any more were to come, they would see right away that there was nothing left to take" (71). In the Russian version of Sarra's diary, emphasis on the destruction of the dwelling place is much stronger; there everything is *razbrosano, raskidano, razbito* (88), "scattered all over, strewn everywhere, broken to pieces," with the repetition of the prefix *raz-* and its connotations of disintegration. When we observe that the *Amidah*, the daily prayer of the Jews, ends with a blessing on the peace or the *shalom* that comes only from God, we are reminded that the word for "peace" is a cognate of the word for "whole," *shalem*. Life takes on meaning and direction only where it becomes whole, hale, and holy, all of which belong to the wholeness of home and family; when a home or a family loses its significance, it is said to be "broken." In the Shoah, however, the fragmentation of home and family comes not from the inside but from the outside. As was noted in chapter 6, the terror outside finds its way to the inside, so that there is no inside and therefore no home, no place to be a human being, no place for the *Shekhinah* to dwell.

This proves to be the case even in homes that are not literally broken to bits by the Nazis; even there the darkness of the spiritual fragmentation on the outside finds its way to the inside, as we see when Adam Czerniakow writes, "At home loneliness and gloom" (89). The darkness and isolation Czerniakow describes are antithetical to the light that signifies the home and that emanates from the home into the world; like the bits of furniture and home fixtures, the light too has been broken. Just as the home and its light are broken, so are people broken away from their homes, as we see when Yitskhok Rudashevski writes: "I go around with bleary eyes among the bundles, see how we are being uprooted overnight from our home. Soon we have our first view of the move into the [Vilna] ghetto, a picture of the Middle Ages—a gray black mass of people goes harnessed to large bundles" (31). The image of darkness associated with the breaking up of and the breaking away from the home repeats itself. The people carry the broken pieces of their homes and of their lives with them, but these fragments cannot constitute a home. Left with only these fragments, these people are left outside the time and the season of the earth itself, as Helena Dorembus indicates in her diary from the Warsaw Ghetto: "On this bright blue spring day I feel like crying. But I have no place to vent my anguish" (59). This, of course, does not mean that the anguish is not vented; rather it is vented in a non-place, which is to say that the anguish vented is drained of meaning.

Here we realize that one function of the Holocaust diary is to create a place where this meaning, and with it some trace of a home, might be retrieved. Through the word, the diarist creates a space in which he may vent his anguish not only by weeping but by writing about the weeping. And so Avraham Tory cries out: "They shave off the beards of rabbis and yeshiva students; heads are bashed, arms are twisted. The sound of weeping issues from Jewish homes in Kovno. The destruction is complete. The Jews are overcome by despair. They wonder: What will happen next?" (9). The sound of weeping from Jewish homes is the sound of the destruction of those places as places of dwelling; dwelling is the opposite of despairing, as the despair within denotes an internal fragmentation that parallels the external fragmentation of the home. Again, this fragmentation is the fragmentation of an interior, so that in the home that is not a home, the Jews are led to seek an interior—not, however, where they can dwell, but where they can hide. "A new psychosis pervades the Ghetto," says Tory. "The inmates are building hiding places in their homes. . . . I also applied myself to this task, even though I do not believe it will save me in time of trouble. Calamities wear different disguises, and never fail to catch us off guard" (235). The people are caught off guard because they cannot know what to expect. Where humans being dwell, by contrast, they have some notion of what the next day might bring. With the destruction of the dwelling place, then, comes the destruction of the future and, therefore, the destruction of time.

Here the diary, at least for a moment, comes to the aid of the human being. Measuring the days of the time of destruction, it attempts to recover the time that belongs to the home, just as it struggles to recover the inner space of a home. Thus the longing for home dominates many of the pages of the Holocaust diaries. "I must draw upon all the strength I have," asserts Renata Laqueur, "in order to keep a hold on myself and not succumb to madness from the misery of my longing for home" (15). And: "I long for home, have a terrible longing for all that 'once was'" (29). In another diary from Bergen-Belsen, Hanna Levy-Hass writes, "There burns within us a glowing longing for home" (33). And in the diary she kept while wandering through Transnistria, the Romanian teenager Mirjam Korber wonders: "Will we ever go home again? This is the word we eternally repeat" (83). The madness tied to this longing, the heat with which it burns, and the question it continually raises all lie in the fear and the knowledge that for the Jews there is no home to return to. That is why each day, with resolve but without resolution, the diarist returns to the diary, for even if he happens to return home, as Dawid Rubinowicz returns for a moment from the Bodzentyn Ghetto to his home in Krajno, the home is no longer familiar to him, no longer welcomes him. "I went to our house," he relates. "When I went in, the dwelling seemed so strange, as if we'd never lived there" (65). In the Polish text of this diary, the word translated as "dwelling" (*mieszkania*), has the same root as the word translated as "lived" (*mieszkali*) (81), a verb that means "to dwell." Here too the implication is that the home is not merely a place to live but a place to establish a center of meaning for life. Whereas the entries in Tory's diary, moreover, point up the loss of a future, this entry indicates a loss of the past: it is as if the home has never been there. As we saw in chapter 3, where the past and the future are obliterated, so is the present and the capacity for establishing a presence in life. And that presence is established originally and primordially in the home.

We realize, then, that the imposed absence discussed in the last chapter is connected to the absence of the home. And the absence of the home, in turn, amounts to the absence of the family that dwells in the home. Michael Zylberberg makes this point in his diary when, during the summer of 1943, he hides in a Polish home that was once owned by Jews and that still bears the signs of the absent Jewish family. In this structure with the *mezuzah* still on the door, he notes, "a small statue of the Virgin Mary now stood on a small table between the two windows of the main room, while the table was covered with a small white cloth on which was embroidered in Hebrew, 'Remember The Sabbath Day to Keep It Holy!'" (108). The Hebrew words out of sync with the Christian statue coincide with the Jews forced out of the dwelling place; the alien symbol imposed upon the home signifies the alienation and absence of a people driven not only from their home, not only from their land, but from the face of the earth, from being itself. In a word, the Jews are excluded from the ontological sum of all that is. And, as always, the external manifestation is expressive of an internal condition, as we see in the diary of Josef Katz: "We march through the still-dark streets of Liepaja. Most of the houses in the Bahnhofstrasse have been destroyed. For the first time I see the ravages of war. A Czech Jew who walks beside me says the houses are like our lives: destroyed, and what's left is ruins" (82). What these entries from the diaries of Zylberberg and Katz reveal is perhaps obvious but nevertheless must be stated: the destruction of the dwelling place amounts to nothing less than the destruction of lives. A family once gathered around the table with the cloth embroidered in Hebrew letters to light Sabbath candles, say *Kiddush*, and break *challah*; a father once sang the *Eshet Chayil* to his wife and pronounced blessings upon his children. With the destruction of the dwelling place comes the murder of these relations, these prayers, and these blessings that sanctify life in the sanctification of the home. With the destruction of the dwelling place comes the obliteration of the family.

THE OBLITERATION OF THE FAMILY

In the diary he kept at Westerbork, the Dutch journalist Philip Mechanicus observes that, without exception, each of the camp's inmates "points out how his family has been torn asunder, how he has been robbed of his possessions and humiliated. All these are tragic variations of one and the same fate, but they always claim your attention" (71). The "same fate" referred to here is not just the fate of the family torn asunder; it is the fate of extermination that the Nazis imposed on the Jews and all they stand for. In order to murder not only the Jews but the sanctity of life and human relation that they signify, the family must be torn asunder in the process.

The Jewish teaching that all people stem from one person, from Adam, is an affirmation of the essence of humanity as a family. And why the tradition of a single ancestor who comes from the hand of God? So that no one may say to another, "My family is better than your family"; so that each may understand himself to be related to all and to the Creator of all (see, for example, Wiesel, *Messengers* 10). The Jews, then, understand the relation of human being to human being and of humanity to God in terms of a family relation; in the words of the fifteenth-century sage Rabbi Don Isaac Abrabanel, "The fatherhood of God inevitably leads to the brotherhood of man" (Chill 136). But, as we have seen, the Nazis set out to murder God in their murder of the Jews. With that murder they would annihilate the fatherhood of God and the brotherhood of man; they would murder not just families but the family as such. For, as Andreas-Friedrich suggests, where death invades the family, the brotherhood of humanity is slain: "Ten times over death strikes in a single family. Truly, with the Grim Reaper we have lost all brotherhood" (122). More precisely, however, what strikes these families is not the Grim Reaper, who comes to claim us all; it is the SS, who comes to murder the Jews and to obliterate the family. It is not the one who leads families to gather around a grave and recite the *Kaddish*, the prayer for the dead; it is the one who casts entire families into mass graves and snatches all prayer from their lips. "The death of entire families in the course of one or two days is a very common occurrence," says Emmanuel Ringelblum of "life" in the Warsaw Ghetto. "There has been an enormous increase in the number of orphans, since the grown-ups die first, particularly the men. [But] there are practically no children under two, simply because there's no milk at all, either for the infants or the nursing mothers" (206). And in the Vilna Ghetto, Herman Kruk writes: "The word [*Ponary*] is in the mouths of all. It 'sustains' many a home. Ponary means the mention of a father, a mother, a sister, a fiancée, and so on" (36). Of course, *Ponary* also means a mass grave.

At the beginning of this chapter we cited Salmen Gradowski's comparison of his new "home" at Auschwitz with a new grave. What constitutes this new home as a grave is not that so many people die there, since people die everywhere, both in the world and in the anti-world; rather the home is transformed into a grave by what Gradowski describes as "the first commandment of camp life": namely, "Abandon all care for your family" (102). And yet in the first pages of his diary Gradowski writes, "I dedicate it [this diary] to the memory of my family burnt alive at Birkenau" (77). Like many Holocaust diaries, the aim of this diary that recounts the obliteration of the family is to preserve the memory and the meaning of the family. Seeking not only to record the collapse of life but to recover a trace of it, the Holocaust diary invariably attests to the dearness of the family. If Gradowski tells us that the first commandment of camp life is to abandon all care for the family, he is reminding us of what must be cared for above all else; he is attesting to what is obliterated, without precedent, in the Shoah. As Gradowski understands it (and who would presume to understand it better?), this is the first commandment of Auschwitz because this is the first target of Auschwitz: the first thing to befall the Jews upon their arrival at the camp is not death but the breakup of their family. Hence on "planet Auschwitz," he says: "the only thing that one still feels is the pain of separation. If women and children are sent away separately and husbands are unable to keep them, then the hope which had sustained them all the way here was only a phantasy, an illusion" (95). Of course, in many cases the destruction of the family transpires before a family can reach the camp, in the dark and suffocating recesses of the sealed trains. Commenting on one such case, another member of the *Sonderkommando*, Salmen Lewental, writes, "The mother with five children perished [in transit], only the father left alive, who wept but without . . . tears" (131). Once again we see that to murder Israel and the God of Israel is to murder the family. Just as the Nazis would deprive the heavenly Father of His children and thereby make Him other than a Father, so they tore the human father from his family. The annihilation of the one demanded the obliteration of the other.

This tearing of a man from his family, however, was not confined to the sealed trains and the concentration camps; for these Jews, in all their homelessness, the whole of Europe was a concentration camp, a "concentrationary universe," as it has been called. Among the first things that Zylberberg reports in his *Warsaw Diary*, for example, is this: "I had said good-bye to my family; I would never see them again" (23). So begins Zylberberg's collapse of life and his diary's attempt to recover some trace of it. And so the testimony to the fragmentation of the family abounds throughout these diaries, regardless of the background or the upbringing of the diarists. Speaking of a group of people taken to the Lukishki Prison in the fall of 1941, for instance, Rudashevski is conscious not only of the violence done to these individuals but of the assault on their families: "The ghetto is full of lamentation. Sobbing, dejected people. One has a father, another a mother, a third a child. Families have been torn apart. One left to save his life, a second was carried off by force" (40). Rudashevski is careful to name each member of the family—father, mother, and child—as if to describe the live dissection of a single body; to be sure, the Baal Shem Tov, founder of Hasidism, taught that "each person of Israel is a member of the *Shekhinah*" (Dov Ber 59). Once more the wholeness or the *shalem* of the dwelling place comes to mind, reminding us that the wholeness of the home, like the holiness of a people, lies in the wholeness and holiness of the family. Therefore, hundreds of miles away and nearly a year after Rudashevski made his entry in his diary, Anne Frank is struck by the same horror: "Day and night more of those poor miserable people are being dragged off, with nothing but a rucksack and a little money. On the way they are deprived even of these possessions. Families are torn apart, the men, women, and children all being separated. Children coming home from school find that their parents have disappeared" (74). Can any of us imagine our own children in such a situation? Can we comprehend this emptiness imposed upon these children and the anguish forced upon their parents? Do we want to comprehend it? Do we dare?

One can be certain that this horror inflicted upon parents and their children was carefully calculated; it happened too often, too precisely, and too routinely, not to be. Dawid Rubinowicz points it out repeatedly. On 10 April 1942, for example, he says, "They've taken away a man and a woman from over the road, and two children are left behind" (55). A week later he notes a similar case: "They've taken away the parents from across the road, leaving two little children on their own. Next door they've again taken the husband away; if you look into the window you can see sadness there" (61). The Polish word here rendered as "sadness," *zaloba* (76), conveys more than sadness; it means "mourning," "grief," and "affliction," implying a sadness that follows in the wake of a certain violence or violation, and not just the mood or emotion of "feeling blue." Diarists who have to endure such a separation from their families are frequently preoccupied with those from whom they are separated, as if by writing about them in their diaries they might somehow move closer to them. "I think of nothing now but my mother and brother," writes Hannah Senesh, to take one example. "I am sometimes overwhelmed by dreadful fears. Will we ever meet again?" (126). And of her mother she says: "I've never longed for her the way I long for her now. I'm so overwhelmed with this need for her at times, and with the constant fear that I'll never see her again. I wonder, can I bear it?" (125). We shall explore some of the deeper implications of this desire for the mother in the next chapter. What is to be emphasized here is the interconnection between the longing for home that we saw earlier in this chapter and the longing for the family. The object of this desire is not a place or a thing or even a person; it is a living presence that reveals itself in the midst of the relation that constitutes the family. It is the presence symbolized by the father, which before the war Hannah was able to sense despite the death of her father. "I feel that even from beyond the grave," she affirms, "Daddy is helping us, if in no other way than with his name. I don't think he could have left us a greater legacy" (14). Once the war begins, however, and she is separated from her family, this sense of the presence of the father no longer appears in her diary—not because of the passage of time but because of the murder of parenthood and, with it, the significance of the father.

THE MURDER OF PARENTHOOD

According to the Talmud, "a man is commanded concerning the duty of propagation but not a woman" (*Yevamot* 65b); therefore at the heart of parenthood and at the head of home and family, as viewed by the Jewish tradition, is fatherhood, a relation that parallels the relation of God to His creation and His children.[4] While the mother of a household recites the blessing on the Sabbath candles and thus ushers in the Sabbath Bride, or the *Shekhinah* (which is Indwelling Presence of God in a feminine aspect), the father pronounces the blessing on the children and the family. Both, to be sure, are necessary to the existence and the wholeness of home and family, but in our examination of parenthood we shall focus on the father in the Holocaust diaries. Far from diminishing the importance of the mother or the female (chapter 9, it will be seen, is devoted to the assault on the feminine), the aim here is to draw a distinction that affirms the sanctity of both father and mother.

The Talmud teaches us that "for all [other] dead one rends only the uppermost [garment] even though he be wearing ten; but for one's father or mother one rends them all" (*Mo'ed Katan* 22b). The Holocaust diarists rend their very souls over their mothers and fathers; indeed, next to the children, who will be discussed in chapter 10, the ones with whom the diarists are most concerned are their parents. The Warsaw Ghetto diarist Hersh Wasser, for example, writes: "I am most uneasy about my parents in the Lodz Ghetto. No clothes, no money" (211). And in the diary he kept at Janowska, Leon Wells says: "I dream about my father and mother. They are crying because their last child is going to be killed by the same assassins that killed their other children" (148). Of course, it is not just the anguish of their parents that haunts these diarists; more often it is the death of their parents, and here we note that a distinguishing feature of the antiworld is that it is a world made up of orphans. Thus, in a diary he kept while hiding in a field in Galicia, Aryeh Klonicki-Klonymus writes, "It is no use dreaming that our parents might still be alive" (26). And for Sarra Gleykh, one of the few to emerge only wounded from a mass grave, the nightmare of the death of her parents became a stark reality: "Our turn arrived, and the horrible image of a senseless, a wildly senseless and meek death was before our eyes as we set off behind the barns. The bodies of Father and Mother were already there somewhere. By sending them by truck, I had shortened their lives by a few hours. We were herded toward the trenches which had been dug for the defense of the city. These trenches served no other function than as receptacles for the death of nine thousand Jews" (74). What Sarra describes here is the action taken by the Nazis upon their arrival in her town of Mariupol. In keeping with their standard procedure, the Nazis here first marked the parents of the town, the elderly, for death; mothers and fathers were the first to be loaded on trucks, and, says Sarra, "it was rumored that the trucks were taking the elderly out of town to be destroyed" (74). At times the death of elderly mothers was postponed, but, as we see from an entry in the Warsaw diary of Abraham Levin, the fathers and grandfathers were sent immediately to their deaths. "In Pabianice," he reports on 6 June 1942, "all men of 60 and over were shot" (316). Before proceeding, then, we should briefly consider the significance of the father in Jewish tradition and the implications of this assault on the fathers of the community.

Embodied in the father is the truth that provides a ground for life, the wisdom that underlies all thinking about life, and the order that constitutes the reality and substance of life. From an archetypal or symbolic standpoint, then, when the father's existence is rendered illegitimate, truth, thought, and reality lose their substance. From a Jewish perspective, these terms pertain to the truth of tradition, which Saadia Gaon, among others, deems an avenue of revelation (174); to the wisdom of the intellect, which thinkers such as Maimonides (*Guide* 74) and Gersonides (1:157) identify with God; and to the order of reality as it continually issues from the hand and the mouth of the Creator. All of this is lost in the murder of the father, so that the diarists' memory of this murder entails far more than a mournful reminiscence surrounding the head of a household or a community. The attack on the father is, in fact, an attack on the very memory that the diarists set out to recover. For, according to Jewish tradition, memory is associated with the father, who is responsible for remembering and handing down the tradition to his children. Regarding the *zachor veshamor* that pertain to the Sabbath, for example, the *Bahir* teaches us that "'remember' (*zachor*) refers to the male (*Zachar*). 'Keep' (*shamor*) refers to the bride" (70). The male is the bridegroom, the one who is to become a father in the observance of the first of all the commandments, to be fruitful and multiply (Genesis 1:28), that is, to become a parent and create a home where a family may dwell. And, insofar as the Holocaust diary invokes the memory of the father, it too amounts to an observance of that commandment, which the Nazis transformed into a crime.

Thus when diarists such as the sculptor Rivosh of Riga relate that "the street is strewn with the corpses of old men" (340), they offer much more than a report on casualties. When Ringelblum writes that "they put old folks in prison, even Jews over sixty" (64–65), he files much more than a report on arrests. And when Éva Heyman says, "Today they arrested my father," adding that "at night they came to him and put a seal on his door" (73), she implies that what is sealed off is much more than the entrance to a room. It is the center of home and family, the entrance to a life in the world, that is sealed off like a tomb. Just as Jewish souls were crushed before their bodies were destroyed, very often the image of the father was broken before he himself was taken away to death. We find an example of this breakdown of the paternal image when, after she and her family had been forced into the Varad Ghetto, Éva remarks: "I saw Grandpa cry for the first time in my life. From the gate arch you can see the garden, and the garden never looked so beautiful, even though no one had taken care of it for some days now. I will never forget how Grandpa stood there looking at the garden, shaking from his crying" (85–86). If her grandfather is broken, this father of the family, what becomes of the ground that the child Éva stands on? With the collapse of this center of her home and family, all of life, an entire world, collapses; Éva herself loses all sense of herself, so that in turning to her diary, she struggles to retrieve the pieces of what is broken in the convulsions of her grandfather.

In the diary of Dawid Rubinowicz the concern for the father is especially pronounced. From a hovel in the Bodzentyn Ghetto this teenager fears two things above all, each of which may result in the disappearance and death of his father: that his father will obtain a work permit and that his father will not obtain a work permit. On 17 March 1942 he writes: "All sorts of thoughts are going round and round inside my head—whether Father's pass will be signed, how on earth will he come if the pass isn't signed? Often utterly senseless thoughts force themselves upon me. I kept a look-out the whole day to see if Father was coming" (50–51). This waiting for the coming of the father is a waiting for the appearance of some light that may penetrate into the darkness of the ghetto and, at least for a time, bring to the ghetto the semblance of a home and family. His father receives a signed work permit, but this only results in his being taken away on a truck to work at Skarzysko. "The lorry was already at the other market-place," writes Dawid. "I burst out crying, and as they came up I cried out: 'Papa!—Papa, where are you? If only I could see you once more,' . . . and then I saw him on the last lorry; his eyes were red with weeping. I kept on looking at him until he disappeared round the corner, then I had a sudden fit of crying" (69–70). As when Éva Heyman saw her grandfather break down, the image of the father here crumbles before the father disappears. We see the implication of a link between the father and God the Father, moreover, when, during his father's absence, Dawid says: "While praying I felt a deep yearning for Father. I saw other children standing with their fathers, and the parts of their prayers that they didn't know were told them by their fathers, and who is there to tell me? . . . only God alone. God give me good thoughts and lead me in the right way. Never before have I felt my prayers to be such a burden to me as today" (82). In these lines we discover a definitive tie between the assault on the father and the assault on God and Torah, on Israel and the soul of Israel—on prayer.

Elie Wiesel describes prayer as "the substance of language and the language of silence" (*Paroles* 172). It is the father who imparts to his children this substance of life that inheres in the link between word and meaning; he is the bearer not only of the word but of this link.

The father, then, does more than hold his child's hand; he leads his child by the hand, showing him the path to the truth and meaning that sanctify the child's life and make it matter. There can be no home and family where children have no fathers to teach them the prayers. That is what is murdered in the murder of parenthood: not only a people but the higher relation that imparts substance and significance to any people. Therefore Dawid begins the last entry of his diary with the words "a happy day" (85), which in English is a rather weaker expression than the Polish *dzien radosci* (106), meaning "a day of joy" or "a day of exultation." For on that day his father returned from Skarzysko after an absence of four weeks. Approximately three months later, however, he and his father and the rest of his family would perish in Suchediow. One wonders whether it might have been a scene like the one Katz describes: "An SS man comes to tear the child's hand from that of his father, which he is clutching fearfully. But the father is a hero. Tall and strong, with the boy holding his hand, he walks through the rows to stand with his son and the other children" (181). As in the last chapter, where we saw that meaning is ultimately retrievable only through sacrifice, the father remains a father in the midst of this murder of parenthood only by offering himself up—if not for his son, then with his son.

In the *Bahir* we are taught that "the covenant of circumcision and man's mate are considered as one" (30). If the father who bears the sign of the Covenant lies at the foundation of home and family, he assumes this position by virtue of a relation to a wife and mother; if he is a link to the heavenly Father who is the divine Lawgiver, it is because he is tied to a mother who has her own ties to the Supernal Mother. Therefore, where faith and family are debased, as Janusz Korczak indicates in his diary, so is motherhood (185). The fragmentation of home and family that begins with the murder of the father and fatherhood quickly carries over to an assault on the mother and motherhood. "The beginning of November '41," says Ringelblum, for instance, "news from Lodz that the Lodz Jews had been prohibited from marrying and having children. Women pregnant up to three months have to have an abortion" (230). Hence the Nazis take their murder to the very seed of life. As there is no home without marriage, there is no family without childbearing. From the standpoint of Jewish life and thought, this prohibition against marriage and childbearing has even deeper ramifications. To be sure, the eighteenth-century sage Rabbi Yaakov Culi reminds us that marriage "is the foundation of Judaism" (123–24). For in the words of the sixteenth-century teacher Rabbi Moshe Cordovero: "As long as a man has not married, the *Shekhinah* is not with him, since she relates to man mainly via the female aspect. For man stands between two female aspects—his wife below in the physical world, who receives 'sustenance, clothing, and conjugal rights' from him; and the *Shekhinah* above him, who blesses him with all these so that he will give them again and again to the wife he has chosen in the covenant of marriage" (128). Thus the Nazis take their assault on the family to an assault on the feminine, on the very womb of life; it is an assault on the *Shekhinah*.

THE ASSAULT ON THE FEMININE

COMMENTING ON THE BRAVERY OF TWO YOUNG JEWISH women known as Chajke and Frumke, Emmanuel Ringelblum declares, "They are a theme that calls for the pen of a great writer" (273), and he adds, "The story of the Jewish women will be a glorious page in the history of Jewry during the present war" (274). Ringelblum here refers mainly to work of courageous women in the underground who served as couriers, messengers, and spies throughout Poland. Their significance and their glory, however, lie not only in the history they made and the deeds they performed; they also represent the mystery of the origin and the meaning, of the embrace and the compassion, that the Nazis set out to destroy. In this larger context, their glory reveals the glory of the Infinite One Himself.

In the Jewish tradition, the glory of the Holy One lies in His oneness. As it is said in the opening line of the *Shema*, "Hear, O Israel, the Lord our God, the Lord is One." This oneness, moreover, is manifested, among other ways, through the relationship between men and women. "The relationship between men and women," writes Rabbi Adin Steinsaltz, "has the character of a quest for something lost, to use the Talmudic expression. Male and female are essentially parts of a single whole, originally created as one being; but for various reasons—principally the establishment of a different, more complex and perhaps deeper kind of connection between the two—the whole body is divided. The two half bodies are constantly in search of one another and find no fulfillment until they are rejoined, in a new and different unity" (*Biblical* 5). The attack on the God of Israel entails an attack on this unity, and it cannot be carried out without an attack on the women of Israel; the Nazis' affliction of the body of Israel demands the affliction of the mothers and daughters of Israel. The assault on the feminine, therefore, is a definitive aspect of the singularity of the Holocaust. And the testimony to that assault is an important part of the Holocaust diary. But before we examine the diaries themselves, let us consider the significance of the feminine in Jewish life.

THE SIGNIFICANCE OF THE FEMININE IN JEWISH LIFE

In *Ethics and Infinity*, the profound twentieth-century Jewish thinker Emmanuel Levinas states quite simply that "the feminine is described as the *of itself other*, as the origin of the very concept of alterity" (66). Thus understood, the feminine comes to bear not only in the relation between man and woman but in any relation between one human being and another. As the origin of alterity, the feminine makes possible the establishment of a difference from which all issues of meaning and morality, of human understanding and human sanctity, might be derived. For in the midst of this difference, one person comes to *signify* the dearness of another and thereby takes on a significance of his or her own. The feminine lies at the center of the meaningful and the moral, of the intelligible and the sacred, because the feminine represents not only an immemorial past but also an open-ended future and, therefore, the mystery of what is forever yet to be born, yet to be revealed, and yet to be consummated.[1] The alterity represented by the feminine, then, is not an otherness already contained in being; it is the otherness of what is *better* than being, so that what is *there* is not all there is; so that something better is yet to be, something *meaningful*.

Thus, meaning belongs to the future designated by the feminine; meaning is never *my* meaning but rather inheres in the alterity of someone or something other than myself. To have meaning is to have a direction, and to have a direction is to approach a realm where we have yet to arrive: meaning is what is yet to be realized. Similarly, the *ought* that underlies morality and the commandments of the Holy One is tied to a *yet* that underlies the future: morality announces what is yet to be done. The sanctity of the human being which makes morality a matter of urgency is what is forever sought but never touched in every caress that is a caress. And it is embodied in the feminine. "The caress," says Levinas, "consists in seizing upon nothing, in soliciting what ceaselessly escapes its form toward a future never future enough, in soliciting what slips away as though *it were not yet*. It *searches*" (*Totality* 257–58). This searching after the sanctification of what is forever yet to be sanctified is what the Nazis targeted for annihilation in their assault not only on women but on womanhood. Such an assault on womanhood, of course, bears implications for all of human being. With its emphasis on racism, materialism, and power, National Socialism exemplifies the "natural life" that is void of human relation, ethical concern, and meaningful living.[2]

What the feminine signifies, by contrast, in the Jewish tradition can be seen in the tale of the creation of the first woman. Here Levinas comments by saying: "Woman does not simply come to someone deprived of companionship to keep him company. She answers to a solitude inside this privation and—which is stranger—to a solitude that subsists in spite of the presence of God; to a solitude in the universal, to the inhuman which continues to well up even when the human has mastered nature and raised it to thought" (*Difficult* 33). The feminine lies at the core of the human; woman is not just the other but opens up the very otherness of the interrelation that defines humanity, as well as the mystery of divinity, as a giving, over against a conquering. Forever sought and eternally future, the feminine is otherwise than being, which, again, opens up what is better than being. In philosophical terms, then, the Nazi agenda is an instance of ontology transformed into totality; instead of regarding the feminine as something more than what is there, the Nazis situate the feminine in the midst of what is merely there. Woman, and with her the mystery of humanity and divinity, becomes one more item to be conquered, possessed, and crushed.

In the Jewish tradition, which itself was targeted for annihilation, the feminine is represented by the *Shekhinah*. The thirteenth-century mystic Rabbi Joseph Gikatilla, for instance, asserts that the *Shekhinah* "in the time of Abraham our father is called Sarah and in the time of Isaac our father is called Rebecca and in the time of Jacob our father is called Rachel" (204). Therefore, says the *Zohar*, "when a man is at home, the foundation of his house is the wife, for it is on account of her that the *Shekhinah* departs not from the house" (1:159)—or from the world. Because the *Shekhinah* accompanies Israel into exile, the Jews are able to endure life without succumbing to the alienation of exile. What is the sign of this accompaniment? It is the Torah itself, which the Jews bear with them in their wanderings. According to an ancient teaching, the Torah had to be accepted first by the women before it could be received by the men (see, for example, Rashi 2:97); for the House of Jacob mentioned in Exodus 19:3 precedes the reference to the House of Israel, and the House of Jacob refers to the women among the Hebrews. It is through the feminine, the mystery of value and meaning, that we have the Torah.[3] Hence we see that the Nazis' assault on the Torah, discussed in chapter 5, includes an assault on the feminine.

Arguing that the Holocaust is distinguished by an ontological and metaphysical assault exemplified in the assault on the Torah, I noted in chapter 5 the Jewish teaching that the Torah is the basis and the model for creation itself (recall, for example, *Zohar* 1:21). Here we realize why such a tradition includes the idea that the feminine underlies creation itself. To be sure, there are many Jewish texts that attest to this view. The *Zohar* expresses it rather cryptically, saying, "First came *Ehyeh* (I shall be), the dark womb of all. Then *Asher Ehyeh* (That I am), indicating the readiness of the Mother to beget all" (5:57). Bearing in mind the association between the feminine and the House of Jacob, we note that this principle is stated in the *Midrash Rabbah*, in the commentary on Leviticus: "The Holy One, blessed be He, said to His world: 'O My world, My world! Shall I tell thee who created thee, who formed thee? Jacob has created thee, Jacob has formed thee'" (4:460).[4] An insight from Levinas comes to mind in this connection. "*Rakhamim* (Mercy)," he points out, "goes back to the word *Rekhem*, which means 'uterus.' *Rakhamim* is the relation of the uterus to the *other*, whose gestation takes place within it. *Rakhamim* is maternity itself. God as merciful is God defined by maternity. A feminine element is stirred up in the depth of this mercy" (*Nine* 183). From the depths of this mercy, human life itself begins to stir. And that stirring is the movement of the Feminine Essence, as the mystics refer to it. Here we begin to establish a more solid connection between the feminine and the Torah, between the feminine and the Creation, and to see more clearly the implications of the Nazis' assault on the mothers of Israel.[5] The mother links us to the Creator, to the absolutely Other revealed in the absolute non-indifference of love, or *chesed*, which, as Gikatilla notes, is at the root of creation (276). Therefore the mother is at the center of the home, distinguished as it is by love, which in turn signifies the site and the center of creation: it is through the home and the family, which originates in motherhood, that life is born into the world, that the Torah is preserved in the world, and that the world itself is sustained.

Recalling that the first letter of the Torah in its account of the Creation is *beit*, we also recall that *beit* is the Hebrew word for "house."[6] Since, according to the Talmud, "blessing is only found in a man's house on account of his wife" (*Bava Metzia* 59a), the sanctity of the home is linked to the wife and mother of the house. Hence the women, the wives and mothers, of Israel are known as the *House* of Jacob. If the Torah is the foundation of the Creation, the mother, through her association with the *beit* in which the Torah originates, is the foundation of the Torah itself; she is the origin of the origin, the very *heart* of being. In this regard the sixteenth-century mystic Yitzhak Luria once asked, "If Binah or Understanding, which is associated with the Mother, is a mental process, why is it said to be in the heart, and not in the head?" To which Aryeh Kaplan replies, "The heart is actually the Personification of Imma-Mother, which is Binah-Understanding, where She reveals herself" (*Bahir* 127–28; see also Idel 2). If we may be allowed a moment of midrash, we observe that the *lamed* and *beit* which end and begin the Torah form the word *lev*, meaning "heart": it is upon the heart that the Teaching is to be inscribed (Deuteronomy 6:6), for the heart is the receptacle of the Torah. Thus the mother whom the *beit* situates at the beginning of the Torah signifies the sum of the Torah in her personification as the *lev* or the heart of all things.

Taken together, all of these texts from the tradition are laden with ramifications for how we may understand the assault on the feminine in the Holocaust as it is chronicled in the Holocaust diary. Because the feminine is so closely associated with creation itself, we shall first consider the assault on the mothers of Israel.

THE ASSAULT ON THE MOTHERS OF ISRAEL

By now we have at least glimpsed the intricate interconnections linking the mother, Torah, and creation in Jewish tradition. We sense the complexity of all that underlies the seemingly simply midrashic assertion that the greatness of Israel may be compared to "a woman bearing child" (*Midrash Rabbah* 10:327). And we realize the gravity of Emil Fackenheim's insight into the Holocaust, when he asserts: "The conjunction of birth and crime is a *novum* in history. . . . *She'erit ha-pleta*, not a holy but accidental 'remnant of the destruction'—this is how the survivors have described themselves all along. All along, too, they have referred to those who did not survive as *k'doshim*—'holy ones.' The very concept of holiness, is the implication, must be altered in response to the conjunction, unprecedented in the annals of history, of 'birth' and 'crime'" (*Jewish Bible* 87). That the association between pregnancy and crime alters the concept of holiness is made clear by the traditional association between the mother and the Holy One, who is *Ehyeh Asher Ehyeh*, the "dark womb" of the Mother ready "to beget all." Establishing this conjunction and thereby making pregnancy a criminal *condition*, and not just a criminal act, the Nazis demonstrate the totality characterizing the ontological scope of their assault on humanity as it unfolds in their assault on the mother. And the Holocaust diarists thoroughly attest to this assault.

On 5 February 1942 Vilna Ghetto diarist Herman Kruk, for example, wrote: "Today the Gestapo summoned two members of the Judenrat and notified them: No more Jewish children are to be born. The order came from Berlin" (20). What was to become of the Jewish mothers—who simply by *being* mothers violated Nazi "law" and the Nazi order—we discover in an entry from the Westerbork diary of Philip Mechanicus dated 21 July 1943: "All transports are terrible. It is heart-rending [yes, *heart*-rending!] again and again, to see mothers and fathers, or mothers alone with their offspring, a yellow card on their chests, or bent elderly folk laden with their last meager possessions, setting out on the journey callously ordained by a hater of mankind. But there is a crescendo in the feeling of horror—this time pregnant women in their seventh or eighth month and week-old infants with scarlet fever were taken" (97). What places this feeling of horror in a category of its own is the metaphysical significance of the mother outlined above. What breaks here is not just the heart of the diarist but the heart of human being. For what becomes of the condition of the mother we realize from the entry that Mechanicus recorded a month later: "Mothers wheel their babies through the camp in deep prams to let them have some sunshine. They murmur soft words of endearment, but their hearts are heavy and they are thinking of the husband who is not there, of the older children who are not there, of the brother and sister who are not there and about whom nothing is known. The mothers laugh to their babies who just will not grow or thrive. . . . They suckle their children, not with the joy of the mother whose child is going on to a secure future, but with a feeling of anxiety and sorrow" (132). Without the secure future of the child, the essence of the mother is broken. These images offer decisive evidence for the claim that the Nazis' assault was targeted not only against mothers but against mother*hood*. The very joy of the mother—which is not merely one feeling among a variety of feelings but is an essentially spiritual condition of the human being—is annihilated, underscoring once again the ontological nature of the assault on the mothers of Israel.

Which is an assault on the substance and foundation of humanity. In *Art and Answerability*, Mikhail Bakhtin points out that a "child receives all initial determinations of himself and of his body from his mother's lips and from the lips of those who are close to him. It is from their lips, in the emotional-volitional tones of love, that the child hears and begins to acknowledge his own *proper name*. . . . The words of a loving human being are the first and most authoritative words about him; they are the words that for the first time determine his personality *from outside*, the words that *come to meet* his indistinct sensation of himself, giving it a form and a name in which, for the first time, he finds himself and becomes aware of himself as a *something*" (49–50). Thus we recall the "soft words of endearment" uttered by the mothers of Westerbork; but we also recall the sorrow and anxiety that pervade them and that undermine the child's awareness of himself as a *something*—that is what is annihilated in the annihilation of the mother. Nothing proper remains of the proper names that tremble on their lips. These words, which are the first words that call forth the first traces of a world, are muted into the sterile silence of what is merely there. Like the prohibition against birth, then, the Nazis' infamous project of sterilization is designed to sterilize the first words of the mother, the words that make the woman into a mother and the world into a world, and not just a wasteland.

To cite another example, in his diary from the Kovno Ghetto, on 24 July 1942, Avraham Tory notes: "From September on, giving birth is strictly forbidden. Pregnant women will be put to death" (114). And when a pregnant woman is put to death, more than a pregnant woman is murdered, physically and metaphysically, as we see when on 4 February 1943 Tory laments: "It was terrible to watch the women getting on the truck; they held in their arms babies of different ages and wrapped them in more and more sweaters so that they would not catch cold on the way" (195). Exceeding the horror of slaughtering pregnant mothers, it seems that the Nazis waited until many of these mothers held their babies in their arms before murdering them and their infants with them. What are these mothers to say that would declare to their little ones that they are a *something*, as they wrap them in another sweater to keep them from catching cold on their way to the cold and darkness of a mass grave? We do not know what to reply to such a question. The diarists did not know what to reply; all commentary is here transformed into a crescendo of horror. For the word that would determine that the human being is a *something* is murdered with the murder of these mothers. Therefore the horror that overcomes Philip Mechanicus and Avraham Tory oozes from the words of Yitzhak Katznelson when he cries out: "These Jewish mothers with babes in their wombs! This murderous German nation! That was their chief joy! To destroy women with child!" (109). It was their chief joy because it was an expression of their primary aim; it was the joy of those who bask in the satisfaction of a job well done.

Since a mother is a mother by virtue of a certain relation to her child, the assault on the mothers of Israel included an assault on that very relationship, an assault not just on the body but on the being of the mother. Josef Katz records an incident related to him by a woman from the ghetto of Liepaja. "When the SS surrounded the ghetto," she told him, "I thought our last hour had struck. I took my little children and dressed them in their woolen socks and their best little dresses. I thought my children should be nice and warm when they go to their deaths" (103). Nice and warm: one might suppose that this is an example of the invincibility of a mother's care for her children, but it cannot be understood in such a manner, since a mother's care is a caring for life. In the world of humanity a mother dresses her children "nice and warm" for a cold winter's day, not for their last day. Here, then, not just the mother but the loving relation that makes her a mother is twisted out of the world and turned over to the antiworld. Other examples make this perversion even more evident. In her diary from the Warsaw Ghetto, for instance, Mary Berg writes: "Sometimes a mother cuddles a child frozen to death, and tries to warm the inanimate little body. Sometimes a child huddles against his mother, thinking that she is asleep and trying to awaken her, while, in fact, she is dead" (115). Thus the assault on the relation that constitutes the mother as mother entails not only dealing out death but displacing life with death; it entails a *confusion* of life and death, so that where there should be life, there is only death. The result is that death itself is no longer recognized—another sign distinguishing the event we call the Holocaust.

It is no coincidence that the confusion of life and death is imposed upon Jewish life by men wearing the insignia of the death's head. This point is illustrated quite clearly in an entry from Ringelblum's diary dated 28 February 1941. It concerns an SS guard who threw a three-year-old off a truck and into the snow on the way to the Warsaw Ghetto. The little boy's mother, says Ringelblum, "jumped off the wagon and tried to save the child. The guard threatened her with a revolver. The mother insisted life was worthless for her without her child. Then the guard threatened to shoot all the Jews in the wagon. The mother arrived in Warsaw, and she went out of her mind" (131). Whereas in the world of humanity being a mother and saving a child would be a means of sustaining the life of the community, in the antiworld it becomes a threat to the community, so that, once again, we have a deadly confusion between life and death. Indeed, there is no place for a mother in the antiworld, for the construction of the antiworld, of the Holocaust Kingdom, is predicated upon the obliteration of the mother and motherhood. No longer a mother, the n—who abandoned her child for the sake of a community that was no longer a community—was no longer who she was. And so she went mad.

Other, more heinous instances of the assault on the mothers of Israel and their relation to their children involve the murder of the mother *before* she is murdered, by making her into something monstrous that "lives" not for her children but at the expense of her children. One seemingly innocuous case is found in Ringelblum's diary, where he notes, "One mother hid her dead child so as to be able to enjoy his ration card as long as possible" (205). But we see where the terrible logic of such an action leads when we turn to the Warsaw Ghetto diary of Adam Czerniakow and read, "Nossig told me about a Jewish mother who abandoned two children on the street, disclaiming to the crowd that they were hers, although they kept on crying, 'Mummy!'" (228). The mother who fails to respond to this cry is a mother who no longer pronounces in loving tones the proper names, who no longer answers even to her own name: she is no longer a mother, which is just the condition that the Nazis set out to establish. Reading further in Czerniakow's diary, we note that on 20 February 1942 he writes: "At this very moment (11:33) Colonel Szerynski, the chief of the Order Service, has reported a case of cannibalism in the Jewish Quarter. Mother-child" (328). While it would add to the assault on the mother if we were to disregard her responsibility for such an act, disregarding the Nazis' role in this act would amount to ignoring the assault.

Of course, many diarists who address the assault on the mothers of Israel are mindful of their own mothers. Leon Wells, for example, relates a moment in the Janowska camp when he and a friend fell silent in the presence of one another. "Neither of us," he writes, "has the courage to interrupt our silence now or the other's thoughts. Perhaps he is thinking of his parents or family. . . . Mother . . . Mother, you who sold your gold teeth to buy food to send packages to the concentration camp so that your son might not hunger" (147). Neither interrupts the silence of the other because neither wants to break this moment of memory that maintains some tenuous connection to life's origin and therefore to life itself in the midst of the Kingdom of Death, where death is the death of just this connection.[7] Therefore, in his diary from Riga, the sculptor Rivosh laments, "My beloved, poor

Mama, forgive me for being powerless to protect you in your old age" (336). Powerless to protect the source of his life, the man is powerless to live. More than that, he is powerless to bear life into the world, and here too we see the implications of sterilization, for to live is to create life and thus renew the source of life.

As deeply as this renewal is symbolized by the mothers of Israel, it is perhaps even more deeply signified by Israel's daughters.

THE ASSAULT ON THE DAUGHTERS OF ISRAEL

"To me," said the talmudic sage Rabbi Chisda, "daughters are dearer than sons" (*Bava Batra* 141a). And so, just as Rivosh lamented his powerlessness to protect his mother, the Romanian writer Emil Dorian bemoaned his inability to comfort his daughter, saying, "her suffering shatters me" (42). The suffering of Dorian's little girl lies not just in the experience of physical pain but in the collapse of everything that would sanctify life, so that her life becomes abhorrent to her. And even if she could be protected from physical suffering, she cannot be protected from the longing to end her life rather than endure life. Hence her father's life becomes unendurable. Once again we find that a peculiar feature of the horror distinguishing the Holocaust lies not only in bringing death to a people but in the imposition of death on life by displacing the will to live with a yearning to die. We see one instance of this displacement in Katz's account of a conversation he had with a girl in Liepaja. "We dream of things which will never come true," he says. "Suddenly I see a shooting star. 'Make a wish, Marcia, quick!' I call out. 'I'm wishing for freedom. What about you?' 'I wish to die a natural death,' Marcia replies, 'because there will be no more freedom for us.' I am appalled. I was not prepared for such an answer" (95). As soon as Marcia makes this wish, the Nazis' wish comes true. Bent on killing Jewish souls before they kill Jewish bodies, they accomplish this goal by killing the desire to live and to bear life. Thus, even as the mothers of Israel are under assault, the daughters of Israel are assailed before they can become mothers—before they might even have the wish to become mothers. The freedom that Marcia refers to, then, is not just the physical freedom of movement but the metaphysical freedom of maternity.

The project of annihilating the womanhood that might become motherhood, which is a primary aim of the architects of the Holocaust, was often accomplished by first demonstrating to a little girl the fate of other little girls, and then engendering in her an identification with that fate. Two passages from the diary of Anne Frank illustrate this point. "Yesterday evening," she writes on 27 November 1943, "before I fell asleep, who should suddenly appear before my eyes but Lies! I saw her in front of me, clothed in rags, her face thin and worn. Her eyes were very big and she looked so sadly and reproachfully at me that I could read in her eyes: 'Oh, Anne, why have you deserted me? Help, oh, help me, rescue me from this hell!' And I cannot help her, I can only look on, how others suffer and die, and can only pray to God to send her back to us" (131). This prayer—that Lies might be sent back to her—is Anne's prayer that she might recover some part of herself. For a month later, on 29 December, she says, "Lies, I see in you all the time what my lot might have been, I keep seeing myself in your place" (139). But her place is a nonplace, a realm in which there is no place for the feminine. The Nazis, of course, saw to it that Anne's vision would come to pass. But before it came to pass, the little girl's status as little girl, the daughter's condition as daughter, was destroyed, even before she was torn from the arms of her parents.

We find a similar situation in the diary of another teenage girl, Éva Heyman of Nagyvarad, who, like Anne, was murdered by the Nazis. Jealous of her friend Aniko, who has the luxury of living with her own parents, Éva already suffers a separation from her mother and father that threatens her condition as a daughter. "In order to be able to give Agi [her mother] a kiss," she writes, "I usually have to travel quite a long way [to Budapest], and in order to kiss my father I have to walk two blocks on the main street without being sure that I'll even find him at home" (34). Although in this respect her case is not like Anne's, since Anne went into hiding with both of her parents, in another respect there is an important similarity. For, like Anne, Éva has a friend who has been taken by the Nazis and who constantly haunts her thoughts. "Dear diary," we read in her entry of 26 March 1944, "until now I didn't want to write about this in you because I tried to put it out of my mind, but ever since the Germans are here, all I think about is Marta. She was also just a little girl, and still the

Germans killed her. But I don't want them to kill me!" (63). And in an entry dated 19 April 1944 we see where her terrible fear takes her; we see that it tears her from her very soul as a daughter of Israel. "Even though," she says, "it would be very bad not to see Agi and all the rest for such a long time, I would go with Aunt Jakobi, or with Sanyi, to any place in the world where they don't know that I'm Jewish and wherefrom I couldn't be taken to Poland like Marta was" (80). Identifying with the fate of another little girl, this child is led not to a longing for death but—what is perhaps worse—to a longing for the death of who she is, a daughter of Israel. And that is just what the Nazis would achieve: to foster in the child a longing to be neither a daughter nor of Israel.

The opposition to the Nazis, then, would be an opposition to such a longing. Hence we find an important injunction at the end of an entry from David Kahane's diary of the Lvov Ghetto. Speaking of his own daughter and her forced separation from her grandparents, he writes: "The three-year-old granddaughter stood by, her face serious as if she already knew, as if she had understood the gravity of the moment. In a few months' time you shall part, little girl, from your parents on account of bad people. You will be among strangers, who live according to strange customs. You shall be called by a foreign name. Look well, my little girl, let this sight be etched deeply in your memory. Do not forget that you are a daughter of Israel, the daughter of a holy people" (32). The sight that this little one was enjoined not to forget was the deportation of her father's mother and father to Belzec, which is an assault on the holiness that constitutes her as a daughter of Israel. Kahane stands at the center of this scene, in which he witnesses a terrible assault on his mother and daughter, who embody the feminine essence of Jewish life. Just as the life of Israel, embodied in the Torah, begins with the House of Jacob, so does the death of Israel begin with the assault on the House of Jacob. With the assault on the daughters of Israel, who represent the first appearance of the Jewish woman, comes the assault on the women of Israel.

And the Holocaust diarists make special note of this assault. In the diary he kept while working in the *Sonderkommando* of Auschwitz, for example, Leib Langfus comments on the sight of three thousand women standing naked at the gas chambers. "All looked grave and fell silent," he says. "Then they began to recite *Vidduy*, their voices faltering, confessing the sins committed in the past. All feelings were obliterated, all were as if transfixed by one thought, by which they were, so to say, rooted to the ground and electrified: self-examination before death" (115–16). Even as they stood along the edge of annihilation, those who first received the Torah at Sinai stood before the One who gave them the Torah. Because they were the first to receive the Torah, they were among the first marked to be plunged over the edge of annihilation, along with all of Israel. Josef Katz comes to this realization when he says: "The treatment of our women makes me realize how completely hopeless our situation is. It is so dehumanizing and cruel to beat these young girls who later huddle together, sobbing, not knowing what to do" (163). Éva Heyman makes a similar observation on the treatment of women, saying, "Whoever hasn't seen how they beat the women at the fence hasn't the slightest idea of what Fascism is" (43). Hersh Wasser, a member of Ringelblum's *Oneg Shabbat* circle, compresses his commentary on the assault against daughters of Israel into a remark about a single Jewish girl: she "was shot because she was pretty, and 'Jews must not have pretty girls'" (280). And, similar to Wasser, Dawid Rubinowicz writes: "I can scarcely believe it, but everything's possible. A girl as pretty as a picture—if *she* could be shot, then the end of the world will soon be here" (56). We immediately notice that the understanding of the perimeters of the possible is determined by some sense of what the feminine represents. Why does the assault on the feminine represent the transcendence of possibilities for death? Because the feminine is precisely the possibility of life. Why is the murder of the daughters of Israel a sign of the end of the world? Because, as the wives and mothers of Israel, they are the very ones who sustain the world.

Thus, in the midst of his terrible distress, Adam Czerniakow is especially distressed when "a mistreated woman pleads for intercession"; for, as he says, "there is nothing I can do" (102). In another entry we read: "Mrs. Tempel, all tears, screams, and recriminations, said that I failed to do anything to help her husband and that he was sent away at 6:00 a.m. today. To calm her down I drove to the Gestapo with her and did my best to intervene" (163). But, of course, to no avail. What these entries from Czerniakow's diary tell us is that the assault on the women of Israel also assails the men of Israel. If blessing comes to the men of Israel because of their mothers, wives, and daughters, then the men of Israel must protect and provide for the women of Israel. When they are robbed of that capacity, then blessing and the life it confers on humanity are removed from Israel, and all are turned over to death. For this protection of and provision for the women of Israel is what makes the renewal of life possible for both men and women: it is what makes it possible to bear children into the world.

Therefore the fate of women is often tied to the fate of children. "Women and children wander aimlessly," notes Eliezer Yerushalmi, for example, in his diary from the Siauliai Ghetto. "There is no way to measure the despair of all these women" (277). Their despair, which is Yerushalmi's despair as well, is without measure because the life of the children whom they would bear is without a future and thus without meaning or direction. Hence they wander aimlessly, these daughters of Israel who are condemned never to become mothers of Israel. And so a passage from an ancient text is ridden with the ramifications of a horror that exceeds anything that the ancients might have conceived: "A cry went up in Ramah, lamenting and bitter weeping: it is Rachel weeping for her children and refusing to be comforted. For they are no more" (Jeremiah 31:15). The Holocaust diarists, too, refuse to be comforted. And they refuse to forget the children of Rachel. If the mothers and daughters of Israel make it possible for all to receive the Torah, the children of Sarah, Rebecca, Rachel, and Leah make it possible to keep the Torah. For in the *Midrash Tanchuma* it is written: "In the hour when the Holy One, blessed be He, was to offer the Torah to Israel, He said, 'Preserve My Torah.' They told Him, 'We shall.' He said to them, 'Give Me a guarantee that you will keep it.' They said to Him, 'Abraham, Isaac, and Jacob will be our guarantee.' He told them, 'Your fathers themselves need a guarantee. . . . They told Him, 'Our children will be our guarantee'" (1:170–71). And, the *Midrash on Psalms* adds, God "asked the sucklings and the embryos: 'Will you be sureties for your fathers, so that if I give them the Torah they will live by it, but that if they do not, you will be forfeited because of them?" They replied: 'Yes'" (1:125). And so we proceed from the assault on the feminine to the suffocation of the child, to which the authors of the Holocaust diary bear witness.

THE SUFFOCATION OF THE CHILD

ON 5 MAY 1942 ADAM CZERNIAKOW TOOK CARE TO NOTE: "Today [is the] Jewish children's holiday: *Lag B'Omer*" (350). *Lag B'Omer* is the thirty-third day in the counting of the omer, which numbers each day of the seven weeks from the second night of Passover to the giving of the Torah on the Sixth of Sivan, the holy day known as Shavuot. Why is the thirty-third day of the omer the Jewish children's holy day? Perhaps because it is eighteen days away from the giving of the Torah at Sinai, with the number eighteen signifying *chai*, or life. When the Torah was given at Sinai, life was given to the world, for in the Jewish tradition the Torah is life itself; and, as we recall from the last chapter, our children are the guarantors of that life. This truth surrounding the children is so strongly embraced among the Jewish people that when Czerniakow was ordered to personally turn over the children for deportation to Treblinka, as he indicates in his suicide note written on 23 July 1942, he chose instead to take his own life. Perhaps he knew on some level that to participate in this murder of the children would amount to becoming an accomplice in the murder of God, if one may speak in such a manner. This is a point made all too clearly in a haunting and horrifying scene from Elie Wiesel's *Night*. When the prisoners of Buna were forced to witness the hanging of a child, a man standing behind Eliezer whispered, "Where is God now?" And, we read, "I heard a voice within me answer him: 'Where is He? Here He is—He is hanging here on this gallows'" (62).

How deeply ingrained is the status of the child in the Jewish soul we begin to realize when we recall the passage from the *Midrash Rabbah* attributed to Rabbi Judah the Prince: "Come and see how beloved are the children by the Holy One, blessed be He. The Sanhedrin were exiled but the *Shekhinah* did not go into exile with them. When, however, the children were exiled, the *Shekhinah* went into exile with them" (7:106). Teaching in the name of Rabbi Judah, the talmudic sage Resh Lakish said, "The world endures only for the sake of the breath of the school children" (*Shabbat* 119b). Why? Because in the breath of the children, both at prayer and at play, vibrates the spirit of the *Shekhinah* herself. Thus, says the *Zohar*: "From the 'breath' which issues out of the mouth the voice is formed, and according to the well-known dictum, the world is upheld only by the merit of the 'breath' of little school children who have not yet tasted sin. Breath is itself mixture, being composed of air and moisture, and through it the world is carried on. Esoterically speaking, the breath of the little ones becomes 'voice,' and spreads throughout the whole universe, so that they become the guardians of the world" (3:121). Not by might but by spirit, the world endures as long as it attends to the "voice" that speaks from within the breath of the children. Very often what the Holocaust diarist seeks is not his or her own inner voice, but this voice of the children which makes life meaningful. For that voice is just what the Nazis set out to silence; that breath is just what they aimed to suffocate, consciously and deliberately. At the core of the Nazis' assault on God and creation, on the family and the feminine, then, is the calculated attempt to suffocate the breath and to silence the voice arising from the mouths of Jewish children. "It is as though the Nazi killers knew precisely what children represent to us," says Wiesel. "According to our tradition, the entire world subsists thanks to them" (*Jew* 178–79). An examination of the Holocaust diaries, however, will lead us to make a correction in Wiesel's statement: it is not "as though" but in fact.

The Holocaust diarists universally attest to this murder of the children, and, either explicitly or implicitly, they pursue the ontological and metaphysical implications of this crime that lies at the core of the Shoah. If there are exceptions to this claim, they are found among the diaries kept by those who were themselves children, all of whom were victims of the murderers: Anne Frank, Yitskhok Rudashevski, Moshe Flinker, Éva Heyman, Mirjam Korber, Elisabeth Block, and Dawid Rubinowicz, to name just a few. The suffocation of the child lies at the core of the Shoah because it is the starkest, most horrifying evidence (though not the only evidence) of the singularity of the Event. This point did not escape the notice of Emmanuel Ringelblum. On 10 June 1942, along the edge of this annihilation, he asserts: "In the past, whatever was done with grownups, the children were always permitted to live—so that they might be converted to the Christian faith. Even in the most barbaric times, a human spark glowed in the rudest heart, and children were spared. But the Hitlerian beast is quite different. It would devour the dearest of us, those who arouse the greatest compassion—our innocent children" (293–94). Therefore when Eliezer arrives at Birkenau in Wiesel's *Night*, a prisoner asks him his age, and thc youth replies, "I'm not yet fifteen." To which the prisoner answers, "No. Eighteen" (28). For anyone regarded as a child was sent straight to the gas chamber. The matter of being "useful" or able to work was not an issue.

As we shall see, this devouring of the child begins with an assault on the ontological status and symbolic significance of the child, so that when the innocents are themselves slaughtered, so too is the messianic hope associated with them. Let us consider, then, the thinking on these things most dear as it unfolds in the Holocaust diary.

THE ONTOLOGICAL CONDITION OF THE CHILD IN THE SHOAH

The suffocation of the children that characterizes the Shoah lies not only in the destruction of the bodies of these little ones but also includes the perversion of their very being. One example of how this perversion reveals itself is found in Aryeh Klonicki-Klonymus's *Diary of Adam's Father*. "How many times," he writes on 5 July 1943, "would I look at my little child, so handsome and full of life, and it would seem to me that it is not a child I am looking at but a box filled with ashes" (24). This undoing of the image of the child is the first manifestation of the undoing of his essence; where the child is concerned, image and essence are of a piece. It is worth noting that the Hebrew word used for "box" in the original text of the diary is *tevah* (19), which also means "word." When the child is reduced to a box filled with ashes, the word itself is reduced to ashes, torn from its meaning and choked into emptiness. With the draining of meaning from the word, the future opened up by meaning and signified by the child—both for the child and for men and women—is also reduced to ashes. *Tevah* also means "ark": what is borne over the face of the deep during this time of the world's destruction is not the remnant of humanity but its ashes. In the same entry, Klonicki-Klonymus illustrates how such a condition emerges. While hiding in a cellar with his three-month-old son, he relates, "I had some heated encounters with fellow Jews who were hiding. They demanded that I allow the strangling of my child. Among them were mothers whose children had already met this fate. Of course I replied to them that as long as I was alive such a thing would not come to pass" (31). Here we see the nefarious nature of the Nazis' project. Their aim? To turn Jew against Jew in a struggle to preserve the life of a child, thus annihilating in the assault on the child the very soul of the Jew whose life is sustained by the breath of the child. Just as the word is torn from its meaning, the Jew is torn from his child and therefore from his essence.

This rending of the soul from the heart of its being manifests itself in other ways. Many children, for example, were torn away from their parents in an effort to spare their young lives, as it happened with David Kahane and his three-year-old little girl. "Tomorrow," he says with devastating despair, "our child will leave us; who knows whether we shall see her again? Who will bring her up? What fate awaits her?" (61). Behind the overwhelming sadness that cries out from these lines is the hidden sadness of the child: the three-year-old little girl kept no diary. Surely more devastating than a father's despair is the terrible fear that becomes a definitive feature of the child's ontological condition: in the time of the Holocaust the Jewish child is the one whose very being is abject fear, with "death as a cradle and the curse of death as a cradle song," as Edmond Jabès expresses it (*Return* 195). Thus, says Hanna Levy-Hass in her Bergen-Belsen diary: "the children know no joy. They know only fear, nothing but fear. These poor, humiliated little creatures stand erect for hours on end, with fear racking their bodies, as they stare in paralyzed anticipation of things that will surely befall them" (15). The paralyzing effect of knowing only fear suggests a *rigor mortis* that takes over the soul before the body is laid into the earth or reduced to ashes. And so the children do not move; they do not speak and they do not play—they are not children but only the vanishing shadows of children. "One never sees even one child playing," says the sculptor Rivosh, for example, writing from the Riga Ghetto. "All of them, like beasts at bay, cling timidly close to their mothers or sit in the gateways" (324). Why? Because they "instinctively sense their own destruction—they are quiet and dejected" (336). And they are afraid. Ridden with fear, their bodies are all but emptied of life's spirit, which is the spirit of the child, who in turn sustains the spirit of a people and a world.

Indeed, dwelling along the edge of the origin, the child is our link to the earth itself. But the edge of the origin has been transformed into the edge of annihilation. Philip Mechanicus hints at this point in the journal he kept at Westerbork, saying: "The road from Hooghalen to Westerbork groaned under the misery of the Jews and the callousness and shamelessness of their persecutors. A sea of dispirited, defeated human beings—among them children and yet more children, who pushed and stumbled over one another in the throng" (56–57). In the Dutch text of the diary, *moedeloze* and *geslagen*, rendered as "dispirited" and "defeated" (51), might be translated more literally as "spiritless" and "beaten down." The blows aimed at these frail bodies are calculated to break the spirit of a world, so that in the suffocation of the child the spirit is itself suffocated, and the earth itself, the Great Mother, groans all the way from Hooghalen to Westerbork. With the assault on the being of the child, the status of the origin is obliterated. For the child is an emanation of the origin, which consists of a compassion that is the opposite of the cruelty to which these children are subjected.

The ontological status of the child whose being now lies in being suffocated, however, is established long before any children are marched or shipped off to a camp. Indeed, establishing this condition of the child is one of the aims of forbidding children to attend schools in the ghetto. "The soul of the child," says Hersh Wasser in his Warsaw Ghetto diary, "grows more and more tainted. The lack of schools, the gutter, absolute demoralization, leave their terrible mark. What sort of generation will grow out of all this?" (223). The answer, of course, is that no generation will grow out of this: these children belong to a generation consigned to the gas chambers. What taints them, moreover, is not any moral corruption but the absence of a future, the absence of meaning and mission. Drained of life, they are emptied of the time that goes into a life, each of them a victim of an ontological progeria. "Children were old, and old men were as helpless as children," Wiesel puts it (Patterson 21), a statement illustrated by the image of two children in a ghetto pushing an old man in a baby carriage in Ka-tzetnik's *House of Dolls* (44). Says Simon Wiesenthal, for the children of the ghetto, "days were months and months were years. When I saw them with toys in their hands, they looked unfamiliar, uncanny, like old men playing with childish things" (47). What Wiesel, Ka-tzetnik, and Wiesenthal recall, the Holocaust diarists carefully record. In his Romanian diary, for example, Emil Dorian comments on a nine-year-old little girl named Claruta, saying: "She is an old person. Suffering has worn out all the spontaneity of childhood and dried out the sources of feeling" (308). Similarly, Janusz Korczak, the noted physician who was the head of an orphanage in the Warsaw Ghetto, writes, "The Children's Home is now a home for the aged" (166). The implications of the divorce from the future discussed in chapter 3 here unfold in graphic ways. If time is a fundamental horizon of human being, then this collapse of time in the children fundamentally alters their being. It steals their life away before they are sent to their death, making them more ancient than the Ancient of Days. These little ones are forced into an awareness of every breath sucked forth from their young souls.[1]

This death before death that befalls the children is the reason behind Willy Cohn's lament, "I myself have lived my life, but the little children ought to have a happy life before them" (61). But, of course they have no life before them. For these little creatures who have very little of a past, the past is all they have. And, since they have no future, they do not even have a past. They are suspended in a being without time. The days they live are not the days of their lives but the days of their death. That is why "the situation of the children is especially tragic," as Tuvia Borzykowski states it. "Now that their parents are dead, the children do not even remember them, and have become accustomed to their foster parents, but still they are constantly aware of the fact that they have no right to live" (120–21). With the elimination of life's origin, all of life is orphaned, and this condition is exemplified by the ontological status of the children as orphans. They have no right to live because they have no origin of life to which they are attached. Robbed of their time, they are robbed of their place, so that any place they occupy is a nonplace, and their presence is out of place. Peretz Opoczynski makes this point in his Warsaw Ghetto diary, where he sees the essence of the ghetto "symbolized by one- and two-year-old children sitting on a sofa in the middle of the street and crying, 'Mama,' while Jews, their hearts bleeding, were passing by, watching the horrible scene and crying. The Germans had probably done it deliberately. They could have taken the children away, but they did not. On the contrary—let the Jews see and grieve" (104–5). One may be certain that in this action, as in all their actions, the Germans acted deliberately. These orphaned children symbolize the orphaned condition of a world in which not only mothers and fathers are under assault but, as argued in the last two chapters, motherhood and fatherhood are targeted for removal from being. With the elimination of motherhood and fatherhood comes the erasure of childhood. With the erasure of childhood, the child's ontological condition is made into a noncondition; having no right to live, he has no place in being. Subsequently, being has no place in the child. The bread of life, the bread that joins the body with being, is therefore snatched from his mouth.

Starvation, then, comes to define the ontological condition of the child, and the diarists repeatedly point this out. "I know full well," says Moshe Flinker, "how bitter it is when children have nothing to eat and when their parents can give them nothing" (84). Similarly, in Czerniakow's diary we read: "They [the children] are living skeletons from the ranks of street beggars. Some of them came to my office. They talked with me like grownups—these eight-year-old citizens. I am ashamed to admit it, but I wept as I have not wept for a long time. I gave a chocolate bar to each of them. They all received soup as well. Damned be those of us who have enough to eat and drink and forget about these children" (366). Czerniakow's entry reveals the link between being removed from life's time and being removed from life's sustenance. If being entails being with, that condition is exemplified in the act of sharing food. When the child is reduced to the status of beggar, he is isolated from other beings, that is, from the tables of other beings. And yet, of all the beings in the world, it is precisely the child who is entrusted to the care of other beings. Thus the ontological condition to which the Nazis relegated the child exemplifies an ontological aspect of the assault on the people of Israel. As the Jews are cut off from the world, the children are cut off from the Jews. Indeed, once *being* becomes the crime of the Jews, Jewish children have to be relegated to this condition of beggary and starvation. And this condition affects and infects the condition of all. Illustrating this point, Ringelblum, for example, notes: "Three-year-old children are out begging in the streets. You can't rest nowadays in a Jewish apartment. You hear beggars rapping on doors on either side of your own apartment" (158). Elsewhere Ringelblum describes a six-year-old boy who "lay gasping all night, too weak to roll over to the piece of bread that had been thrown down to him from the balcony" (204–5). Soon the starvation of the child rapping at the door and lying below the balcony becomes a definitive feature of the entire ghetto. The very being of the ghetto is joined with the ontological condition of the starving child. He is not part of the landscape—he is the sum of the landscape, from which there is no escape.

In the ontological condition of the ghetto—a condition embodied in the condition of the child who has no right to live—the "there is"[2] announces itself in the wailing of the child. "A terrifying, simply monstrous impression is made," Ringelblum declares, "[by] the wailing of children who . . . beg for alms, or whine that they have nowhere to sleep. At the corner of Leszno and Karmelika Streets, children weep bitterly at night. Although I hear this weeping every night, I cannot fall asleep until late. The couple of groschen I give them nightly cannot ease my conscience" (241). Once again we realize that the diarist's conscience cannot be eased because he knows that the child, by definition, is precisely the being who has been placed in his care. And yet, the condition of the child is such that he has been removed from the care of all. The absence of everything that returns as a presence is this absence of care for the child. In a word, this absence of care is the absence of the holy, so that this assault on the child becomes an integral part of the assault on the Holy One. Paradoxically, it is an absence as omnipresent as the Holy One Himself. "Frozen children are becoming a general phenomenon," notes Ringelblum. "Children's bodies and crying serve as a persistent background for the Ghetto. People cover the dead bodies of frozen children with the handsome posters designed for Children's Month, bearing the legend, 'Our Children, Our Children Must Live—A Child Is the Holiest Thing'" (233–34). Thus we see the ultimate overturning of the ontological condition of the child: the sign that was to signify and celebrate the life of the child as a center of community life becomes the burial shroud laid over the little one. What may sound innocuous when described as an "overturning," of course, is the calculated imposition of starvation upon these children. They do not starve to death—they are murdered by means of starvation, as well as by other means.

THE SLAUGHTER OF THE INNOCENTS

Among the children of the Holocaust, as we have seen, the murder of their bodies begins with the undermining of their being; before they are killed, their child*hood* is killed. Korczak elaborates on this point by noting, "The body of a dead boy lies on the sidewalk. Nearby, three boys are playing horses and drivers. At one point they notice the body, move a few steps to the side, go on playing" (121). This is the death before death, the slaughter before the slaughter, which is a slaughter of the innocents in their innocence: it is the child's indifference toward the death of the child. This slaughter is the substance of the waking dream that brings on the nightmare Korczak describes when he says that in his sleep he sees "bodies of dead children. One dead child in a bucket. Another skinned, lying on the boards in the mortuary, clearly still breathing" (146). Still breathing and yet shrouded in death: this is the breath emptied of soul, the *neshiymah* drained of *neshamah*, not the last breath but the breath that is continually the last, suffocated before the last breath is drawn. It burns not only on their trembling lips but in their eyes, as we see when Dr. Henryk Shoshkes writes in his Warsaw Ghetto diary, "I cannot forget the little boys with their wild, burning eyes and their curly locks, as they repeated their [Torah] lessons by heart" (44). These eyes are aflame not with the fire that is Torah but with the inferno that consumed a generation of children. The wild, burning eyes of these children are eyes that have seen death overtake their companions; they are the eyes of innocents awaiting slaughter, filled with the flames of the crematoria that await them. It is through such eyes that the teenager from the Lodz Ghetto, David Sierakowiak, beholds one of his classmates: "Yesterday a pupil of the parallel class died. He died of exhaustion and starvation. Because of his terrible appearance he was permitted to eat as much soup [at school] as he liked, but it did not help him any more. This is already the third victim in our class" (19). These lines are haunted by a fearsome question that the boy is too terrified to ask: Am I next? For he knows that there is "an unbelievable increase in consumption among the children and the youth. The death cart is working at full steam" (21). Less than three months after making this entry dated 28 May 1941, the death cart came for David Sierakowiak himself.

One may recall at this juncture Emil Fackenheim's observation that "the murder camp was not an accidental by-product of the Nazi empire. It was its pure essence" (*Jewish Return* 246). If the essence of the Nazi empire is the murder camp, the essence of that murder is the murder of the children, which transcends the barbed-wire boundaries of the camps. The Nazis were not merely murderers—they were, in their heartless essence, child hunters and child murderers who relentlessly tracked down their prey. "Before my eyes," says Hersh Wasser, "I saw a small boy shot down, corner of Chlodna-Zelazna. Heartrending. In the evening, on Bonifraterska, a little lad was wounded" (218). This rending of the heart is the "true suffering" that one of Wiesel's characters describes when he says, "Suffering, true suffering, is watching death—dark, cunning death—drawing close to children too weak to cry" (*Zalmen* 49). What is rent here is not only the heart of the diarist but the heart of all humanity. For the life-giving heart of humanity lies in the life that it bears into the world; when that life is murdered, the heart—the very core of human being—is lost. "How much of the future have they destroyed with the children?" Hillel Seidman asks (107). And yet he knows that there is no answer, because everything that would make any answer meaningful has been destroyed with the destruction of this future, which is the heart torn out by the Nazis' heartlessness. As for those who were hiding from this open season on their lives, we may refer to the entry in Menahem Kon's diary from the Warsaw Ghetto, dated 6 August 1942: "The children are being hidden since they are the most sought after by the murderers. I make up my mind not to go into the cellar, I shall not take up room where some more children could be hidden. The children have preference to be saved" (80). But, of course, they cannot be saved. Or rather, a world that might have saved them has abandoned them.[3]

The Talmud teaches us that the body of an infant must be placed in a casket designed not to be carried on the shoulders but to be cradled in our arms (*Mo'ed Katan* 24b): instead of a casket, the diarist bears in his arms the chronicles that he has written. With words he conveys what he cannot carry in his arms, knowing all the while that his efforts are as insane as they are needful. The child who whispers to him—and, through him, to us—was not spared, not even when the man gave up his place of safety for the child. That whisper was suffocated before it could be uttered. All that was left for the diarists was to summon the courage to attest to the slaughter of the innocents, thus to take up a spiritual resistance when all other avenues of resistance were closed. So they wrote, these diarists. They wrote as tirelessly as the Nazis murdered. "On the streets," says Ringelblum, for instance, on 22 November 1941, "one regularly comes across children frozen to death" (237). On 7 June 1943 Mechanicus writes, "Infant mortality is high—one child dies every day" (37), and ten days later he notes, "Mortality among the children continues to be alarming" (50). One each day, each day ten, a hundred, a thousand: the diurnal entries of the Holocaust diary are measured not according to the sands of time, not as the clock ticks and the earth revolves, but according to a very different scale, a very different axis—according to the blood of children. Each time the diarist turns a page a child is turned to ashes. And the authors of these diaries, which are therefore unlike any other diaries, know it.

Unable either to save the children or to die for them, the diarists can only follow them along the edge of annihilation. And follow them they do. "Children with scarlet fever and diphtheria," Mechanicus attests on 9 February 1944, "were carried weeping to the long snaking train. Children without parents from the orphanage. Perhaps the most abominable transport that has ever gone" (248). What becomes of such transports is recorded in the diaries of the members of the *Sonderkommando* at Auschwitz. Leib Langfus, for example, bears witness to the gassing of six hundred children who arrived in the camp towards the end of 1943. "A transport was brought," he says, "consisting entirely of children. They came from Shaulen [Siauliai] in Lithuania, region of Kaunas, where they were seized from their mothers' homes and were put into lorries during their fathers' absence, who were working" (118). Similarly, Salmen Lewental records the gassing of a thousand boys that took place on 20 October 1944: "The young, clear, boyish voices resounded louder and louder with every minute [when at last they passed] into bitter sobbing. This dreadful lamentation was heard from very far. We stood completely aghast and as if paralysed by this mournful weeping . . . [while] the SS men followed them, beat and belaboured them, until they had mastered the situation and at last drove them [into the bunker]. Their joy was indescribable. Did they not [have] any children ever?" (178). And what is multiplied by six hundred, by a thousand, in these scenes is the infinite horror and suffering that floods Lewental's description of a single child: "A shiver passed through the body of the young girl, she called desperately, 'Mamma!' And she spoke no more, those were her last words" (145). As the Nazis tear meaning from words, they tear the life from these children, tearing from their mouths all words, until at last all that remains is either sobbing or the single word, the child's first and last word, uttered in the midst of this slaughter: Mamma. What, then, is the diarist to do with this word? How is he to take it into his mouth and place it in ours? "The life of the word," says Mikhail Bakhtin, "is contained in its transfer from one mouth to another" (*Problems* 202). But what becomes of that transfer when the word uttered is the last word to contain any meaning, when even the meaning of this last word, the child's utterance of "Mamma," is under assault?

That this word, the first and the last to come from the mouth of the child, is under assault, becomes all too evident when we recall an entry dated 26 October 1943 from the diary that Leon Wells kept in the Janowska camp. "Mothers undress their children," he relates, "and the naked mother carries her child in her arms to the fire. However, sometimes a mother will undress herself but will fail to undress the child, or the child refuses to let itself be undressed out of panic. When this happens, we can hear the voices of the children. 'What for?' or 'Mother, mother, I'm scared! No! No!' In these cases one of the

German SD's takes the child by its small feet, swings it, crushing its head against the nearest tree, then carries it over to the fire and tosses it in. This is all done in front of the mother. When the mother reacts to this, which happens a few times, even if only by saying something, she is beaten and afterward hung by her feet from a tree with her head down until she dies" (206). Even if only to say something: here too the slaughter of the innocents is accompanied by the obliteration of the word, so that the task of the diarist is not merely to search his soul or to record the events of the day but to become a voice for those who have been rendered voiceless.

It happened therefore that the lives of the little ones were snuffed out before any words could ever come to their lips. Even before they emerged from the womb, the word waiting to be born from the womb was silenced, as we see when we read in Yitzhak Katznelson's *Vittel Diary*: "Only those babes who were yet in their mothers' womb died thus, alongside their mothers. Those children that were already born were snatched from their mothers' arms and taken to the slaughter" (62). Similarly, Sarra Gleykh's diary contains a description of a mass murder that she survived near her home town of Mariupol: "Somewhere beneath the corpses babies were crying. Most of them had been carried by their mothers and, since we were shot in the backs, they had fallen, protected by their mothers' bodies. Not wounded by the bullets, they were covered up and buried alive under the corpses" (75). And so we see the extremity of the heinous inversion: the bodies of those who had borne the babes into the world and had nourished them now suffocate them. Finally, in his diary from the Kovno Ghetto, Avraham Tory writes: "Babies were taken out and placed on the ground in the stone-paved hospital courtyard, their tiny faces turned skyward. Soldiers of the third squad of the German Police passed between them. They stopped for a moment. Some of them kicked the babies with their boots. The babies rolled a little to the side but soon enough regained their belly-up position, their faces turned toward the sky" (41). And all of the sky, the infinite silence of the heavens, is gathered into their faces. Even beneath the corpses, buried face-down in a mass grave, their faces are turned toward the sky. For the Holocaust diarist who gazes into these faces turns them toward the sky. From the mouth of the diarist, the babes who have never spoken a word speak volumes unto the sky.

And so we may better understand Elie Wiesel when he declares: "The death of a man is only the death of a man, but the death of a child is the death of innocence, the death of God in the heart of man. And he who does not drink deeply of this truth, who does not shout it from the rooftops, is a man devoid of heart, of God" (*Beggar* 99). What more can be said when the death of a child is the slaughter of a child, the slaughter of innocence and of God? Looking for a way to say more, Michael Zylberberg cites a poem by Chaim Bialik in his Warsaw diary:

> Cursed be the man who cries, "Vengeance for this."
> Vengeance for this—the blood of little children—
> The devil has not framed.
> The blood will pierce the abyss,
> To the gloomy depths the blood will worm its way,
> Devour in darkness, gnaw upon the earth's
> Foundations in decay. (66)

There can be no vengeance, no "settling the score" for the little ones because they are the vessels of the infinite as it penetrates from on high into our lives, and an infinite score cannot be settled. Therefore, if the earth's foundations rot, they rot from the top down, from the heavens to the earth. For our looking down into the face of a child is a looking up, into that dimension of height that ordains and sanctifies all of being. Indeed, even in the midst of the slaughter of the innocents, the diarists turn their gaze in this upward direction. And there they behold the face of a savior.

THE STRUGGLE TO SAVE THE SAVIOR

Echoing the tradition's teachings on the significance of the child, Wiesel's character Moshe from *The Oath* asserts: "The Messiah. We seek him, we pursue him. We think he is in heaven; we don't know that he likes to come down as a child. And yet, every man's childhood is messianic in essence" (132). One of the texts from the Jewish tradition that articulates this view of the child as savior is the *Even Sheleimah* of the Vilna Gaon, the renowned sage of the eighteenth century. There he writes, "The child redeems his parent from Gehinom and causes him to be brought to Gan Eden" (45). The Maggid of Dubno, a contemporary of the Vilna Gaon, illustrates this significance of the child with a parable about a family that lived in a house in the forest. Every evening the father of the family would barricade the windows and doors of the house to protect his wife and children from danger. One night, however, a fire broke out in their home. And somehow a heavy stone had fallen outside to seal the door, so that they could not get out. Since the windows were locked from the outside, they had no way of crying out to their neighbors for help. One of the youngest of the children, however, discovered the dormer window, and, because he was so small, he was able to climb outside and go for help. The villagers came and rolled away the stone from the entrance to the house. And so the family was saved thanks to the courageous efforts of a small child. "Even as this one little boy triumphantly flung open the door of his father's house and thereby saved his family," says the Maggid, "so, too, the study, prayers and tears of our children can open the lofty gates of Heaven and thus bring about the deliverance of their elders" (Heinemann 200–1). Thus the diarists who attest to the suffocation of the child also bear witness to this messianic significance of the child as a savior. What is slaughtered with the slaughter of the innocents, then, is salvation itself.

Recall in this connection Katznelson's description of the Jewish police in Warsaw, who took away "these young children, tender, pure, our hope, our future, our very best, our messiahs, our saviors!" (53). And among those taken away were Katznelson's own wife and children. From the camp in Vittel, on 15 August 1943, he writes: "Yesterday, I could not hold my pen to continue writing about the annihilation of our people. It was a year to the day since they took away my Chanah, and my sons, Ben Zion, fourteen years of age, Binyamin, eleven years of age" (128). In many cases the diarist views the writing of his diary as a source of salvation (see, for example, Kaplan 233); but with the loss of the child, the ability to write is itself compromised. Why? Because the child signifies not only one who speaks but also a reader to whom the word is offered; the child bears the meaning sought in the word; the child is the flesh imparted to the word. As long as children are born into our midst, creation continues, and the chaos of the void is kept at bay. That is why Herman Kruk comments on a program presented by the children of the Vilna Ghetto, where the little ones bring to their audience the words of the Yiddish author Isaac Loeb Peretz, "Do not think that chaos rules the world" (28). That is why Zelig Kalmanovitch asserts, "Our comfort are the children" (76). A world whose streets are emptied of its children is a world plunged into chaos, without comfort or consolation. Therefore the murder characterizing the Holocaust is a murder not only of these little bodies but of the world's soul—that is the meaning of the term *antiworld*, as it is used to refer the Holocaust Kingdom. It is a chaos devoid not just of law and order but of significance and substance—of the care, comfort, and compassion which, according to Jewish tradition, lie at the heart of creation. In the Holocaust Kingdom the child is precisely the one who is eternally *elsewhere* because chaos is everywhere. Hence salvation is to be found nowhere.

This aspect of the realm to which the diarists attest becomes especially clear when we consider diaries written by parents separated from their children. From his hiding place in Holland, for instance, Julian Castle Stanford writes in December 1944: "We have managed to survive the whole of this past year, and now we cling to the hope that we might be able to see our children once again. When will that be?" (134). But this is a *when* without answer, since the future and therefore the meaning signified by the child have been obliterated, making the question meaningless. The stages by which this meaninglessness sets in are chronicled in Czerniakow's dairy, which is full of references to his child, Jas, a lad who had fled to Lvov never to return. On 1 June 1940, for example, he writes, "What is Jas thinking about us today?" (156), and on 2 June 1940, "My thoughts are with Jas" (157). While he had received a letter from his son on 23 March 1940—a letter from the other shore of life—soon his link to the child is confined to his anxious thoughts, for on 9 July 1940 he laments, "I can no longer write to Jas" (172). Without this offering of the word to his child, all words are broken. It parallels precisely and without coincidence the collapse of life in the ghetto, until the only entry that Czerniakow makes on 28 October 1940 is the single word "Jas" (211), which he then crossed out, as though without the presence signified by that word all other words were pointless. And yet, as long as he lives he longs for the child, for that is the substance of his living, the stuff of his being. Therefore he invokes the child, if only to give voice to the absence of the child, as on 6 July 1941, when he writes, "Today is our 28th wedding anniversary, without Jas" (256), and on 23 July 1943, when he notes, "There has been no news of Jas" (260). Finally, in one of the diary's last mentions of his son, all the diarist has left of any hope or salvation is a question that breaks forth on 13 February 1942, "And where is Jas, my only child?" (325). This *where*, like Stanford's *when*, has no answer other than the *elsewhere* that has overtaken the being of the child and the meaning of the world. It is a variation on the questions "Where is God?" and "Where is humanity?" that reverberate throughout the Holocaust diary.

The one means left to the diarist for making the *elsewhere* into a *here* is to engage in a struggle to save the children. That is what makes the children our saviors: they provide us with meaning by offering us something of infinite value that we might struggle to preserve and protect. Realizing this truth, Czerniakow sets out to gain the release "of several hundred youngsters" from prison, declaring "I am doing my best to bring this about" (356). And it becomes a matter of the utmost urgency for him to create in this antiworld that is a nonplace some kind of place where children may be children. Thus, after a great deal of labor, Czerniakow accomplished one of his greatest achievements as head of the Jewish Council of Warsaw: he managed to get a playground opened. For where children are at play, God is at work. "The playground," he writes on 7 June 1942, "was handed over to the [younger] children by the [older] children. Three delegates, two men and a woman, did the announcing in Polish, Yiddish, and Hebrew. I spoke twice. The ceremony made a great impression on those present. Balm for the wounds. The street is smiling!" (363–64). Beholding children at play, the soul receives, if only for a moment, the salve of salvation. The street smiles because the world rejoices in the shouts and the laughter of the children that resound with the *ki tov*, with the utterance of "it is good," pronounced in the beginning to sustain all creation.[4] The children are our saviors because they embody the good without which the world cannot endure.

Every word that overflows with meaning, every instant that teems with presence, is replete with the good that reverberates in the laughter of the children. Hence in his diary Michael Zylberberg comments on the opening of the playground in the Warsaw Ghetto, saying: "It is surely more than coincidence that the playground should be opposite the community centre. Whenever we hear children laughing and singing our windows will be open to let in the sound. This will give us hope and courage to go on and fight for the future" (52). What enters these windows in the laughter and song of the children is the light of day, which is the light of a new beginning. "This potentiality," says Martin Buber, "streaming unconquered, however much of it is squandered, is the reality *child*: this phenomenon of uniqueness, which is more than just begetting and birth, the grace of beginning again and ever again" (*Between* 83). God is the One who begins, but the human being, thanks to the presence of the children, is the one who begins again with the dawning of the light of each day. It is the children who make the dawning of that light a moment of grace; if we are not saddled with our past, it is because they open up for us the hope of a future in which we can be better than we are. As essential as the light of day that enters our windows, then, is the sound of children; indeed, their laughing and singing comprise the light of day, the light of our lives, so that the people who preserve that light preserve their own lives. And the Holocaust diary is just such a window: it opens up a portal through which the salvific light of the child may enter, even in the midst of the dying—of the murder—of that light. This too is among the unique aspects of the Holocaust diary.

The care for the salvation of the child who brings us salvation, as well as the testimony to that care, is found in numerous other diaries. *Oneg Shabbat* diarist Abraham Levin, for example, applauds the efforts of Jews who pose as Poles into order to go from town to town and save as many children as possible. "May these heroes be blessed," he writes, "who risk their lives to save pure and innocent Jewish children" (318). Similarly, Eliezer Yerushalmi agonizes over the issue of saving the little ones in the Siauliai Ghetto. "What can I do to avert a danger such as this?" he puts the terrible question to himself concerning the fate hanging over the children, which Yerushalmi sees as the fate hanging over all humanity (189). And six months later, on 15 November 1943, he enters into his diary once more the question that will not go away: "What can be done to save these children from destruction, when they have no place to work? This Ghetto of women and children has been consigned to the flames" (315). While in some ghettos children could receive a stay of execution by being forced into labor fit only for adults, in others they were marked for death under the very pretense of being cared for as children. Such was the perversion characteristic of the Nazis. Avraham Tory, for instance, comments on the Nazis' plan to establish a kindergarten—a garden of children—in the Kovno Ghetto. Says Tory: "We are not at all happy about the idea of concentrating 1,000 children in one place. We do not want to expose our children to the Germans. The Germans cast greedy glances in their direction" (483). While in the world this gesture might be viewed as an act of compassion, in the antiworld it is a genuine cause for concern over the lives of the little ones. For this measure was a common ploy used by the Nazis for gathering together children to be murdered, as one may conclude from Wiesenthal's account of a similar design implemented by SS Group Leader Katzmann in the Lvov Ghetto. After he set up a kindergarten in the Ghetto, "one morning three SS trucks arrived and took all the children away to the gas chambers. And that night, when the parents came back from work, there were heart-rending scenes in the deserted kindergarten" (50).

The question that arises from the suffocation of the child is this: what becomes of the human image when it is twisted into greedy glances aimed at the children? Does the image of the human being, indeed, retain any of its humanity when it is so twisted? Before proceeding further, it must be noted that this perversion of the human image is something not only inflicted upon the Jews and Jewish children but is something also suffered by the perpetrators and the onlookers, something that they inflict upon their own children. Shimon Huberband, for example, relates that Polish schoolteachers would take their children on field trips to watch Jews being hanged (272). And Shlomo Frank points out that Polish children were encouraged to assume the bestial aspect of their elders: as "guards stand by and laugh," he tells us, these "children" beat Jews with sticks and stones (86). To be sure, children invariably come to resemble their elders. The humanity that they come to resemble is the subject of the next chapter.

THE HUMAN IMAGE DEFILED

EMIL FACKENHEIM HAS NOTED THAT "THE NAZI STATE had no higher aim than to murder souls while bodies were still alive. The *Musselmann* was its most characteristic, most original product" (*To Mend* 100). Embodied in the horrific image of the *Musselmann* is something more than the emaciated body of a human being. His eyes emptied of the light of life, the *Musselmann* embodies the destruction of the very notion of a human being. "At Auschwitz, not only man died, but also the idea of man," we recall one of Elie Wiesel's most famous remarks. "It was its own heart the world incinerated at Auschwitz" (*Legends* 230). But what exactly is the idea of man, that is, of the human being? And how does it die? Or better: how does it come to be murdered in the murder of the human being which characterizes the Shoah?

Perhaps most fundamental to "the idea of man" that Wiesel invokes is the idea of the sanctity of the human being. That is why the human being, in his image, can be not only murdered—he can be *defiled*. When the human image is defiled, the meaning and significance of humanity are destroyed, beyond the slaughter of bodies and souls. Indeed, the calculated defilement of the human image is part of the singularity of the Holocaust, because it is a distinctive part of the Nazis' singular assault on the essence of the Jews and Judaism. What are the Jews, as God's Chosen, chosen for? They are chosen for the task of attesting to the chosenness of every human being. That is why the Jewish tradition maintains that all of humanity stems from a single human being: so that no one can take himself, his race, or his tribe to be better than another. But, as Leo Baeck explains, the essence of "the idea of man" that comes to the world from the Jewish tradition lies in something more, which belongs to the idea of the first man and thus to the idea of the human being as such: "The most important thing which Judaism gave to man—the contribution which enables man to feel the ethical consciousness of his dignity as an individual human being—is the idea of his likeness to God" (153). The Koretzer Rebbe, a disciple of the Baal Shem Tov, makes precisely this point in his commentary on the Hebrew word for "man," *ish*. "'Aleph,'" he explains, "means the 'Source, the Leader.' The word *Ish* (Man) is composed of the 'Aleph' and the word *Yesh* (There Is). This signifies that there is in Man the Source, that Divinity abides in Man" (Newman 83). Not just in the Jew, mind you, but in Man, in every human being—such is the idea of the human being that comes to the world through the Jews. Undertaking the extermination not only of the Jews but of every idea they symbolize, the Nazis set out to destroy this very idea of a trace of something holy, of something beyond the accidents of nature, that abides at the heart of humanity. In a word, they sought the defilement of the human image, beginning with the defilement of the Jew.[1]

"Species or man of God," says Rabbi Joseph Soloveitchik, "this is the alternative which the Almighty [has] placed before man" (125). Opting to regard the human being in terms of his species—that is, in terms of his race—the Nazis opted to destroy every notion of the "man of God" through the defilement of the human image. To be sure, we have seen that they chose to destroy the very One who places these alternatives before us. For one cannot destroy the man of God, the human being created in the image of God, without also assailing God. The reverse, we shall soon discover, is also true: one cannot set out to murder God without also annihilating the divine image in which the human being is created and by which the human being is sanctified. Hence the human being cannot be determined as a species racially defined without the defilement and destruction both of the human image and of the Divine Presence. "Man is the creature created for the purpose of being drawn close to God," says the eighteenth-century sage, Rabbi Moshe Chayim Luzzatto, in *The Way of God* (45). To harbor the Source is to seek the Source through a relation to our fellow human being which is expressive of a higher relation. Thus, according to their grim and horrifying logic, the Nazis understood that both the Source and its seekers had to be destroyed.

Perhaps even more horrifying than the Nazis' logic was their exploitation of the Jews' idea of humanity, to use it as a weapon against them; this point comes out particularly in the diarists' accounts of the disbelief that plagued the Jewish communities. Yitzhak Zuckerman, for example, writes, "In many a place people responded to the news about German murders which we had disseminated by saying, 'Nothing like that could happen here'" (64). Why? Because, as Hillel Seidman notes, the best and most humane features of the Jewish soul prevented many from comprehending the cruelty of their murderers (67). This incredulity on the part of the victims cannot be attributed to stubbornness, blindness, stupidity, or naive optimism. Any attempt to explain it in such terms would amount to aligning oneself with the murderers. No, they disbelieved in the Nazi horrors because they continued to believe in the idea of the human being that was given to the world through the Torah. "Blessed are we that we could not believe it!" Yitzhak Katznelson cries out from the pages of his *Vittel Diary*. "We could not believe it because of the Image of God that is in us. . . . We did not believe it could happen because we are human beings" (83–84). For to be a human being, drawn close to God, is to affirm the humanity of our fellow human beings. That is why *Oneg Shabbat* diarist Hersh Wasser asserts: "Man, no matter how shamed and suffering, still inwardly preserves God's image, and believes in justice. Things can't really be so hideous. Change must come" (248). To believe in justice is to believe in the humanity of the other human being; to inwardly preserve the divine image is to hold to the sanctity of the other human being as a being who believes in justice. Therefore, as we shall see, the Nazis defile the human image by desecrating the basis of interhuman relation. They defile the human image in others by assuming the image of a beast within themselves. And they take on the image of the beast by turning others into beasts.

And yet, Emmanuel Ringelblum insists, "Let it be said that though we have been sentenced to death and know it, we have not lost our human features" (299), that is, our *mentshlekhen partsuf*, his Yiddish texts reads, our "human face" (243). That is where the image of the divine, where not only the idea but the reality and the holiness of the human being, shows itself: in the face. Remarkably and mysteriously, in those days of destruction and defilement there were those who, in an act of spiritual resistance, retained their human image in spite of the assault on it. And one means of retaining it was to speak, to bear witness to the assault on the human image through the testimony offered to us from the heart of these diaries. What, then, does this tell us about the event that transpires between the Holocaust diarist and the page before him? In his study of the diary as a literary genre, Alain Girard argues: "The diarist does not accept himself. . . . He wants to be other and awakens forces that lurk within him. Knowledge of himself is not an end but a means to an end. . . . The aim is neither to abandon nor to admire himself but to collect himself" (533). But what is unique to the Holocaust diarists is that this collecting of oneself entails a gathering together of the divine image within oneself through an affirmation of the divinity that abides in the heart of humanity. When Yitskhok Rudashevski asks, "Into what kind of helpless, broken creature can man be transformed?" (38), it is a means of resisting a certain insidious transformation within himself. Thus it is not so much that the Holocaust diarist does not accept himself; rather, he does not accept the image of the animal that is forced upon him and upon all of humanity. With his every fiber he struggles to sustain the idea of the human being in the midst of the slaughter of humanity and the defilement of the human image. Let us consider, then, the nature of that struggle.

THE ASSAULT ON THE FACE OF HUMANITY

"Judaism speaks of the good man," Leo Baeck reminds us. "The words 'a good Jew' are alien to the Bible and the Oral Law" (70). Central to the Jewish notion of the Jew is the idea of the human being as a sacred being. Central to the Nazis' assault on humanity, then, is an assault not only on the Jew but on the notion of the Jew as a human being. That is why Emmanuel Ringelblum, for instance, is careful to record a statement made by a Nazi to his friend Rabbi Velvele, "You're not human, you're not animal, you're Jew" (24). That is why Josef Katz relates a conversation that he had with a German guard at Kaiserwald.

After reporting to the guard that he had brought thirty men to be washed, the guard asked, "What men? What do you mean?" And Katz corrected himself, saying, "Thirty Jews for washing." To which the guard replied, "Okay" (153). How is the Jew, then, transformed into something other than human in the eyes of the Nazi? The process begins by regarding the human being as a species, and not as a child of God. And it proceeds by replacing the face with a physiognomy. The title that Günther Marcuse gave to the diary he kept at Gross-Breesen, *The New Face of the Labor Camp*, may therefore bear implications deeper than the nineteen-year-old suspected. For the Aryan physiognomy that the Nazis imposed on the world, from the ghetto to the camp, consisted of the calculated erasure of the humanity couched in the Jewish face.

Such a project was, of course, in keeping with the general aim of erasing from the world the Jewish being manifested in the face, and with it all that it represents. The great sage of the Talmud, Rabbi Akiba, maintained that the humanity and the dignity of the human being are revealed in the face; in the face, he held, lies the image of the Holy One (see Finkelstein 103).[2] When the human image is defiled, the mystery and the meaning of the face are obliterated in a twisting and torturing of the face itself. And so Harry James Cargas has included just such a Jewish face in the photos he collected from the Yad Vashem archives for his book *Shadows of Auschwitz*. Here the assault on the face of humanity is graphic indeed: it is the face of a man beaten to death with a hammer. "This was a face," he writes, "the face of a man who lived, and dreamed and died a ghastly death. We cannot look at this face—and yet we dare not avert our eyes lest . . . " (117). Lest what? Lest we lose our own face.

Among the Holocaust diarists, Abraham Lissner, a leader in the Jewish Partisan Unit in Paris, attests to the mutilation of the Jewish face when he notes, "I was in Douai when the walls of the houses were covered with posters the Gestapo had distributed all over France under the heading 'The Army of Criminals.' I saw the faces of my comrades-in-arms, swollen and distorted from all the tortures they had endured" (295). The distorted face is a definitive aspect of the image of the criminal: a criminal in this case is he who has lost the humanity expressed in the face, reduced to the status of animal or object.

To transform the Jew into a criminal, then, is to defile his human image. This point becomes all too evident when we consider some observations from the diarists of the Auschwitz *Sonderkommando*, Salmen Gradowski and Salmen Lewental. "We came dressed like men and left in wet rags," Gradowski recalls his entry into the camp. "In these clothes we look like criminals or like confirmed lunatics" (98)—but not like human beings. "We were ashamed of one another," says Lewental, "and dared not look one another in the face. Our eyes swollen with pain, shame, tears and lamentations, each of us burrowed into a hole to avoid meeting one another" (136). The hole they burrow into swallows up their humanity, because what is buried in this hole that resembles a grave is the human face. This distancing between one human being and another, this avoiding of any encounter with the other, creates a void into which every trace of humanity disappears. For the human image belongs not just to this person or that but rises up where two come together face to face.[3] Creating a condition that precludes the proximity of one human being to another, the Nazis defile the human image.

Lewental's remark suggests, moreover, that the forced imposition of shame is not the only thing that characterizes the assault on the face of humanity. Along with shame are tears and lamentations, sorrow and terror, which become not just the transitory emotions that may pass over any face but the essential features of the Jewish face—essential because here the sorrow and the terror in the face are the outward signs of an irreversible cataclysm at the core of the human being. Hence, as the Jews are plunged more and more into the definitive sorrow and terror that the Nazis impose on them, they are less and less able to retain the traces of the human image. For the human life that had shone in their eyes is drained into a sorrow and a terror that by degrees displace the human image of the Jew. Thus it happened that Jews could be recognized not only by the insignia on their sleeves, as Chaim Kaplan points out, but "by the sorrow implanted on their faces" (129)—*implanted* there, mind you, as though the face would not be a Jewish face without this sorrow that is rooted in it. As for the imprint of terror, recall Michael Zylberberg's comment on what had come to be the identifying feature of the Jew: "Their years of tragedy had left their mark on all the Jews. The eyes were still filled with the terror of what had been" (160). What strikes this grown man from Warsaw also overwhelms a teenage girl in Hungary: commenting on her stepfather's return from being held by the Nazis, Éva Heyman writes, "Grandma has noticed that in his eyes you can still see the fear that he brought back with him" (45). The human face is lined with the life that the human being has lived; the Jewish face is marked with the erasure of the human image that might distinguish a human life. For the fear that marks these faces signifies an assault on the face of humanity that is intended to defile the image and the essence of the human being, to the point where that very being is dissipated into sheer terror.

But terror is not the last stage in the attempt to render the Jew faceless. As the assault on the face of the Jew runs its course, his face is gradually emptied of every expression of life that would animate the face. Éva Heyman makes note of this stage in the degeneration of the face in the last entry of her diary. "The gendarme," she writes, "says that he doesn't understand these Jews [as they were being herded into cattle cars]: not even the children cried; all of them were like zombies; like robots. They walked into the wagons so mechanically, without making a sound" (104). Similarly commenting on Jews awaiting deportation from the Lvov Ghetto, David Kahane describes them by saying: "Their faces bespoke quiet, meditative resignation, devoid of fear and theatrics. They had come to the simple conclusion: 'We are Jews and therefore we must die. There is no alternative'" (67). It is not life that animates these faces; rather, they lose their animation to a death that has disfigured them before they are dead. The human image defiled is defiled by the death that imprints itself on the face, making the Jewish face into nothing more than a breathing death mask. And so we begin to see a progression in this mutilation of the face, from shame to sorrow to terror to emptiness.

Indeed, diaries written by a variety of people in a variety of places, from the ghetto to the concentration camp, make this very point about the draining of life from the heart of the human being. Tuvia Borzykowski, for example, claims he could always spot those Jews who, because of their facial features, were trying to pass as Aryans. But the Aryan features were not enough to hide what had become the definitive feature of the Jewish face. "I could tell they were Jews," he says, "by the lifeless eyes, which reflected their inner collapse" (151). In what was once a business school at 12 Prosta Street in Warsaw, to take another example, Chaim Kaplan encounters a group of refugees from Danzig "whose eyes are without a ray of hope or a spark of life" (260). In the Vilna Ghetto, Zelig Kalmanovitch notes that "people are downcast. Their eyes stare into empty space" (59). In Auschwitz, Gradowski raises an outcry over "those who were men once and are now walking ghosts" (97). And in Bergen-Belsen, Hanna Levy-Hass struggles against the same fate creeping over herself. "It is as though my innermost being has grown numb," she relates on 16 August 1944, "and I feel my apathy toward the outer world growing each day" (7). Months later, in March of 1945, she recounts how this undermining of her own being has eaten its way into all humanity: "Everything to be seen here, all that unfolds before our eyes, causes us to begin to doubt the human quality of our being. A dark and heavy doubt rises up—the doubting of humanity" (54). Such is the heinous progression that characterizes the defilement of the human image: the one whose human image is defiled comes to doubt both her own humanity and the humanity of all.

What, then, is the image that the human being assumes as this defilement proceeds? It is the image of the beaten animal imposed upon the Jews by their bestialized oppressors. "There was another transport this morning," Philip Mechanicus writes in this connection. "The men and women who feared they would be deported packed yesterday evening with a resignation that could have been mistaken for courage, but was simply the resignation of human beings not familiar with the passion of indignation and opposition. It is the resignation of caged beasts who have lost their natural impulses and have got used to the cage" (148). During the time of the Shoah every Jew in Europe was caged: each man, woman, and child was locked into a struggle for survival in a camp, a ghetto, or a hiding place. If they were not locked up or in hiding, they were on the run, with dogs on their heels, which is not a human condition—it is a bestial condition. Rendered nameless and homeless, the Jews were rendered faceless. Thus the assault on the home as a center of the sanctity that makes dwelling possible—as the site where the human image is affirmed—resulted not only in making the Jews into homeless wanderers. It transformed them into caged or fleeing beasts. Similar to the journalist Philip

Mechanicus, then, the Romanian teenager Mirjam Korber writes, "We have become beasts. We gaze upon the misfortune of another, and we cannot help" (71). Here we realize that the eclipse of the human image by the image of the beast brings about an eclipse of the relation to the other human being. With the waxing of the bestial image, the distance between one human being and another takes on another dimension. Charlotte Wardi has noted that in naming their dogs "Man" and referring to the Jews as dogs, the SS engineered "the psychological destruction of the Other" (51). But a further consideration of the Holocaust diaries demonstrates that this destruction born of the bestialization of the human being goes beyond the psychological to include the ethical, the physical, and the metaphysical.

In what may be viewed as a chronicle of shame and disgrace, the transformation of the human image into the image of the beast unfolds in the diarists' comments on the Jewish police. "This is a tragedy as deep as the abyss," Chaim Kaplan, for instance, speaks of his horror at these Jews who thought they could save themselves by becoming accomplices to murder. "To help your enemy with your own hands, to save him from his misfortune so that he may turn around and kill you" (375). Killing you is not enough: before the Nazi kills you he defiles you by turning you against your brother, a turning that does violence not only to the brother who is assaulted but to every Jew who lives in fear of the Jewish police. Says Shimon Huberband in May 1942: "All night long, we heard the constant tramping of policemen's boots on the cobblestone streets. This is one of the most horrible misfortunes of the war—the footsteps of the Jewish policemen and one Jew's fear of another Jew" (103). Thus, becoming an accomplice to the imprinting of abject fear on the face of the Jew, the Jewish police have a hand in this defilement of the human image, beginning with themselves, extending to their brother, and ending with all. Like Kaplan and Huberband in the Warsaw Ghetto, then, Aryeh Klonicki-Klonymus of Pinsk writes, "You will no doubt be astonished to learn of the existence of a creature known as a 'Jewish policeman' whose task is to beat up Jews" (40). For reasons that will soon become clear, it is worth translating more literally from the original Hebrew text of Klonicki-Klonymus's diary: "A 'Jewish policeman?!' One is certainly astonished at such a creature. The sole aim of this creature fashioned by Hitler is to beat us with Jewish hands" (27). To this statement we add what Kalmanovitch records in his horror at the Jewish police of the Vilna Ghetto: "What occurred the day before yesterday surpasses in inner tension everything that happened before. Jews raised hands against Jews. The arms intended for the protection of Jewish lives took Jewish lives" (64). And finally we discover an important implication of this testimony from the Holocaust diaries: the human hand is the instrument of the affirmation or the defilement of the human image, both in oneself and in the other. The human image is not some theological or psychological or sociological abstraction; it is embodied in the actions undertaken by human hands.

Therefore Kahane makes an important distinction between the Jewish policemen of the Lvov Ghetto and the Hebrew overseers of ancient Egypt. It is a distinction between what one laid his hands on, and what the other refused to hand over. "Jewish policemen in the Lvov Ghetto," he explains, "did not appear at all like their prototypes—the policemen in ancient Egypt. The latter did not hand over to the Egyptian Gestapo those of their brethren who failed to produce the required quota of bricks. The Midrash interprets the verse 'And the officers of the children of Israel, which Pharaoh's taskmasters had set over them, were beaten' (Exodus 5:14) as meaning that Jewish policemen were risking their lives, beaten and killed by the Egyptian taskmasters, but did not turn over their brethren to their oppressors" (17). Indeed, the *Midrash Rabbah* tells us that this refusal to turn on one another was among the reasons for the Israelites' liberation from Egypt (6:818–19); only a humanity that retains its human image can merit the revelation of the Divine which is the culmination of the exodus out of slavery. And how is that image retained? In the refusal to raise a hand against one another; in the refusal to hand over one's fellow Jews to the oppressors. The *hand* is the key: the hand is the link between one person and another. Which tells us that the human image, whether affirmed or defiled, arises *between* two: there is but a single image.

One's own violence and the violence inflicted by one's fellow Jews can result in self-hatred. This self-hatred is, indeed, the ultimate aim of the assault on the face of humanity. As Fackenheim has noted, "this—nothing less—was the ultimate goal. The Nazi logic of destruction was aimed, ultimately, at the victim's *self*-destruction. . . . Nazism can seek nothing higher from the 'non-Aryan' 'race'-enemy than self-destruction, preceded by self-transformation into the loathsome creature which, according to Nazi doctrine, he has been since birth" (*To Mend* 209). And Wiesel points out an important metaphysical aspect of the self-hate that the Nazis attempt to impose on the Jew: "Self-hate is more harmful than hate toward others. The latter questions man's relationship with man; the first implicates man's relationship to God" (*Oath* 88). Hence the assault on God which is intricately tied to the defilement of the human image generates a hatred of oneself, not just as a human being but as a Jew. "Instead of loathing and despising those foulest dregs of humanity, the accursed German nation," writes Katznelson, "we have begun to hate ourselves" (94). As Fackenheim suggests, this self-hatred is more than the hatred of oneself as a person; it is a hatred of oneself as a Jew. This, then, is the height of the Nazis' defilement of the human image of the Jew: they engender among the Chosen a longing to be unchosen—which would mean abandoning the sacred task of attesting to the sanctity of each human being, a task from which the very image of the human being is derived.

"When you remove from a child his 'Jewish gene,'" Katznelson states it, "you remove from him the 'human gene'" (152). When the assault on the face of humanity is successful, it results in a longing on the part of the Jew to be rid of his Jewish face. When it works most nefariously, it works on a child. Among the diarists who are children, in fact, there are some who fall prey to this horror. The thirteen-year-old Éva Heyman, for example, writes, "I would go with Aunt Jakobi, or with Sanyi, to any place in the world where they don't know that I'm Jewish and wherefrom I couldn't be taken to Poland like Marta was" (80). Ringelblum comments on a more extreme instance, noting, "In a refugee center an eight-year-old child went mad. Screamed, 'I want to steal, I want to rob. I want to eat, I want to be a German.' In his hunger he hated being Jewish" (39). And yet to be Jewish in the Nazi antiworld is to be trapped in the throes of a hunger that eats away at the humanity of the face, eats its way into the soul, until the human being succumbs to the madness of longing to be the enemy. Since it was impossible for a Jew to become a German, some did the next best—or the next worst—thing, as Ringelblum indicates. "A great many cases of conversion," he laments. "At Hoshana Raba time more than fifty Jews were converted (data from the Council). The reason being that the Catholics look after their converts. . . . This is a pathological phenomenon" (225–26). This last phrase is crucial. For even more than Ringelblum's previous remark about the madness of the eight-year-old child, it points up a fragmentation of identity indicative of the defilement of the human image. Instead of the image of man, what the Nazis imposed on humanity was the image of the madman.

THE SPECTER OF MADNESS

Imposed not only on the Jew but on the humanity embodied by the Jew, madness manifests itself during the Holocaust on a massive scale. "The popular unrest is dreadful," says Ringelblum in October 1941. "The populace has lost its head" (218). Why? Because the erasure of the reference points by which these people make sense of the world leads to a loss of the senses. But madness is not just a later development arising out of the defilement of the human image; rather, it is engineered from the start as an aspect of that defilement. The onset of madness, then, is something that Ringelblum comments on in one of the first entries of this diary in which the concern with madness is a recurring motif. "Noticeable increase in the number of madmen," he writes on 21 February 1940. "Heard about a good-looking ten-year-old boy beaten on the head who went mad" (21). On 24 March 1940 he notes, "Mietek Zucker from Lodz, who defended his father from an attack by soldiers, is in the madhouse" (35). And recall his mention of the woman on the truck headed for Warsaw, the one who tried to save her three-year-old child after a guard had thrown him to the side of the road; as she was about to jump off the truck and go to her child, the Nazi threatened to shoot all the Jews on the truck, if she did not abandon the little one. "The mother arrived in Warsaw," Ringelblum finishes this terrible tale, "and here went out of her mind" (131). What these last two examples have in common is that they are cases of people who struggled to keep their hold on their human image by attending to the need of a loved one. Those who are sane, hale and whole, derive their sanity from their relation to the humanity closest to them. Plunged into the absolute isolation of madness, that relation is lost. And the image of their own humanity is therefore defiled.

Hence, in their concern with the human image defiled, many Holocaust diarists enter into their diaries a testimony on those driven mad. "We met Naomi Vag," says the sculptor Rivosh from Riga. "She has decided to give up on life since her husband Monya was burned alive in a synagogue. She creates the impression of being somewhat unbalanced" (324–35). The phrase from the original Russian text of this diary translated as "give up on life" is *uiti iz zhizni*, which literally means she has decided to "depart from life" (328). That is the mark of her being unbalanced, or *ne vpolne normal'noi*, "not altogether normal" (328): buried in the solitude of insanity, her madness is tied to the breaking of all ties with a life that sustains the human image. The engineered isolation of Jewish humanity into ghettos and camps is calculated to create an absolute isolation of the human being from life—a departure from life, as in the case of Naomi Vag—which, among many of these victims, culminates in the isolation of madness. Indeed, turning to an entry from Josef Katz's diary, we see a madness that manifests itself as a severing from the very wellspring of life. "A young Jew from Lodz," he relates, "goes insane. 'Mama,' he screams incessantly, 'Mama!'" (244). Madness entails a tearing of all signifiers from what they signify. If Katz takes this scream of "Mama!" to signify madness, it is because this scream invokes the signifier of life—the mother—from which the young Jew has been torn; torn from the source of his human being, he is twisted into madness. As though falling into a black hole, the man recedes from the mother who first uttered his name with love and in that utterance announced his humanity. When his humanity is undone, he cries out for the one who first affirmed his humanity, but he receives no response. Receiving no response from his human origin, he slips away from all humanity; receding from the source of his humanity, he recedes into insanity.

The metaphor of the black hole has other implications. It suggests, for example, a certain field of gravity surrounding the madman which draws others into its depths; just as a black hole swallows up all light, madness can swallow up the light of reason in all who are near it. In this connection Katz describes a scene from a barge floating down the Vistula on its way to Danzig in the fall of 1944: "I don't know whether from hunger or pain, but crying women are dangerous because their crying is contagious and can cause a panic. We try to comfort them as best we can and apply improvised bandages, but the prolonged hardships of the voyage without sleep or food have found their ultimate expression in this one hysterical scream" (206). Thus, like the human image that is lost in the abyss of madness, madness is itself a condition that arises between people. This hysteria that spreads like a contagion throughout the barge bound for Danzig also spreads throughout the ghetto. On 26 November 1940, for instance, Kaplan writes, "Jewish Warsaw has turned into a madhouse" (226). And nearly four months later, on 11 March 1941, he reiterates, "In reality, we don't have a ghetto, but a madhouse" (255). In reality, there occurs here a complete perversion of reality into the unreality of madness. Within the realm of human being, reality is a human reality that rests upon the sanctity and the meaning of the human image as it is revealed in open-armed human relation. The defilement of that image, then, is accompanied by a collapse of humanity into itself, where the real and the unreal exchange places; instead of arms open to relation we find arms folded in isolation, as though constrained by a straitjacket. Taking up his task within the confines of this constraint, the Holocaust diarist must engage his labor amidst the ruins of a collapsing reality, without being sucked into the overwhelming gravitational field of madness. Like a man clinging to his craft in the eddy of a maelstrom, he clings to the word that he brings to his diary.

Hence we find many diarists who struggle to maintain a hold on their own humanity in the midst of the madness rising around them and threatening to rise up within them. This struggle comes out when Moshe Flinker, for instance, writes: "My sister told me that Mrs. Keller, who was taken away with her whole family, has gone mad! I never before imagined that from the immensity of one's troubles one can go mad, but now I have found that even this affliction has not been spared us. Madness, too, is among us. When I heard that this good woman had gone mad I suddenly understood what I had been fearing until now" (75). In Flinker's original Hebrew text there is a sentence following "Madness, too, is among us" that was omitted from the English translation. It is "The affliction unfolds and literally congeals before my eyes" (66). What unfolds before his eyes is a darkness gathering in his eyes. Striving to sustain his human image, he gazes upon the image of the other, only to behold that image defiled by madness. In the case of Janusz Korczak, to take another example, the image before his eyes is the image of his father. But it is not a source of comfort: "I used to be desperately afraid of the lunatic asylum. My father was sent there several times. So I am the son of a madman. A hereditary affliction" (164). If he used to be afraid of what might befall him, he is now terrified that madness is indeed creeping over him. "More than two score years have gone by," he says, "and to this day this thought is a torment to me" (165). And as the thought torments him, it threatens to twist his image into the very thing he fears. For in the faces of the Jews who surround him, contorted as they are with madness, Korczak beholds the face of his father, as well as the image of his own face. It is a face that he is less and less able to recognize.

Because the face of a human being is a face that speaks, the diarist may retain the traces of his humanity by speaking through his diary. With words he endeavors to sustain a humanity that the delirious discourse of madness endangers. But the words he must speak—the words pertaining to *this* event—are such that the very thing offering a refuge for him also poses a danger to him. Katznelson makes this point by saying: "I am seized with mental nausea as I scrape these running sores day by day. It depresses and maddens me" (47–48). These running sores are not only the wounds inflicted in the defilement of humanity but also the words that issue from those wounds. The Holocaust diarist scrapes these wounds with words that are themselves like open wounds, from which all meaning is bleeding away. And so the words he writes are haunted by the very madness that he seeks to overcome and that he knows will consume him. For in the same entry, dated 21 July 1943, Katznelson declares, "When the nations will have concluded peace and their peoples will come trampling over the unmarked graves of our slain, in the towns and villages, then I shall certainly go insane" (48–49). Here we see that the sanity of the human being inheres in having a future in which the fullness of humanity may be realized. The human image is an image of a what is yet to be. As madness, then, undoes the human image, isolating the man from his humanity and from the humanity of others, it isolates him from a future: the madman is locked into the torment of an eternal present divorced from time. Thus, similar to Katznelson, the Romanian diarist Emil Dorian writes, "I was dizzy with everything that happened and so terrified that I felt close to madness at the thought of what is yet to come" (129). This dizziness steeped in terror is a dizziness that comes with hanging by one's heels over a future transformed into an abyss, a future devoid of all human presence, itself defiled in the defilement of the human image. The difficulty facing the Holocaust diarist, who day by day measures out the time of this obliteration of time, is to move along the edge of madness without falling prey to it and without turning away from it. It is the difficulty of remaining human, when remaining human may itself be a form of madness.

And so Elie Wiesel writes, "'It came to pass in those days,' said Rabbi Michael Dov Weismandel, 'that normal beings had to lose their reason, and those who did not lose it—were not normal'" (*Six Days* 48). It happened that those who were not normal chose to resemble the murderers rather than lose their reason. And yet to resemble the murderers is to take on the image of the beast emptied of reason which they themselves have assumed. We have seen the horror of this phenomenon in the diarists' comments on the Jewish policemen. Let us now consider how they deal with "the others," with those whose human image is defiled by assuming the image of evil.

THE INHUMANITY OF THE OTHERS

In the *Tosefta*, a collection of teachings and commentaries from the talmudic period which were not included in the Talmud, we are taught that Adam was created after all the animals "so that he would not join with them and act after their manner" (*Sanhedrin* 8:7). Now the name *Adam*, of course, means "human being." What does it mean to act in a manner in keeping with being human? It is to act with compassion and loving kindness toward our fellow human being, so that we may be free of the struggle for survival, for power and pleasure, that characterizes an animalistic existence. In a word, to act as a human being, as a child of Adam, is to do good. That is why the *Tosefta* teaches us further that "it is hard for a person to hate evil without fulfilling what is written against idolatry, open wantonness, and the spilling of blood"

(*Menachot* 23:22). For these are the means by which people prey upon one another like beasts, thereby losing their human image; and a good deal of our humanity lies in shunning evil. In the time of the Shoah, the Nazis represent the epitome of idolatry, wantonness, and the spilling of blood.[4] The perfect representatives of idolatry, wantonness, and murder, the Nazis are the perfect representatives of the evil that is more than the contrary of good. It is the contrary of humanity, "a counternature," as Levinas expresses it, "a monstrosity, what is disturbing and foreign of itself" (*Collected* 180). What is a monstrosity? It is not the animal found in the realm of the animal, situated in the animal kingdom, but is rather the joining of the animal to the image of the human, where the face becomes a snout and hands turn into claws.

Understood as monstrosity, then, the evil that would defile the human image in the victim ends in a defilement of the perpetrator's humanity.[5] The horror is that the other man is not a man, that this other who resembles a man is in fact inhuman; while the killer may have facial features, he does not have a face—that is the horror. He does not have a face, despite his appearance, because he is deaf to the prohibition against killing that comes to us in a face-to-face encounter. "I look at the faces of the Germans," says Avraham Tory, for example. "I wonder: it would seem that they are human beings like everyone else; where, then, does their cruelty come from? What is the source of their lust for blood? Of hatred for hatred's sake?" (427). Tory's questions arise from a radical incongruity lying at the heart of what is foreign of itself. In this very incongruity, then, lie the monstrosity of evil and the horror over the image of the other man. And yet behind this horror there lurks a greater horror: this monstrous other looks very much like everyone else, very much like *me*.[6] Once again we realize that the image of the divine is implicated in the human image. The question is: how do the Holocaust diarists answer to this implication?

One means adopted by the diarists is to call into question the Nazi's status as a son of man. Kalmanovitch, for instance, describes the SS officer Martin Weiss by saying: "His face, the face of a murderer, becomes him. He drinks blood and is not sated. I am stupefied. How does a man like this live? The very thought that nearby at the table, before the electric light, sits such a monstrous creature is dreadful. He is inscrutable. There has never been anything like it" (38). Never anything like it: here too the diarist collides with the foreign of itself, with the man who is not a man. Indeed, what is translated simply as "man" in this passage is the Hebrew phrase *ben adam*, which means son of man, or son of Adam (90). Once again we find that the monstrosity of the other lies in an alien incongruity: he is not what he appears to be, not a son of man who bears the face of Adam, but a murderer of man. And, once again, we see that in assaulting the face of humanity, the Nazis lose their own faces. Ringelblum underscores this point with an anecdote from the Warsaw Ghetto. "A police chief," he writes, "came to the apartment of a Jewish family, wanted to take some things away. The woman cried out that she was a widow with a child. The chief said he'd take nothing if she could guess which of his eyes was the artificial one. She guessed the left eye. She was asked how she knew. 'Because that one,' she answered, 'has a human look'" (84). What does the face of the killer look like; what is the face that becomes him? It looks like a face that is not a face. It has eyes that are like yours and mine and yet are blind to human suffering; it has hands—yes, hands—that, like yours and mine, are made for nourishing life but insist on taking life. The face that is not a face does not respond to the other; it does not commune or communicate.[7] Entombed in himself, the Nazi is blind to his own artificial eye. Blind to his blindness, this faceless beast does not see his face in the face of the Jew. Instead, he sees a creature who has no face.

But the diarist who attests to this horror is not faceless. From the pages of his diary his face speaks in an effort to maintain his vision of the human image, despite the inhumanity of the others. Recall, for example, the questions that Kaplan wrestles with when he writes: "How is it possible to attack a stranger to me, a man of flesh and blood like myself, to wound him and trample upon him, and cover his body with sores, bruises, and welts, without any reason? How is it possible? Yet I swear that I saw all this with my own eyes" (242). Like the disbelief of those who were told of the Nazis' atrocities, Kaplan's disbelief is couched in his own humanity. Because he struggles to retain his human image, he is incredulous at the defilement of the human image even as it transpires before his very eyes. Realizing that what the Jews suffer in the ghetto is unlike any other instance of brutality, Kaplan points out what distinguishes the Nazis from others who have reveled in torturing the Jews. "Even the sadists," he says, "used to be tempered with a sense of shame; their cruelty was perpetrated in secret places, not in public. But since the coming of Nazism public shame has ceased, and the more one practices cruelty in public, the better" (331). Even when covered with shame, the face of the human being still retains the traces of a face; to have a face is to be capable of being shamefaced. Incapable of shame, the Nazis' pride in the public display of their cruelty is a major part of what links their assault on the human image to a defilement of the human image within themselves. Not only do they spill blood—they wallow in it. Refusing to turn their faces away in shame and insisting upon showing their faces in public, they show themselves to be without a face: they show themselves to be inhuman.

Among the "others" who lost their humanity were those who were all too eager to become the accomplices of the Nazis. They too are the subject of the diarists' testimony on the human image defiled. To the Gentiles of Romania, says Dorian, for example, the Jews were nothing more than "a target for stones" (9). And, commenting on a march of Jews into the Siauliai Ghetto, Eliezer Yerushalmi writes: "Many Lithuanians follow these sorrow-ridden people along the sidewalks out of curiosity. Very few have anything in common with their affliction; the vast majority either look upon this migration with indifference or shout insults at them" (229). While Dorian and Yerushalmi comment on those who throw stones and shout insults at the Jews, the diarists writing from the ghettos of Poland attest to much more severe cases of the inhumanity of the others. Consider, for instance the questions that Shlomo Frank raises about the humanity of the good Christians who surround the Jews of Lodz: "Where are the 'good-hearted' people who once spoke of saving humanity from a holocaust? Of what use is their care for the world when they have all fallen asleep? Of what use will they be when in the final hour there is no relief from despair?" (333). The humanity of the human being is distinguished by a capacity to transform difference into non-indifference—that is the meaning of the human being's wakefulness. When difference collapses into the sleep of the same, people die.

And people kill: the reaction of the Polish others is not confined to the sleep of indifference. During the bombing of Silev on 4 September 1939, Shimon Huberband notes a level of inhumanity more dangerous than indifference: "Jews cried out the *Shma*, recited confessions and the *Al Chet*. The Gentiles, to distinguish between the holy and the profane, crossed themselves and recited their prayers. But soon the Gentiles began to scream loudly that the Jews ought to be slaughtered" (20). No sooner do the Polish Christians here invoke the name of God, with their prayers still warm on their lips, than they cry out for the death of the Jews. Thus defiling their prayers, they defile their souls, as they turn the blessing of God into a curse on humanity. In a similar vein, Adam Czerniakow reports a conversation that he had with a priest, saying: "I returned a visit to Reverend Poplawski, who called on me at one time on the subject of assistance to the Christians of Jewish origin. He proceeded to tell me that he sees God's hand in being placed in the ghetto, that after the war he would leave as much of an anti-Semite as he was when he arrived there, and that the Jewish beggars (children) have considerable acting talent, even playing dead in the streets" (261). There is perhaps no greater mark of the inhumanity of the others than this blindness to the death of children. And it is an inhumanity found in a creature called a Christian, who claims to adore the one known as the Son of Man.

Of course, those Polish Christians who are blind to the death of children are easily inclined either to ignore or to participate in the murder of men and women. During the Warsaw Ghetto Uprising of April 1943, Helena Dorembus, who was in hiding on the Aryan side of the wall, asserts: "Groups of Poles watch women with children in their arms leap from the blazing balconies. The Aryan tables are set. The smell of Easter dishes nauseates me. My landlord shuts the window to keep out the smoke of the ghetto" (59). When Jesus presided over the Last Supper, he enjoined his followers to remember him whenever they place bread and wine in their mouths (see Luke 22:19). But the ones who here eat and drink their Easter suppers in remembrance of the Last Supper have forgotten both these words from Jesus and his Jewish brethren. When those who have become inhuman do remember the Jews, it is often in the way that Dorembus describes when she relates: "In the evening a young Pole passed our house carrying a set of jaws which had belonged to a Jew. Among the two rows of teeth were several gold ones. 'A hundred, a hundred, the best quality gold!' he cried, as though conducting an auction" (61). Thus we see what becomes of the mouth of the Jew when the Gentile loses his humanity, filling his mouth with his Easter morsels. In some cases, even when a Pole took a Jew into hiding, he would still adopt a stance like the one adopted by the Christian who hid Tuvia Borzykowski immediately after the Uprising. "The Polish government after the war ," his host declared, "will have to finish off what Hitler started to do with the Jews" (145–46). One can see why Katznelson was convinced that he would go insane after the war, or why Dorian had such a maddening dread of the future. For the inhumanity of the others comes to this obliteration of any future for the Jews.

During the Shoah, then, the scope of the defilement of the human image is total. It includes both the defilement of human identity and the destruction of human time. Which is to say: it includes the defilement of human life and the desecration of human death. Hillel Seidman notes that, after visiting the Warsaw cemetery one day, he "left with the feeling that no human beings were buried there" (49). Why? Because each destroyed and desecrated memorial not only signified a grave in which the dead lay buried; it also signified a life that had placed death on its proper ground through a sanctification of the living. Therefore a humanity defiled was a humanity removed both from life and from death. "As some were deprived of their identity," Wiesel points out, "so others were deprived of their death" (*Six Days* 46). If at Auschwitz not only was man killed but also the idea of man, then at Auschwitz not only were lives consumed but death itself was made into something other than death.

DEATH AND THE DEATH OF DEATH

"CHOOSE LIFE," GOD ENJOINS ALL JEWS IN HIS TORAH (Deuteronomy 30:19). Indeed, to be among the Chosen of God is precisely to make this choice. Choosing life, we do not choose merely to be alive—we choose to affirm the holiness of a life that has its origin in the Holy One. Making this choice, then, does not mean that we do not pass away from this earth; it does not entail the removal of death from the world. Rather, it means that in choosing life we understand death to be part of the process of sanctifying life, the testimonial outcome of living a life steeped in Torah study, religious observance, and deeds of loving kindness. Thus death is not eliminated; like life, it is situated within the contexts of the sacred. Death is the culmination, not the negation, of life.[1] It is not opposed to life as evil is opposed to good; rather it is a task that confronts us in the course of life. Murder is evil; in itself death is not. Standing by while people die is evil; in itself dying is not. Taking death to be part of life, one begins the *Kaddish*, the Prayer for the Dead, with a magnification and sanctification of the Name of God, in whom all life originates, and one ends by declaring, "Amen." Placed on its proper ground, on its hallowed ground, death in the Jewish tradition becomes an occasion for humanity's affirmation of the dearness of life.

Franz Rosenzweig elaborates on this Jewish understanding of the proper place of death in the realm of creation when he writes: "Within the general Yea of creation, bearing everything individual on its broad back, an area is set apart which is affirmed differently, which is 'very' affirmed. Unlike anything else in creation, it points beyond creation. This 'very' heralds a supercreation within creation itself, something more than worldly within the worldly, something other than life which yet belongs to life and only to life, which was created with life as its ultimate, and which yet first lets life surmise a fulfillment beyond life: this 'very' is death. The created death of the creature portends the revelation of a life which is above the creaturely level. For each created thing, death is the very consummator of its entire materiality. It removes creation imperceptibly into the past, and thus turns it into the tacit, permanent prediction of the miracle of its removal. That is why, on the sixth day, it was not said that it was 'good,' but rather 'behold, very good!' 'Very,' so the sages teach, 'very'—that is death" (*Star* 155). To choose life is to choose this "very good" that distinguishes the living from the inanimate. It inheres in the *nefesh* or soul that is life itself. Therefore choosing this "very good" means realizing that the basis of our ethical relation to another soul—underlying all love for our neighbor—is our fear for his death. In our fear for the death of the other person, we draw nigh unto him in an act of offering. This "approach," says Emmanuel Levinas, "inasmuch as it is a sacrifice, confers a sense on death. In it, the absolute singularity of the responsible one encompasses the generality or generalization of death" (*Otherwise* 129). So encompassed, death is overcome through an ultimate declaration of "Here I am" before the other. What Levinas here describes is martyrdom, which is an assertion that life is "very good" in the very midst of a dying for another that encompasses death. Unless one is able to connect death with this "very good," one becomes entrenched in the proposition that there is no higher good than one's own survival. Thus left with nothing but oneself to live for, one has nothing to die for. And, without the fulfillment of life beyond life, one's life is emptied of meaning.

During the Shoah, the Jewish struggle to situate death within the contexts of the "very good" is what Harry James Cargas describes as "another form of struggle which some consider to be on an even higher plane than that of physical courage." Quoting Dr. Leo Eitinger, he goes on to explain: "There has been a Jewish religious tradition throughout the centuries, where 'dying as a man' means something quite different from what Western people usually understand by this expression. To die as a man, or as a Jew—for the religious Jew it is the same thing—means to die with the 'Shema' and with the Holy Name of God on their lips, without resistance, without 'falling into the abyss of the aggressor, namely to kill just as he did'" (*Reflections* 25). Ultimately, to live as a human being is to die as a human being. And to die as a human being is to affirm even in death that life is very good, speaking even in death the Name of the One who is the origin of life in a declaration of "*Shema Yisrael!*" This utterance of "Hear, O Israel" is itself an offering of life to all who hear it. Therefore, even as the tide of death is rising all around him, Josef Katz is able to see that, at least in his mother's case, death was not all encompassing but rather was encompassed. For soon after he arrived at the camp in Jungfernhof he received a message that read: "My dear Josef, your mother died last night of a stroke in the arms of Chief Rabbi Carlbach. She recited the 'Shema Yisrael'" (37). What transpires in the Nazis' imposition of death upon all of European Jewry, however, is not only the end of Jewish life but the end of the Jewish affirmation of life that lies in dying as a human being.[2] And so we see a connection between the defilement of the human image and what is here referred to as "the death of death." Indeed, *this* death belongs to the singularity of the Holocaust itself: casting the Jews into a deluge of death calculated to destroy their humanity, the Nazis deprive the Jews of the death—of the "very good"—that forms the foundation of their life as human beings.

Because this death and the death of death are definitive features of the Holocaust, they are a significant part of what is addressed in the Holocaust diary. "We die anonymously," writes Ruth Andreas-Friedrich, for example (179): stifling the Name of God on the lips of the dying, the Nazis render the Jews themselves not only lifeless but nameless, literally anonymous. They are not laid to rest in a grave, with their names inscribed on a memorial—they are forced to "live" in a grave that must remain unmarked lest they be murdered, in what Hillel Seidman calls the "underground world" of bunkers and hiding places (221). While Helena Dorembus delighted in the sight of SS men being killed during the Warsaw Ghetto Uprising (58), those German dead retained a certain place in death that connected them to life, a place that was denied to the Jews: they retained their names.[3] But the Nazis saw to it that the Jewish dead had no such link to the living. Each Jew was murdered many times over, in body, in soul, in memory, in name, in substance—and in death. Perhaps that is why Adam

Czerniakow kept a model of a Jewish gravestone on his desk (90): to remind himself not only of the ubiquitous death that overwhelmed the Jews but of the calculated obliteration of death that was a distinctive aspect of the Nazis' metaphysical assault on humanity. It was a marker for a people who had no other marker, a sign of their link to life in a realm devoid of all such signs. And as soon as he situates this sign among the signifiers that comprise his diary, the diary itself becomes such a sign: unlike any other diary, the Holocaust diary is a gravestone that links the dead to the living in an effort to recapture the attachment of life to life.

"In Judaism," Rabbi Adin Steinsaltz teaches us, "holiness is first and foremost the sanctity of life. Where life abounds, holiness is at hand. 'Life' is a synonym for all that is most exalted in Creation. One of the names of God is 'the God of life.' The Torah is described as 'the Torah of life.' The Torah itself speaks of 'life and goodness' as of one and the same thing" (*Strife* 192–93). And all of these things that are life—Torah, God, and goodness—the Nazis sought to exterminate by flooding the Jewish world with death. In this chapter, then, we shall consider the nature of the death with which the Nazis overwhelmed Jewish life and how that death went into the murder of death itself. For this murder, not only of life but of a sanctified death in life, belongs to the singularity of the Holocaust. And the account of this murder is a singular feature of the Holocaust diary.

THE ENCOMPASSING UBIQUITY OF DEATH

If, as Levinas has indicated, death takes on some sense when the totality of death is encompassed, life is rendered void of all sense and meaning when death is itself the totality. Just such a totality confronts the Romanian teenager Mirjam Korber, when she declares, "Hundreds of people die, and usually it is the best ones who die" (75). The best ones are those who choose life. And yet in choosing life they are chosen by death. Why? Because, in an overturning of meaning, the very traits of generosity and loving kindness that in the world of humanity engender life are turned against those who possess those traits in the antiworld, until finally the ones who choose life end by succumbing to death. "There are times," writes Korber, "when I might manage to hope for the end of this war and to see once more the beautiful days that used to be. But death is better" (99). Which is to say: death is more than those days of life. When such words are forced into the mouth of a child—when a girl in the flower of life deems death to be better than life—death is indeed all-encompassing. No longer a task to be engaged over the course of three score and ten years, death here becomes the stuff of a life transformed into an antilife before it is lived. That is what the death's head, the symbol set like a frontlet between the eyes of the SS, signifies: the life of the Jew is defined by and confined to an all-encompassing death.

Indeed, for the Jew trapped in the Holocaust Kingdom, the encompassing hand of death reaches even into the womb. "Most of us," we remember Isabella Leitner's address to an infant born in Auschwitz, "are born to live—to die, but to live first. You, dear darling, you are being born only to die. How good of you to come before roll call though, so your mother does not have to stand at attention while you are being born. Dropping out of the womb onto the ground with your mother's thighs shielding you like wings of angels is an infinitely nicer way to die than being fed to the gas chamber. But we are not having *Zeil Appell*, so we can stand around and listen to your mother's muffled cries. And now that you are born, your mother begs to see you, to hold you. But we know that if we give you to her, there will be a struggle to take you away again, so we cannot let her see you because you don't belong to her. You belong to the gas chamber" (31–32). To be sure, the term *Holocaust* means that every Jew in Europe belongs to the gas chamber, born not to live first and then die but to die, first and last. Leitner reminds us that for the Jews under the Nazi regime, death was the punishment for giving birth, so that here we have a connection between the assault on motherhood, discussed in chapter 9, and the reign of death. In order that their mothers at least might be spared, infants were put to death by the loving hands that delivered them into the world . For the Jews, then, living itself became a dying. The angel's wings that surrounded them are wings covered with eyes: they are the wings of the Angel of Death.

And so in his Warsaw Ghetto diary Seidman asserts, "the dark wings of the Angel of Death spread over the extinguished sparks of life" (63). So pervasive is death in the Warsaw Ghetto that the Angel becomes as seductive as it is dreadful, leading many to spend the days of their lives seeking death. "The number of suicides among the Jews," Czerniakow records in his diary on 10 October 1940, "has been greatly increasing during the last months" (205). Instilling in the Jews a desire for death, the Nazis achieve just what they set out to achieve: not only would they kill the Jews, but they would force them into a longing for death. And those who do not succumb to suicide succumb to death nevertheless. "Typhus is raging," says Czerniakow on 4 December 1941. "Friends and acquaintances are dying all around me" (305). A sea of death rises all around the diarist, until death becomes as all-encompassing to him as the sea is to a drowning man. The breath of life and the air upon which that breath is drawn—the *neshamah* and *ruach*—are no longer there. The atmosphere of the Holocaust Kingdom is not one in which a Jew can breathe, and, like the atmosphere surrounding a planet, it extends throughout that Kingdom. Hence, in another ghetto, fifteen-year-old Dawid Rubinowicz writes: "Already a lot of Jewish blood has flowed in this Bieliny, in fact a whole Jewish cemetery has already grown up there. When will this terrible bloodshed finally end? If this goes on much longer then people will drop like flies out of sheer horror" (55). The horror arises here not just at the spectacle of death and murder but at the sense that death and murder are the only reality. Indeed, the horror is itself a kind of death that steals over the living before they are dead. Planet Auschwitz, which extends far beyond the confines of the death camps, has an immense field of gravity that tugs on the soul of every Jew, and its deadly, ashen atmosphere fills every Jewish mouth. Unlike other diaries, the Holocaust diary is not the daily record of a life but is the account of a daily struggle against death.

Thus the Romanian diarist Emil Dorian cries out: "I try to tear myself out of the vortex that is pulling me down. I did manage to complete a translation, it sits ready on my desk, but everything has a taste of ashes and sticks in my throat like a foretaste of death" (167). The lifeline to which the diarist clings as he struggles against the vortex of death is the word that he consigns to the pages of his diary. Returning meaning and life to the word is his one means of resisting the overturning of meaning in the realm of death. For the work of this overturning also arises from words, from words used not to join word to meaning and life to life, but to tear the life from the souls of the Jews. The foretaste of death that fouls the mouth of the diarist, then, issues from the mouths of the Nazis and their minions, whose death-orders vibrate on their breath and foul the air. In this connection Herman Kruk comments on an announcement of death made by the notorious Jacob Gens, head of the Jewish Council in the Vilna Ghetto, saying: "A loud weeping breaks out as he begins. A gust of Ponary bursts into the hall, a breath of death, memories of men, women, and children snatched away" (41). Once again, like the atmosphere surrounding Planet Auschwitz, the breath of corruption rises up from Ponary to flood the Vilna Ghetto. "The district Ponar," Yitskhok Rudashevski cries out, "is soaked in Jewish blood. Ponar is the same as a nightmare, a nightmare which accompanies the gray strand of our ghetto-days" (41). And the nightmare is as everpresent—and ultimately as mundane—as the day itself. The nightmare is a daymare, as banal and diurnal as the setting of the sun. But in the Kingdom of Night the sun does not set—it turns to darkness. Instead of living in the light of day, the diarist is turned over to the gray of the ghetto-day, which swallows up any life that may issue from the earth.

Indeed, the death that the Nazis spread about the world is so pervasive that the earth itself seems to wither at its touch. "Throughout the summer," laments David Kahane, for example, "I have seen no green vegetation or the shape of a flower. . . . Are there any Jews left in the world? . . . Do Jews still rise to say Selikhoth somewhere?" (3). Here we have the interconnections linking the absence of Jews to the absence of prayer, and the absence of prayer to the absence of life. And so, in the ghetto, what becomes commonplace is not the beds of flowers seen in the neighborhoods of humanity, but pools of blood. "Puddles of blood have become an ordinary sight," writes Rivosh from the Riga Ghetto. "We walk past them, step in them" (340). Hence the blood of the dead clings to the living: the Jew who walks these streets leaves behind him a trail of death, tracking it everywhere he goes, down the sidewalks where he lives and into his home. This trail of blood is the trace of the death that not only awaits him but is all around him. Thus established as the condition assigned to Jewish existence, death is not only an ontological ubiquity. It is altogether ordinary. "We become quite used to the sight of women walking to their death," Josef Katz comments on the situation at Stutthof, "and the chimney, too, no longer bothers us" (216). The clouds bellowing from the chimney are as mundane as the clouds in the sky. To be sure, they take the place of the clouds in the sky, eclipsing those clouds that God set in the heavens, eclipsing God Himself. For in their assault on God, the Nazis have set other clouds on high, clouds of death that bring all things low, to the same level of empty indifference, erasing the difference between life and death. "There is a marked, remarkable indifference to death, which no longer impresses" says Emmanuel Ringelblum of the attitude that pervades the Warsaw Ghetto. "One walks past corpses with indifference" (194). The Yiddish word used here for "indifference" is *gleikhgiltikeit* (153), which literally means "having the same value." The same value as what? The same value as life: there is no qualitative distinction between life and death. The lines of demarcation have been erased.

No longer, then, is one human being joined to another according to an everyday life shared; their only interhuman link, which is not inter*human* at all, is a death endured each day. Indeed, the borderlines between the living and the dead are literally and graphically blurred, as Leon Wells suggests in his remarks about the prisoners working on the Janowska Death Brigade, those who were assigned to dig up mass graves and burn the bodies: "Their hands are caked with the fluids from the corpses so that one cannot differentiate between the flesh of their hands and the flesh of the corpses" (151). Like those who track blood everywhere they walk, these men who are seized by death bring death to everything they touch. For they have been touched by the hands of the dead. The previous day, on 15 June 1943, Wells had written in his diary: "Some of the bodies in the fire have their hands extended. It looks as if they are pleading to be taken out. Many bodies are lying around with open mouths. Could they be trying to say: 'We are your own mothers, fathers, who raised you and took care of you. Now you are burning us.' If they could have spoken, maybe they would have said this, but they are forbidden to talk too" (141–42). Once again we see the erasure of life—the obliteration of the difference between life and death—in the erasure of the word. What makes the living indistinguishable from the dead, and at times indifferent toward the dead, is this deathly silence imposed on both. "Death is silence," says André Neher, "silence overtaking life" (*Exile* 37), and as the Nazis flood the world with death, they deluge the world with silence. Both opposing this silence and transmitting it, the diarist fetches the words from the mouths of the dead and brings them to his diary, where, perhaps, the difference between life and death may be re-established, even if for only a moment. And the difference is re-established by making that difference into a nonindifference.

But the diarist cannot take on a stance of nonindifference toward the death of the other without being implicated by that death and by the indifference that would collapse the distinction between life and death.[4] In our relation to the other person we see more than he can see: we see his face, in which are inscribed both his sanctity and his mortality. In the realm of the Holocaust the encompassing ubiquity of death blinds us to the face of the other, which is a blindness to life and death, just as it is a blindness to light and dark. Through the words he sets to the page in an act of nonindifference, the diarist sees excessively; that is, he comes to see more than the totality of death that surrounds him. And where does he see the life and death, to which a ubiquitous death threatens to blind him? In the other person. "Death," says Levinas, "is *present* only in the Other, and only in him does it summon me urgently to my final essence, to my responsibility" (*Totality* 179). Therefore, getting rid of the other, we get rid of death. And if we can get rid of death, then we can get rid of the other. Only others lie in the cemeteries. But during the Holocaust those who lay in their graves in the cemeteries—indeed, as we shall see, the cemeteries themselves that situated death in the midst of life and placed it on its proper ground, on its sacred ground—were under attack. For eliminating the "others"—the Jews—was the Nazis' aim, and this they did, in part, by eliminating the cemeteries.[5] Such was the project that the Nazis undertook in the murder of death: removing Jewish death from Jewish life, they sought to remove the Jew from life.

Let us consider how this process might be understood.

THE DEATH OF DEATH

In the foregoing, horror was described as a form of death that steals over the living before they are dead. Thus, if horror is a kind of death, it may well be viewed not as a *fear* of death but as the *death* of death. "Horror is nowise an anxiety about death," Levinas makes this point. "In horror a subject is stripped of his subjectivity, of his power to have a private existence. . . . It is a participation in the *there is*, in the *there is* which returns in the heart of every negation, in the *there is* that has 'no exits.' It is, if we may say so, the impossibility of death, the universality of existence even in its annihilation" (*Existence* 61). Stripped of his subjectivity, both the human being and his world are stripped of all significance. To be a subject who lives and dies is to take up the project of making sense of a world. Bereft of both world and sense, the human being is not alive—he is simply there; the world has no inherent meaning or value—it is simply there. The "there is," then, consists of being in the midst of an indifferent being that is merely there, where there is no evaluation of life or death and therefore no distinction between life and death—no human *being*. Bodies are not consigned for burial; like trash, they are collected for disposal. Mourners offer up no prayers; they simply go about the business of survival, so that they are not mourners at all. Here death is not so much impossible as it is meaningless. In the "there is" that descends upon the ghetto, death is not a rite of passage; neither a rite nor a passage, it simply is. And one means by which death is thus rendered meaningless is through the removal of the signs, of the gravestones and cemeteries, that would impart to it a significance. Hence, death dies.

Or rather, it is murdered. For in the Shoah the conditions and contexts that would make death matter are not just absent; they are annihilated. Fackenheim explains: "In Ezekiel's image [of the dry bones], the dead have fallen in battle. The dead of the Holocaust were denied battle, its opportunity and its honours. Denied the peace even of the bones, they were denied also the honour of graves, for they, the others, ground their bones to dust and threw the dust into rivers. To apply Ezekiel's image of Jewish death to the Holocaust, then, is impossible. The new enemy, no mere Haman, not only succeeded where Haman failed, for he murdered the Jewish people. He murdered also Ezekiel's image of Jewish death" (*Jewish Bible* 67). In chapter 5 we examined the assault on the sacred texts in connection with assailing God, who sanctifies both life and death. Taking note of Fackenheim's reference to the prophet Ezekiel, we realize that a significant portion of the sacred texts addresses the sanctification of death; as God breathes life into Adam, so He claims life in the kiss that He places on the mouth of Moses, the mouth that uttered His Holy Word. Therefore we see that the assault on the Holy Word and the meaning it confers upon life is once again tied to an assault on death. How is a Jew, then, removed from life? By removing him from the kiss of the Divine that is death. And he is removed from death when he is removed from the signifier and sanctifier of life that is his grave. For God not only kisses Moses; He lays him in his grave. Thus, usurping God, the Nazis are literally grave robbers: they rob the Jews of their graves. "Is a Jew so low that a Jew cannot even have a grave?" Isabella Leitner asks. "Even death is too good for a Jew?" (23). To this question the Nazis shout, "Yes," which is a shouting of "No" to life. According to their design, there will be no ascent of the dry bones from the earth. That is why the Hungarian survivor Miklos Nyiszli describes Auschwitz as a "cemetery of millions, a cemetery without a single grave" (151). It is a cemetery in which the bones of Ezekiel have been ground to dust, in which death itself lies dead and buried beneath the ashes of the dead.

In the Holocaust diaries, then, we encounter the chronicle of a calculated onslaught against death that undermines all significance in life. But what exactly does this chronicle contain? First of all, the diarists note that for the Nazis, to whom the Jews were not human beings at all, the Jewish dead were not only objects of contempt; they were sources of curiosity and amusement. In this regard Michael Zylberberg reports from the Warsaw Ghetto that the Germans "gleefully photographed the dead and their accompanying relatives, and even went as far as taking snapshots of the corpses as they were laid out in the mortuary. The Nazis were particularly active in this respect on Sundays, when they would visit the cemeteries with their girlfriends. This, rather than the cinema, was a place of amusement for them" (31). And so the Sunday routine for many of these Nazis was church, the cafe, and then the mortuary, where, no doubt, they would spend their day of rest admiring the results of their week's labor. Of course, when a mortuary becomes a place of amusement, it is no longer a mortuary, and the dead are no longer the dead. To be sure, once the Jew is robbed of his status as person and is reduced to an object, he cannot die because he is not alive in any meaningful sense. But in their desecration of the dead and their murder of death the Nazis went far beyond such amusements.

Turning to Chaim Kaplan's diary from the Warsaw Ghetto, we recognize the stages by which the termination—or the extermination—of death unfolds. On 6 August 1940, for example, he writes, "Every great man or leader of his people who passes on in these evil times is carried to his grave alone, with his death and burial unknown to anyone" (176). The great men and leaders to whom Kaplan refers are those who engendered life in their communities; that is what made them great. What distinguishes these times as evil is precisely the absence of any recognition of that life which these dead fostered. The absence of such recognition belongs to the erasure of life's sanctity, so that the dead too lose their sanctity. Hence, says Kaplan on 9 October 1941: "the dead have lost their traditional importance and sanctity. The sanctity of the cemetery is also being profaned; it has been turned into a marketplace" (267). Finally, a month later, he notes, "Henceforward people accompanying their dead for burial will be denied permission to enter the cemetery grounds. They will be permitted to come only as far as the gate and then strangers will accompany the departed to their graves" (275–76). Just as the murder of death is linked to the assault on God, so too is it tied to the destruction of the family (see chapter 8) in this divorce of the family from the dead. Bodies are desecrated in their being torn from the hands of loved ones and turned over to strangers who have lost their human image. Denied entry into the cemetery, the family members are denied their status as family—as mothers and fathers, as sons and daughters, and ultimately as Jews. Since mourning is a form of prayer in the Jewish tradition and prayer was forbidden (see chapter 5), the Nazis will brook no Jewish mourners. The Hungarian survivor Lily Gluck Lerner recalls in this connection her mother's insistence that "the greatest *mitzvah*, the greatest respect, one can give is to accompany a dead person to burial" (35). To be sure, the Talmud tells us that even "the study of Torah may be suspended for escorting a dead body to the burying place" (*Megillah* 29a; also *Ketuvot* 17a). Denied the performance of this *mitzvah* for the dead, the Jews are denied the *mitzvah* of choosing life: a Jew cut off from the *mitzvot* pertaining to death is a Jew cut off from life. And so the *mitzvah* that the diarist performs in bearing witness to this horror becomes all the more pressing: the diarist becomes the only remaining mourner to accompany the dead to the graves that they are denied. And his diary becomes a form of prayer.

Such are the implications of the notation that Czerniakow makes in his diary about a Jew who committed suicide. "The body of a stoker who hanged himself three days ago," he writes, "is still in the boiler room at Jagiellonska Street. He cannot be buried since the workers in the funeral home cannot obtain the passes. To make things more difficult they have forbidden burials at the Praga cemetery" (218). Here death is slain by refusing the living the means of burying the dead and thereby observing the passage of those who in life had borne the image of the Holy One. This point becomes all the more clear when in Czerniakow's diary we read: "Continuous complaints that there is nothing to bury the dead in. They have to be left naked in holes dug in the ground. There isn't even any paper which could be used as a substitute for linen shrouds" (300). Very often the linen burial shroud for a man was the *talis* or the *kitl* that he wore in prayer, so that once again we have the connection between the assault on prayer and the death of death. Notice also that in this entry, instead of referring to a grave in the cemetery where a loved one is laid to rest, Czerniakow speaks of a hole in the ground where a corpse is left. But a grave is not a hole. A grave is a tract of ground made sacred through the ritualistic interment of a human body in the earth and the marking of the site with a memorial stone and flowers. When the grave takes on the status of a hole, this marking, too, loses its status. "I looked out my window," says Czerniakow on 21 May 1942, "and saw a hearse full of flowers which were being taken from the cemetery to the ballroom" (357). And what transpires in the ballroom decked out with these flowers is neither the dance of life nor the dance of death. It is the dance of the death of death.

Just as the flowers are among the fixtures that adorn this macabre revelry, so are the bodies of human beings among the fixtures that adorn the Warsaw Ghetto. "Not having the money to bury their dead," Ringelblum relates on 26 August 1941, "the poor often throw the corpses into the street. Some houses shut their gates and refuse to permit tenants to leave until they have had the body buried. On the other hand, the police district chiefs, not wanting to bother with the formalities connected with corpses, simply throw the bodies from one streetcar to the next" (196–97). And so we have the image of the murdered riding around the ghetto alongside the yet to be murdered: the tram is turned into a hearse bound for every stop except the cemetery. Before long, then, not only would the Jews have no money to bury their dead—they would have no place to bury them. In an entry dated 12 May 1942 Ringelblum writes: "The Praga cemetery, which is more than 150 years old, is being leveled. The devils won't even let the dead rest. They've done the same sort of thing elsewhere in Poland and Germany" (267). Thus the assault on death is taken to the dead themselves in a campaign to destroy Jewish cemeteries. And the diarists are careful to record this campaign. Walking among the ruins of the Warsaw Ghetto, for example, Zylberberg says: "The cemetery wall had been destroyed—it seemed to break down the division between the worlds of life and death. I walked back through the ruins of the ghetto. My footprints were clear in the snow, and they were the only ones" (212). The collapse of the division between life and death is indeed the mark of the death of death. It signifies the onset of the indifferent "there is" that Levinas refers to above, where the impossibility of death lies in the loss of a difference between life and death. And it demonstrates very graphically the point that when death loses its distinction, so does life lose its meaning.

In a similar vein David Kahane comments on "the wanton, barbaric profanation of the Jewish cemetery" in Lvov. "The Nazis," he says, "were not content with tormenting the living Jews; they also vented their spleen upon the dead. A special labor battalion of Jewish workers from the camp was ordered to uproot and smash all the tombstones in the cemetery" (53). And in yet another example Leon Wells writes from Stojanov, "The so-called *Friedhofskolonne* (cemetery brigade) works at the Jewish cemetery, bringing the gravestones that are used here for road construction" (137). Not only, then, do the Nazis undertake the task of desecrating the dead and removing death from Jewish life; they force Jewish hands to engage this task of destroying the graves where they once said the *Kaddish*, the Prayer for the Dead, over their mothers and fathers. Here an important connection between death and the death of death comes to light. The encompassing ubiquity of death is coupled with the death of death, when death becomes so pervasive as to undermine the rites of prayer associated with the burial of the dead. For the Jews who have no cemeteries, the world is itself a cemetery, which is to say, it is not a world at all. For the world is a place in which the living define a realm where people are laid to rest and prayers are said at their graves. When the graves and the prayers over them are obliterated, the world and the life that constitutes it are also obliterated.

"During the last few days," Josef Katz observes the rising tide of death at Jungfernhof, "wę have had twenty to twenty-five deaths in our barracks every day. It is strange how quickly people die" (46). And, as we have seen, this tidal wave of death soon leads to the elimination of the rites and rituals of death. "In the beginning," says Katz, "when we did not have so many casualties yet, we had a *minyan* for everybody and recited the *Kaddish*. While the dead were carried from the barracks we chanted, '*El molei rachamim*.' But now that has stopped. There are too many deaths" (47). Or better: there are too many murders. Even the word *death* here becomes a euphemism that threatens to veil the truth of the Nazis' project. "Natural death no longer exists," declares Emil Dorian (322), a point that Yitzhak Katznelson makes more powerfully still in his *Vittel Diary*, when he cries out, "Throughout the era of Hitler, the agent of the whole non-Jewish world, not a single Jew died, they were just murdered, murdered" (228). That is why the Nazis targeted the old and the ailing for murder, as they flooded the earth with death: refusing to simply wait for them to expire, they were determined to see to it that no Jew would die. To see to it that Jewish death itself would be eliminated from the world. For this erasure of Jewish death from existence was a key to the elimination of the significance of Jewish existence itself.

What, then, do we learn about the singular significance of the Holocaust diary from its testimony to the death and the death of death among the Jews? Written along the edge of this annihilation, the pages of the Holocaust diary are akin to a grave from which the voices of the dead reverberate; to be sure, most of these diarists were themselves fated to lie in unmarked trenches or to ascend to the clouds on fading columns of smoke. Much of what went into the diaries they kept is like a prayer said for those who were robbed of prayers, a memorial inscription consecrated to take the place of the desecrated memorials that once marked the lives and the deaths of European Jews. Witnesses of the death of Jewish death, the Holocaust diarists faced the overwhelming task of transforming this Jewish death into a moment of witnessing. And so we return to the issue of martyrdom that was breached at the beginning of this chapter.

In one of his most famous statements, Albert Camus opens *The Myth of Sisyphus* by saying, "There is but one truly serious philosophical problem, and that is suicide" (3). To this remark Rabbi Abraham Joshua Heschel replies, "There is only one really serious problem: and that is martyrdom" (*Wonder* 45). Why? Because suicide negates the sanctity of life, while martyrdom affirms it. "In martyrdom," Leo Baeck asserts, "death is no longer a mere end of life, a mere fate. It becomes a deed of freedom and of love for God" (174)—and, we may add, of love for humanity. For martyrdom is "an ethical affirmation of the soul," as Baeck states it (174), and ethical affirmation entails both the relation to God and the relation to humanity.[6] In the Sanctification of the Name, the Jew's conduct of his life carries him even unto death, to the point where life and death intersect in the testimony of martyrdom. "In martyrdom," Neher maintains, "human history receives a meaning. Martyrdom is the negation of the absurd. Everything receives a meaning through the ultimate testimony of the man who accepts that meaning to the very limit. Everything is oriented in relation to that testimony. Everything becomes *sanctified* through it" (*Prophetic* 338–39). Therefore every Holocaust diarist, no matter how inarticulate, offers up his testimony to the sanctity of human life. Thus he becomes a messenger who is a martyr to Jewish martyrdom.

But that is just where the difficulty arises: obliterating the signs of sanctity surrounding both Jewish life and Jewish death, the Nazis undertook an assault on Jewish martyrdom itself. "In making the teaching of the Jewish book a capital crime," Fackenheim explains, "Hadrian had created the possibility of Jewish martyrdom for Jewish believers. In making Jewish existence a capital crime, Hitler murdered Jewish martyrdom itself" (*Jewish Return* 247). Confronted with the erasure of every visible sign of Jewish existence, both in life and in death, the Holocaust diarist confronts the task of reestablishing martyrdom in Jewish life and death through an affirmation of the invisible. Unlike any other diary, then, what underlies the Holocaust diary is a desire for the invisible—or for the Invisible One, a metaphysical desire for the metaphysical—that arises precisely where, by all that meets the eye, it should not arise. It is the desire that Levinas invokes when he says, "The very dimension of height is opened up by metaphysical Desire. That this height is no longer the heavens but the Invisible is the very elevation of height and its nobility. To die for the invisible—that is metaphysics" (*Totality* 34–35). And that is martyrdom. Dying for the invisible—dying in the midst of a living that, from every visible indication, should not be there—is what characterizes the Holocaust diarist's affirmation of life in the midst of an ontological assault on the metaphysical. That is how he restores Jewish death to its proper, sacred ground. And that is how he clings to life.

CLINGING TO LIFE

"WISDOM AND LIFE ARE ONE AND THE SAME IN HIM," SAYS Maimonides (*Existence* 199). And in the Talmud, Rabbi Eliezer ben Azariah declares, "The disciples of the wise increase peace in the world" (*Tamid* 32b). Who are the wise? They are those who embrace the wisdom of God's Torah. And to embrace the wisdom of the Torah, which is the Torah of Life, is to embrace peace: as the issue of wisdom, peace is the core of life. Clinging to the wisdom of the Torah, we cling to peace; clinging to peace, we cling to life. Therefore the *Midrash Tanchuma* teaches that "all that is written in the Torah is written for the sake of peace" (2:494). Therefore the prayer of the Eighteen Benedictions ends by blessing the Holy One for imparting to Israel *shalom* or peace. There is no dwelling in the world without dwelling in peace. And peace means: the other human being *matters*. Peace, then, is a condition that abides not just in the soul of the individual but *between* one human being and another, as well as between the human being and God. To be sure, these are the very relationships that are central to the Torah.[1] There is no clinging to life—no adherence to God and to His Torah—without this relation of benevolence to our fellow human being. In this relation, and not just inside the individual, lies the humanity that bears the likeness of the divinity. In this relation lies what the Nazis set out to destroy and what the Holocaust diarists strive to recover.

If the Holocaust diarists strive to recover life and cling to it, they do so by affirming a relation to the other human being which is expressive of the relation to God and thus to all that is threatened in the Holocaust.[2] As we have seen throughout this book, the Nazis' assault on Jewish life entails an assault on God, home, and family; on truth, meaning, and sanctity; on justice, mercy, and humanity. For these are the ingredients of the life that unfolds in a human relation expressive of a relation to the divine. How, then, do the Holocaust diarists cling to this life that is targeted for annihilation? By clinging to the other human being through their testimonies and their actions.

In almost every instance, this clinging to life entails a sacrifice for the other that far exceeds the parameters of life delineated by the diary itself. One will recall, for example, Adam Czerniakow's repeated attempts to offer himself up in exchange for others. "I pleaded to be arrested," he writes on 8 November 1939, "in exchange for the 24 hostages" (88); on 24 November, "I informed Brandt of my willingness to offer myself as a hostage" (92); and on 1 December, "Who could serve this purpose [of being a scapegoat] better than I?" (95). If, as we have seen in the last chapter, the Nazis set out to destroy death, the diarists struggle to regain a proper ground for death that sanctifies and attests to life through a responsibility for others that goes beyond the horizon of one's own life. In this way they approach the infinite that is life itself, the infinite that lies in the infinite dearness of life and that therefore summons an infinite sacrifice for life.[3] Sacrifice, then, forms a definitive part of the subject matter addressed in the Holocaust diary. Indeed, the very act of writing these diaries is an act of sacrifice steeped in the consciousness not of the diarists' own sacrifice but of the sacrifice made by others. This being for the other is precisely the clinging to life that distinguishes the Holocaust diary.

Articulating her longing to fulfill a mission for the sake of others, the words and deeds of Hannah Senesh represent another good example of how the Holocaust diarist clings to life through a sacrificial being for the other. In her diary she says that she was faced with two choices: "to seek personal happiness and shut my eyes to all the faults in my surroundings, or else to invest my efforts in the difficult and devastating war for the things I deem good and proper" (113). Opting for the latter, she determined that her speech was to concur with her acts. And so she undertook her famous mission to Yugoslavia and Hungary that ended in the sacrifice of her life. Perhaps less dramatic than Hannah Senesh's secret mission—but no less significant—is the diarists' testimony to the willingness of people to give to one another even when they have the least to offer. "Today," Rivosh, the sculptor of the Riga Ghetto, affirms, "everyone is generous and is sharing everything sincerely. Today there is no 'mine' and 'yours'; today there is only 'ours'" (336). Similarly, upon his family's removal to a Polish ghetto, the teenager Dawid Rubinowicz notes: "Although we've only just arrived, we're not strangers in Bodzentyn. Everyone treats us well, like brothers" (50). While the diarists do not always comment on the benevolence of the community, they often bear witness to the loving kindness of an individual. In the Warsaw Ghetto, for example, Hersh Wasser offers a comment on a fellow diarist: "Friend Menahem Kon is a rare person. In every respect. Unique in our [*Oneg Shabbat*] society. His intelligent, good, human face attracts people and inspires respect, esteem, awe. How good it is to come across such a person today" (232). Likewise, Michael Zylberberg expresses his admiration for Janusz Korczak, commenting on how the suffering of the Jews "affected Dr. Korczak's thinking and outlook. He became strongly attracted to the spiritual significance of Judaism and to the Jewish people as an entity, and he identified himself with every aspect of the Jewish catastrophe" (27). Of course, one recalls that Janusz Korczak ended by sacrificing his own life so that the children of his orphanage could have a few final hours of his comforting presence: when ordered to turn his children over for deportation to Treblinka, he insisted on joining them, even though he could have saved himself.

Attesting to the humanity that unfolds in times and places where there should be no humanity, all of these entries from Holocaust diaries amount to the affirmation that life means something, despite the Nazis' demonstrations to the contrary. The life of the Holocaust diarist—the life that he or she seeks to recover—is characterized by this clinging to life that surpasses rational understanding. And, as we shall see, it shows itself not only in a concern for the Jewish community but also in a gratitude for the kindness, however rare, shown toward the Jews by the Gentiles. It manifests itself in the all but insane song and dance and laughter summoned in this realm that conspires to silence such things. It unfolds in the embrace of creation, where the diarist joins his voice to the Voice of the Creator in his pronouncement of "It is good," in spite of his imprisonment in a universe that is antithetical to the good. And so, amidst the sea of darkness from which these diarists cry out, there are beacons of humanity that perhaps justify the diarists' endeavor. Clinging to the life that emanates from those points of light, the Holocaust diarists are themselves part of the light to which they attest. Let us consider, then, this light that the darkness cannot comprehend.

THE HUMANITY OF THE OTHERS

In the Talmud, Bar Kappara (*Berakhot* 63a) and Rabbi Hillel (*Avot* 7a), both declare that in a place where there are no men, one must be a man. And what, according to the Jewish tradition, does it mean to be a man, that is, to be a human being? It means affirming the sanctity of one's fellow human being through deeds of loving kindness. It means, in the words of the Talmud, that "if a person sees flood waters approaching someone else's field, he must build a dam before them" (*Bava Metzia* 31a). While most of the others, the non-Jewish neighbors of the Jews, either ignored or contributed to the flood of death that swallowed up European Jewry, in this realm where humanity was all too rare there were a few human beings who struggled to erect a dam here and there. These are not the ones who, in the words of Emmanuel Ringelblum, engaged in "soul snatching" (336), saving Jews in order to convert them to the religion of their historical oppressors. Rather, they are the truly Righteous among the Nations, who attended to the suffering of Jewish bodies, not the "salvation" of Jewish souls.[4] If one must be a human being in a land where there are no human beings, then one must be this subject who signifies the dearness of the other human being—in the flesh. In the Holocaust Kingdom there was no enjoyment of life that did not come at the expense of life. But there were a few among the Nations who, instead of enjoying the pleasures of life, rejoiced in the sanctity of life by saving the life of another, even if it meant snatching a piece of bread from their own mouths—or worse. Thus they retained their human image by attending to the hunger of the other human being.

When speaking of the Shoah, however, we speak not only of the hunger that ravages the other person; we speak of the murder that devours him. Therefore the humanity of the others, of those Righteous Gentiles who signified the sanctity of the Jew, lay in their realization of a prohibition against murder, a prohibition that comes from *on high*. Coming face to face with the Jew, those who remained human in this time encountered the face as such. For they encountered "the Other," as Levinas puts it, who "paralyzes possession, which he contests by his epiphany in the face. He can contest my possession only because he approaches me not from outside but from above. The same cannot lay hold of the other without suppressing him. But the untraversable infinity of the negation of murder is announced by this dimension of height, when the Other comes to me concretely in the ethical impossibility of committing this murder" (*Totality* 171). The Nazis' assault on life, then, is an assault on the epiphany of the face; it is a rendering faceless—and thus lifeless—the Jew whom they determine to be other than human. For "the epiphany of a face is alive," says Levinas (*Collected* 95). Indeed, it is more than alive: it is an affirmation of the infinite dearness of life, a dearness that bespeaks an essential oneness of life. "Every human being is a part of the single soul that is the spirit of the entire universe," Rabbi Adin Steinsaltz teaches us (*Thirteen* 171), so that the humanity of those who helped the Jews lay in their affirmation of a connectedness to the Jews and, through the Jews, to all human life. Their being for the other was a being for all, and the life that the diarists here attest to is the life of all. This link between each life and the life of all underlies the teaching in the Talmud that to save a single life is like saving the entire world (*Sanhedrin* 37a). Therefore the scope of the Shoah extends over the entire world: if, as we have seen, the Nazis' murderous project was ontological and metaphysical, it was also cosmic, both including and exceeding the realm of historical time and geographical space. And this excess shows itself not only in the destruction of life that characterized the Nazis' activities, but also in the saving of life undertaken by the Righteous.

Thus diarists such as Julian Stanford include in their account of the slaughter of humanity an account of the preservation of humanity. "The Dutch are genuine Christians," he writes from his hiding place in Holland on 1 November 1942. "They cannot understand the actions and the psychology of the Germans" (75). Indeed, their humanity precludes such understanding. Stanford adds that when the Jews of Holland were ordered to wear the yellow star in April of 1942, the Dutch greeted them not with ridicule and derision, as the Nazis had intended, but with honor and respect (93)—something that the

Nazis could not understand. Anne Frank, another German Jew hiding among the Dutch, declares: "It is amazing how much noble, unselfish work these people are doing, risking their lives to help and save others. Our helpers are a very good example" (159). Here we see that what the diarist affirms, what she clings to in her clinging to life, is a humanity that lies in a radical vulnerability. Those who encounter the Jews as the most vulnerable of people assert their humanity by assuming a similar—not the same, certainly, but a similar—vulnerability.[5] Because humanity is tied to vulnerability, to be human is not so much to be what we are as it is to be more than what we are, despite what we are. But we cannot become more than what we are without moving outside of ourselves, into the openness of the face-to-face encounter, and thereby becoming vulnerable. Humanity, then, is an *event*: it is a tearing of oneself from from oneself, where the human being acts not from his own need but from a responsibility that is more than his need or his inclination. Indeed, we find that at times the humanity of the human being can overwhelm his inclination, so that his movement into a position of vulnerability is truly despite himself.

Helena Dorembus notes this phenomenon in her comments on a good Pole named Lenski. "Lenski is an enigma," she says. "He keeps trying to convince us that he can't stand the Jews. But the Stock family and the others he is hiding assure us that he loves the Jews more than the Poles" (59). Zylberberg is among the other diarists of Poland who in the midst of a general Polish indifference or outright cruelty also points out the rare instance of Polish kindness. "I met an elderly lady," he remarks in September 1944, "who noticed my sorry state and asked me sympathetically about the fight in the Old City, and what was going to happen to me. She was moved by what I told her and invited me into her house. This seemed like divine intervention at the eleventh hour" (176). To be sure, this act of kindness is a sort of divine intervention, or a moment of epiphany, when one human being responds to the sanctity that shows itself in the face of the other. Sometimes it was an intervention undertaken by representatives of the Church, by priests, in Christian Poland. And the evidence of the Holocaust diaries demonstrates that a single word from a single priest—a word that came all too rarely—could move many others to help. Rabbi Shimon Huberband, for example, points out in his remarks about his stay in a labor camp that the priest of Kampinos "called upon the Christian population to assist us in all possible ways. And he also attacked the guards and the Christian camp administrators, referring to them as Antichrists. He harshly condemned the guards who beat and murdered the unfortunate Jewish inmates so mercilessly. As a result, the peasants began to bring various food items to the labor sites" (95). Words create angels, according to an ancient Jewish teaching, and those angels go out into the world to do good or evil, which is to say: our words have consequences for the lives of the people around us. And the example of the priest of Kampinos demonstrates the truth of this teaching; a word is truly a deed, inasmuch as it can foster other deeds. Thus the human being's testimony to the humanity of the Jews calls forth the humanity of the others and moves them to act.

Of course, there were some priests who themselves took action. According to Yehuda Bauer, in fact, four thousand of these clergymen perished at the hands of the Nazis (137). Czerniakow comments on such a priest, saying: "Somewhere in the provinces, as I was told, another pastor was in the habit of soliciting aid from both a priest and the [Jewish] Community. When asked why he was turning to the Community, he replied that in the present hard times relying on one God is not enough" (345). Which is to say: there is but one God, and He is relying on us, Jew and Gentile alike. The priest who turned to the Jewish community, however, turned to a community that for the most part was already characterized by a sense of responsibility for one's neighbor. He turned to a community steeped in the teaching articulated by the twelfth-century sage Bachya ibn Paquda: "He who does no more than his duty is not doing his duty" (2:37). Among the Holocaust diarists, then, if anything is greater than their gratitude for the help received from the Righteous Gentiles, it is their own sense of responsibility for their fellow Jews. And asserting this responsibility for the other is a key component of their clinging to life.

RESPONSIBILITY FOR THE OTHER

"I have set before you this day," it is written in the Torah, "life and good, death and evil" (Deuteronomy 30:15). Choosing life, we choose good over evil, so that clinging to life is possible only where we struggle to cling to good and preserve ourselves from evil. And how do we do that? "By each taking upon himself the responsibility of the others," Levinas explains. "Nothing is more foreign to me than the other; nothing is more intimate to me than myself. Israel would teach that the greatest intimacy of me to myself consists in being at every moment responsible for the other" (*Nine* 85). It is no coincidence that Israel is the name both of an individual and of a people; each is definitively tied to the other through an absolute claim made upon both by the God Who reveals Himself as the Good.[6] Therefore a life of infinite value and an infinite responsibility for that life are of a piece. They are one because a Good that is One has already chosen each Jew—and every human being—for the task of being there for the sake of the other. And to choose life is to realize this condition of having already been chosen by the Good for this responsibility.

If this is the lesson that comes to the world through Israel, it is proclaimed most powerfully in the pages of the Holocaust diaries. For there this teaching cries out to the world in the midst of the assault on Israel. There we have incontrovertible evidence that, in the words of Levinas, "the tie with the Other is knotted only as responsibility" (*Ethics* 97). And the tie with the other is the tie with life; seeking to recover life in the midst of its collapse, the Holocaust diarists seek to maintain this tie to life through a responsibility for the other. To be sure, this truth that is demonstrated in the Holocaust diaries is a definitive feature of the most ancient of Jewish teachings. "All Israel are sureties for one another," we are told in the Talmud (*Shevu'ot* 39a), a point that Rashi underscores in his commentary on the Torah, saying, "All Israelites are held responsible for one another" (3:128b).[7] Such is the Jewish message, the Jewish testimony, to the Jews and to all of humanity. For the Jewish Holocaust diarist, then, clinging to life lies in clinging to his Jewishness, which in turn lies in his responsibility to his fellow Jews. While an embrace of the Torah has rightly been understood to be the distinguishing feature of the Jew, this embrace of the other human being is the distinguishing feature of the Torah. Those who would receive the Torah of life must be involved with life; those who have only the Torah do not even have the Torah. Says Maimonides, "One who occupies himself with the needs of the community is in the same class with one who is occupied with the study of the Torah" (*Mishneh* 2:105a). Insofar as the Holocaust diary is a Jewish diary, it is characterized by such an occupation. Just as the Torah is the Tree of Life, so is life to be found in the concern for the community; a Jew cannot live as a severed branch. And the consciousness of life in the Holocaust diarist lies in the consciousness of this concern, of this connection, of this responsibility.

One way in which that consciousness manifests itself in the Holocaust diary is through the awareness of a certain indebtedness to the other, the awareness that the life enjoyed by each of us comes at the expense of another life. That is why, during her time in Israel, Hannah Senesh writes, "I'm conscience-stricken that I have it so good and easy while others are suffering, and I feel I ought to do something—something exerting, demanding, to justify my existence" (105). The conscience of the diarist is stricken, however, not because of the geographical distance from her fellow Jews but because of her distance from fulfilling an infinite responsibility. Therefore, while hiding in the heart of Poland, Zylberberg asserts, "I could not suppress my frequent pangs of conscience about my enforced idleness at the expense of others" (190). And from the depths of the concentrationary universe, from the crematoria of Auschwitz-Birkenau, the *Sonderkommando* diarist Salmen Lewental writes, "There was a time in this camp, in the years 1941–1942, when each man, really each man, who lived longer than two weeks, lived at the cost of the other victims, at the cost of lives of other people or on what he had taken from them" (147). Among many diarists, then, there is a sense that one's own life has been purchased at a cost too dear, at a cost of life for life. Hence a fear of death becomes a feature of the responsibility that distinguishes my life—not, however, a fear of one's own death but a fear for the death of the other. "The fear for the death of the other," Levinas makes this point, "is certainly the basis of the responsibility for him" (*Ethics* 119). And so, taking himself to be the one who is responsible, Czerniakow dreads every announcement of the casualties in the Warsaw Ghetto. "On Saturday, as usual," he writes, "I received a list of the deceased. I am always tense when I receive that list lest I see a familiar name" (273). Of course, every name is familiar to someone. Names signify lives and deaths. Names announce responsibility. And responsibility declares our essential connection to the other, to the community.[8]

Unlike most diarists, who often focus on the inner torments of their own souls, the Holocaust diarists are all but obsessed with the suffering of their fellow Jews. Czerniakow, for example, relates: "In the afternoon I was working at home—with interruptions of the moans of beggars under the window—'Bread, bread! I am hungry, hungry!'" (247). Recognizing his responsibility for that hunger, Czerniakow makes the outcry of the hungry part of his own outcry: it echoes throughout the outcry that he enters into his diary. Similarly, when Tuvia Borzykowski wonders, "How many Jews hiding in Warsaw perished today?" (123), he is wondering how much of his own soul has been slain in this slaughter of his fellow Jews; those silenced lives belong to the silence between the words that make up his diary. In yet another example, Chaim Kaplan writes, "Sometimes, from among tens of thousands of the ravaged, your eyes are drawn to a face which haunts you no matter where you turn, does not leave you alone, follows you like a shadow and disturbs your rest" (75). Indeed, precluding all rest, that face haunts all who encounter these diaries. It peers at us from between the lines on the page, just as the roar of the slaughter echoes throughout its margins. "These lines are being written after midnight," Kaplan tells his reader, "and out of the silence of the night, the rumble of the wheels of the cars hurrying on their way to Pawiak, the house of slaughter, reaches my ears. A ray of light showing through the window would endanger my life. The victims are bound inside the cars. This very night they will ascend the scaffold. God of Gods! Shall the sword devour thy sons forever?" (363). And from the heart of the same ghetto, Hersh Wasser cries out for the sake of those entering the ghetto: "These legions of newly sentenced to a slow but certain death are being hurled into the half-dark, but fully-starved Warsaw by the force of murderous ordinances. From their bright provincial heaven, from their momentarily relatively safe refuge, the unfortunates march into darkened, petrified, heartless Warsaw. Welcome! Woe to the clear-eyed children, woe to the young maidens' hearts!" (268). As these people enter the ghetto, they enter the soul of the ghetto diarist. Conscious of his responsibility for them, he is tormented by the knowledge that he cannot save them. All he can do is to make their plight central to the pages of his diary and there affirm his tie to them.

The consciousness of a tie to the other that is found in these mature men of Warsaw is also found in the sixteen-year-old Mary Berg, who mourns: "I gaze at the faces of the passers-by, blue with cold. I try to learn by heart the look of the homeless women wrapped in rags and of the children with chapped and frozen cheeks. . . . Every day there are more such 'dreamers of bread' in the streets of the ghetto. Their eyes are veiled with a mist that belongs to another world" (47–48). Why does Mary Berg inscribe these faces on her heart, on the place where a Jew is to inscribe the words of the Holy One? Because, as we are taught by the tradition, the heart is God's favorite dwelling place. And, from the depths of those faces engraved on the heart, He proclaims our responsibility for the other, for the one who has no dwelling place. On the day of reaffirming that relation of responsibility to God and humanity, the holiest day of the year, another teenager in another ghetto, Yitzkhok Rudashevski of Vilna, writes: "Today is Yom Kippur. . . . In the morning the terrible news spreads. Several thousand people were uprooted from the ghetto at night. These people never came back again" (35). And this anxiety over the suffering of others is found throughout the diary of the most famous of the teenage diarists. "Our many Jewish friends are being taken away by the dozen," says Anne Frank on 9 October 1942. "These people are treated by the Gestapo without a shred of decency, being loaded into cattle trucks and sent to Westerbork. . . . We assume that most of them are murdered. The English radio speaks of their being gassed" (49–50). On 19 November 1942: "I get frightened when I think of close friends who have now been delivered into the hands of the cruelest brutes that walk the earth. And all because they are Jews!" (65). On 27 March 1943: "These wretched people are sent to filthy slaughterhouses like a herd of sick, neglected cattle" (87). And on 1 May 1943: "If I just think of how we live here, I usually come to the conclusion that it is a paradise compared with how other Jews who are not in hiding must be living" (91). Certainly the stereotype of the selfish, self-centered teen does not apply to these youngsters who had every reason to worry only about themselves and their own survival. Their clinging to life is characterized by a selfless fear for the suffering and death of the other. And the substance of their lives derives from their sense of an obligation to respond to that suffering and death.

Just as these youths share a sense of responsibility with the grown men of the Warsaw Ghetto, so do they share it with the men of other ghettos. From Romania, for instance, Emil Dorian asserts, "Whatever I do, wherever I am—at the table, at my writing desk—the thought of what is happening to these human beings poisons every moment of my life with its silent scream, its barren hopelessness, its mute rage" (194). And, commenting on the time when he was hiding in a monastery near Lvov, David Kahane laments: "Time and again I was woken in the middle of the night by weeping, crying, and heartrending voices of hunted Jews flushed out of their hiding places in the district where the monastery was located. My heart felt the torments of the Jews going to their deaths, and I languished in pain and powerlessness" (131). In all of these instances of the diarists' concern for the suffering of others—a concern that, as we see, transcends all differences in age and circumstance—their sense of powerlessness is the sign of their sense of responsibility. Only those who know that they must act would agonize over the fact that they cannot act. And because they cannot meet that responsibility, they languish in pain, the days outlined in their diaries poisoned by the shriek of silence that will not stop, by the Jewish screams that call out their Jewish names. So insistent is that summons that many of the diarists voice a longing to be among the members of their community, no matter what their fate. For they are deeply aware of the wisdom that comes to us from sages such as Sforno, the noted Torah commentator of the early sixteenth century, who maintains that "the purpose intended in his being in the likeness and image (of God) will not be realized if (man) will have to occupy himself alone" (1:25). These diarists know that if their lives are to mean anything, if they are to live as human beings, they cannot allow themselves the complacency of curling up in the isolation of self-interest. They know that any substance or significance in their lives rests on their ability to become a sign of the depth and the dearness of other lives—that is the meaning of this responsibility for the other.

Therefore the diarists embrace the truth that comes to us from the Talmud: "A man should share in the distress of the community" (*Ta'anit* 11a). This Jewish teaching, too, is reflected in these Jewish diaries. In his Kovno Ghetto diary, for example, Avraham Tory remarks on the many letters that he receives from Jews outside the ghetto. "They cry for help," he explains in an entry dated 30 July 1942. "Recently, letters such as these are not uncommon. Their content is nearly identical. Their authors long to live in a Jewish milieu, among Jews. They are prepared to share the Jewish fate—come what may. The 'ingathering of exiles' from the neighboring townlets to the Kovno Ghetto has begun" (118). And, once again, this interest in sharing in the distress of the community is not confined to age or upbringing, to geographical location or ideological outlook. To be sure, it is one of the dominant features of the diary that the sixteen-year-old Moshe Flinker kept while hiding with his family in Brussels. At times, for example, he will close an entry with the words "Good night, my people!" (35). More often he explicitly affirms this bond to Jewish life, without which he would have no life. On 4 December 1943 he writes: "I often have a great yearning for my brothers who are in Poland and elsewhere. The Lord alone knows where they are" (58). Two weeks later he returns to the same theme: "He knows how thankful I am to Him that He protects my parents and my sisters and brother, but even so something devours my heart, a vast yearning to participate with my brothers in all that happens to them" (66). And three months later, again: "Thoughts of my people never leave my mind, not even for a minute. They are with me everywhere" (83). The terrible irony of these sentiments is that in April of 1944, on the Eve of Passover, the Gestapo would see to it that young Moshe Flinker would indeed join his brothers. Nevertheless, despite the hopelessness and the powerlessness of his situation—despite the death that awaited him—Moshe's longing to be with his community was a clinging to life. For it is an affirmation of a tradition that affirms the sanctity of life and therefore a responsibility for life, even unto death.

But, it must be asked, how is the diarist to respond to that hopelessness and powerlessness? How does one cling to life, when every day and every hour there is less life to cling to? Elie Wiesel suggests one response to this dilemma. "Revolt is not a solution," he has said. "Neither is submission. Remains laughter, metaphysical laughter" (*Souls* 199). Laughter becomes metaphysical when it arises in a realm where everything conspires against it. During the Shoah laughter becomes metaphysical when it remains the only means of clinging to a life that is no longer there, a means not only of clinging to life but of recovering life. Let us consider, then, the role of laughter in its various forms as it appears in the Holocaust diary.

METAPHYSICAL LAUGHTER

In the diary she kept while struggling to survive in the Warsaw Ghetto, Mary Berg states that laughter "is our only weapon in the ghetto—our people laugh at death and at the Nazi decrees. Humor is the only thing the Nazis cannot understand" (111). They cannot understand it because the merchants of death cannot understand the clinging to life that characterizes laughter. They cannot understand it because it is a language unknown to them, the language of the soul that animates life and affirms its dearness. Suddenly bellies emptied of bread are filled with laughter. In the moment of laughter the fear with which the Nazis would terrorize the Jews is defeated, if only for a moment, and the horror into which they plunge the Jews is overcome—inexplicably. Rabbi Shimon Huberband, in fact, includes among his chronicles of that time many jokes—yes, jokes!—told in the Warsaw Ghetto. For example: "We eat as if it were Yom Kippur, sleep in *succahs*, and dress as if it were Purim" (113). And: "A teacher asks his pupil, 'Tell me, Moyshe, what would you like to be if you were Hitler's son?' 'An orphan,' the pupil answers" (113). And: "Where does Hitler feel best? In the toilet. There, all the brown masses are behind him" (120). These jokes, of course, are no laughing matter. Hence the laughter that arises from them is a laughter *despite*: therein lies something of its metaphysical essence.

A passage from Wiesel's *A Beggar in Jerusalem* that echoes Mary Berg's assertion and Rabbi Huberband's testimony comes to mind. There Moshe the Madman declares to the prophet Elijah: "My weapons? Not tears, not prayers, but laughter, only laughter. Admit then that laughter too can provoke miracles." And the prophet replies, "In our day, Moshe, laughter itself is a miracle, the most astonishing miracle of all" (33). Why a miracle? Because in the deluge of death, this sound of life should not be there. Thus understood as a miracle, laughter is understood to be metaphysical. That Moshe would make this remark specifically to Elijah is especially appropriate, given the tale related in the Talmud about Rabbi Beroka Hoza'ah, who was walking through the marketplace one day with none other than the prophet himself. He asked Elijah whether there was anyone in the market that day who would have a place in the World to Come. Elijah looked around and pointed out two who seemed to Rabbi Beroka to be very unlikely candidates for redemption: the jesters of the market place. "They bring laughter to the world," Elijah explained. "And with laughter they bring peace. Therefore they have a place in the World to Come" (*Ta'anit* 22a). If the disciples of the wise increase peace in the world, they also increase laughter in the world; increasing laughter, they increase life. To the extent that such laughter increases peace in the world—and is thereby linked to the World to Come—it is metaphysical laughter, a laughter that not only resounds but speaks. "Laughter is words," says André Neher. "Tears are silence" (*Exile* 236). If laughter is words, then, like life, it arises between people. If laughter is words, then laughter is spirit, the wellspring of life. In the beginning there is laughter, and it is through laughter that we begin again. Therefore it is worth noting Czerniakow's comment on the passing of Zofia Feigenbaum, a woman who succumbed to typhus in the Warsaw Ghetto. "Here was a human being who could laugh," he asserts (296), that is, who *knew how* to laugh, as the verb *umial* from the Polish text indicates (226): Zofia Feigenbaum had not only the ability but the wisdom to laugh. Knowing how to laugh, she was among the disciples of the wise, as her laughter brought to the world a moment of peace.

If the laughter that brings peace is metaphysical, then it can assume a variety of forms and sounds, not the least of which is song. "Beautiful singing in a man's voice is heard," writes Salmen Gradowski in the dairy he kept while serving on the *Sonderkommando* of Auschwitz. "What is this? Here, in this cemetery, a song about life? Here, in this island of death, the voice of life is still heard? Here, in this extermination camp, people are still able to sing? . . . How is it possible?" (103). Perhaps the Rebbe from Wiesel's *The Gates of the Forest* can explain: "The man who goes singing to death is the brother of the man who goes to death fighting. I take this song and make it mine. Do you know what the song hides? A dagger, an outcry. . . . There is joy as well as fury in the Hasid's dancing. It is a way of proclaiming, 'You don't want me to dance; too bad, I'll dance anyhow. You've taken away every reason for singing, but I shall sing. I shall sing of the deceit that walks by day and the truth that walks by night, yes, and of the silence of the dusk as well. You didn't expect my joy, but here it is; yes, my joy will rise up; it will submerge you'" (198). What comes to us from the pages of this novel returns to us from the pages of the diary of another member of the Auschwitz *Sonderkommando*, the one kept by Leib Langfus, who takes note of the rabbi who "entered the undressing-room and then the bunker, dancing and singing" (112). With these images of the dance added to the song we realize that the vehicle of metaphysical laughter is not only the mouth or the voice; it is the whole body. Overcome with dancing, the body overcomes itself—its hunger and fear and pain—to move *beyond* itself through a metamorphosis into the metaphysical. No body is less confined to the flesh than the body of the dancer. Dancing along the very edge of annihilation, it overcomes the gravity of annihilation, even as it is drawn down into the maelstrom of death.

Thus the Nazis' assault on the metaphysical is resisted in this manifestation of the metaphysical that characterizes the dance. "When somebody asks something impossible of me," said the Hasidic master, Rabbi Moshe Leib of Sassov, "I know what I must do: I must dance" (Wiesel, *Somewhere* 110). Nothing could be more impossible than to affirm the dearness of life in the midst of this sea of death. "My dancing was more important to God than all my prayers," said another Hasid, Rabbi Leib, son of Rabbi Abraham the Angel (Rabinowicz 331). In this realm where God may seem to have fallen silent, He perhaps makes His appearance in the dance of the Jews. What their masters taught in the days before the Event the Hasidim, as well as other Jews, exemplified from the depths of the Event. And the Holocaust diarists see to it that their example is recorded. Ringelblum, for instance, relates: "In the prayer house of the Pietists [Hasidim] from Braclaw on Nowalipie Street there is a large sign: Jews, Never Despair! The Pietists dance there with the same religious fervor as they did before the war" (125). Through their fervor they bring peace to a realm where there is no peace. And so the dance becomes the antidote to the fragmentation of despair, a mark of wisdom and a means of becoming whole again—of becoming *shelem*, which is a cognate of *shalom*—even as life is crumbling apart. Likewise, then, on 25 October 1940 Kaplan bears witness to a group of Hasidim who led a crowd dancing down Mila Street (214), and on 20 February 1941 he asserts: "It is almost a *mitzvah* to dance. The more one dances, the more it is a sign of his belief in the 'eternity of Israel.' Every dance is a protest against our oppressors" (245). Clinging to life, both the dancers and the diarists cling to this eternity. A *mitzvah* is a sacred deed, a prayer in the form of a deed, as Abraham Joshua Heschel has pointed out (*Man's Quest* 69). Therefore a dance that is a *mitzvah* is a dance transformed into prayer, with all the metaphysics—and here all the laughter—that belong to prayer.

In the dance, then, not only is the image of humanity seen, but the voice of life is heard, a voice that burns with an affirming flame when every reason for such an affirmation has gone up in flames. Let us attend to that voice as it rises up from the Holocaust diary and see exactly what it affirms. And let us attend to the life that it voices.

THE VOICE OF LIFE

Giving utterance to the voice of life, the diarists come to hear life's voice. Therefore their speaking is a hearing, and what they hear is something that penetrates the anonymous rumbling and the stark horror of a cruel and indifferent being. It rises above the roar of tanks and trucks and reverberates in the cry of humanity to declare that suffering matters because life is dear. Thus, like the dance of the Hasidim, the voice of life carries the diarist into a dimension of height, where the holiness of life is affirmed. And where the Holy One, perhaps, is heard. "The very foundation of the Jewish People's link with God," says the Breslover Rebbe, "is through *hearing*" (*Tikkun* 56). The link lies in hearing because the Jew not only hears the voice but also knows that he is heard; even though he may speak from the confines of his garret, he does not speak to a void. The voice of life rests upon this hearing and being heard. The voice of life, then, is the voice of language itself, for language itself, in its hearing and being heard, is our link to life.[9] As an attending to the other, language is a listening to the other, even as we speak. And when this listening to the other takes us into the heights, into the realm of life's holiness, it opens up a relation to a Third, who is the Holy One Himself.[10] We have seen the manifestations of the diarists' responsibility for their neighbor; in the voice of life that rises up from these dairies we discover a Third to whom their response is addressed and by whom they are addressed. If Yitskhok Rudashevski insists that "everything should be recorded and noted down" (84), it is because he knows that in this address he is being addressed, that in his own bearing witness, the voice of life summons him. Therefore he knows that he must adhere to the integrity of the word, if he is to have any hope of adhering to life.

The Nazis, too, have some sense of the connection between the integrity of the word and the voice of life. That is why they are careful to distort the language, tearing words from meaning at every turn. "That is the way of the Nazi murderers," writes Chaim Kaplan. "They cloak every cruelty in a beautiful phrase. You are swayed by the prose and pay no attention to the content" (246). In order not to be swayed by this perversion of the language, the diarist struggles to return meaning to the word and the word to life. "In keeping this diary," Kaplan says, "I find spiritual rest" (16). For in keeping this diary he keeps to the word that gives voice to spiritual life. Why? Because, once again, language is fraternity: his link to the word is a link to humanity. Indeed, Michael Zylberberg expresses this very idea in his own diary. "It is now dark outside and I am thinking about today's victims," he makes an entry in July of 1942. "In recording it, I feel temporarily less isolated. Writing has briefly replaced the need for human contact" (101). The need for human contact is a need to hear and be heard, and since writing is a hearing and being heard, it is tied to the life that unfolds in human contact. Hence many diarists exhibit a sense of profound gratitude for their writing, and in this gratitude, too, the voice of life can be heard. Indeed, if the voice of life says anything, it says, "Thank you"—thank you for this giving thanks, for this language, this voice, this writing. "I am grateful to God," says Anne Frank, "for giving me this gift, this possibility of developing myself and of writing, of expressing all that is in me" (211). And yet, she declares, "God has not left me alone and will not leave me alone" (207). Why, then, her gratitude? Because life stirs in her soul as she is disturbed by God; because the disturbance of God is an awakening to responsibility. And in responsibility the voice of life summons us to respond, not only to God's creatures but to creation itself. "I've found that there is always some beauty left," Anne writes, "in nature, sunshine, freedom, in yourself; these can all help you. Look at these things, then you find yourself again, and God, and then you regain your balance" (184). And the sense of balance lies in the sense of hearing: both physically and spiritually, the ear is the organ of balance.

The balance regained is a balance proclaimed. It is the balance exemplified by the Psalmist who cries, "Day utters speech unto day, and night unto night declares knowledge" (Psalms 19:2). Inasmuch as the voice of life is heard in the Holocaust diaries, this utterance and declaration that resound throughout creation makes themselves heard. "To look up at the sky, the clouds, the moon, and the stars makes me calm and patient," says Anne Frank (266). Thus, opposite the crumbling of creation that was examined in chapter 6, we have this affirmation of creation, of the height and therefore of the holiness opened up in creation. Just as Anne looks up, so does a very different diarist look up, despite their differences. "The sun and the light," writes the journalist Philip Mechanicus from Westerbork, "had given us back our feeling of freedom and made us brave. In our outdoor clothes we felt we were human beings again" (70). And in the Vilna Ghetto, Rudashevski asserts, "I revel in the spring breeze, catch the spring rays and my heart is full of strange yearning" (136). To feel like a human being is to feel alive; the yearning that arises from the spring sunshine is life's yearning for life. That is how day utters speech unto day, and that is the utterance heard in the Holocaust diary as it struggles to give voice to life.

Throughout these diaries written in a darkness devoid of all light, this utterance, this struggle, is as pervasive as sunlight itself. Indeed, the urge to enter into the midst of creation is so powerful that it can overpower the fear of death. "The desire to be under the open sky," writes Tuvia Borzykowski from his hiding place, "to breathe fresh air, to walk undisturbed became stronger than the fear of the Gestapo and 'schmaltzovniks' [Poles who would harass Jews and extort money from them]. I decided to take a chance" (150). If the longing for the light of the sky exemplifies a longing for the height and the holiness that sanctify life, an equally intense yearning for the earth expresses itself in a yearning for the origin of life. Emil Dorian, for example, comments on attending to his garden, saying, "As the spade penetrates the earth, a feeling of contentment runs through you, the voluptuous pleasure of being in direct and total contact with the source of life" (153). From the combination of earth and sky nature is born. It is not for nothing that Martin Buber includes "life with nature" among what he identifies, along with life with humanity and life with God, as one of the three "spheres of relation" (*I and Thou* 56–57). Nor is it surprising, then, to find that nature is a frequent topic of testimony among the Holocaust diarists who struggle to give voice to life. "The nature groups are very interesting," relates Rudashevski, for instance. "In general it is very interesting to read and to occupy yourself in the ghetto with nature. It shows that we are not cut off from nature in spirit, we feel it and have a sound understanding of it" (78). The spirit that establishes a connection between the diarist and nature is the spirit of affirmation with which he engages his diary. Joining the diarist to nature, it establishes a dwelling place in a world that is antithetical to dwelling. That spirit manifests itself in the diary of Philip Mechanicus, who affirms: "A bright sky—soft sunlight over a wide autumn landscape. Nature gives a sense of peace" (182). Nature *ademt vrede*, the original Dutch text reads (192), that is, nature "breathes peace." Once again the motif of peace shows up in the effort to cling to life. Once again there is a certain wisdom in that breath of peace, the wisdom that day utters unto day and night declares to night in a restoration of balance. In this breathing of peace and wisdom the diarist draws a breath of life. And vibrating on that breath is the voice of life.

Parallel to the diarists' affirmation of nature is their affirmation of nature's Creator. This affirmation imparts to the diaries a religious dimension that manifests itself in many ways. Hannah Senesh, for instance, writes: "I think religion means a great deal in life, and I find the modern concept—that faith in God is only a crutch for the weak—ridiculous. It's exactly that faith which makes one strong, and because of it one does not depend upon other things for support" (32). In many cases, then, the diarists attest to the life-affirming significance of religious life, particularly as it is manifested through prayer, which is an effort to join one's voice to the voice of the Creator of life.[11] This testimony to the importance of religious life imparts to the diary itself something of an aspect of prayer; in that realm where, as we have seen, prayer was under assault, the voice of prayer becomes the voice of life.[12] Clinging to life, therefore, the Holocaust diarists bear witness to the life of prayer. On the first day of Passover in 1940, for example, Kaplan notes, "The synagogues are closed, but in every courtyard there is a holiday service, and cantors sing the prayers and hymns in their sweet voices" (140). While Kaplan was perhaps more religiously observant than other diarists, the testimony to religious life and the admiration of the religious Jews is not confined to the religious or highly observant diarists.

Emmanuel Ringelblum is a case in point. "There is an apartment in a Jewish courtyard," he attests, "where traditional studies are secretly going on. The door of the apartment is opened only to the password (one knock). When you come in, you see a large group of Talmudic students sitting over their studies" (138). Here we are reminded that in the Jewish tradition study is a form of prayer. "When two sit together and words of Torah are spoken between them," says Rabbi Chaniniah ben Teradion, "the *Shekhinah* too abides there" (*Avot* 8b), and the voice heard in prayer is the voice of the *Shekhinah*. In terms even stronger than Ringelblum's, Avraham Tory expresses his admiration of the faithful, saying, "I admired those pious Jews and envied them their ability to set themselves free from the yoke of the Ghetto. . . . Happy is the one who believes" (503). Similarly, Michael Zylberberg writes: "I see in my mind's eye all the Jewish characters of former times. Particularly the religious Jews, who, till the last, believed that there was some order, some pattern in life, that everything was not chaos. They felt there was a deep meaning in their suffering and death which would be perpetuated in Jewish history. These people seem more real to me every day. I feel that they accompany me wherever I go" (54–55). Here too we have an instance of a certain peace instilled in the diarist by the disciples of the wise. "Faith is Wisdom and Wisdom is Faith," as the thirteenth-century kabbalist, Rabbi Jacob ben Sheshet of Gerona, has said (Dan 116), and in that linkage the diarists discover a basis for clinging to life. These visions of prayer and faith, then, constitute a vision of life and of all that sustains life. Voicing that vision, the diarists give voice to life. For without their voicing of this vision, they would succumb to despair and to death; without it they cannot live.

In Zylberberg's case, as it must happen in every case, this faith in the Holy One on high underlies a faith in humanity below. "Though I was fighting for my life," he asserts, "I always tried to assume that the people I met tended to be compassionate and not vindictive. It was a guiding principle of mine to refuse to believe that everyone was bloodthirsty" (102–3). This guiding principle for Zylberberg's life is a principle of meaning in life. As such, it opens up the horizon of the future, which is precisely the horizon of meaning and of life: to have life is to have a future, and to have meaning is to have a direction to pursue into the future. And what constitutes that horizon? It is hope. Therefore the voice of life in the Holocaust diary often takes the form of the voice of hope, as when Abraham Levin declares, "I think that the present war will remove from our world much of its foulness and savagery. Winds of freedom and love of mankind will blow towards us from the east and the west" (320). Or as when Yitskhok Rudashevski cries, "I live confident in the future. I am not conflicted about it, and I see before me sun and sun and sun" (104). And: "I shall live with tomorrow, not with today. And if for every 100 ghetto children my age 10 can study, I must be among the fortunate ones, I must take advantage of this" (120). Nor are these voices of hope merely the voices of naive wishful thinking, since such voices can be found among those who harbor no illusions about their own survival. Chaim Kaplan is a good example. Even in the midst of the death all around him, even in the face of his all but certain death, he declares: "Our existence as a people will not be destroyed. Individuals will be destroyed, but the Jewish community will live on. Therefore every entry [in this diary] is more precious than gold" (58). More precious than any value placed on gold, every entry places an infinite value on life, despite the deluge of death.

Thus, even as we are flooded with the undeniable darkness and death that lurk in every page of the Holocaust diary, we are overwhelmed with a stubborn, Jewish clinging to life. And in this clinging to life we encounter—or perhaps collide with—a clinging to the living. As the diarist's hand descends to the page, it reaches into our souls and will not let go. It inscribes its testimony on the souls of those who come to meet the diary, and from the midst of that testimony arises the first question put to the first man: Where are you? And so we come to our closing remarks. Or rather to our reopening remarks: for those who come before the Holocaust diary are never done with it.

REOPENING REMARKS: THE ASSIGNATION OF THE READER

WE HAVE DETERMINED THAT THE HOLOCAUST DIARY DOES not conform to the categories that define the general genre of diaries; that it offers a testimony surpassing the information offered by other historical archives; that there are elements common to nearly all of the diaries, despite differences in the diarists; and that the Holocaust diary opens up metaphysical and ontological aspects of the Holocaust. While we may draw these conclusions from our examination of the Holocaust diary, we are not done with the implications of the investigation. For one thing that these diaries have in common is this: they continually lay claim to us and implicate us in our capacity to respond to the onslaught against life known as the Holocaust. The Talmud tells us that "the path of a funeral cortege has no limit, in deference to the dead" (*Bava Batra* 100b). Entrusted to us by the dead, these diaries line up in a funeral procession that has no limit, no end. And where does the procession lead? Into the soul of the reader. As we delve into each entry, it enters into us to put to us the first question that God put to the first man, the unceasing question that decides the value of the human being and all human values: Where are you? "It's hard, almost impossible to read," says Elie Wiesel. "These pages of these diaries were found in the ashes. Then you say to yourself that if they had the courage and the desperate faith, if they had the strength to write such words, we must have the strength to read them" (*Dimensions* 11). Yes, the strength: for in deciding something about these diaries, we decide something about our own lives, about the future of life. These diaries that come to us from the dead are about life, about all that sustains and threatens life. Unless we respond to the summons that comes to us from their depths, the summons to which the diaries themselves respond, we can have no life.

Through their example of answering to a "voice," as Mary Berg describes it, these diarists make it incumbent upon us to answer to their voices. "Who is interested in my diary?" she writes. "I have thought of burning it several times, but some inner voice forbade me to do it. The same inner voice is now urging me to write down all the terrible things I have heard" (227). More than "urging," the Polish text reads *nakazuje*, or "commanding" (243): writing the diary is not an option—it is an order. Where does the order come from? It comes from within. But this "within" is a synonym for "above," so that the commanding voice that speaks from within Mary Berg stands above us all. It arises from that dimension of height which, as Emmanuel Levinas has shown, "ordains being" and imparts meaning to life (*Collected* 100). If, as I step before the Holocaust diary, I bear a responsibility, then it "presupposes one who addresses me primarily," in the words of Martin Buber, "that is, from a realm independent of myself, and to whom I am answerable. He addresses me about something that he has entrusted to me and that I am bound to take care of loyally" (*Between* 45). Therefore when Renata Laqueur asks, "What will become of this diary?" (57), it is not only she who asks herself; the voice that commands her to write also asks us, "What will become of this diary?" And we must answer not only from the standpoint of academic curiosity or scholarly investigation but, more important, with our very lives: what becomes of the diary is determined by how we live and the testimony we bear in the light of having received this testimony.

Indeed, given the conditions under which these diaries were written, it is all but miraculous not only that they were written but that we have received them. But they have come to us, like letters that have somehow reached a destination that was their destiny, like the letters Hannah Senesh refers to when on 25 December 1943 she wrote to her brother George, "Letters one must write without asking oneself, 'I wonder whether this will ever reach its destination?'" (132). If these diaries may be compared to such letters, then we are their destination. And whether they reach their destination depends not only on whether we have them in hand but on whether we respond to them in the wholeness of the responsibility that constitutes the substance of our lives. To be sure, these diaries contain not only the voices of the diarists but legions of voices that were silenced in the Event. These voices, too, are like letters that the diarists themselves must deliver, a point that becomes clear when in the diary of Josef Katz we read: "My ears are humming. Soon all my pockets are filled with little notes, and still more people arrive with more requests. Erlanger warns me not to take too many letters, for there is a death penalty for smuggling mail" (101). So, too, were these diaries, for the most part, written under penalty of death by Jews already sentenced to death.

That is why they were generally hidden. And in some cases the diarists reveal their hiding places. Avraham Tory, for example, tells us, "After the death of the last Jew on Lithuanian soil, he, the priest Vaickus, will be the one to know where to find my notes, and to pass them to the person who, after the war, stands at the helm of world Jewry" (446). And the *Sonderkommando* diarist Salmen Gradowski writes: "Dear finder, search everywhere, in every inch of soil. Tons of documents are buried under it, mine and those of other prisoners, which will throw light on everything that was happening here. It was we, the Kommando workers, who expressly have strewn them all over the terrain, as many as we could, so that the world would find material traces of the millions of murdered people. We ourselves have lost hope of being able to live to see the moment of liberation" (76). Why declare to the reader who has already found the diary where the diary lies hidden? Because these diaries lie hidden not only in the care of a good priest or in the soil of the earth but in the souls of the diarists who in turn entrust their diaries to our own souls. Thus even after we have found them we must search for them—inside of *us*. Recall in this connection the entry dated 16 September 1943 in Yitzhak Katznelson's *Vittel Diary*: "At this later hour—for I do not sleep these nights—as I write these words, I want to weep. And if perchance I shed a tear, then Chanah, Ben Zion and Binyamin [his wife and children] are there within it, in miniature. They, together with the whole of my people, are reflected in its brightness. . . . Do not seek them out in Treblinka, nor in other mounds of earth, for you will find no trace of them. You must look for them in my tiny tear" (232–33). What shall we say to that tiny tear? It is not enough to add to it our own tears. We must add to it our living testimony, as Katznelson himself did, and not just our passive commentary.

Thus when Katznelson refers to "us" in a summons to remembrance, we may understand it to include *us*: "On and on, up to seven million . . . count! Count! . . . you must not stop! For us, a few utterly wretched ones, still living—alas that this should be called living!—this is a memorial service for the departed souls. Count on, count on, until your lips and tongue dry up in your mouth. . . . As for the lives [lost], they are an abyss, unfathomable depths and towering heights. As for the names, call out! Abraham, Isaac and Jacob! Every one of those lives, seven million lives, had something of Abraham, of Isaac and of Jacob" (194). Engaging in this counting, we come before an accounting for what the diarists place in our care. For those names that we count are the names of our fathers, and as we call them out we are called by name. Indeed, only by calling out those names can we hope to know our own names. Only by answering can we hope to hear. "He who ceases to make a response," we recall Buber's insight, "ceases to hear the Word" (*Between* 45). Although the Holocaust diary comes to us from the past, "it demands nothing of what is past," to borrow another line from Buber. "It demands presence, responsibility; it demands you" (*Between* 114). The days of the lives dated and measured in each entry of the Holocaust diary measure our own lives. Whatever we are, whatever we may aspire to, is measured by the response of the Holocaust diarist, who announces our responsibility.

That is what the assignation of the reader is about: responsibility. Indeed, in the Holocaust diary's account of this massive assault on life—in its testimony on the collapse of life and its struggle to recover it—I discover that this responsibility is what life itself is about. "I am I," Levinas states it, "in the sole measure that I am responsible, a non-interchangeable I. I can substitute myself for everyone, but no one can substitute himself for me. Such is my inalienable identity" (*Ethics* 101). Added to the first question put to the first man, then, are the two questions put to his firstborn, the questions put to Cain: Where is your brother? And: What have you done? Therefore as these voices call us forth, they send us forth: coming to the end of this exploration, we do not step away from the Holocaust diary—we are sent away, transformed into witnesses and messengers, "sent back to the other man," as Levinas puts it, "to the neighbor for whom I have to fear" ("Bad" 40). Such is the fear that we must learn to acquire from the Holocaust diary; as these diarists feared for the fate of their fellow human being, so must we fear for the lives of those all around us. To be sure, that is the Jewish message that comes to us from these Jewish diaries. It rises up from the connections we have established between these Jewish texts and the teachings of the Jewish tradition, between the ineluctable voices of the Jews who were slaughtered and the millennial voices of the Jews who preceded them. And if those connections have anything to teach the Jews, it is that they must be Jews.

In the Talmud it is said that "when there is an epidemic in a town, one should not walk in the middle of the road, as the Angel of Death walks then in the middle of the road" (*Bava Kama* 60b). Both during the Shoah and in its aftermath, an epidemic spreads not only through town after town but over the face of the earth. "There is no longer any difference between day and night," Levinas addresses this point, "between outside and inside. Do we not smell here, more strongly than a while back, beyond all violence, the odor of the camps? Violence is no longer a political phenomenon of war and peace, beyond all morality. It is the abyss of Auschwitz or the world at war. A world which has lost its 'very worldliness.' It is the twentieth century. One must go back inside, even if there is terror inside" (*Nine* 190–91). Answering to an inner voice, to a voice that is both within and above, the Holocaust diary is written from the inside; answering in a Jewish voice, the Holocaust diary is written from inside Jewish teaching and testimony. For the Jew, it is only from this inside that any mending, any *tikkun*, of what was torn asunder can be achieved. Thus the Jew who steps before the countenance of the Holocaust diary is summoned to return to the inside of Jewish teaching and testimony precisely because in the diary such a mending was already underway. "*The Tikkun which for the post-Holocaust Jew is a moral necessity*," Emil Fackenheim insists, "*is a possibility because during the Holocaust itself a Jewish Tikkun was already actual.* This simple but enormous, nay, world-historical truth is the rock on which rests any authentic Jewish future, and any authentic Jewish identity" (*To Mend* 300). In a very important sense, Jews today owe their very being to these diarists who held to their Jewish being during those days of destruction. If Jews today are to proceed toward a Jewish future, then Jews most especially must answer to these Jewish diarists.

Any reader who comes to these diaries encounters a responsibility to bear witness to life through his words and deeds. But the Jew encounters one responsibility more. And here Fackenheim's famous 614th Commandment enters the picture. He explains: "A Jew cannot take upon himself the age-old task of testifying to the divine image in man without believing his own testimony. In our time, however, he cannot authentically believe in this testimony without exposing himself *both* to the fact that the image of God was destroyed, *and* to the fact that the unsurpassable attempt to destroy it was successfully resisted, supremely so, by the survivor. *Hence the wish to bear witness turns into a commandment, the commandment to restore the divine image to the limits of his power*" (*Jewish Return* 251). To "survivor" we may add "Holocaust diarist," even though most of those who wrote these diaries did not survive. If the Jewish diarist was commanded to write, the Jewish reader is also commanded—commanded to bear witness, as a Jew, to the truth of human sanctity in word and deed, to lay this teaching, this Torah, on his heart, to place it as a sign on his hand and between his eyes. For the Holocaust diary confronts the Chosen with a choice: either be a Jew in a return to the inside or become an accomplice to those who would murder both the children of Abraham and the God of Abraham. Thus we arrive once more at an ancient teaching, one that comes to us from the talmudic sage Rabbi Shimon ben Yochai: "'Only when ye are My witnesses, am I God. But when ye are not My witnesses, I'—if one may speak thus—'am not God'" (Kahana 232). The Holocaust diarists understood this teaching. And if we are to understand the Holocaust diary, we must understand it as well.

One who understood it all too well was young Moshe Flinker, who wrote, "Even if we already deserve to be redeemed because of our great sufferings, there is the danger that the Jews themselves will not want to be redeemed" (29). And so every Jew is implicated by the sufferings of every Moshe Flinker. The pages of his diary, like the pages of all the diaries, are spread out before humanity like the bloodstained rags that Janusz Korczak refers to when he says: "There are problems that lie, like bloodstained rags, right across the sidewalk. People cross to the other side of the street or turn their eyes away in order not to see" (164). But if we are to refuse the Nazis a posthumous victory, we cannot avert our eyes. What, then, must we do in our analysis of these bloodstained texts that were written along the edge of annihilation? In Korczak's diary we may find an answer but not a solution: "To analyze in order to know? No. To analyze in order to find, to get to the bottom of things? Not that either. Rather to analyze in order to ask further and further questions" (170). And the first of these question comes to us from the diaries themselves, as when Philip Mechanicus asks: "Where are you, you thousands and tens of thousands who have been carried away from one place to another—what has been your fate? You are silent because they will not let you speak" (240). And yet they speak in the silence between the words of the Holocaust diary. They speak in the silent interior of the Jewish soul. They speak in the Jewish response called forth from the depths of these Jewish diaries. For these diaries contain the remnants of a myriad of Jewish voices and Jewish lives.

Like the Israelites who bore the bones of Joseph into the wilderness on their way to the Promised Land, we must bear these voices into our own wilderness. And, if we are ever to reach the Land of the Promise, we must bear them, as the Israelites bore the bones of Joseph, alongside the ark that contained the Torah.

NOTES

OPENING REMARKS

1. I am the translator of all quotes from sources for which an English title is not given.—D.P.

2. "All relations between man and God," writes Edmond Jabès in this connection, "pass through the word. That's why the Jew, unable to bear the silence of the Book, has always busied himself commenting on it. Every commentary is first of all a commentary on a silence" (*Desert* 102).

3. Here too Jabès offers a helpful insight: "Every question is tied to becoming. Yesterday interrogates tomorrow, just as tomorrow interrogates yesterday in the name of an always open future. The famous 'Who am I?' finds its justification only in a universal questioning of which we would be but the persistent echo" (*Desert* 74).

4. "I write," says Jabès in *The Book of Yukel*, "and right away I become the word which escapes me and thanks to which I am, the word which leads to other words and asserts itself as such. I am multiplied in my sentence as a tree unfolds its branches" (56).

5. Emmanuel Levinas makes this point by saying, "The true substantiality of a subject consists in its *substantivity*: in the fact that there is not only, anonymously, being in general, but there are beings capable of bearing names" (*Existence* 98).

THE WRITER AND THE WRITING

1. "My determination of myself is given to me," Mikhail Bakhtin expresses this notion, "not in the categories of temporal being, but in the categories of *not-yet-being*, in the categories of purpose and meaning—in the meaning-governed future" (*Art* 123).

2. "He who ceases to make a response ceases to hear the Word," we are reminded of Martin Buber's insight (*Between* 45).

THE CONSCIOUSNESS OF THE BOOK

1. Fackenheim elaborates: "*Ha-makom* [the Place] is He who can be present, and who is present when scholars study Torah in earnest. The *shechina* is the 'indwelling' of what, for want of a better rendering, we must refer to as the spirit of God between those studying Torah, provided they direct their hearts to heaven. Here lies the innermost secret of Torah study, and the source of its life" (*Judaism* 163–64).

THE MEASURE OF TIME

1. Rabbi Joseph Lehmann of the Reform movement, for example, believed that the Jews of Nazi Germany could continue their struggle for a place in their German homeland; and Zionist Robert Weltsch maintained that Jews could overcome the new oppression by displaying their Jewishness with greater pride (*see* Dawidowicz 175–76).

2. Emmanuel Levinas adds to our understanding of this point when he says, "Time is precisely the fact that the whole existence of the mortal being—exposed to violence—is not for death, but the 'not yet' which is a way of being against death" (*Totality* 224). Here Levinas opens up the connection between the collapse of the present and the divorce from the future, a matter we shall soon examine in detail.

THE CHRONICLE OF THE HOLY

1. And so it is written in the *Zohar*: "Festivals, Sabbaths, and all days of moment in Israel have this 'remembrance' [of the Covenant] for their object and basis, therefore the deliverance from Egypt is mentioned in connection with such days. Truly, this 'remembrance' is the foundation and root of the whole Torah" (3:118–19). One recalls in this regard that many Jews date the days and the weeks of a given time of year according to the Torah portion for that week: the Torah, which is the Voice of the Eternal One, is itself the measure of time.

2. "Prayer," says Nachman of Breslov, "is a battle against evil" (*Advice* 285).

3. "The Seder," Rabbi Steinsaltz explains, "is a 'family offering,' the Jewish family celebration par excellence. The ceremony renews the ties that bind the family together and link it to the past and future" (*Teshuvah* 117).

4. One is reminded of the teaching handed down from Nachman of Breslov, that at Passover "speech emerges from Exile. This is the main idea of the Exodus" (*Wisdom* 205).

5. We recall Heschel's assertion that "time is the presence of God in the world of space" (*Sabbath* 100).

6. In the words of Rabbi Menachem Schneerson: "'Light' is the purpose of each Jew: that he transforms his situation and environment to light. Not merely by driving out the darkness (evil) by refraining from sin, but by changing the darkness itself to light" (4).

ASSAILING GOD

1. The idea that an assault on the Chosen is an assault on God is at least as old as Rashi, who in his eleventh-century *Commentary on the Torah* asserts, "Whoever attacks Israel is as though he attacks the Holy One, blessed be He" (4:146). In modern times Abraham Joshua Heschel elaborates on this notion by saying: "With Israel's distress came the affliction of God, His displacement, His homelessness in the land, in the world. And the prophet's prayer, 'O save us,' involved not only the fate of a people. It involved the fate of God in relation to the people" (*Prophets* 1: 112).

2. One cannot help but recall here the prayer taken from tractate *Avot* of the Talmud, where we ask God that He grant us a portion in His Torah (*Avot* 5:20)—not *of* His Torah but *in* His Torah, as though each Jew were himself a letter that goes into the making of the Torah, himself a syllable in God's utterance—a notion that is in keeping with the teaching of Rabbi Levi Yitschak of Berditchev (*see* Rabinowicz 61) and that implies once again a definitive association of Israel with the Torah, of the Torah with God, and of God with Israel.

3. "For all things," Buber reminds us of a Jewish teaching, "above and below, are a *single* unity. 'I am the prayer,' speaks the *Shekhinah*. A zaddik said, 'Men believe they pray before God, but this is not so, for the prayer itself is divinity" (*Legend* 27).

4. The diarist's condition in this regard is akin to the condition of the soul that Wiesel describes when he writes: "God's final victory, my son, lies in man's inability to reject Him. You think you're cursing Him, but your curse is

praise; you think you're fighting Him, but all you do is open yourself to Him; you think you're crying out your hatred and rebellion, but all you're doing is telling Him how much you need His support" (*Gates* 33).

5. We have another good example in Rabbi Levi Yitschak of Berditchev, who studied with another disciple of the Besht, the Maggid of Mezeritch. "On the Day of Atonement," we are told, "he once urged the town's humble tailor to speak up in front of the whole congregation; the man publicly made his confession: 'I, Yankel, am a poor tailor who, to tell the truth, has not been too honest with his work. I have occasionally kept remnants of cloth that were left over, and I have occasionally missed the afternoon service. But You, O Lord, have taken away infants from their mothers, and mothers from their infants. Let us on this Day of Days, be quits. If You forgive me, then I will forgive You.' At this the rabbi sighed: 'Oh, Yankel, Yankel, why did you let God off so lightly?'" (Rabinowicz 63).

6. Therefore Wiesel raises his cry: "I no longer ask You to resolve my questions, only to receive them and make them part of You" (*One* 241).

THE CRUMBLING OF CREATION

1. This midrashic teaching is reiterated, at times with variations, by later texts, such as the seventh-century *Pirke de Rabbi Eliezer*; there, in a repetition of a teaching from the Talmud (*Pesachim* 54a; *Nedarim* 39b), we read, "Seven things were created before the world was created. They are: The Torah, Gehinnom, the Garden of Eden, the Throne of Glory, the Temple, Repentance, and the Name of the Messiah" (10–11). And in his thirteenth-century *Commentary on the Torah*, Nachmanides explains, "The reason for the Torah being written in this [third-person] form is that it preceded the creation of the world" (1:8).

2. Like an architect turning to the plan in his soul, says the *Zohar*, God consulted theTorah not once but four times before taking up His task: "The account of the creation commences with the four words *Bereshith Bara Aelohim Aith* ('In-the-beginning created God the'), before mentioning 'the heavens,' thus signifying the four times which the Holy One, blessed be He, looked into the Torah before He performed His work" (1:21). One sees a correspondence between these four times and the four letters in the divine Name, from which creation derives and which, as noted in the last chapter, is synonymous with Torah. Nor is this teaching a mystical aberration of the Middle Ages, since it appears on the first page of the earlier, seventh-century text, the

Midrash Tanchuma, where we are taught, "When He created His world, the Holy One, blessed be He, consulted the Torah and created the world" (1:1).

3. Of course, Rabbi Steinsaltz draws on the teachers and the traditions that precede him. Rabbi Nachman of Breslov, for example, declares, "Letters of Torah are present throughout the Creation" (*Advice* 81). Rabbi Israel Meir HaKohen, the sage known as the Chofetz Chaim (1838–1933), maintains, "If not for Torah study, the entire universe would revert to chaos" (*Light* 31).

4. "When I killed my brother," says Cain in Elie Wiesel's *Twilight*, "it was really Him I wanted to kill. And He knows it. Any fool knows that whoever kills, kills God" (58).

5. "When those of flesh and blood build a palace," says Rabbi Yitzhak in the *Midrash Tanchuma*, "they first build the lower part, and then they build the upper part. But the Holy One, blessed be He, first created the upper part and then created the lower part" (1:9). "Height ordains being," Levinas explains. "Height introduces sense into being. It is already lived across the experience of the human body. It leads human societies to raise up altars. It is not because men, through their bodies, have an experience of the vertical that the human is placed under the sign of height; because being is ordained to height the human body is placed in a space in which the high and the low are distinguished and the sky is discovered" (*Collected* 100).

MEANING UNDONE

1. In *Ethics and Infinity* he adds: "'There is' is the phenomenon of impersonal being: 'it.' My reflection on this subject starts with childhood memories. One sleeps alone, the adults continue life; the child feels the silence of his bedroom as 'rumbling,' . . . as if the emptiness were full, as if the silence were a noise. . . . It is a noise returning after every negation of this noise. Neither nothingness nor being. I sometimes use the expression: the excluded middle. One cannot say of this 'there is' which persists that it is an event of being. One can neither say that it is nothingness, even though there is nothing" (48–49).

2. The words of Bachya ibn Paquda, spoken a thousand years ago, come to mind: "The [evil] inclination became firmly fixed in them and the pitcher [of iniquity] was full. What had been strange in this world became known to them, while the right way was strange to them" (2:297).

3. Alvin Rosenfeld describes this silence when he notes that writers such as the Holocaust diarists are in a position "analogous to that of the man

of faith, who is likewise beset by frustration and anguish and, in just those moments when his spirit may yearn for the fullness of Presence, is forced to acknowledge the emptiness and silence of an imposed Absence. The life centers of the self—intelligence, imagination, assertiveness—undergo paralysis in such moments, which, if prolonged, have the effect of a total detachment or the profoundest despair. Yet to indulge in silence is to court madness or death. At just those points where, through some abiding and still operative reflex of language, silence converts once more into words—even into words about silence—Holocaust literature [beginning with the Holocaust diary] is born" (*Double* 14–15).

4. Elsewhere Levinas describes this condition as "a vigilance without possible recourse to sleep, . . . a vigilance without refuge in unconsciousness, without the possibility of withdrawing into sleep as a private domain. This existing is not an *in-itself* [*en-soi*], which is already peace; it is precisely the absence of self, a *without-self* [*sans-soi*]" (*Time* 48–49).

5. To be sure, like meaning, repentance is the basis of human life, a point made by Rabbi Nachman of Breslov when he asserts, "Previous to repentance a man has no real existence" (Newman 382).

6. Levinas describes this transformation by saying: "There is a non-coinciding of the ego with itself, restlessness, insomnia, beyond what is found again in the present. There is the pain which confounds the ego or in vertigo draws it like an abyss, and prevents it from assuming the other that wounds it in an intentional movement when it posits itself in itself and for itself. Then there is produced in this vulnerability the reversal whereby the other inspires the same, pain, an overflowing of meaning by nonsense. The sense bypasses nonsense—that sense which is the-same-for-the-other. The passivity or patience of vulnerability has to go that far! In it sensibility is sense; it is by the other and for the other, for another. Not in elevated feelings, in 'belles lettres,' but as in a tearing away of bread from the mouth that tastes it, to give it to the other" (*Otherwise* 64).

7. One is reminded of the commentary on Moses's selection of the judges of Israel in the *Midrash Rabbah*; there we are told that these elders of Israel were those "who submitted their bodies to be smitten for the people's sake in Egypt on account of the total of bricks" (7: 665).

THE FRAGMENTATION OF HOME AND FAMILY

1. We are reminded of a passage from the *Midrash Rabbah*: "The Holy One, blessed be He, said to His world: 'O My world, My world! Shall I tell thee

who created thee, who formed thee? Jacob has created thee, Jacob has formed thee'" (4:460). Hence Jacob is symbolized by a house and a home, by the *beit* from which the world is created.

2. "The familial upbringing (*emun*)," says Rabbi Abraham Isaac Kook, "is a product and linear extension of that great faith (*emunah*) that rests in the depth of love, which works in a spirit of life, with glorious, sublime intelligence, in harmony and coordination in the totality of the multitude of creatures and worlds. Betrayal of the family is a betrayal that destroys the foundations of the creation" (136–37).

3. Recall, for example, the teaching found in the *Pesikta de-Rab Kahana* (341) and in the *Midrash Tanchuma* (1:378) that the windows of the Temple were designed not so as to let light in but to let light out; it is the light emanating from the Temple, which is the paradigm for the dwelling place, that illuminates our path into the world and that creates for us a place in the world.

4. In his commentary on the Hebrew letter *beit*—which, as already noted, means "house" or "home"—Rabbi Ginsburgh explains: "The root of *bereshit* [the word with which the Creation and the Torah begin], *rosh*, means 'head.' Thus the most 'natural' permutation of *bereshit* reads: *rosh beit*, 'the head of the house.' One permutation of the letters *rosh* is *asher*, 'happiness.' When the *tzadik* draws G–d, the 'Head,' into His 'House,' it becomes a house of true and eternal happiness. The drawing down of the 'Head' to dwell in His 'House' below, in true happiness, is the secret of blessing (*brakhah*) which begins with the letter *beit*" (39). The *beit* that begins "blessing" is itself where blessing begins. And, as Rabbi Samson Raphael Hirsch maintains, this blessing that comes into the world through the home enters through the honor shown toward our parents: "In order to become an instrument of blessing, learn first to honor your parents as messengers to you of God, mankind and Israel" (80).

THE ASSAULT ON THE FEMININE

1. The relationship with the feminine, Levinas explains, is a relationship "with the future, with what (in a world where there is everything) is never there, with what cannot be there when everything else is there—not with a being that is not there, but with the very dimension of alterity" (*Time* 88).

2. Without the feminine, argues Levinas, man knows "nothing which transforms his natural life into ethics, nothing which permits living a life, not even the death that one dies for another" (*Difficult* 34).

3. That is why in the sixteenth century Rabbi Yehuda Loeve, the Maharal

of Prague, declared, "Woman is the consummation of man's existence, for through her, man becomes complete. When a man has his own woman [a bride], his existence is essential, not casual. When he has an illicit relationship with a woman, however—when the lust strikes him—his very existence is casual. Thus 'He who has illicit relations with a woman lacks a heart.' The Torah, too, completes man; it is often compared to a woman [see, for example, *Kiddushin* 30b] because, like woman, it makes man complete" (106).

4. This ancient truth finds expression in more modern times through the teachings of Rabbi Nachman of Breslov, who states it by saying, "Compassion is at the root of all Creation" (Aron 160), for compassion is at the root of the feminine.

5. In his commentary on the *Sefer Yetzirah*, Aryeh Kaplan points out that the Feminine Essence belongs to the domain of Understanding or *Binah* (16), a word derived from *beyn*, which means "between." Understanding arises from the difference *between* two, and, as the highest manifestation of the Feminine Essence, the mother transforms the radical difference that underlies understanding into the absolute non-indifference of love.

6. Here Rabbi Yitzhak Ginsburgh explains, "At the level of Divinity the house symbolizes the purpose of all reality: to become a dwelling place below for the manifestation of G–d's presence. 'Not as Abraham who called [the Temple] "a mountain," nor as Isaac who called it "a field," but as Jacob who call it "a house"'" (46).

7. One recalls in this regard the comment from the Talmud that "when Rabbi Joseph heard the sound of his mother's footsteps, he would stand and say, 'I rise before the approaching *Shekhinah*'" (*Kiddushin* 31b). Central, then, to the annihilation of the Jew in his care for the *Shekhinah* is the annihilation of his care for his mother.

THE SUFFOCATION OF THE CHILD

1. "She was six years old," Wiesel tells the tale of a little girl who embodies the ontological condition of all these children, "a pale, shy and nervous child. Did she know what was happening around her? How much did she understand of the events? She saw the killers kill, she saw them kill—how did she translate these visions in her child's mind? One morning she asked her mother to hug her. Then she came to place a kiss on her father's forehead. And she said, 'I think that I shall die today.' And after a sigh, a long sigh: 'I

think I am glad'" (*Jew* 128). The child who is glad of dying has been robbed of her life before that life has been extinguished.

2. Recall in this connection the notion of the "there is" as Emmanuel Levinas defines it, where, he says, "the absence of everything returns as a presence, as the place where the bottom has dropped out of everything, an atmospheric density, a plenitude of the void, or the murmur of silence" (*Time* 46).

3. Therefore the diarist is thrown into the position of the persona who speaks in Wiesel's *Ani Maamin*: I run / As far as my legs will carry me, / Like the wind, / With the wind, / Farther than the wind. / I run, / And while I run, / I am thinking: / This is insane, / This Jewish child / Will not be spared. / I run and run / And cry. / And while I am crying, / While I am running, / I perceive a whisper: / I believe, / Says the little girl, / Weakly, / I believe in you (89 and 91). The Holocaust diarist's method of running with the child in his arms—the only means of running that is open to him—is to write.

4. When the *ki tov* is removed from the world, says the thirteenth-century mystic Rabbi Joseph Gikatilla, "the whole world is destroyed and *tov* [the good] is not to be found in the world" (87).

THE HUMAN IMAGE DEFILED

1. Fackenheim makes the connection between the annihilation of the Jew and the assault on the idea of humanity as clear as it is incontrovertible. "Never was a more exalted view of man conceived than that of the divine image, and never one more radically antiracist," he writes. "It was therefore grimly logical—if to be sure uniquely horrifying—that the most radical racists of all time decreed a unique fate for the Jewish people" (*Judaism* 109).

2. Attesting to this tradition, Rabbi Abraham Joshua Heschel writes, "A face cannot be grafted or interchanged. A face is a message, a face speaks, often unbeknown to the person. Is not the human face a living mixture of mystery and meaning?" (*Wonder* 48).

3. "True union or true togetherness," Emmanuel Levinas points out, is not the togetherness of being merely alongside one another "but a togetherness of face to face" (*Ethics* 77).

4. In his novel *The Parnas*, for instance, Silvano Arieti develops his title character's fear of animals into a fear of the Nazis who ultimately set upon him and beat him to death. Over and over, as the beasts pound him, he repeats, "Animals with a snout, fur, four claws, and a tail," as though in a hypnotic trance. "But what was to be hypnotic for others," we read, "was for him

the stupendous unveiling of his life secret. Yes, God was with him. By making the Nazis appear as animals, God was revealing that his past fears were indeed the fear of human evil, of which the Nazis were the most perfect representatives in all of human history" (140).

5. Thus "the horror of the evil aimed at me," in the words of Levinas, "becomes the horror over the evil in the other man" (*Collected* 185).

6. Therefore one may cry out, as Ka-tzetnik cries out: "Oh Lord of Auschwitz heavens, illumine my ignorance of your handiwork, so that I might know who is the being within me now delivered to the crematorium—and why? And who is the being within him delivering me to the crematorium—and why? For you know that at this moment the two of us, dispatcher and dispatched, are equal sons of man, both created by you, in your image" (*Shivitti* 11).

7. "Evil—or bestiality—is non-communication," says Levinas. "It is being completely enclosed within oneself, to the point of not revealing oneself even to oneself!" (*Nine* 108).

DEATH AND THE DEATH OF DEATH

1. In the words of the eleventh-century sage Rabbi Bachya ibn Paquda: "Life and Death are brethren, dwelling together closely to one another, inseparable, holding fast to the two ends of a tottering bridge over which all the world's creatures pass. Life is at its entrance; Death is at its exit. Life builds, Death breaks up. Life sows, Death reaps. Life unites, Death divides. Life strings together, Death scatters what has been strung together" (2:389).

2. For "the Nazi murder machine," we recall an insight from Emil Fackenheim, "was systematically designed to stifle this *Shema Yisrael* on Jewish lips before it murdered Jews themselves" (*God's Presence* 74).

3. Simon Wiesenthal makes this very point in *The Sunflower*. In a scene that explains the title of his book, he recalls gazing upon a German cemetery with sunflowers growing on the graves of SS soldiers. Noticing the butterflies that were flitting from one flower to the next, he wonders: "Were they carrying messages from grave to grave? Were they whispering something to each flower to pass on to the soldier below? Yes, this was just what they were doing; the dead were receiving light and messages. Suddenly I envied the dead soldiers. Each had a sunflower to connect him with the living world, and butterflies to visit his grave" (20).

4. "The other man's death," Levinas states it, "calls me into question, as

if, by my possible future indifference, I had become the accomplice of the death to which the other, who cannot see it, is exposed" ("Ethics" 83).

5. "My generation has been robbed of everything," Elie Wiesel reminds us, "even of our cemeteries" (*Legends* 25).

6. "In Judaism," Baeck explains, "only the ethical deed makes possible the 'sanctification of the Name,' the *Kiddush ha-Shem*. Every good action born of pure intention sanctifies God's name; every base action desecrates it. The good that one practices is the best witness of God that one can give; at the same time it is the most impressive sermon about the truth of religion that can possibly be delivered. Everyone, no matter how inarticulate, can thus become the messenger of his faith among men. Every Jew is called upon to manifest the meaning of his religion by the conduct of his life" (270–71).

CLINGING TO LIFE

1. That is why Nachman of Breslov asserts, "The Torah is revealed through peace" (*Aleph-Bet* 137). Because the relation of peace between God and humanity lies at the heart of the Torah, the fourteenth-century sage Rabbi Yitzchak Abohav declares: "No other *mitzvah* carries as strong an emphasis on the pursuit of it as does the *mitzvah* of living at peace with other people. The achievement of social harmony is the culmination of civilization. The climax of the *kohanim*'s benediction to the people is that they be blessed to live in harmony" (251). Indeed, a sage who lived a century after Rabbenu Abohav, Rabbi Don Isaac Abrabanel, asserts that "one of God's names is *Shalom*—Peace, because God binds all peoples together and establishes for them an organized pattern of life" (Chill 62). What Abrabanel refers to as "an organized pattern of life" is a pattern of benevolence toward our fellow human being.

2. God, in the words of Emil Fackenheim, "confronts man with the demand to turn to his human neighbor, and in doing so, turn back to God Himself. . . . For there is no humble walking before God unless it manifests itself in justice and mercy to the human neighbor" (*Encounters* 49). Hence walking before God means walking toward our fellow human being; indeed, such "walking" is the essence and meaning of *halakhah*. Emmanuel Levinas makes this point by saying: "The justice rendered to the Other, my neighbor, gives me an unsurpassable proximity to God. It is as intimate as the prayer and the liturgy which, without justice, are nothing" (*Difficult* 18).

3. "I approach the infinite," Levinas states it, "insofar as I forget myself

for my neighbor who looks at me; I forget myself only in breaking the undephasable simultaneity of representation, in existing beyond my death. I approach the infinite by sacrificing myself. Sacrifice is the norm and the criterion of the approach. And the truth of transcendence consists in the concording of speech with acts" (*Collected* 72).

4. It was these *Hasidei Umot HaOlam*, the Righteous among the Nations, who exemplified the sense and sensibility that Levinas describes: "Sensibility has meaning only as a 'taking care of the other's need,' of his misfortunes and his faults, that is, as a giving. But giving has meaning only as a tearing away from oneself despite oneself, and not only *without* me. And to be torn from oneself despite oneself has meaning only as a being torn from the complacency in oneself characteristic of enjoyment, snatching the bread from one's own mouth. Only a subject that eats can be for-the-other, or can signify. Signification, the one-for-the-other, has meaning only among beings of flesh and blood" (*Otherwise* 74).

5. No one who is to remain a human being "can remain in himself," Levinas insists. "The humanity of man, subjectivity, is a responsibility for the others, an extreme vulnerability" (*Collected* 149).

6. "In Judaism, the certainty of the absolute's hold over man," says Levinas, "burns *inwards*, as an infinite demand made on oneself, an infinite responsibility" (*Difficult* 174).

7. Therefore, addressing his Jewish audience, Rabbi Nachman of Breslov insists, "The duty rests upon *you*: this single person who is standing in *this* generation at *this* point in the whole of eternity. It has to be done by you. 'Not an angel! Not a seraph!'" (*Restore* 47–48).

8. Emphasizing the definitive link between the life of the individual and the community of Israel, the *Mekilta* declares, "The people of Israel are compared to a lamb. What is the nature of the lamb? If it is hurt in one limb, all its limbs feel the pain" (2:205–6).

9. "Language is fraternity," Levinas holds, "and thus a responsibility for the other" (*Collected* 123).

10. "Speech, in its original essence," Levinas makes this point, "is a commitment to a third party on behalf of our neighbor" (*Nine* 21).

11. "Our devotion in prayer," Bachya ibn Pakuda states it, "is nothing but the soul's longing for God" (2: 211).

12. "Life is fashioned by prayer," says Abraham Joshua Heschel, "and prayer is the quintessence of life" (*Man's Quest* 12).

BIBLIOGRAPHY OF WORKS CITED

PRIMARY SOURCES

ANDREAS-FRIEDRICH, RUTH. *Der Schattenmann: Tagebuchaufzeichnungen 1938–1945*. Berlin: Suhrkamp, 1947.

BERG, MARY, *The Warsaw Ghetto: A Diary.* Trans. Norbert and Sylvia Glass. Ed. S. L. Schneiderman. New York: L. B. Fischer, 1945. [*Dziennik z Getta Warszawskiego*. Warsaw: Czytelnik, 1983.]

BLOCK, ELISABETH. *Erinnerungszeichen: Die Tagebücher der Elisabeth Block.* ed. Manfred Treml, Peter Miesbeck, Evamaria Brockhoff. Rosenheim: Bayerische Staatskanzelei, 1993.

BORZYKOWSKI, TUVIA. *Between Tumbling Walls.* Trans. Mendel Kohansky. 2nd ed. Tel-Aviv: Hakibbutz Hameuchad, 1976. [*Tsvishen falndike vent*. Warsaw: Nakladem Wydawnictwa Hechaluc, 1949.]

COHN, WILLY ISRAEL. *Als Jude in Breslau—1941: Aus der Tagebücher von Studienrat a.D. Dr. Willy Israel Cohn*. Ed. Joseph Walk. Bar-Ilan: Bar-Ilan University Press, 1975.

CZERNIAKOW, ADAM. *The Warsaw Ghetto Diary of Adam Czerniakow.* Trans. Stanislaw Staron, *et al.* Ed. Raul Hilberg, Stanislaw Staron, Joseph Kermisz. New York: Stein and Day, 1979. [*Adama Czerniakowa dziennik getta warszawsjiego: 6 IX 1939–23 VII 1942*. Warsaw: Panstowowe Wydawnictwo Naukowe, 1983.]

DOREMBUS, HELENA ELBAUM. "Through Helpless Eyes: A Survivor's Diary of the Warsaw Ghetto Uprising," *Moment*, April 1993:56–61.

DORIAN, EMIL. *The Quality of Witness.* Trans. Mara Soceanu Vamos. Ed. Marguerite Dorian. Philadelphia: Jewish Publication Society, 1982.

FLINKER, MOSHE. *Young Moshe's Diary.* Trans. Shaul Esh and Geoffrey Wigoder. Jerusalem: Yad Vashem and Board of Jewish Education, 1971. [*Hana'ar Moshe: yoman shel Moshe Flinker*. Jerusalem: Yad Vashem, 1958.]

FRANK, ANNE. *The Diary of a Young Girl.* Trans. B. M. Mooyaart-Doubleday. New York: Modern Library, 1952. [*Het Achterhuis.* Amsterdam: Uitgeverij Contact, 1955.]

FRANK, SHLOMO. *Togbukh fon Lodzsher geto.* Tel-Aviv: Menorah, 1958.

GLEYKH, SARRA. "The Diary of Sarra Gleykh (Mariupol)," trans. John Glad and James S. Levine, in *The Black Book*, ed. Ilya Ehrenburg and Vasily Grossman. New York: Holocaust Library, 1980, pp. 70–76. [In *Chernaya kniga*, ed. Ilya Ehrenburg and Vasily Grossman. Kiev: MIP "Oberig," 1991, pp. 87–92.]

GRADOWSKI, SALMEN. Manuscript of Sonderkommando Member, trans. Krystyna Michalik, in *Amidst a Nightmare of Crime: Manuscripts of Members of Sonderkommando*, ed. Jadwiga Bezwinska. Oswiecim: State Museum, 1973, pp. 75–108.

HEYMAN, ÉVA. *The Diary of Eva Heyman.* Trans. Moshe M. Kohn. Jerusalem: Yad Vashem, 1974.

HUBERBAND, SHIMON. *Kiddush Hashem: Jewish Religious and Cultural Life in Poland during the Holocaust.* Trans. David E. Fishman. Ed. Jeffrey S. Gurock and Robert S. Hirt. Hoboken, NJ: Ktav and Yeshiva University Press, 1987.

KAHANE, DAVID. *Lvov Ghetto Diary.* Trans. Jerzy Michalowicz. Amherst: University of Massachusetts Press, 1990. [*Yoman gito Lvov.* Jerusalem: Yad Vashem, 1978.]

KALMANOVITCH, ZELIG. "A Diary of the Nazi Ghetto in Vilna," trans. and ed. Koppel S. Pinson, *YIVO Annual of Jewish Social Sciences* 8 (1953):9–81. [*Yoman bagito Vilna.* Tel-Aviv: Sfrit Poelim, 1977.]

KAPLAN, CHAIM A. *The Warsaw Diary of Chaim A. Kaplan.* Trans. and ed. Abraham I. Katsh. New York: Collier, 1973. [*Megilat yisorin: yoman gito Varshah.* Tel-Aviv: Am Oved, 1966.]

KATZ, JOSEF. *One Who Came Back: The Diary of a Jewish Survivor.* Trans. Herzl Reach. New York: Herzl Press and Bergen-Belsen Memorial Press, 1973.

KATZNELSON, YITZHAK. *Vittel Diary.* Trans. Myer Cohn. 2nd ed. Tel-Aviv: Hakibbutz Hameuchad, 1972. ["Pinkas Vitel," in *Ktavim achronim: bagito Warshah v'bamachnah Vitel*, ed. Menachem Dorman. Tel-Aviv: Ghetto Fighters House and Hakibbutz Hameuchad, 1988, pp. 29–110.]

KLONICKI-KLONYMUS, ARYEH. *The Diary of Adam's Father.* Trans.

Avner Tomaschaff. Tel-Aviv: Ghetto Fighters House and Hakibbutz Hameuchad, 1973. [*Yoman avi Adam*. Tel-Aviv: Ghetto Fighters House and Hakibbutz Hameuchad, 1969.]

KON, MENAHEM. "Fragments of a Diary (August 6, 1942–October 1, 1942)," trans. M. Z. Prives, in *To Live with Honor and Die with Honor: Selected Documents from the Warsaw Ghetto Underground Archives "O.S.,"* ed. Joseph Kermish. Jerusalem: Yad Vashem, 1986, pp. 80–86.

KORBER, MIRJAM. *Deportiert: Jüdische Überlebensschicksale aus Rumänien 1941–1944: Ein Tagebuch*. Trans. Andrei Hoisie. Konstanz: Hartung-Garre, 1993.

KORCZAK, JANUSZ. *Ghetto Diary*. Trans. Jerzy Bachrach and Barbara Krzywicka. New York: Holocaust Library, 1978. [*Pamietnik*, ed. Alicja Szlazakowa. Poznan: Wydawnictwo Poznanskie, 1984.]

KRUK, HERMAN. "Diary of the Vilna Ghetto," trans. Shlomo Noble, *YIVO Annual of Jewish Social Sciences* 13 (1965):9–78. [*Togbukh fon Vilner geto*. New York: YIVO, 1961.]

LANGFUS, LEIB. Manuscript of Sonderkommando Member, trans. Krystyna Michalik, in *Amidst a Nightmare of Crime: Manuscripts of Members of Sonderkommando*, ed. Jadwiga Bezwinska. Oswiecim: State Museum, 1973, pp. 112–22.

LAQUEUR, RENATA. *Bergen-Belsen Tagebuch*. Trans. Peter Wiebke. Hannover: Fackelträger, 1983.

LEVIN, ABRAHAM. "Extract from the Diary of Abraham Levin," *Yad Vashem Studies* 6 (1967):315–30.

LEVY-HASS, HANNA. *Vielleicht war das alles erst der Anfang: Tagebuch aus dem KZ Bergen Belsen 1944–1945*. Ed. Eike Geisel. Berlin: Rotbuch, 1969.

LEWENTAL, SALMEN. Manuscript of Sonderkommando Member, trans. Krystyna Michalik, in *Amidst a Nightmare of Crime: Manuscripts of Members of Sonderkommando*, ed. Jadwiga Bezwinska. Oswiecim: State Museum, 1973, pp. 130–78.

LISSNER, ABRAHAM. "Diary of a Jewish Partisan in Paris," trans. Yuri Suhl, in *They Fought Back*, ed. Yuri Suhl. New York: Crown, 1967, pp. 282–97.

MARCUSE, GÜNTHER. "The Diary of Günther Marcuse (The Last Days of the Gross-Breesen Training Centre)," trans. and ed. Joseph Walk, *Yad Vashem Studies* 8 (1970):159–81.

MECHANICUS, PHILIP. *Year of Fear: A Jewish Prisoner Waits for Auschwitz.* Trans. Irene S. Gibbons. New York: Hawthorne, 1964. [*In Depot: Dagboek uit Westerbork.* Amsterdam: Polak and Van Gennep, 1964.]

OPOCZYNSKI, PERETZ. "Warsaw Ghetto Chronicle—September 1942," trans. M. Z. Prives, in *To Live with Honor and Die with Honor: Selected Documents from the Warsaw Ghetto Underground Archives "O.S.,"* ed. Joseph Kermish. Jerusalem: Yad Vashem, 1986, pp. 101–11.

RINGELBLUM, EMMANUEL. *Notes from the Warsaw Ghetto.* Trans. and ed. Jacob Sloan. New York: Schocken, 1974. [*Notizn fon Warshever geto.* Warsaw: Yiddish Books, 1952.]

RIVOSH. "From the Diary of the Sculptor Rivosh (Riga)," trans. John Glad and James Levine, in *The Black Book*, ed. Ilya Ehrenburg and Vasily Grossman. New York: Holocaust Library, 1980, pp. 324–46. [*Chernaya kniga*, pp. 327–47.]

RUBINOWICZ, DAVID. *The Diary of David Rubinowicz.* Trans. Derek Bowman. Edmonds, WA: Creative Options, 1982. [*Pamietnik Dawida Rubinowicza.* Warsaw: Ksiazka i Wiedza, 1960.]

RUDASHEVSKI, YITSKHOK. *The Diary of the Vilna Ghetto.* Trans. Percy Matenko. Tel-Aviv: Ghetto Fighters House and Hakibbutz Hameuchad, 1973.

SEIDMAN, HILLEL. *Tog-bukh fon Warshever geto.* New York: Avraham Mitlberg, 1947.

SENESH, HANNAH. *Hannah Senesh: Her Life and Diary.* Trans. Marta Cohn. New York: Schocken, 1972.

SHEINKINDER, S. "The Diary of S. Sheinkinder," *Yad Vashem Studies* 5 (1963): 255–69.

SHOSHKES, HENRYK. *Bleter fon a geto-tog-bukh.* New York: H. H. Glanz, 1943.

SIERAKOWIAK, DAVID. "Extracts from the Diary of David Sierakowiak," *Yad Vashem Bulletin* 12 (1962): 15–21.

STANFORD, JULIAN CASTLE. *Tagebuch eines deutschen Juden im Untergrund.* Darmstadt: Darmstädter Blaetter, 1980.

TORY, AVRAHAM. *Surviving the Holocaust: The Kovno Ghetto Diary.* Trans. Jerzy Michalowicz. Ed. Martin Gilbert. Cambridge, MA: Harvard University Press, 1990.

WASSER, HERSH. "Daily Entries of Hersh Wasser." Trans. Joseph Kermish, *Yad Vashem Studies* 15 (1983): 201–82.

WELLS, LEON. "The Death Brigade," trans. Leon Wells, in *ibid., The*

Death Brigade (The Janowska Road). New York: Holocaust Library, 1978, pp. 131–224.

YERUSHALMI, ELIEZER. *Pinkas Shavli: yoman megito Litai*. Jerusalem: Yad Vashem, 1950.

ZUCKERMAN, YITZHAK. "From the Warsaw Ghetto," *Commentary*, December 1975: 62–69.

ZYLBERBERG, MICHAEL. *A Warsaw Diary*. London: Valentine, Mitchell & Co., 1969.

SECONDARY SOURCES

ABOHAV, YITZCHAK. *Menoras Hamaor: The Light of Contentment*. Trans. Yaakov Yosef Reinman. Lakewood, NJ: Torascript Library, 1982.

ABRAHAM IBN EZRA. *The Commentary of Ibn Ezra on Isaiah*. Trans. Michael Friedlander. New York: Feldheim, 1943.

———. *The Secret of the Torah*. Trans. H. Norman Strickman. Northvale, NJ: Aronson, 1995.

ARIETI, SILVANO. *The Parnas*. New York: Basic Books, 1979.

ARON, MILTON. *Ideas and Ideals of the Hasidim*. Secaucus, NJ: Citadel, 1969.

BACHYA IBN PAQUDA. *Duties of the Heart*. 2 vols. Trans. Moses Hyamson. New York: Feldheim, 1970.

BAECK, LEO. *The Essence of Judaism*. Revised edition. Trans. Victor Grubenwieser and Leonard Pearl. New York: Schocken, 1948.

The Bahir. Trans. with commentary by Aryeh Kaplan. York Beach, ME: Samuel Weiser, 1979.

BAKHTIN, MIKHAIL. *Art and Answerability*. Trans. Vadim Liapunov. Ed. Michael Holquist and Vadim Liapunov. Austin: University of Texas Press, 1990.

———. *The Dialogic Imagination*. Trans. Caryl Emerson and Michael Holquist. Austin: University of Texas Press, 1981.

———. *Problems of Dostoevsky's Poetics*. Trans. Caryl Emerson. Minneapolis: University of Minnesota Press, 1984.

———. *Speech Genres and Other Late Essays*. Trans. Vern W. McGee. Ed. Caryl Emerson and Michael Holquist. Austin: University of Texas Press, 1986.

BAUER, YEHUDA. *A History of the Holocaust*. New York: Franklin Watts, 1982.

BENJAMIN, WALTER. "Über einige Motive bei Baudelaire," in *Gesammelte Schriften*, vol. 1, part 2. Frankfurt: Suhrkamp, 1974, pp. 605–53.

———. "Zum Bilde Prousts," in *Gesammelte Schriften*, vol. 2, part 1. Frankfurt: Suhrkamp, 1977, pp. 310–24.

BETTELHEIM, BRUNO. "Ignored Lessons of Anne Frank," *Harper's*, November 1960:45–50.

BITTON-JACKSON, LIVIA E. *Elli*. New York: Times Books, 1980.

BUBER, MARTIN. *Between Man and Man*. Trans. Ronald Gregor Smith. New York: Macmillan, 1965.

———. *I and Thou*. Trans. Walter Kaufmann. New York: Charles Scribner's Sons, 1970.

———. *The Legend of the Baal Shem*. Trans. Maurice Friedman. New York: Schocken, 1969.

———. *On Judaism*. Trans. Eva Jospe. Ed. Nahum N. Glatzer. New York: Schocken, 1967.

CAMON, FERDINANDO. *Conversations with Primo Levi*. Trans. John Shepley. Marlboro, VT: Marlboro Press, 1989.

CAMUS, ALBERT. *The Myth of Sisyphus*. Trans. Justin O'Brien. New York: Random House, 1955.

CARGAS, HARRY JAMES. *Reflections of a Post-Auschwitz Christian*. Detroit: Wayne State University Press, 1989.

———. *Shadows of Auschwitz: A Christian Response to the Holocaust*. New York: Crossroad, 1990.

CHILL, ABRAHAM, trans. and ed. *Abrabanel on Pirke Avot*. New York: Sepher-Hermon, 1991.

CHOFETZ CHAIM. *Ahavath Chesed*. Trans. Leonard Oschry. Jerusalem: Feldheim, 1976.

———. *Let There Be Light*. Trans. Raphael Blumberg. Jerusalem: Feldheim, 1992.

COHEN, NATHAN. "Diaries of the *Sonderkommandos* in Auschwitz: Coping with Fate and Reality," *Yad Vashem Studies* 20 (1990):273–312.

CORDOVERO, MOSHE. *The Palm Tree of Devorah*. Trans. Moshe Miller. Southfield, MI: Targum, 1993.

CULI, YAAKOV. *The Torah Anthology: MeAm Lo'ez*. Vol. 1. Trans. Aryeh Kaplan. New York: Maznaim, 1977.

DAN, JOSEPH, ed. *The Early Kabbalah*. Trans. Ronald C. Kiener. New York: Paulist Press, 1986.

DAWIDOWICZ, LUCY S. *The War against the Jews: 1933–1945*. New York: Bantam, 1976.

DOV BER. *In Praise of the Baal Shem Tov*. Trans. and ed. Dan Ben-Amos and Jerome R. Mintz. New York: Schocken, 1970.

DRESNER, SAMUEL H. *The Zaddik: The Doctrine of the Zaddik according to the Writings of Rabbi Yaakov Yosef of Polnoy*. New York: Abelard-Schuman, 1960.

DRIBBEN, JUDITH. *And Some Shall Live*. Jerusalem: Keter Books, 1969.

En Jacob: Agada of the Babylonian Talmud. 5 vols. Trans. S. H. Glick. New York: Hebrew Publishing Co., 1916–1921.

FACKENHEIM, EMIL L. *Encounters between Judaism and Modern Philosophy*. New York: Basic Books, 1973.

———. *God's Presence in History: Jewish Affirmations and Philosophical Reflections*. New York: Harper, 1970.

———. *The Jewish Bible after the Holocaust*. Bloomington: Indiana University Press, 1990.

———. *The Jewish Return into History*. New York: Schocken, 1978.

———. *To Mend the World: Foundations of Post-Holocaust Jewish Thought*. New York: Schocken, 1989.

———. *What Is Judaism?* New York: Macmillan, 1987.

FEUERBACH, LUDWIG. *The Essence of Christianity*. Trans. George Eliot. New York: Harper, 1957.

FINKELSTEIN, LOUIS. *Akiba: Scholar, Saint and Martyr*. New York: Atheneum, 1981.

FOLEY, BARBARA. "Fact, Fiction, Fascism: Testimony and Mimesis in Holocaust Narratives," *Comparative Literature* 34 (Fall 1982): 330–60.

GERSONIDES. *The Wars of the Lord*. 2 vols. Trans. Seymour Feldman. Philadelphia: Jewish Publication Society, 1984.

GIKATILLA, JOSEPH. *Sha'are orah: Gates of Light*. Trans. Avi Weinstein. San Francisco: Harper, 1994.

GINSBURGH, YITZCHAK. *The Alef-Beit: Jewish Thought Revealed through the Hebrew Letters*. Northvale, NJ: Aronson, 1991.

GIRARD, ALAIN. *Le journal intime*. Paris: Presses Universitaires de France, 1963.

GOETHE, JOHANN WOLFGANG VON. *Poems of Goethe*. Selected by Ronald Gray. Cambridge: Cambridge University Press, 1966.

GRAESER, ALBERT. *Das Tagebuch: Studien über Elements des Tagebuchs als Kunstform*. Saarbrücken: West-Ost Verlag, 1955.

GUTMAN, YISRAEL. "Adam Czerniakow: The Man and His Diary," in *The Catastrophe of European Jewry*, ed. Israel Gutman and Livia Rothkirchen. Jerusalem: Yad Vashem, 1976, pp. 451–89.

HALEVI, JUDAH. *The Kuzari*. Trans. Hartwig Hirschfeld. New York: Schocken, 1964.

HANDELMAN, SUSAN A. *The Slayers of Moses: The Emergence of Rabbinic Interpretation in Modern Literary Theory*. Albany: SUNY Press, 1982.

HEINEMANN, BENNO. *The Maggid of Dubno and His Parables*. 3rd ed. New York: Feldheim, 1973.

HELLER, CELIA S. *On the Edge of Destruction: Jews of Poland between the Two World Wars*. New York: Schocken, 1980.

HESCHEL, ABRAHAM JOSHUA. *The Earth Is the Lord's*. New York: Farrar, Straus and Giroux, 1978.

———. *God in Search of Man*. Farrar, Straus and Giroux, 1955.

———. *I Asked for Wonder*. Ed. Samuel H. Dresner. New York: Crossroad, 1983.

———. *Israel: An Echo of Eternity*. New York: Farrar, Straus and Giroux, 1969.

———. *Man's Quest for God: Studies in Prayer and Symbolism*. New York: Charles Scribner's Sons, 1954.

———. *The Prophets*. 2 vols. New York: Harper & Row, 1962, 1975.

———. *The Sabbath: Its Meaning for Modern Man*. New York: Farrar, Straus and Giroux, 1981.

HILLESUM, ETTY. *An Interrupted Life*. Trans. Arno Pomerans. New York: Pantheon, 1983.

HIRSCH, SAMSON RAPHAEL. *The Nineteen Letters on Judaism*. Trans. Bernard Drachman. Ed. Jacob Breuer. Jerusalem: Feldheim, 1969.

IDEL, MOSHE. *Language, Torah, and Hermeneutics in Abraham Abulafia*. Albany: SUNY Press, 1989.

JABÈS, EDMOND. *The Book of Yukel and Return to the Book*. Trans. Rosemarie Waldrop. Middletown, CT: Wesleyan University Press, 1977.

———. *From the Desert to the Book: Dialogues with Marcel Cohen*. Trans. Pierre Joris. Barrytown, NY: Station Hill, 1990.

JASPERS, KARL. *Truth and Symbol*. Trans. Jean T. Wilde, William Kluback, and William New Haven, CT: College and University Press, 1959.

KAHANA, RAB. *Pesikta de-Rab Kahana*. Trans. William G. Braude and Israel J. Kapstein. Philadelphia: Jewish Publication Society, 1975.

KA-TZETNIK 135633. *House of Dolls*. Trans. Moshe M. Kohn. New York: Pyramid, 1958.

———. *Phoenix over the Galilee*. Trans. Nina De-Nur. New York: Harper, 1969.

———. *Shivitti: A Vision*. Trans. Eliyah Nike De-Nur and Lisa Herman. San Francisco: Harper, 1989.

KOOK, ABRAHAM ISAAC. *Orot*. Trans. Bezalel Naor. Northvale, NJ: Aronson, 1993.

LEITNER, ISABELLA. *Fragments of Isabella: A Memoir of Auschwitz*. Ed. Irving A. Leitner. New York: Thomas Y. Crowell, 1978.

LERNER, LILY GLUCK. *The Silence*. Secaucus, NJ: Lyle Stuart, 1980.

LEVI, PRIMO. *The Drowned and the Saved*. Trans. Raymond Rosenthal. New York: Vintage Books, 1989.

———. *Survival in Auschwitz*. Trans. Stuart Woolf. New York: Collier, 1961.

LEVIN, MEYER. *Hasidic Stories*. Tel-Aviv: Greenfield, 1975.

LEVINAS, EMMANUEL. "Bad Conscience and the Inexorable," in *Face to Face with Levinas*, ed. Richard A. Cohen. Albany: SUNY Press, 1986, pp. 35–40.

———. *Collected Philosophical Papers*. Trans. Alphonso Lingis. Dordrecht: Martinus Nijhoff, 1987.

———. "Dialogue with Emmanuel Levinas," in *Face to Face with Levinas*, ed. Richard A. Cohen. Albany: SUNY Press, 1986, pp. 13–23.

———. *Difficult Freedom: Essays on Judaism*. Trans. Sean Hand. Baltimore: Johns Hopkins University Press, 1990.

———. *Ethics and Infinity*. Trans. Richard A. Cohen. Pittsburgh: Duquesne University Press, 1985.

———. "Ethics as First Philosophy," trans. Sean Hand and Richard Temple, in *The Levinas Reader*, ed. Sean Hand. Oxford: Basil Blackwell, 1989, pp. 75–87.

———. *Existence and Existents*. Trans. Alphonso Lingis. The Hague: Martinus Nijhoff, 1978.

———. *Nine Talmudic Readings*. Trans. Annette Aronowicz. Bloomington: Indiana University Press, 1990.

———. *Otherwise than Being or Beyond Essence*. Trans. Alphonso Lingis. The Hague: Martinus Nijhoff, 1981.

———. "The Paradox of Morality," trans. Richard A. Cohen, in *The Provocation of Levinas: Rethinking the Other*, ed. Robert Bernasconi and David Wood. London: Routledge, 1988, pp. 168–80.

———. "Revelation in the Jewish Tradition," trans. Sarah Richmond, in *The Levinas Reader*, ed. Sean Hand. Oxford: Basil Blackwell, 1989, pp. 190–210.

———. *Time and the Other*. Trans. Richard A. Cohen. Pittsburgh: Duquesne University Press, 1987.

———. *Totality and Infinity*. Trans. Alphonso Lingis. Pittsburgh: Duquesne University Press, 1969.

LOEVE, YEHUDA. *Nesivos Olam: Nesiv Hatorah*. Trans. Eliakim Willner. Brooklyn: Mesorah, 1994.

LUBETKIN, ZIVIA. *In the Days of Destruction and Revolt*. Trans. Ishai Tubbin. Tel-Aviv: Ghetto Fighters House, 1981.

LUZZATTO, MOSHE CHAYIM. *The Way of God*. Trans. Aryeh Kaplan. 4th ed. New York: Feldheim, 1988.

MAIMONIDES. *The Existence and Unity of God: Three Treatises Attributed to Maimonides*. Trans. Fred Rosner. Northvale, NJ: Aronson, 1990.

———. *The Guide for the Perplexed*. Trans. M. Friedlaender. New York: Dover, 1956.

———. *Mishneh Torah Volume One: The Book of Knowledge*. Trans. Moses Hyamson. Jerusalem: Feldheim, 1981.

———. *Mishneh Torah Volume Two: The Book of Adoration*. Trans. Moses Hyamson. Jerusalem: Feldheim, 1981.

MARTIN, BERNARD. *A History of Judaism—Volume 2: Europe and the New World*. New York: Basic Books, 1974.

MEIR IBN GABBAI. *Sod ha-Shabbat*. Trans. Elliot K. Ginsburg. Albany: SUNY Press, 1989.

Mekilta de-Rabbi Ishmael. 3 vols. Trans. Jacob Z. Lauterbach. Philadelphia: Jewish Publication Society, 1961.

Midrash on Psalms. Trans. William G. Braude. 2 vols. New Haven, CT: Yale University Press, 1959.

Midrash Rabbah. 10 vols. Trans. and ed. H. Friedman, Maurice Simon, *et al*. London: Soncino, 1961.

Midrash Tanchuma. 2 vols. Jerusalem: Eshkol, 1935.

NACHMAN OF BRESLOV. *Advice*. Trans. Avraham Greenbaum. Brooklyn: Breslov Research Institute, 1983.

———. *The Aleph-Bet Book*. Trans. Moshe Myhoff. Jerusalem: Breslov Research Institute, 1986.

———. *Rabbi Nachman's Wisdom: Shevachay HaRan and Sichos HaRan*. Trans. Aryeh Kaplan. New York: A. Kaplan, 1973.

———. *Restore My Soul (Meshivat Nefesh)*. Trans. Avraham Greenbaum. Jerusalem: Chasidei Breslov, 1980.

———. *Tikkun*. Trans. Avraham Greenbaum. Jerusalem: Breslov Research Institute, 1984.

NACHMANIDES. *Commentary on the Torah*. 5 vols. Trans. Charles B. Chavel. New York: Shilo, 1971.

———. *Writings and Discourses*. 2 vols. Trans. Charles B. Chavel. New York: Shilo, 1978.

NEHER, ANDRÉ. *The Exile of the Word: From the Silence of the Bible to the Silence of Auschwitz*. Trans. David Maisel. Philadelphia: Jewish Publication Society, 1981.

———. *The Prophetic Existence*. Trans. William Wolf. New York: A. S. Barnes, 1969.

———. *They Made Their Souls Anew*. Trans. David Maisel. Albany: SUNY Press, 1990.

NEWMAN, LOUIS I., ed. *The Hasidic Anthology*. New York: Schocken, 1963.

NIETZSCHE, FRIEDRICH. *Thus Spoke Zarathustra*. Trans. Walter Kaufmann. New York: Penguin, 1966.

NYISZLI, MIKLOS. *Auschwitz*. Trans. Tibere Kremer and Richard Seaver. New York: Fawcett Crest, 1960.

PATTERSON, DAVID. *In Dialogue and Dilemma with Elie Wiesel*. Wakefield, NH: Longwood Academic, 1991.

PELI, PINHAS H. *The Jewish Sabbath: A Renewed Encounter*. New York: Schocken, 1988.

Pirke de Rabbi Eliezer. Trans. Gerald Friedlander. New York: Hermon Press, 1970.

RABINOWICZ, HARRY M. *Hasidism: The Movement and Its Masters*. Northvale, NJ: Aronson, 1988.

RASHI. *Commentary on the Torah*. 5 vols. Trans. M. Rosenbaum and N. M. Silbermann. Jerusalem: The Silbermann Family, 1972.

ROSENFELD, ALVIN. *A Double Dying: Reflections on Holocaust Literature*. Bloomington: Indiana University Press, 1980.

———. "Popularization and Memory: The Case of Anne Frank," in *Lessons and Legacies: The Meaning of the Holocaust in a Changing World*, ed. Peter Hayes. Evanston, IL: Northwestern University Press, 1991, pp. 243–371.

ROSENZWEIG, FRANZ. *On Jewish Learning*. Trans. and ed. N. N. Glatzer. New York: Schocken, 1955.

———. *The Star of Redemption*. Trans. William W. Hallo. Boston: Beacon Press, 1972.

ROSKIES, DAVID. *Against the Apocalypse: Responses to Catastrophe in Modern Jewish Culture*. Cambridge, MA: Harvard University Press, 1984.

SAADIA GAON. *The Book of Belief and Opinions*. Trans. Samuel Rosenblatt. New Haven, CT: Yale University Press, 1976.

SCHNEERSON, MENACHEM M. *Torah Studies*. Adapted by Jonathan Sacks. 2nd ed. London: Lubavitch Foundation, 1986.

SCHNEIDAU, HERBERT. *Sacred Discontent: The Bible and Western Tradition*. Berkeley: University of California Press, 1976.

Sefer Yetzirah: The Book of Creation. Trans. with commentary by Aryeh Kaplan. York Beach, ME: Samuel Weiser, 1990.

SFORNO. *Commentary on the Torah*. 2 vols. Trans. Raphael Pelcovitz. Brooklyn: Mesorah, 1987–1989.

SHAPIRA, KALONYMUS KALMAN. *A Student's Obligation*. Trans. Micha Odenheimer. Northvale, NJ: Aronson, 1991.

SOLOVEITCHIK, JOSEPH B. *Halakhic Man*. Trans. Lawrence Kaplan. Philadelphia: Jewish Publication Society, 1983.

SPALDING, P. A. *Self-Harvest: A Study of Diaries and the Diarist*. London: Independent Press, 1949.

STEINSALTZ, ADIN. *The Essential Talmud*. Trans. Chaya Galai. New York: Basic Books, 1976.

———. *The Long Shorter Way: Discourses on Chasidic Thought*. Trans. Yehuda Hanegbi. Northvale, NJ: Aronson, 1988.

———. *On Being Free*. Northvale, NJ: Aronson, 1995.

———. *Biblical Images: Men and Women of the Book*. Trans. Yehuda Hanegbi and Yehudit Keshet. New York: Basic Books, 1984.

———. *The Strife of the Spirit*. Northvale, NJ: Aronson, 1988.

———. *The Sustaining Utterance: Discourses on Chasidic Thought*. Ed. and trans. Yehuda Hanegbi. Northvale, NJ: Aronson, 1989.

———. *Teshuvah: A Guide for the Newly Observant Jew.* New York: Free Press, 1987.

———. *The Thirteen-Petalled Rose: A Discourse on the Essence of Jewish Existence.* Trans. Yehuda Hanegbi. New York: Basic Books, 1980.

SYRKIN, MARIE. "Holocaust Literature 1: Diaries," in *Encountering the Holocaust: An Interdisciplinary Survey*, ed. Byron L. Sherwin and Susan G. Ament. Chicago: Impact Press, 1979, pp. 226–43.

VILNA GAON. *Even Sheleimah.* Trans. Yaakov Singer and Chaim David Ackerman. Southfield, MI: Targum Press, 1992.

WARDI, CHARLOTTE. *Le génocide dans la fiction romanesque.* Paris: Presses Universitaires de France, 1986.

WEINTRAUB, KARL J. "Autobiography and Historical Consciousness," *Critical Inquiry* 1 (June 1975): 821–48.

WEISS, RENATA LAQUEUR. "Writing in Defiance: Concentration Camp Diaries in Dutch, French and German." Doctoral dissertation. Ann Arbor, MI: University Microfilms, 1971.

WIESEL, ELIE. *Against Silence: The Voice and Vision of Elie Wiesel.* 3 vols. Ed. Irving Abrahamson. New York: Holocaust Library, 1985.

———. *Ani Maamin: A Song Lost and Found Again.* Trans. Marion Wiesel. New York: Random House, 1973.

———. *A Beggar in Jerusalem.* Trans. Lily Edelman and Elie Wiesel. New York: Randon House, 1970.

——— and others. *Dimensions of the Holocaust.* Evanston, IL: Northwestern University Press, 1977.

——— and Philippe de Saint-Cheron. *Evil and Exile.* Trans. Jon Rothschild. Notre Dame, IN: University of Notre Dame Press, 1990.

———. *The Forgotten.* Trans. Stephen Becker. New York: Summit, 1992.

———. *From the Kingdom of Memory: Reminiscences.* New York: Summit, 1990.

———. *The Gates of the Forest.* Trans. Frances Frenaye. New York: Holt, Rinehart and Winston, 1966.

———. *The Golem.* New York: Summit, 1983.

———. *A Jew Today.* Trans. Marion Wiesel. New York: Random House, 1978.

———. *Legends of Our Time.* New York: Avon, 1968.

———. *Messengers of God: Biblical Portraits and Legends.* Trans. Marion Wiesel. New York: Random House, 1976.

———. *Night*. Trans. Stella Rodway. New York: Bantam, 1982.

———. *The Oath*. New York: Avon, 1973.

———. *One Generation After*. Trans. Lily Edelman and Elie Wiesel. New York: Pocket Books, 1970.

———. *Paroles d'étranger*. Paris: Éditions du Seuil, 1982.

———. *Sages and Dreamers*. Trans. Marion Wiesel. New York: Summit, 1991.

——— and Albert Friedlander. *The Six Days of Destruction: Meditations Towards Hope*. Trans. Cynthia Lander and Evelyn Friedlander. Oxford: Pergamon, 1988.

———. *Somewhere a Master*. Trans. Marion Wiesel. New York: Summit, 1982.

———. *Souls on Fire: Portraits and Legends of Hasidic Masters*. Trans. Marion Wiesel. New York: Vintage, 1973.

———. *The Testament*. Trans. Marion Wiesel. New York: Summit, 1981.

———. *Twilight*. Trans. Marion Wiesel. New York: Summit, 1988.

———. *Zalmen or The Madness of God*. Adapted for the stage by Marion Wiesel. New York: Random House, 1974.

WIESENTHAL, SIMON. *The Sunflower*. Trans. H. A. Piehler. New York: Schocken, 1976.

YOUNG, JAMES E. "Interpreting Literary Testimony: A Preface to Rereading Holocaust Diaries and Memoirs," *New Literary History* 18 (Winter 1987): 403–23.

———. *Writing and Rewriting the Holocaust: Narrative and the Consequences of Interpretation*. Bloomington: Indiana University Press, 1988.

ZALMAN, SCHNEUR. *Likutei Amarim Tanya*. Trans. Nissan Mindel, *et al.* Brooklyn: Kehot, 1981.

The Zohar. 5 vols. Trans. Harry Sperling and Maurice Simon. London: Soncino, 1984.

INDEX